Computer Communications and Networks

Series editor
A.J. Sammes
Centre for Forensic Computing
Cranfield University, Shrivenham Campus
Swindon, UK

The **Computer Communications and Networks** series is a range of textbooks, monographs and handbooks. It sets out to provide students, researchers, and non-specialists alike with a sure grounding in current knowledge, together with comprehensible access to the latest developments in computer communications and networking.

Emphasis is placed on clear and explanatory styles that support a tutorial approach, so that even the most complex of topics is presented in a lucid and intelligible manner.

More information about this series at http://www.springer.com/series/4198

Nick Antonopoulos • Lee Gillam
Editors

Cloud Computing

Principles, Systems and Applications

Second Edition

 Springer

Editors
Nick Antonopoulos
University of Derby
Derby, Derbyshire, UK

Lee Gillam
University of Surrey
Guildford, Surrey, UK

ISSN 1617-7975   ISSN 2197-8433   (electronic)
Computer Communications and Networks
ISBN 978-3-319-85443-4   ISBN 978-3-319-54645-2   (eBook)
DOI 10.1007/978-3-319-54645-2

Printed on acid-free paper

This Springer imprint is published by Springer Nature
The registered company is Springer International Publishing AG
The registered company address is: Gewerbestrasse 11, 6330 Cham, Switzerland

Foreword

Since the first version of this book was published in 2010, with a foreword by my colleague Mark Baker (University of Reading), considerable developments have taken place in Cloud computing. Today, Cloud computing is no longer a niche research area but now closely embedded in our everyday computing environment. This is the ultimate success of a technology, which initially starts out as a specialist domain-specific interest, but becomes so successful that it becomes invisible to us as users. Systems such as Dropbox, Apple iCloud, Microsoft Office 365 and Google Drive (amongst many others) are now regularly made use of and considered very much a core fabric of our computing infrastructure. Social media platforms such as Facebook, Twitter and Instagram all make use of Cloud systems and make use of novel concepts such as "eventual consistency" (amongst others) as part of their implementation. A mobile app that does not make use of a Cloud-based back end is now an anomaly rather than a norm, a considerable change that has taken place since 2010. Early scientific Cloud systems, such as Eucalyptus, Open Cirrus, etc., once considered the domain of computer science research, are now regularly used within a variety of other communities, from biological sciences to arts and humanities.

Figure 1 shows change in interest (via Google trends) for the three terms "Cloud computing" (dashed line, descending), "Internet of Things" (dashed line, slowly ascending) and "big data" (dotted line) since the first edition of this book was published in 2010. These three trends are closely related, as many applications that generate or process large data sizes make use of Cloud-based infrastructure. Similarly, many IoT devices act as data generators or consumers. It is also interesting to see that programming models such as MapReduce, featured in the 2010 book, also appear in this version of the book but with a specific focus on a dynamic Cloud computing environment. This programming model has now been implemented across a variety of systems, from Hadoop (Cloudera, Apache) to in-memory systems such as Apache Spark and Mesos (amongst others). This programming model demonstrates how Cloud computing mechanisms have also transformed data analysis and processing and has found wide-scale adoption in industry and academia.

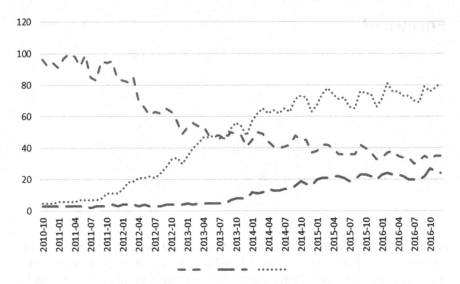

Fig. 1 Google trends for Cloud computing, Internet of Things and big data

With significant commercial interest in Cloud computing due to its transformative impact on industry, the most prominent example of which is Amazon Web Services (AWS), understanding how academic research could complement rather than compete has been difficult. Whereas Cloud computing infrastructure developers (Google Cloud, AWS, Microsoft Azure, Salesforce, etc.) often make use of large-scale data centres with a large pool of servers, specialist energy infrastructure and scalable/configurable networks, the academic community often has limited access to such resources. Better understanding on how academic researchers could respond to specialist challenges that may be commercially risky for commercial vendors has changed since 2010. This book demonstrates many such challenges that have been chosen by the academic community, such as (1) Cloud federation, (2) adaptive and elastic resource allocation and (3) reproducibility supported through Cloud-based systems. Whereas a particular industry vendor would prefer a user to always make use of a single Cloud system, purchasing and acquisition of computational infrastructure may not conform to this model, often requiring a multi-system/Cloud environment. Understanding how commercial Cloud systems could be "bridged" with private in-house systems, how a sudden increase in workload could support "bursting" across multiple Cloud systems and how services which are specialised for deployment over particular types of infrastructure (such as GPUs) need to be integrated with services hosted on other platforms (e.g. analytics or database services only available on a given platform) remains an important challenge. Managing resources and efficient allocation within such a federation remain important academic research challenges, which often complement work being carried out in industry.

The significant growth and capability of edge devices, and how these can be combined with Cloud-based data centres, has also seen considerable interest over recent years. In 2010, edge devices generally comprising of sensors were primarily used as mechanism for data capture. With increasing advances in semiconductor technologies, edge devices today have significant processing capability (e.g. the use of Arduino, Raspberry Pi 3, Intel Edison, etc.) enabling data to be preprocessed and sampled at the network edge, prior to being transmitted to a centralised data centre. Another significant trend since 2010 has been the wider adoption and availability of programmable networks through software-defined networks and network function virtualisation technologies. The availability of a more complex capability at the network edge, along with in-network programmability, changes the role of a data centre. This perspective requires researchers to better understand how edge devices and data centres can be used collectively. Understanding what should be done at the network edge vs. in the data centre becomes an important consideration. In 2010, a key requirement was to understand how processing and data could be "offloaded" from a mobile/edge device to a Cloud data centre (to conserve battery power of the edge device and avoid the impact of intermittent network connectivity). Today the focus has shifted to "reverse offloading", i.e. understanding how processing to be carried out within a Cloud data centre could be shifted to edge devices – to limit large data transfer over a public network and avoid latency due to such transfers. Better and more effective use of edge devices (alongside the use of a data centre) also leads to useful ways of supporting data security (i.e. a user can decide what should remain on the devices vs. what to shift to the data centre). The programming models needed to support this collaborative and opportunistic use of edge devices and data centres remain in short supply at present. Recent availability of low-overhead (in terms of memory/storage requirements and scheduling delay) "container" technologies (such as Docker, Kubernetes, Red Hat OpenShift) also provides useful mechanisms for supporting edge device/Cloud data centre integration, enabling services to be migrated (offloaded) from edge devices to data centres (and vice versa) – Villari et al.[1] refer to this as "osmotic computing".

Virtualisation technologies have also seen a considerable improvement since 2010. The capability to virtualise various parts of our computing infrastructure (from processors, networks, edge devices, storage, etc.) and services (such as a firewall) has seen considerable growth. The "virtualised enterprise" vision now dominates thinking in many resource management systems, aiming to make more effective use of resources across different applications. Understanding how the memory requirements and switching overhead of virtual machines (VMs) could be

---

[1] M. Villari, M. Fazio, S. Dustdar, O. Rana and R. Ranjan, "Osmotic Computing: A New Paradigm for Edge/Cloud Integration", IEEE Cloud Computing, December 2016. IEEE Computer Society Press.

reduced has led to interest in container technologies. Some predict that the days of VM-based deployments are limited, due to benefits observed with containers. How such approaches can be made multiplatform and support federation remain important challenges in this context.

The editors of this book have selected an excellent combination of chapters that cover these emerging themes in Cloud computing – from autonomic resource management, energy efficiency within such systems and new application requirements of such technologies. The book will provide valuable reference material for both academic researchers and those in industry to better gauge current state of the art in Cloud-based systems.

Professor of Performance Engineering   Omer F. Rana
Cardiff University, Cardiff, UK

Preface

1. Introduction

The first edition of this book, back in 2010, started by identifying the relatively recent emergence of Cloud and the increasing demand for Cloud systems and services that was apparent. We suggested, back then, that its meaning was hotly debated and identified specific IT and e-commerce vendors – Amazon, Google, IBM, Microsoft and Sun – who seemed to be leading the charge in making pay-per-use access to a wide variety of third-party applications and computational resources on a massive scale available widely. We also identified how the notion of Clouds seems to blur the distinctions between grid services, web services and data centres.

In the time that has elapsed between the first edition and this second edition, it would be fair to say that Cloud has not only emerged but has become a go-to for both experimental and developmental uses and is variously at the core of numerous businesses across the globe. For some, the use of Cloud in many of their activities is either second nature or is otherwise unavoidable. The definitional debates at a broad level have subsided, with a purportedly final perspective – at the 16th version – offered by the US National Institute of Standards and Technology (The NIST Definition of Cloud Computing, *NIST Special Publication 800–145*).[2] This is completed by the subsequent production in 2014 of ISO/IEC 17788, Cloud computing – Overview and vocabulary, although these two are not perfectly aligned, as well as ISO/IEC 17789, Cloud computing – Reference architecture. Of the five vendors we had acknowledged before, four remain and would probably now be considered the biggest Cloud players at this point in time, not least because their reported Cloud revenues are now in the billions of dollars *per quarter*: Sun's Network.com which had originally appeared to be a well-timed foray is, for most and perhaps unfortunately, a slightly distant memory following Sun's acquisition by

---

[2]http://nvlpubs.nist.gov/nistpubs/Legacy/SP/nistspecialpublication800-145.pdf – doi:10.6028/NIST.SP.800–145.

Oracle, with the memory of Sun as a company becoming equally distant. And for these big four, not only is the scale of their Cloud operations substantial, as it needs to be, but the range of services now available is also substantial and growing. And in terms of blurred distinctions, Cloud variously supports or subsumes these – running in, and across, multiple data centres in a large number of geographical jurisdictions and supporting grid, web and mobile services amongst others.

As the subject has grown, so topic coverage has extended. Many new Cloud-based services are a commoditisation of decreasingly common computational needs, albeit with a few with broad application. Given the inherent economies of scale brought to such commoditisation, this is likely to put further pressure on companies that are (still) trying to compete in Cloud. And, indeed, this has already led to some companies who have tried to compete withdrawing their attempts to keep pace and in one particular large company case closing down their public Cloud entirely. Various reasons may be cited: one key reason will be the sheer scale of investment needed to address the inherently high costs of building and running large new data centres and of continuing to ensure these comprise the latest and most capable hardware within a highly competitive pricing environment. The result, of not being able to compete at this level, tends to be that the arena for competition shifts up the stack, with consultancies and commentators of various hues espousing the benefits to be gained using multiple, and potentially federated, Clouds (multi-Cloud). This also adds opportunities in Cloud brokerage, in adding value or getting the best performance per unit of cost, and also in Cloud orchestration, with the need to simplify the complexities of using a multiplicity of services simultaneously. And the continued focus on Cloud security shows no sign of abating at any time soon.

Cloud is also, arguably, the springboard for the emergence of various other significant topics of interest. The scale of storage and computational capability available supports the treatment of big data, not only of large static collections but also of the kinds of streaming sensor data important in the Internet of Things and the combination of big and streaming data. In turn, Cloud acts as an enabler for activities in so-called smart cities and in supporting operation of connected and autonomous vehicles. And although software, platform and infrastructure remain the mainstay of service models, these also now address containers (e.g. with Docker in Amazon's Elastic Container Service, Microsoft Container Service, Google Container Engine and IBM Containers) and microservices (AWS Lambda, Microsoft Azure Functions, Google Cloud Functions and IBM OpenWhisk); the latter abstracts away from the lower levels of the stack, as well as offering pricing based on compute time used as multiples of milliseconds rather than hours. With the relative maturity of such offerings, as well the emergent next generations of mobile telecommunications related to network function virtualisation and mobile edge Cloud computing, increased focus on distributed computation and computational offloading may also be anticipated.

Given the extent described above, any collection such as this can only ever offer insights into select subsets of what exists – as, indeed, have the paragraphs above. Research around these areas abounds and will continue to grow, with the growth in number and diversity of Cloud conferences and workshops and special issues of very many journals that are variously Cloud flavoured, as a crude but effective measure of reach, coverage and scope. However, the four cornerstones of quality of service, embodied in the first edition, remain consistent:

1. Efficiency: The need for execution and coordination of the services to be optimised in terms of data traffic and latency remains, even with lower-latency communications, in part due to growth of data and ability to process it. Data traffic is typically one of the main cost factors in any distributed computing framework, and thus its reduction is a standard long-term goal of such systems. Latency is arguably one of the most important factors affecting customer satisfaction, and therefore it should also be within specified acceptable limits. And efficiencies in performance per unit cost are of particular importance.
2. Scalability: Cloud service offerings of various kinds continue to need to scale well to support massive customer bases. They must continue to withstand demand of a great many bursty applications during peak times and endure the "flash crowd" phenomenon familiar in overly successful marketing strategies and provisioning for popular websites at key times. There is evidence to suggest, also, that great scale can dissipate distributed denial of service attacks, albeit at a price. However, applications must also be architected to be able to operate at scale.
3. Robustness: Cloud services still need continuously high availability by design, with effective use of redundancy and graceful failover. With users charged for the expected successful use of computational facilities, it remains imperative to understand and address the risk of failure, either to help to mitigate the probability of failure or to use this information to offer appropriate compensation schemes. Some high-profile Cloud users are known to make deliberate efforts to disrupt their own systems in order to prove to themselves that any impact on the services is minimised, which again relates to appropriate architecting.
4. Security: Appropriate security provisions are now, quite simply, a fundamental expectation for both data and applications to protect both the providers and consumers from malicious or fraudulent activities and must recognise the responsibilities of each with respect to the other.

In respect to various Cloud topics, this edition carries the following key objectives:

1. To present and explore the principles, techniques, protocols and algorithms that are used to design, develop and manage Clouds
2. To present current Cloud applications and highlight the use of Cloud technologies to manage data and scientific analysis
3. To present methods for linking Clouds and optimising their performance

All three objectives are firmly rooted in extant discourse of distributed computing and a desire to understand the potential of all these technologies in constructing purpose-specific Cloud solutions that successfully address commercial demand and shape successful business.

2. Expected Audience

This book should be of particular interest for the following audiences:

- *Researchers and doctoral students* working on certain aspects of Cloud computing research, implementation and deployment, primarily as a reference publication. Similarly, this book should be useful to researchers in related or more general fields, such as distributed computing, software engineering, web services, modelling of business processes and so on.
- *Academics and students* engaging in research-informed teaching in the above fields. This book can serve as a good collection of articles to facilitate a good understanding of this subject and as such may be useful as a key reference text in such teaching.
- *Professional system architects and developers* who could decide to adapt and apply in practice a number of techniques and processes presented in the book.
- *Technical managers and IT consultants* who would consider this as a book that demonstrates the potential applicability of certain methods for delivering efficient and secure commercial services to customers globally.

These audiences will find this publication appealing as it combines three distinct scholarly contributions: firstly, it identifies and highlights current techniques and methods for designing Cloud systems and optimising their performance; secondly, it presents mechanisms and schemes for developing Clouds to manage data and produce scientific analysis and economic activities; and thirdly, it provides a coverage of approaches and technologies used to link Clouds together and manage heterogeneity.

3. Book Overview

The book contains 14 chapters that were carefully selected based on peer review by at least two expert and independent reviewers. The chapters are split into five parts:

Part I: General Principles

This part aims to cover the essential technical characteristics and concepts behind the new developments in Cloud computing. The chapters included in this part collectively introduce the reader to essential architectural principles behind the new developments and how these advances are influencing the applications, how to measure the performance of new Cloud architectures and how to do effective resource management in the emerging Clouds for improved quality of service and performance.

Chapter 1 provides a taxonomy and survey to highlight the rapid technological advancements in Cloud computing and how it will transform silos into to the so-called Internet of Things (IoT). This chapter discusses the principles and taxonomy behind emerging trends in Cloud computing such as edge computing (Cloudlets and fog computing), IoT (smart grids, smart cities) and big data.

Chapter 2 describes the resource estimation problem that, if not addressed, will either overestimate or underestimate the resources, leading to wasted resources or poor performance. This chapter addresses the problem of dimensioning the amount of virtual machines (VMs) in Clouds and presents approaches that estimate in a static or dynamic way the amount of VMs for several types of applications.

Chapter 3 reviews the important approaches for resource monitoring in virtual machines. Taxonomy is presented that, when applied to different solutions that use or augment virtual machines, can help in determining their similarities and differences. The process of classification and comparing systems is detailed, and several representative state-of-the-art systems are evaluated.

Part II: Science Cloud

This part builds on the principles and approaches of Part I and provides an in-depth coverage of how Clouds can be designed to produce scientific insights and analysis. This part describes important aspects of scientific applications such as agility, reproducibility, consistency and scalability. It includes chapters that propose novel techniques and systems for making Clouds reproducible, agile and consistent.

Chapter 4 introduces elasticity, which helps in determining the most appropriate set of resources for running scientific applications whose requirements cannot be determined in advance. It describes elasticity taxonomy and how this can be used in running scientific applications. A discussion about good practices as well as an analysis of the state of the art is described.

Chapter 5 characterises terms and requirements related to scientific reproducibility. Clouds can play a key role by offering the infrastructure for long-term preservation of programmes and data. This chapter describes how Clouds can aid the development and selection of reproducibility approaches in science.

Chapter 6 describes the challenges in integrating clinical and genomic data and producing insights from it. Integration complexity, data inconsistency and scalability of the underlying data infrastructures have been highlighted as the main challenges. Cloud approaches to storing huge amounts of clinical and genomic data and producing value from it are also described.

Part III: Data Cloud

This part provides an overview of novel approaches in producing scalable, high-performance and decentralised Cloud systems. This provides an overview of how emerging technologies such as P2P and graph systems fit with Cloud computing to enable fault-tolerant, scalable and high-performance data-intensive Clouds.

Chapter 7 describes the challenges of implementing graph-based systems and frameworks. The focus is on the problem of creating scalable systems for storing and processing large-scale graph data on HPC Clouds. It highlights a graph database benchmarking framework and its use in analysing the performance of graph database servers.

Chapter 8 describes a framework that exploits a peer-to-peer (P2P) model to manage systems failures of MapReduce and their recovery in a decentralised but effective way. It describes the architecture and performance results of the proposed model, which shows a higher level of fault tolerance compared to a centralised implementation of MapReduce.

Part IV: Multi-clouds

This part presents ideas on achieving federation and interoperability across Clouds and using autonomic computing and other intelligent approaches to self-manage the federated Clouds. It includes chapters that propose novel techniques and systems for making Cloud data and application interoperable as well as achieving data and compute interoperability through automated means.

Chapter 9 presents an architecture to facilitate federated Clouds for achieving interoperability between Clouds, especially application and data-level interoperability. It describes the design of the architecture, implementation choices and some practical evaluations for monitoring multiple Cloud deployments to make informed decisions.

Chapter 10 provides an overview of the concepts that are being used in practice and theory in order to advance the field of self-managing and self-healing Clouds. It describes approaches to providing self-managed data- and compute-intensive services to the users by overcoming heterogeneity in terms of computing resources.

Part V: Performance and Efficiency

This part covers a range of challenging issues associated to Cloud data centres that, if not addressed properly, may limit its adoption. It includes chapters on

Cloud operations and Cloud economy offering approaches that can bring down Cloud operation costs. It also includes chapters on resource management approaches leading to energy efficiency and predictive workload management.

Chapter 11 presents a Cloud brokering model, which can reduce Cloud customers' costs when compared to traditional on-demand renting costs. It proposes a number of online and offline heuristics to efficiently manage the resources of the broker in order to optimise its revenue, as well as the QoS level offered to the customers.

Chapter 12 proposes a resource management model with the aim of improving energy efficiency and reliability. The model manages the problem of over-provisioning of resources and to an underutilisation of the active servers. Using an evolutionary optimisation algorithm, the model can efficiently map user requests with the available hardware resources.

Chapter 13 describes an approach to manage Cloud data centres by observing workload behaviours and server usage patterns in the past. The analysis presented in this chapter can support Cloud providers for achieving efficient data centre management and prediction analytics in Cloud data centres.

Chapter 14 presents energy-efficient browsing approach that ranks URL and web domains based on web page-induced energy consumption. The approach can achieve substantial resource reduction for CPU and memory usage. It is also able to reduce bandwidth usage without any degradation to user experience.

Acknowledgements

The editors are grateful to the peer review panel for supporting this book including Miyuru Dayarathna, Daniel de Oliveira, Vincent C. Emeakaroha, Teodor-Florin Fortiş, Imen Ben Fradj, Luiz Manoel Rocha Gadelha Júnior, Guilherme Galante, Santiago Iturriaga, Sara Kadry, Somnath Mazumdar, Bhaskar Prasad Rimal, José Simão and Domenico Talia.

The editors are also grateful to their respective families for continuing to afford them the time to produce works such as this.

The editors wish to thank Springer's team for their strong and continuous support throughout the development of this book.

The editors are also deeply apologetic to anyone that they may have forgotten.

Derby, UK   Nick Antonopoulos
Guildford, UK   Lee Gillam
Winter 2016

Contents

Part I
General Principles

Chapter 1
The Rise of Cloud Computing in the Era of Emerging Networked Society

Bhaskar Prasad Rimal and Ian Lumb

1.1 Introduction

In 2009, Rimal et al. [1] published a very first taxonomy and survey that defined the field, described many issues and opportunities, and summarized the developments of cloud computing up to that point. We refer readers to our original paper [1] to better understand the fundamentals of cloud computing and the descriptions of potential applications. Since then, the role and scope of cloud computing has remarkably changed. In this chapter, our aim is a complement to that taxonomy and survey, denoting the rapid technological advancements since then. Cloud computing has been widely deployed and become a major backbone of every other technology – from cellular phones through to wearables, connected vehicles, and the future *networked society*. The networked society is the *networks of everything (NoE)*, that is, beyond the upcoming 5G networks.

Our vision of networked society is not only about wired/wireless communications but creating an ecosystem of device vendors, application developers, network operators, telecom operators, and cloud services/infrastructure providers to create a foreseeable new business value chain that will not only accelerate every area but also bring new innovative ideas and services. Those services are accessible to anyone (e.g., devices, human, robots, automobiles) to connect each other and share data from anywhere and anytime. However, there is still no well-defined standard definition and requirements of the networked society. Therefore, there is

B.P. Rimal (✉)
University of Québec, INRS, Montfeal, QC, Canada
e-mail: b.bprimal@gmail.com

I. Lumb
York University, Toronto, ON, Canada
Univa Corporation, Hoffman Estates, IL, USA

© Springer International Publishing AG 2017
N. Antonopoulos, L. Gillam (eds.), *Cloud Computing*, Computer Communications and Networks, DOI 10.1007/978-3-319-54645-2_1

3

a need for a taxonomy of enabling technologies of networked society to better understand the concept and advance the state of the art. This chapter provides a holistic understanding of networked society.

Furthermore, given the wide variety of communications (e.g., machine-to-machine communications, human-to-machine communication, human-to-robot communications) and applications in the networked society, a single communication technology is likely not able to meet such heterogeneity. We may need a convergence or integration of different wired/wireless communication technologies to truly address the complexity of the networked society. Cloud computing technologies are the major backbone for networked society, where billions of devices will be connected anytime to each other and access a wide variety of services anywhere. Toward this end, the focus and contributions of this chapter are as follows:

- First, we revisit the scope and role of cloud computing and extend them in the context of networked society, paying particular attention to scope and emerging areas of cloud computing.
- Second, we propose a taxonomy of enabling technologies of networked society. This will be an instrument to understand the vision, the overall concept, and the enabling technologies of networked society. To the best of the authors' knowledge, this is a first taxonomy of enabling technologies of the networked society.
- Third, we describe each enabling technology of networked society based on the proposed taxonomy and pay close attention to some of the particular challenges and opportunities that may be used by other researchers as a baseline for future research in the area of networked society.

The remainder of the chapter is structured as follows. Section 1.2 provides an overview of cloud computing in a nutshell, including cloud service modes and deployment modes. Section 1.3 introduces a networked society and presents a proposed taxonomy of enabling technologies of networked society. Further, each enabling technology is discussed, including issues and opportunities in great detail. Finally, Sect. 1.4 concludes the chapter.

1.2 Cloud Computing in Nutshell

Cloud computing implements the idea of utility computing, which was first coined by Professor John McCarthy in 1961, where computing was viewed as a public utility just as the telephone system. Later, this idea resurfaced in new forms as *cloud computing*. There is a plethora of definitions for cloud computing, from both academia and industry. Among them, Rimal et al. [2] defined cloud computing as, *a model of service delivery and access where dynamically scalable and virtualized resources are provided as a service over the Internet.* Cloud computing provides a paradigm shift of business and IT, where computing power, data storage, and services are outsourced to third parties and made available as commodities to enterprises and customers. Cloud computing is a center point for the most highly impactful technologies such as mobile Internet, automation of knowledge work, the Internet of Things (IoT), and big data. Further, cloud offers tremendous economic benefits. For example, the total economic impact of cloud technology could be $1.7–$6.2 trillion annually in 2025, and the proliferation and sophistication of cloud services could become a major driving force in making entrepreneurship more feasible in the coming decade [3]. However, there are several challenges to be addressed. The taxonomy, survey, challenges, and opportunities of cloud computing are thoroughly studied in [4].

1.2.1 Service Models and Deployment Modes of Cloud Computing

Cloud service models can be classified into three groups: Software-as-a-Service (SaaS), Platform-as-a-Service (PaaS), and Infrastructure-as-a-Service (IaaS). The deployment modes can be categorized into three groups: public cloud, private cloud, and hybrid cloud. We discuss them briefly in the following subsections.

1.2.1.1 Cloud Service Models

(1) Software-as-a-Service (SaaS): SaaS, commonly referred to as the Application Service Provider model, is heralded by many as the new wave in application software delivery. Further, SaaS can be view as a multi-tenant cloud platform [5]. It shares common resources and a single instance of both the object code of an application as well as the underlying database to support multiple customers simultaneously. Key examples of SaaS provider include SalesForce.com,[1] NetSuite,[2] Oracle,[3] IBM,[4] and Microsoft (e.g., Microsoft Office 365[5]).

(2) Platform-as-a-Service (PaaS): It is the big idea to provide developers with a platform including all the systems and environments comprising the end-to-end life cycle of developing, testing, deploying, and hosting of sophisticated web applications as a service delivered by a cloud. It provides an easier way to develop business applications and various services over the Internet. Key examples of

---

[1] SalesForce: https://www.salesforce.com/, Accessed Nov. 2016.

[2] NetSuite: http://www.netsuite.com/, Accessed Nov. 2016.

[3] Oracle: https://www.oracle.com/cloud/saas.html, Accessed Nov. 2016.

[4] IBM: https://www.ibm.com/cloud-computing/solutions/, Accessed Nov. 2016.

[5] Microsoft Office 365: https://products.office.com/en-us/office-online/documents-spreadsheets-presentations-office-online, Accessed Nov. 2016.

PaaS are Google AppEngine[6] and Microsoft Azure,[7] just to name two. PaaS can slash development time and offer hundreds of readily available tools and services compared to conventional application development.

(3) Infrastructure-as-a-Service (IaaS): IaaS is the delivery of resources (e.g., processing, storage, networks) as a service over Internet. Aside from the higher flexibility, a key benefit of IaaS is the usage-based payment scheme. This allows customers to pay as you grow. Key examples are Amazon EC2,[8] GoGrid,[9] Flexiscale,[10] Layered Technologies,[11] AppNexus,[12] Joyent,[13] and Mosso/Rackspace.[14]

1.2.1.2   Cloud Deployment Modes

(1) Public Cloud: It describes the cloud computing in the traditional mainstream sense, whereby resources are dynamically provisioned on a fine-grained, self-service basis over the Internet, via web applications/web services, from an off-site third-party provider who shares resources. Some examples are Zimory,[15] Microsoft Azure, Amazon EC2, GigaSpaces,[16] Rackspace, and Flexiscale.[17]

(2) Private Cloud: Data and processes are managed within the organization without the restrictions of network bandwidth, security exposures, and legal requirements that using public cloud services across open, public networks might entail. Some examples are Amazon VPC,[18] Eucalyptus,[19] OpenStack,[20] VMWare,[21] and Intalio.[22]

---

[6]Google AppEngine: https://console.cloud.google.com/projectselector/appengine, Accessed Nov. 2016.

[7]Microsoft Azure: https://azure.microsoft.com/en-us/?b=16.26, Accessed Nov. 2016.

[8]Amazon EC2: https://aws.amazon.com/ec2/, Accessed Nov. 2016.

[9]GoGrid: https://www.datapipe.com/gogrid/, Accessed Nov. 2016.

[10]Flexiscale: http://www.flexiscale.com/, Accessed Nov. 2016.

[11]Layered Technologies: https://www.datapipe.com/layered_tech/, Accessed Nov. 2016.

[12]AppNexus: https://www.appnexus.com/en/platform, Accessed Nov. 2016.

[13]Joyent: https://www.joyent.com/, Accessed Nov. 2016.

[14]Mosso/Rackspace: https://www.rackspace.com/cloud, Accessed Nov. 2016.

[15]Zimory: http://www.zimory.com/, Accessed Nov. 2016.

[16]GigaSpaces: http://www.gigaspaces.com/HP, Accessed Nov. 2016.

[17]Flexiscale: http://www.flexiscale.com/, Accessed Nov. 2016.

[18]Amazon VPC: https://aws.amazon.com/vpc/, Accessed Nov. 2016.

[19]Eucalyptus: http://www8.hp.com/us/en/cloud/helion-eucalyptus.html, Accessed Nov. 2016.

[20]OpenStack: https://www.openstack.org/, Accessed Nov. 2016.

[21]VMWare: https://www.vmware.com/, Accessed Nov. 2016.

[22]Intalio: http://www.intalio.com/, Accessed Nov. 2016.

(3) Hybrid Cloud: The environment is consisting of multiple internal and/or external providers. Some examples are RightScale,[23] Asigra Hybrid Cloud Backup,[24] QTS,[25] and Skytap.[26]

1.3 Networked Society

A conventional definition of networked society states that *a number of major social, technological, economic, and cultural transformations came together to give rise to a new form of society, the so-called networked society.* A focal point of the networked society is the transformation of the realm of communications [6, 7]. In a broader perspective of information, communications and technologies (ICTs), and beyond 5G networks (refer Sect. 1.3.1), networked society can be defined as a new paradigm and is not only about technology, but it creates *an ecosystem of device vendors,* application developers, network operators, telecom operators, and cloud services/infrastructure providers to create a foreseeable *new business value chain* that will not only accelerate every area but also *brings new innovative ideas and services.* Cloud technologies became a major part of networked society.

Figure 1.1 presents a hypothetical scenario that is suggestive of the near future we hope to create by leveraging the benefits of cloud computing in the networked society. The networked society is beyond future 5G networks. It is more than *more data* and *massive end-to-end connectivity* of the things. Networked society is not just incremental research but game changers for the quality and experience of people's life that will be more intelligent, more immersive experience enriched by context-aware services (e.g., mixed augmented and virtual reality) and automated, secure, sustainable, green, and more knowledgeable society. Furthermore, that will also create a new scientific concept toward industrial and social innovations.

> *Jony is 65 years old and medically paralyzed man. One day Jony feels sick and asks personal assistant robot to call the hospital. The personal assistant robot then calls the hospital emergency number and requests further assistance. The hospital authority then sends self-driving car to Jony's home. The personal assistant robot puts Jony into the self-driving car. Then the self-driving car takes him to the hospital. On the way to hospital doctors were monitoring Jony's health status remotely. At the hospital, a specialist doctor performs remote surgery with actuating robots to save his life.*

Fig. 1.1 Hypothetical scenario of the next generation of cloud computing: connecting everything from everywhere via cloud in the networked society

---

[23]http://www.rightscale.com/, Accessed Nov. 2016.

[24]Asigra: http://www.asigra.com/cloud-backup-software, Accessed Nov. 2016.

[25]http://www.qtsdatacenters.com/, Accessed Nov. 2016.

[26]https://www.skytap.com/, Accessed Nov. 2016.

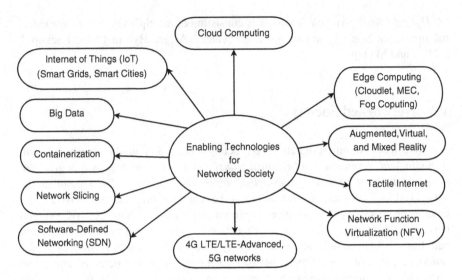

Fig. 1.2 Proposed taxonomy of enabling technologies of the networked society

1.3.1 Taxonomy of Enabling Technologies of Networked Society

Pervasiveness and emerging technological trend of cloud computing disrupts industries across the world, and companies look forward to maximize and implement cloud as a strategic and integral technology to create value chain and business agility. This will create a huge opportunity in the networked society era of disruptive innovation. The proposed taxonomy of enabling technologies of networked society is shown in Fig. 1.2. In the next section, we provide a more detailed description of each enabling technology.

1.3.1.1 Edge Computing: Cloudlet, Fog Computing, and Mobile-Edge Computing

Cloudlet: A cloudlet (also known as edge cloud) is a powerful computer or computer cluster that can be viewed as a *data center in a box* whose goal is to bring the cloud one wireless hop away from the mobile devices, thereby maintaining logical proximity (low latency, high bandwidth). Further, it can be viewed as a new architectural element that represents the middle tier of a three-tier hierarchy: mobile device, cloudlet, and cloud [8]. The cloudlet host runs a hypervisor (e.g., KVM) in order to host multiple virtual machines (VMs). Those VMs publish information (e.g., OS and other properties) to the network. The cloudlet client (e.g., smart phones, PDAs, wearable devices) discovers the cloudlet server through information (cloudlet server IP address and port) broadcasted by the discovery service residing in a cloudlet host. The client then establishes an HTTP connection to the cloudlet server for VM overlay[27] transmission and uploads the overlay [8–10]. The cloudlet decompresses this overlay and applies it to the baseVM to derive the launchVM and then creates a VM instance from it. Afterward, the mobile client starts offloading operation on that instance. The mobile device uses Wi-Fi or cellular data service of 4G LTE depending on the deployment scenarios of cloudlet to reach Internet and then remote cloud (e.g., Amazon EC2).

Cloudlet supports resource-intensive and interactive mobile applications by providing computing resources to mobile devices with low latency. Key features of cloudlets include near-real-time, just-in-time provisioning of applications to edge nodes and handoff of virtual machines seamlessly from one node to another once a user has moved away from its first node.

Potential application areas of cloudlet are enormous. More specifically, the applications (e.g., video streaming, speech processing, cognitive assistance applications, augmented and virtual reality, edge analytics in IoT, new automotive services, drone, just to name a few) which have stringent QoS requirements, such as low latency and real time, can all benefit from cloudlets.

Fog Computing: Cisco envisioned the concept of Fog computing in 2012. Fog computing is a highly virtualized platform, which extends the cloud computing to the edge of networks, thereby enabling applications and services on billions of connected devices, especially, in the Internet of Things (IoT) [11]. Example includes Cisco IOx that combines IoT application execution within the fog computing and offers highly secure connectivity with Cisco IOS technology. Some of the major characteristics of Fog computing are listed below:

- Fog nodes (i.e., provide compute, storage, and network capabilities) are typically located away from the main cloud data centers.
- Fog nodes provide applications with awareness of device geographical location and device context.
- Fog nodes offer special services that may only be required in the IoT context (e.g., translation between IP and non-IP transport).
- Support for online analytics and interplay with the cloud

Fog computing may have a wide range of applications such as connected vehicle, smart grid, smart cities, pipeline monitoring, connected rail, smart traffic light systems, machine-to-machine (M2M) communications, or human-machine interaction (HMI), just to name a few.

Mobile-Edge Computing: The European Telecommunications Standards Institute (ETSI) launched an industry specification for mobile-edge computing (MEC) in September 2014. The ETSI defined MEC as: *Mobile-edge Computing transforms*

---

[27]The compressed binary difference between the *baseVM* (i.e., a VM with a minimally configured guest operating system installed) image and the *launchVM* (i.e., VM image used for offloading) image is known a VM overlay [8, 9].

base stations (e.g., 2G/3G/4G/5G) into intelligent service hubs that are capable of delivering highly personalized services (IT and cloud computing capabilities) directly from the very edge of the network within the radio access network (RAN) while providing the best possible performance in mobile networks [12]. Some typical use cases of MEC are as follows:

- Intelligent video acceleration service
- Active location-aware application services
- Video stream analysis and video delivery optimization using data caching
- Augmented and virtual reality services
- RAN intelligence for customer experience
- Mobile PBX for large enterprises
- Connected vehicles and IoT gateway services

Examples of some leading MEC solution providers include the Vasona Smart AIR platform, Saguna Open-RAN, Brocade MEC Platform Services, Nokia Liquid Radio Applications Cloud Server, and Intel's Network Edge Virtualization (NEV) SDK MEC application and services.

The major components of the ETSI-MEC architecture [13] are summarized in Table 1.1.

1.3.1.2 Internet of Things: Smart Grids and Smart Cities

Internet of Things: The Internet of Things (IoT) is the *network of networks* where billions of devices/objects connect to each other and create new opportunities and challenges. IoT ecosystem includes any type of devices/technology (smartphones, connected cars, wearables, robots, vertical applications) that can connect to the Internet. The International Telecommunication Union (ITU) Telecommunication

Table 1.1 The major components and its functionalities of the ETSI-MEC reference architecture

Components	Description
Mobile-edge platform	Sets the policy and configuration rules (e.g., traffic rules) for forwarding user plane traffic to MEC applications. It also provides a set of services and access to persistent storage
Mobile-edge orchestrator	Maintains an overall view of the deployed mobile-edge hosts, validates applications rules and requirements, and selects appropriate mobile-edge hosts for instantiating a MEC application
Mobile-edge platform manager	Responsible for life cycle management of applications and provides element management functions to the mobile-edge platform
Virtualized infrastructure manager	Responsible for managing, allocating, and releasing the resources of the virtualized infrastructure and also does rapid provisioning of applications
Mobile-edge applications	Runs on the top of the virtualized infrastructure provided by the mobile-edge host and also interacts with mobile-edge platform to provide services

Table 1.2 Overview of functional requirements of the IoT

Functional requirements	Description
Application support requirements	Programmable interfaces, group management, time synchronization, collaboration, authentication, authorization, and accounting
Service requirements	Service level agreements (SLAs), autonomic service provisioning, service composition, service mobility, user mobility and device mobility, virtual storage, and processing capabilities
Communication requirements	Heterogeneous communications (wired or/and wireless technologies, such as controller area network (CAN) bus, ZigBee (IEEE 802.15.4), Bluetooth (IEEE 802.15.1), Wi-Fi (IEEE 802.11a/b/g/n/ac), 4G LTE/LTE-Advanced, 5G), Low power Wireless Personal Area Networks (IEEE 802.15.4/6LoWPA), communication modes (event-based, periodic, and automatic communication modes), autonomic networking (self-configuring, self-healing, self-optimizing, and self-protecting capabilities), and context- and location-aware communications
Device requirements	Remote monitoring, control and configuration of devices, monitoring of things, and device mobility
Data management requirements	Integrity checking and life cycle management of data; storing, aggregating, transferring, and processing the data; access control of data; and high availability and reliability of data of things
Security and privacy protection requirements	Trust and privacy, mutual authentication and authorization between the devices, integration of security policies and techniques, and security audit

Standardization Sector (ITU-T) in Recommendation ITU-T Y.2066 [14] defined the IoT as *a global infrastructure for the information society, enabling advanced services by interconnecting (physical and virtual) things based on existing and evolving interoperable information and communication technologies.* IoT has an enormous potential to bring innovations to new business. For instance, McKinsey report shows that the IoT has the potential to create economic impact of \$2.7–\$6.2 trillion annually by 2025. Some of the most promising uses are in healthcare, infrastructure, and public sector services [3].

Tables 1.2 and 1.3 summarize the IoT functional (related to the IoT actors[28]) and nonfunctional requirements (related to the implementation and operation of the IoT) [14]. Even though cloud computing and IoT are two very different technologies, both can be converged, giving rise to so-called *IoT-cloud computing* – a novel paradigm and enabler for vast majority of large-scale application deployments. Indeed, the convergence of cloud computing and IoT enables ubiquitous sensing services and powerful computing platforms with large-scale computing and storage capabilities, thus stimulating new innovations in the area of IoT.

---

[28] Actors are external to the IoT and interact with the IoT.

Table 1.3 Overview of nonfunctional requirements of the IoT

Nonfunctional requirements
Interoperability
Scalability to handle a large number of devices, applications, and user
Reliability in communication, service, and data management capabilities of IoT
Service provisioning, data management, communication, sensing, and actuating
Adaptability to new technologies
Manageability – device state and connectivity management and energy consumption management

Cisco predicted that 50 billion devices will be connected to the Internet by 2020 [15]. These devices will produce huge amounts of data. Moving all these data to the cloud for analysis would require vast amounts of bandwidth. Cloud computing is certainly a better way of addressing these requirements. Despite achieving low-latency and ultrahigh reliability (carrier-grade reliability, i.e., 99.999% availability) for mission critical IoT applications (e.g., smart transportation, remote surgery, industrial process automation), designing novel cloud-based sensing algorithms, cloud-based IoT mobility management, and energy-aware communication protocols for IoT are among the important research avenues. However, it is very challenging due to network integration, heterogeneity (of devices, platforms, operating systems, communication protocols), interoperability, and coexistence of human-to-human (H2H) and machine-to-machine (M2M) communications.

Smart Grids: Cloud computing also offers opportunities for significant efficiency savings and for making a huge contribution toward institutional carbon-saving targets, such as smart grids. IEEE Standard 2030 Guide for Smart Grid Interoperability of Energy Technology and Information Technology operation with the Electric Power System (EPS) and End-Use Applications and Loads [16] defines smart grids as the "integration of power, communications, and information technologies for an improved electric power infrastructure serving loads while providing for an ongoing evolution of end-use applications." Ensuring the reliable bidirectional information flow between heterogeneous entities is a key requirement of smart grids. In particular, the integration of IT into smart grids eventually increases the complexity in network design, which motivates large scalable infrastructures for computing and storage.

IEEE P2030 [16] aims at providing interoperability between power and energy technologies, ICT, and customer side applications. Its main objectives include the integration of energy technologies and ICT, seamless data transfer, reliable power delivery, and end-use benefits. Furthermore, IEEE P2030 spans three distinct architectural perspectives: power systems, communication technology, and information technology. The objective of those perspectives is to deal with interoperability among the elements of smart grids. The expected benefits of smart grids are as follows:

- With the help of integrated ICT, smart grids will be able to optimize the system reliability and allow prosumers to adjust their demand during peak hours in order to save money.
- Reduce carbon footprint with the deployment of smart grid-enabled electrical vehicles and efficient use of renewable energy sources that reduce the dependency on fossil fuels.

Besides these advantages, smart grids face some challenges, such as to reduce the capital and operational costs, handling big data, security of cyber and power infrastructures, and regulatory frameworks, among others.

Furthermore, the concepts of smart grids are applicable not only to electrical power grids but are also essential to develop a sustainable high-quality life of citizens in cities. In particular, future smart grids will be intertwined with smart cities to interconnect ICT, energy, water, healthcare, citizens, and governments, as explained shortly.

Smart Cities: The global changes affecting climate, population, urbanization, and advances in urban technology put forward the concept of "Smart Cities" as a new dimension in urban development. There are many definitions of smart cities [17]. The author in [18] defined a smart city as follows: "a smarter city is connecting the physical infrastructure, the IT infrastructure, the social infrastructure, and the business infrastructure to leverage the collective intelligence of the city." Note that no consensus has been reached on what the term smart cities exactly means.

Smart grids can be one of the major domains of smart cities that will address the growing energy demand by integrating renewable resources through demand response and reduce the carbon footprint in the cities. On the other hand, other technologies like cloud computing can provide IT infrastructures to the cities for analyzing, controlling, and monitoring of city council data and applications. Early examples of smart cities include the European Platform for Intelligent Cities, IBM Smarter Cities, Microsoft's CityNext, and Amsterdam Smart City. Among them, the IBM Smarter Cities project promotes the deployment of instrumented, interconnected, and intelligent systems to improve social progress from smart grids and transportation to water management and healthcare. Some of the anticipated benefits of smart cities are as follows:

- Provide city-scale ICT-enabled infrastructures along with unified information and control systems for data collection, analysis, and simulation in order to provide efficient governance and engagement of citizens for planning and decision-making activities of sustainable cities.
- Stimulating the use of sustainable energy efficiency systems to lower carbon emissions.

The research on cloud-based smart cities has started only recently. The authors in [19] proposed a cloud-based architecture for context-aware citizen services for smart cities. Similarly, the Scallop4SC platform [20] was designed to store and process large-scale house data in smart cities. However, there still exist open challenges in realizing smart cities:

- Network edges are becoming themselves complex networks because of increasing data diversity and heterogeneity. Mathematical analysis and modeling of intrinsic network dynamics on the large scale are a complex issue, e.g., distributed demand and supply and destabilized power grid operations, due to integration of renewables and new transmission lines.
- Designing a unified information model that is capable of safely sharing information between applications and services at a city scale is often challenging. It should be based on semantically well-designed information models, which capture data from disparate sources, each having its own attributes, i.e., sampling frequency, latency characteristics, and semantics [21].
- Crowdsourcing can be used for semantic modeling of information from a crowd of people related to a targeted issue and predicting the real-time behavior of traffic. Crowdsourcing has been emerging in smart city applications, e.g., OpenStreetMap,[29] Cyclopath,[30] and Waze.[31] Waze is a crowdsourcing traffic application that uses each driver as a sensor for data acquisition. At the downside, there is no best practice of characterizing crowdsourcing systems. For instance, it is hard to predict the number of influential users, quantifying their range of contributions, and integration of results.

Necessity of Cloud Computing for Smart Grids/Cities

Most of the power grid applications (e.g., SCADA, customer relation management (CRM)) are based on traditional IT models that run over dedicated control centers. They are expensive and rigid, but the scalability of such models in the context of smart grids and smart cities is a major concern. Therefore, instead of deploying such applications in traditional data centers, leveraging existing public computing infrastructures such as cloud computing appears to be a promising solution, e.g., by using an on-demand pricing model of cloud computing for demand response management. Further, virtualized cloud resources and virtualized smart grid resources can be integrated in the form of a unified virtualization layer to decouple smart grid applications from underlying smart grid monitoring and communications physical infrastructures [22]. Some major roles of cloud computing in smart grids and smart cities are as follows:

---

[29]OpenStreetMap Community: https://www.openstreetmap.org, Accessed Nov. 2016.
[30]Cyclopath: http://cyclopath.org/, Accessed Nov. 2016.
[31]Waze: https://www.waze.com/, Accessed Nov. 2016.

- Managing large numbers of events and updating each state of distributed energy resources create scalability issues. In addition, data generated from smart meters, sensors, CRM, electric vehicles, and home appliances are massive and heterogeneous. Due to poor scalability and high cost, traditional data warehouse technologies may not be a viable option for smart grids and smart cities. For instance, for a frequency of 5 min, 1 KB data per power usage reading with one million smart meters generates 2.68 TB/day data. This requires intensive resources to be processed, analyzed, and stored. Cloud computing can satisfy such requirements, as it offers scalable infrastructures. In addition, smart grid data are time series data that can be stored in a distributed structure made up of key-value pairs, which enable the distributed management and horizontal scaling [23].
- The computational workload of smart grid and smart city applications can be spread across geographically distributed cloud data centers, where electricity supply is available at low cost. Redundant instances of smart grid and smart city applications minimize service outages and prevent disaster recovery. The authors in [24] discussed a grid-aware routing algorithm, which improves load balancing in smart grids and renders power grids more robust and reliable with regard to demand variations.
- Simulations of smart grids and smart cities include contingency analysis, dynamic behavior of power systems, load forecasting, and climate and crime models. To perform those tasks, large scalable parallel computing infrastructures are required, which are not easy to realize at low cost with traditional infrastructures. Conversely, cloud computing offers such resources on-demand at low cost.

1.3.1.3 Big Data

The big data scenario includes the collection of many data sets. In the past, typically the source of big data is considered as remote sensors and satellite imaging and scientific visualization [25]. However, the horizon of data sources is not limited. Many of the most important sources of big data are relatively new [26]. The big data scenarios are like conventional data analytics before it. However, there are four major differences:

Volume: The amount of all types of data generated from different sources. For instance, Walmart collects more than 2.5 petabytes of data every hour from its customer transactions [26].

Velocity: The speed of data transfer matters for many applications. For example, real-time information and batch processing.

Variety: The huge amounts of information are generated from different sources such as mobile phones, online shopping, social networks (e.g., Facebook, Twitter), and GPS, just to name a few.

Veracity: It refers to the uncertainty of the data and its value.

There are several tools and frameworks (e.g., Hadoop,[32] MapReduce [27], Spark,[33] Flink,[34] Storm,[35] Samza[36]) available to handle the volume, velocity, and variety of big data. Cloud computing plays a vital role for big data not only providing scalable infrastructures and on-demand high-performance computing and distributed storage to process and manage big data but also providing a new business model, for example, big data as a service – a cloud service that allows users to collect, store, analyze, visualize, and manage their big data. On the other hand, there are open issues in big data such as real-time big data analytics, coordination between database systems, and large-scale visualization.

1.3.2 5G Networks: Technology Requirements and Potential Use Cases

Recently, the fifth generation of mobile technology (5G) has received enormous attention from both academia and industry (e.g., METIS[37] [28], 5G-Crosshaul [29], 5GNOW[38]). There is no common understanding about what 5G will be. Many different visions and requirements can be found in the literature and industry white papers. For instance, the telecommunications industry alliance NGMN's 5G vision states that "*5G is an end-to-end ecosystem* to enable a *fully mobile and connected society*. It empowers *value creation* towards customers and partners, through existing and emerging *use cases*, delivered with *consistent experience*, and enabled by *sustainable business models*" [30]. In fact, 5G will be intertwined communications, computing, and control communities.

The requirements for a 5G system are as follows [31, 32]: (a) aggregate data rate should be 1000x from 4G to 5G, (b) 5G will need to support an end-to-end round-trip latency of about 1 ms, (c) massive device connectivity (10–100x), (d) Joules/bit and cost/bit of data will need to fall by at least 100x, (e) (Perception of) 99.999% availability, (f) (Perception of) 100% coverage, and (g) up to 10-year battery life for low-power, machine-type devices. An important question may arise at this point: What could users do on a network, which meets the 5G requirements mentioned above that is not currently possible on an existing 3G/4G/4.5G networks? To find

---

[32] Apache Hadoop. http://hadoop.apache.org/, Accessed Oct. 2016.

[33] Apache Spark. http://spark.apache.org/, Accessed Oct. 2016.

[34] Apache Flink. https://flink.apache.org/, Accessed Oct. 2016.

[35] Apache Storm. http://storm.apache.org/, Accessed Oct. 2016.

[36] Apache Samza. http://samza.apache.org/, Accessed Oct. 2016.

[37] FP7 European Project – Mobile and wireless communications Enablers for the Twenty-twenty Information Society (METIS).

[38] FP7 European Project – 5th Generation Non-Orthogonal Waveforms for Asynchronous Signalling (5GNOW), http://www.5gnow.eu/

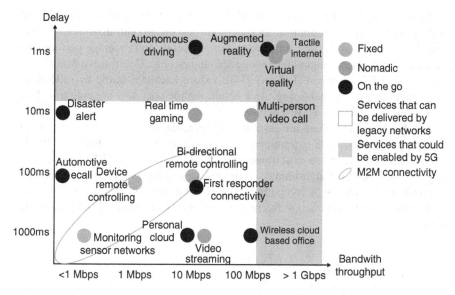

Fig. 1.3 Latency and bandwidth/data rate requirements for generic applications (Source: GSMA Intelligence [32])

the answer of this question, potential use cases should be identified. Some of the requirements identified for 5G can be enabled by existing 4G and/or other networks. Figure 1.3 illustrates the latency and bandwidth/data rate requirements of the various applications, which have been discussed in the context of 5G.

The emerging technologies such as cloud radio access network (C-RAN), software-defined networking (SDN), network functions virtualization (NFV), and edge computing (mobile-edge computing (MEC), fog computing) are the building block for 5G, described in detail in the following.

1.3.2.1 Cloud Radio Access Network (C-RAN)

Cloud computing technology can be beneficial to radio access networks (RANs), e.g., moving RAN functionality to the cloud computing infrastructure. In order to provide mobile broadband Internet access to wireless users with high spectral and energy efficiency, a cloud-based radio access network was envisioned, so-called *cloud radio access network (C-RAN)* [33]. C-RAN is a mobile network architecture where baseband resources are pooled from multiple base stations into centralized baseband units (BBUs) pool. In fact, a C-RAN architecture exploits a combination of virtualization, centralization, and coordination (radio coordination between cells and bands) techniques, all of which interact with each other within the network. Based on the functional splits between BBU and remote radio head (RRH), C-RAN can be fully centralized or partial centralized [33].

Some of the major benefits of the C-RAN are as follows: reduce the network deployment, energy consumption, and operation cost due to centralized maintenance and sharing of infrastructure; improve system, mobility, and coverage performance because of coordinated signal processing techniques (e.g., Coordinated Multi-Point (CoMP) in LTE-Advanced (LTE-A) [34]); reduce backhaul traffic by offloading; and enable better load balancing. As a result, mobile operators are able to deliver rich wireless services in a cost-effective manner.

On the other hand, there are several open research issues to address in C-RAN including high bandwidth requirement for fronthaul (link between BBU and RRH), strict latency and jitter, low-cost transport network, techniques on BBU cooperation (e.g., signal processing algorithms), virtualization techniques for baseband processing pool, and utilization of computing resources (e.g., dynamic resource allocation) in the cloud, just to name a few. Interested readers may refer to [33] and [35] for the details on C-RAN.

1.3.2.2 Tactile Internet

The Tactile Internet enables precise haptic interaction not only machine-to-machine but also human-to-machine relying on 1 ms round-trip latency combining with high availability, ultra-reliability, and high security [36, 37]. Tactile Internet architecture facilitates abstracting and virtualizing sensor/actuator functionalities as well as network resources. The Tactile Internet brings together many disciplines such as healthcare, education, robotics (e.g., industrial robots, service robots, remote-controlled humanoid robots), manufacturing, industrial automation, sports, serious games, and augmented and virtual reality, just to name a few.

Since light travels 300 km within 1 ms, the distance between a control server and the point of tactile interaction can be 150 km, at most [38]. Therefore, to meet the ultralow end-to-end latency and real-time response, Tactile Internet should rely on edge computing (e.g., cloudlets, MEC, Fog computing), and content servers should be located very close to the end users. Possibly such servers are deployed at the base station of every cell, including many small cells (in heterogeneous networks (HetNets)), and importantly any service requiring 1 ms latency has a need for interconnection between operators; this interoperator interconnectivity must also occur within 1 km of the end users [32]. This will likely require a substantial increase in capital expenditure (CAPEX) spent on infrastructure for content distribution and servers [32]. It is worth noting that existing interconnectivity points between operators in 3G/4G networks are very sparse. Meeting 1 ms latency requirement of the Tactile Internet in the era of 5G, there would be also a need of interconnection between base stations (interconnectivity may work in urban areas, but what happens in the case of rural areas?), which not only impact on the CAPEX as mentioned above but also the topology of core network; especially existing mobility model should be revisited.

1.3.2.3 Software-Defined Networking (SDN)

It is a new paradigm in networking (programmable networks), which advocates separating the data plane and the control plane, and facilitates the design, delivery, and operation of network services in a dynamic and scalable manner [39]. Since SDN introduces a centralized approach to network configuration, network operators do not have to configure all network devices individually. Key benefits of the SDN include centralized control, simplified algorithms, commoditizing network hardware, and standard application programming interfaces (APIs). OpenFlow defined by Open Networking Forum[39] is the main southbound API in SDN. Note that there is no currently standardized API for the northbound interactions. A detailed description of the SDN architecture is beyond the scope of this chapter, and interested readers are referred to [39, 40].

SDN has applications in a wide range of networked environments. Importantly, SDN is expected to reduce both capital expenditure and operational expenditures of cloud service providers, enterprise networks, and data centers.

An overview of SDN and some important future research directions are summarized in [41] as follows: controller and switch design, scalability and performance in SDNs, controller-service interfacing, virtualization and cloud service applications, information centric networking, and enabling heterogeneous networking with SDN.

1.3.2.4 Network Function Virtualization (NFV)

Network Function Virtualization (NFV) group of the ETSI [42] defined NFV as follows: "NFV aims to transform the way that network operators architect networks by evolving standard IT virtualization technology to consolidate many network equipment types onto industry standard high volume servers, switches and storage, which could be located in data centers, network nodes and in the end user premises." NFV is applicable to data plane and control plane in both mobile and fixed networks. Some use cases of NFV include security functions, NGN signaling, SLA monitoring functions, gateways, switching functions, and mobile network functions (base station, mobility management entity (MME), radio network controller (RNC), home subscribe server (HSS), packet data network gateway (PDN-GW), serving gateway (SGW), carrier-grade network address translator (CGNAT), and so on). Cloud technologies are the major driving force for NVF, for instance, hardware virtualization (e.g., vSwitch). Indeed, NFV brings several benefits to the telecommunications industry along with cloud computing. More specifically key advantages of NFV are as follows:

- Reduced equipment costs and power consumption
- Availability of network appliance multi-version and multi-tenancy

---

[39]Open Network Foundation. https://www.opennetworking.org, Accessed Oct. 2016.

- Enables a wide variety of ecosystems and fosters openness.
- Enable network operators to reduce the maturation cycle
- Supports multi-tenancy

The building block of NFV architecture mainly consists of virtualized network functions (VNFs – software implementation of network functions), NFV infrastructure (NFVI – virtual compute, storage, and network), and NFV management and orchestration (life cycle management of resources and VNFs). The details of the NFV reference architecture are beyond the scope of this chapter. Interested readers are referred to [43].

Besides these benefits, there are some technical challenges that need to be addressed, such as scalability, seamless integration of different appliances from different vendors, resilience, orchestration of legacy and virtual network appliances, network stability, and so on.

1.3.2.5 Augmented Reality, Virtual Reality, and Mixed Reality

An augmented reality is a system (e.g., Google Glass) that combines the real world with computer-generated virtual objects and appears to coexist in the same space as the real world. AR system registers real and virtual objects to each other [44]. In virtual reality (VR) system, user is immersed in the computer-generated virtual environments. The first VR device called head-mounted display (HMD) was developed by Ivan Sutherland and his team in 1968 (also see his paper "The Ultimate Display" [45]). The examples of recent VR devices include Google Cardboard, Samsung Gear VR, Oculus Rift, HTC Vive, Sony PlayStation VR, Razer OSVR HDK 2, and so on. Mixed reality is the combination of both AR and VR systems (e.g., Microsoft's HoloLens) that means the MR combines real and virtual objects and information.

The AR, VR, and MR systems has a wide range of applications. For instance, AR devices can help improve safety and efficiency in customer service and can be used by doctors, while the VR devices are mainly designed for gaming. However, application areas can be expanded from academic research through to engineering, design, business, gaming (e.g., Pokémon Go), and entertainment. Since AR/VR/MR devices have low computing, processing, and storage capabilities, the best way to achieve good performance of the AR/VR/MR applications is to offload compute-intensive tasks to the remote cloud or edge cloud.

There are several research directions in the AR/VR/MR systems. Among them, performance benchmarking is very important. For instance, finding the relationships among independent variables including field of view, image resolution, scene content, and interactive control, using the presence and performance as dependent variables, is still an open issue [46].

1.3.2.6   Network Slicing

Network slice is an end-to-end logically isolated network, where each slice owns its control plane and data path. The slicing layer provides an abstraction between the control and data plane as well as enforces strong isolation between slices. Users pick which slice controls their traffic [47]. Indeed, slicing policy specifies resource (bandwidth, topology, forwarding rules, etc.) limits for each slice. FlowVisor (i.e., OpenFlow controller) [48] is one of the examples of network slicing. 5G network architecture is expected to provide network slicing feature – so-called *5G slice* – a 5G slice consists of 5G network functions and specific radio access technology settings that are combined together for the specific use case [30].

Network slicing helps operators to manage and operate multiple virtual networks over a shared physical network infrastructure. Since 5G network slicing may involve the combination of different conventional and emerging network technologies (e.g., wired/wireless, different radio access networks, SDN, NFV), network slicing poses new challenges in service instantiation and orchestration and resource allocation/sharing.

1.3.2.7   Containerization

Although it was in principle possible to predict the disruptive impact of containers 5 years ago, it is not clear that anyone actually did. And that is not entirely surprising, as the concept realized with significant success in Solaris Zones,[40] for example, required various enhancements in the Linux kernel (e.g., cgroups, namespaces) as implementation prerequisites. Interestingly in the context of this chapter and indeed this book, the contemporary notion of containers was spun off an internal project from within PaaS company dotCloud in France. Ultimately released to open source in 2013, Docker immediately gained interest, especially following the development of its libcontainer library written in the Go programming language, which replaced the LXC execution environment about a year later. As even a cursory search of Google Trends data emphatically demonstrates, interest in Docker[41] has seen nothing short of a meteoric rise over the past few years and, indeed, since the publication of the first edition of this book. This interest is warranted and can be substantiated on tactical as well as strategic grounds.

Tactically, containers allow applications and all of their dependencies to be packaged, distributed, and executed on any modern Linux server. And although containers have much in common with the virtual machines introduced earlier in this chapter, they also have some significant differences. As Fig. 1.4 indicates, containers share the host's operating system, rather than require their own. Needing only the

---

[40]Solaris   Zones: https://docs.oracle.com/cd/E18440_01/doc.111/e18415/chapter_zones.htm#OPCUG426, Accessed Oct. 2016.

[41]Docker: https://www.docker.com/, Accessed Oct. 2016.

Containers vs. VMs

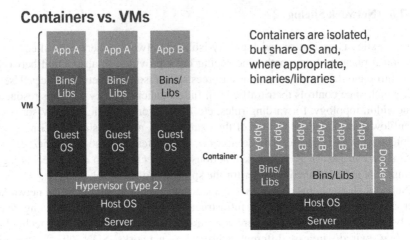

Fig. 1.4 Architectural similarities and differences between containers and virtual machines

runtime provided by the Docker Engine,[42] for example, lighter-weight containers can be instantiated much more efficiently than can a VM that relies on its own OS. Not only is this efficiency appealing in highly dynamic environments, lighter-weight containers are also appealing from a resource management perspective – as a given server can support many isolated containers – as opposed to just a few VMs. Finally, the convenience of containers is responsible for increased portability from development through to deployment and is thus considered significant enablers of the DevOps movement.

From a strategic perspective, containerization is a key enabler for the development of cloud-native applications. Along with an orientation around microservices as well as dynamic scheduling, containerization permits cloud nativity to be architected in at the outset, as opposed to being grafted on as some afterthought. Under the auspices of the Cloud Native Computing Foundation (CNCF),[43] container clusters are already making use of open-source Kubernetes[44] as "seed technology." CNCF is currently incubating a number of projects and promises to further make tangible a number of cloud-native applications.

Although Docker in particular, and containers in general, continue to receive a tremendous amount of interest and attention, it is important to temper this enthusiasm through consideration of a number of concerns. Most importantly, and as is often the case with disruptive technologies, security remains a concern when it comes to containers – so much so – that some organizations run containers within VMs! Security and networking challenges notwithstanding, there is also a degree

---

[42] Docker Engine: https://www.docker.com/products/docker-engine, Accessed Oct. 2016.

[43] Cloud Native Computing Foundation: https://cncf.io/, Accessed Oct. 2016.

[44] Kubernetes: http://kubernetes.io/, Accessed Oct. 2016.

of tension between some proponents of Docker and those who seek to establish standards for containers (e.g., the Open Container Initiative (OCI).[45] Finally, the rapidly evolving ecosystem around containers is both broad and deep, and this certainly creates challenges for those seeking to make future-proofed decisions for enterprise adoption. And that's quite an achievement for a technology that did not really exist, in any significant way, when the previous edition of this book was released some 7 years ago.

1.4 Conclusions

A networked society is a big vision of future information and communications technology world, where everything will be connected and services and application can be accessed anytime from anywhere. Indeed, the networked society is the *networks of everything (NoE)*, that is, beyond the upcoming 5G networks. That will enhance the quality of people's lives not only for information access but in the wide range of sectors including healthcare, education, transportation, education, and entertainment, just to name a few. This chapter has highlighted the new role and scope of cloud computing for the networked society. A taxonomy of enabling technologies of networked society was proposed, and each of them discussed in a great detail. Many technical challenges and opportunities were identified. In order to achieve a full spectrum of benefits of networked society, there is a long journey that may also need new fixed/wireless technologies for long-term realization of networked society. We may need a convergence or combination of different technologies, shown in the proposed taxonomy that can support a wide variety of applications and services. We hope that this chapter will help to understand a long journey toward a networked society.

References

1. Rimal BP, Choi E, Lumb I (2009) A taxonomy and survey of cloud computing systems. In: Proceedings of IEEE fifth international joint conference on INC, IMS and IDC, Aug 2009, pp 44–51
2. Rimal BP, Jukan A, Katsaros D, Goeleven Y (2011) Architectural requirements for cloud computing systems: an enterprise cloud approach. J Grid Comput 9(1):3–26
3. Manyika J, Chui M, Bughin J, Dobbs R, Bisson P, Marrs A (2013) Disruptive technologies: advances that will transform life, business, and the global economy. McKinsey Global Institute, report, May 2013
4. Rimal BP, Choi E (2012) A service-oriented taxonomical spectrum, cloudy challenges and opportunities of cloud computing. Int J Commun Syst 25(6):796–819

---

[45] Open Container Initiative: https://www.opencontainers.org/, Accessed Oct. 2016.

5. Rimal BP, El-Refaey MA (2010) A framework of scientific workflow management systems for multi-tenant cloud orchestration environment. In: Proceedings of the 19th IEEE international workshop on enabling technologies: infrastructures for collaborative enterprises (WETICE), Larissa, June 2010, pp 88–93
6. Castells M (2000) Materials for an exploratory theory of the network society. Br J Soc 51(1): 5–24
7. Castells M (2011) The rise of the network society: the information age: economy, society, and culture, vol 1. Wiley, Somerset
8. Satyanarayanan M, Bahl P, Caceres R, Davies N (2009) The case for vm-based cloudlets in mobile computing. IEEE Pervasive Comput 8(4):14–23
9. Ha K, Pillai P, Richter W, Abe Y, Satyanarayanan M (2013) Just-in-time provisioning for cyber foraging. In: Proceedings of the 11th annual international conference on mobile systems, applications, and services, MobiSys '13, Taipei, June 2013, pp 153–166
10. Simanta S, Lewis GA, Morris E, Ha K, Satyanarayanan M (2012) A reference architecture for mobile code offload in hostile environments. In: Proceedings of the IEEE/IFIP conference on software architecture (WICSA) and European conference on software architecture (ECSA), Helsinki, Aug 2012, pp 282–286
11. Bonomi F, Milito R, Zhu J, Addepalli S (2012) Fog computing and its role in the Internet of things. In: Proceedings of the first edition of the MCC workshop on mobile cloud computing, Helsinki, Aug 2012, pp 13–16
12. ETSI Industry Specification Group (ISG) (2014) Mobile-edge computing – introductory technical white paper. In: ETSI, Sept 2014, pp 1–36
13. ETSI Industry Specification Group (ISG) (2016) Mobile edge computing (MEC); framework and reference architecture, ETSI GS MEC 003 V1.1.1, Mar 2016, pp 1–36
14. International Telecommunication Union (2014) Common requirements of the Internet of Things. Recommendation ITU-T Y.2066, June 2014
15. Evans D (2011) The Internet of Things how the next evolution of the Internet is changing everything. In: Cisco Internet Business Solutions Group (IBSG) white paper, Apr 2011, pp 1–11
16. IEEE (2011) IEEE guide for smart grid interoperability of energy technology and information technology operation with the electric power system (EPS), end-use applications, and loads. IEEE Std 2030-2011, Sept 2011, pp 1–126
17. Chourabi H, Nam T, Walker S, Gil-Garcia JR, Mellouli S, Nahon K, Pardo TA, Scholl HJ (2012) Understanding smart cities: an integrative framework. In: Proceedings of 45th Hawaii international conference on system science (HICSS), Maui, Jan 2012, pp 2289–2297
18. Harrison C, Eckman B, Hamilton R, Hartswick P, Kalagnanam J, Paraszczak J, Williams P (2010) Foundations for smarter cities. IBM J Res Dev 54(4):1–16
19. Khan Z, Kiani SL (2012) A cloud-based architecture for citizen services in smart cities. In: Proceedings of IEEE fifth international conference on utility and cloud computing (UCC), Chicago, Nov 2012, pp 315–320
20. Yamamoto S, Matsumoto S, Nakamura M (2012) Using cloud technologies for large-scale house data in smart city. In: Proceedings of the IEEE 4th international conference on cloud computing technology and science (CloudCom), Taipei, Dec 2012, pp 141–148
21. Naphade M, Banavar G, Harrison C, Paraszczak J, Morris R (2011) Smarter cities and their innovation challenges. Computer 44(6):32–39
22. Yufeng X, Baldine I, Chase J, Beyene T, Parkhurst B, Chakrabortty A (2011) Virtual smart grid architecture and control framework. In: Proceedings of the IEEE international conference on smart grid communications (SmartGridComm), Brussels, Oct 2011, pp 1–6
23. Rusitschka S, Eger K, Gerdes C (2010) Smart grid data cloud: a model for utilizing cloud computing in the smart grid domain. In: Proceedings of the first IEEE international conference on smart grid communications (SmartGridComm), Gaithersburg, Oct 2010, pp 483–488
24. Mohsenian-Rad A-H, Leon-Garcia A (2010) Coordination of cloud computing and smart power grids. In: Proceedings of the first IEEE international conference on smart grid communications (SmartGridComm), Gaithersburg, Oct 2010, pp 368–372

25. Cox M, Ellsworth D (1997) Managing big data for scientific visualization. In: ACM Siggraph, Los Angeles, Aug 1997
26. McAfee A, Brynjolfsson E (2012) Big data. Harv Bus Rev 90(10):61–67
27. Dean J, Ghemawat S (2008) Mapreduce: simplified data processing on large clusters. Commun ACM 51(1):107–113
28. Osseiran A, Boccardi F, Braun V, Kusume K, Marsch P, Maternia M, Queseth O, Schellmann M, Schotten H, Taoka H, Tullberg H, Uusitalo MA, Timus B, Fallgren M (2014) Scenarios for 5G mobile and wireless communications: the vision of the METIS project. IEEE Commun Mag 52(5):26–35
29. La Oliva AD, Perez XC, Azcorra A, Giglio AD, Cavaliere F, Tiegelbekkers D, Lessmann J, Haustein T, Mourad A, Iovanna P (2015) Xhaul: toward an integrated fronthaul/backhaul architecture in 5G networks. IEEE Wirel Commun 22(5):32–40
30. NGMN Alliance (2015) NGMN 5G white paper, Feb 2015, pp 1–125
31. Andrews JG, Buzzi S, Choi W, Hanly SV, Lozano A, Soong ACK, Zhang JC (2014) What will 5G be? IEEE J Sel Areas Commun 32(6):1065–1082
32. GSMA Intelligence (2014) Understanding 5G: perspective on future technological advancement in mobile. White paper, Dec 2014, pp 1–26
33. China Mobile Research Institute (2011) C-RAN: the road towards green RAN. White paper, Oct 2011
34. Lee D, Seo H, Clerckx B, Hardouin E, Mazzarese D, Nagata S, Sayana K (2012) Coordinated multipoint transmission and reception in LTE-advanced: deployment scenarios and operational challenges. IEEE Commun Mag 50(2):148–155
35. Checko A, Christiansen HL, Yan Y, Scolari L, Kardaras G, Berger MS, Dittmann L (2015) Cloud ran for mobile networks – a technology overview. IEEE Commun Surv Tutor 17(1):405–426. Firstquarter 2015
36. Fettweis G, Alamouti S (2014) 5G: personal mobile Internet beyond what cellular did to telephony. IEEE Commun Mag 52(2):140–145
37. Fettweis GP (2014) The tactile Internet: applications and challenges. IEEE Veh Technol Mag 9(1):64–70
38. ITU (2014) The tactile Internet. ITU-T technology watch report, pp 1–24
39. Kim H, Feamster N (2013) Improving network management with software defined networking. IEEE Commun Mag 51(2):114–119
40. Sezer S, Scott-Hayward S, Chouhan PK, Fraser B, Lake D, Finnegan J, Viljoen N, Miller M, Rao N (2013) Are we ready for SDN? Implementation challenges for software-defined networks. IEEE Commun Mag 51(7):36–43
41. Nunes BAA, Mendonca M, Nguyen XN, Obraczka K, Turletti T (2014) A survey of software-defined networking: past, present, and future of programmable networks. IEEE Commun Surv Tutor 16(3):1617–1634. Third Quarter 2014.
42. ETSI Industry Specification Group (ISG) (2012) Network functions virtualisation (NFV), white paper, Oct 2012, pp 1–16
43. ETSI Industry Specification Group (ISG) (2012) Network functions virtualisation (NFV); architectural framework, ETSI GS NFV 002 V1.1.1, Aug 2012, pp 1–21
44. Azuma R, Baillot Y, Behringer R, Feiner S, Julier S, MacIntyre B (2001) Recent advances in augmented reality. IEEE Comput Graph Appl 21(6):34–47
45. Sutherland IE (1965) The ultimate display. In: Proceedings of the IFIP congress, New York City, Aug 1965, pp 506–508
46. Duh HB-L, Lin JJW, Kenyon RV, Parker DE, Furness TA (2002) Effects of characteristics of image quality in an immersive environment. J Presence: Teleoper Virtual Environ 11(3):324–332
47. Feamster N, Motiwala M, Vempala S (2007) Path splicing with network slicing. In: Proceedings of the ACM SIGCOMM HotNets, Nov 2007
48. Sherwood R, Gibb G, Yap K-K, Appenzeller G, Casado M, McKeown N, Parulkar G (2009) Flowvisor: a network virtualization layer. OpenFlow switch consortium, technical report, TR-2009-1, Oct 2009, pp 1–15

Chapter 2
Mirror Mirror on the Wall, How Do I Dimension My Cloud After All?

Rafaelli Coutinho, Yuri Frota, Kary Ocaña, Daniel de Oliveira, and Lúcia M.A. Drummond

2.1 Introduction

Clouds have already proven their utility and importance in commercial and scientific domains over this decade [58]. Although most of its huge success is mainly due to existing commercial providers (e.g., Amazon AWS,[1] Google Cloud,[2] IBM Cloud,[3] Rackspace[4] and Microsoft Azure[5]) and frameworks such as Hadoop [22, 32] and Apache Spark [52], it opened a new dimension of possibilities for building complex scientific applications that demand high performance computing (HPC) capabilities to process large sets of scientific data and combinations of parameters based on distributed resources [30, 58]. Until 2010, there was still a lot of questioning whether clouds were suitable for HPC scientific applications, but several researches

---

[1] https://aws.amazon.com/

[2] cloud.google.com/

[3] http://www.ibm.com/cloud-computing/

[4] https://www.rackspace.com/

[5] https://azure.microsoft.com/

R. Coutinho (✉)
Federal Center of Technological Education, Nova Iguaçu, Brazil
e-mail: rafaelli.coutinho@cefet-rj.br

Y. Frota • D. de Oliveira • L.M.A. Drummond
Fluminense Federal University, Niterói, Brazil
e-mail: yuri@ic.uff.br; danielcmo@ic.uff.br; lucia@ic.uff.br

K. Ocaña
National Laboratory of Scientific Computing, Petrópolis, Brazil
e-mail: karyann@lncc.br

© Springer International Publishing AG 2017
N. Antonopoulos, L. Gillam (eds.), *Cloud Computing*, Computer Communications and Networks, DOI 10.1007/978-3-319-54645-2_2

showed the advantages of cloud computing for science [2, 17, 30, 33]. In addition, some approaches such as Magellan[6] and Nebula[7] offer to the scientific community HPC-optimized Clouds.

Currently, traditional HPC resources are already available in cloud offerings [47]. Applications from different domains of science can take advantage from these resources since scientists commonly need to execute large-scale experiments that require high processing power, memory, storage capacity, etc. to run [56]. Many existing experiments are executed through a single application that encapsulates all the computational steps of the experiment. On the other hand, many experiments have a more complex structure, being composed of a set of programs and the data dependencies among them, thus forming a scientific workflow [42, 56]. Scientific workflows may be defined as an abstraction that models the experiment in terms of activities (steps of the scientific process) connected by a dataflow. Scientific workflows are managed by scientific workflow management systems, and they are at the interface of scientists and computing infrastructures.

Standalone HPC applications are commonly executed by creating several parallel jobs using a HPC scheduler such as PBS/TORQUE [23] or Condor [26]. On the other hand, scientific workflows are managed by complex engines called Scientific Workflow Management Systems (SWfMS) [56] that provide parallel capabilities for managing and executing workflows in HPC environments. Both application types (standalone and workflows) commonly rely on traditional HPC environments such as clusters and grids [24] but many of them have already migrated to clouds [58].

One interesting example of scientific application migrated to clouds is found in the genomic bioinformatics domain: The BLAST application [1]. BLAST is a suite of programs that aims at finding regions of local similarity among biological sequences (DNA or protein). It is used to generate alignments among a sequence, referred to as a "query," and sequences within a database, referred to as "subject." In fact, BLAST serves as basis for many bioinformatics protocols, scripts, pipelines, and workflows [3, 36, 43, 45, 51, 54, 59], and much effort was spent in the last years on optimizing this tool. One of the most interesting optimizations of BLAST is a cloud-based version named CloudBLAST [41], which encapsulates in a VM (or in a set of VMs) the parallelized BLAST using MapReduce [13] model. Experiments showed that CloudBLAST presented speedups of 57 compared with 52.4 of its MPI version running on 64 processors [41].

Although CloudBLAST proved that scientific applications that demand HPC capabilities could benefit from clouds, there is a tricky factor that must be considered before to start using CloudBLAST (or any other scientific application that needs to execute in parallel in the cloud): what is the most suitable type and the amount of resources that "fits" with my scientific problem? Differently from clusters and grids, clouds are based on an "on demand" model, where resources are not available a priori. They need to be deployed only when the user needs them. Also, since

---

[6]http://magellan.alcf.anl.gov

[7]http://nebula.nasa.gov

the cloud follows a pay-as-you-go model, over- or underestimations of resources can produce a negative impact in the scientific experiment both in terms of total execution time and financial costs. However, it is not simple to estimate the necessary amount of resources for a specific application.

Still considering CloudBLAST example, for each execution of the application, the scientist firstly needs to estimate the necessary computing power based on the provided input data (biological sequences) and parameters and then choose one (or more) VM types to deploy based on a (commonly huge) set of VM types. This ad hoc estimation can be tedious and error prone especially because cloud providers such as Amazon AWS offer more than 30 VM types to be deployed, some of them provide high parallel processing capability, others provide high storage capacity, etc. Choosing the right type and the amount of VMs to deploy is a top priority for scientists since under- or overestimations can made the experiment unviable, and/or financial costs can spiral out of control if scientists make the wrong VM type choice.

This chapter addresses the problem of dimensioning the amount of VMs in clouds for executing scientific applications that demand HPC and parallel capabilities. The aim of this chapter is to present existing approaches that estimate in a static or dynamic way the amount of VMs for several types of applications from stand-alone applications to complex simulations modeled as scientific workflows.

This chapter is organized in five sections besides this introduction. Section 2.2 discusses about scientific applications, scientific workflows, and their HPC requirements. Section 2.3 presents the static cloud dimensioning and Sect. 2.4 the dynamic dimensioning approach. Section 2.5 brings a survey on existing approaches for cloud dimensioning, and, finally, Sect. 2.6 concludes this chapter and points some future work.

2.2 Desiderata for HPC Applications and Scientific Workflows

This section presents the main definitions regarding scientific applications and scientific workflow concepts, which will be used along this chapter.

2.2.1 Scientific Applications

Many of the existing scientific applications are compute intensive and/or data intensive [28]. This means that these applications demand HPC capabilities to produce results in a timely manner. Even when scientists have access to HPC environments such as HPC VMs, the execution of some applications may last for several hours or days. Thus, it is fundamental to understand the HPC requirements of scientific applications in order to discover if the chosen resource in the cloud is able to offer the necessary computational power to execute the application. However, it is not trivial to generalize the HPC requirements for scientific applications since there are several different types of applications and their categorization is very complex.

One of the prominent solutions to categorize scientific applications is proposed by Colella [7], which categorized seven computational methods that he believed to be the basis of most scientific applications in science and engineering. In [7] the "Seven Dwarfs" of scientific computing is proposed. Each Dwarf is associated to one type of scientific applications. They represented entire families of applications with common computational properties. After the work of Collela, the parallel computing team at the University of California at Berkeley extended the list for 13 Dwarfs, as follows:

1. Dense linear algebra
2. Combinational logic
3. Sparse linear algebra
4. Graph traversal
5. Spectral methods
6. Dynamic programming
7. N-body methods
8. Backtrack and branch-and-bound
9. Structured grids
10. Graphical models
11. Unstructured grids
12. Finite state machines
13. MapReduce

Some works use the Dwarfs characterization to check if they are suitable for cloud computing environments. Examples using Dwarfs to predict performance and analyze cloud suitability are [21, 40, 48]. These papers showed that clouds provide a suitable environment for executing applications that demand HPC capabilities, since they provide the necessary processing power and storage that are required by those categories of applications. However, how to choose the right type of resource and the amount to deploy for those applications remains an open, yet fundamental, challenge.

2.2.2 Computer-Based Scientific Experiments

Computer-based scientific experiments are composed of complex scientific applications that consume and produce large datasets and allocate huge amounts of computational resources [42]. A computer-based scientific experiment follows a specific life cycle [42], which presents three main phases that describe the experiment from its conception, implementation until its final results, where provenance [25] is a key issue to promote the integration: (i) composition - deals with the experiment configuration steps as defining the activity scope, choosing the adequate scientific application; (ii) execution - focuses on the distribution and monitoring programs and data in a computational environment; and (iii) analysis - focuses on evaluating results from scientific experiments as whole, including steps as data visualization, mining results, or querying provenance databases. These computer-based experiments are commonly modeled as scientific workflows, which are explained in the next subsection.

2.2.3   Scientific Workflows

A scientific workflow is an abstraction that models a set of activities (i.e., program invocations) connected through a dataflow. Scientific workflows are commonly represented as a graph where each node is associated to the invocation of a program and the edges are data dependencies among programs [14, 56]. Scientific workflows can be managed by Scientific Workflow Management Systems (SWfMSs), such as Kepler [37], Taverna [61], Pegasus [14], SciCumulus [16], and Swift/T [62]. SWfMSs allow for defining, executing, and monitoring workflow execution. Most of existing SWfMSs also collect provenance [25], that is, the historical information about the experiment and can be used for reproducibility and data curation. SWfMSs have been successfully used in several domains of science such as chemistry, physics, bioinformatics, oil & gas, and astronomy. Nowadays, several scientific workflows are large scale, since they may process many TBs of data [28], thus requiring parallel execution in HPC or HTC environments, such as clouds. Also, since these workflows are composed of applications that demand HPC capabilities, they also demand HPC environments to run in a timely manner. Thus, the problem of dimensioning the amount of resources in the cloud is also fundamental for cloud-based scientific workflows.

2.3   Static Cloud Dimensioning

Vaquero et al. [58] cite various different objectives for cloud computing. Despite the fact that most of these objectives are important, the focus of this chapter is on the infrastructure-as-a-service model (IaaS), where scientist that wants to run large-scale applications needs computing resources (VMs) for a specific amount of time and pays only what they use. However, deploying the exact number of VMs for a scientific application execution is a hard task because it is not trivial for scientists to estimate the time needed for an application to execute, the size of the files generated, and the associated transfer times. As a matter of fact, if the amount of resources to be deployed is overestimated or underestimated, it may produce a high financial cost of the execution or a negative impact on the performance of applications. This deployment is a complex task because cloud providers commonly have a great number of VM types (e.g., computer and GPU clusters, micro, high performance

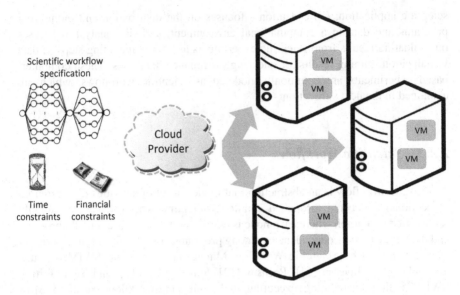

Fig. 2.1 VM allocation scenario [8]

CPU, etc.), where each resource is associated with a performance characteristic and a financial cost, designed to reach the requirements of all kind of users. In this scenario, clients (users/scientists) have to decide the type and the amount of VMs they should deploy with the objective to minimize financial cost or execution time (or both). Figure 2.1 illustrates this scenario, where users pay for a specific set of VMs to a cloud provider, in order to execute their application. On the other hand, the provider offers a group of VM types to users. To prevent a cloud environment with an over- or an under-dimensioning, the user needs to use some strategy to allocate the VMs in an optimal or at least a near-optimal configuration. One type of strategy is the static dimensioning. In this type of dimensioning, all the deployment plan is produced **before** the execution of the application or the workflow. It allows for optimizing the deployment plan, but it is susceptible to performance variations in the cloud VMs.

2.3.1 Mathematical Formulation

The VM allocation problem described in the last section can be described as the following mathematical formulation. Let P be the set of available VM types. A set of users' requirements such as the maximum execution time T_M, memory capacity M_C, maximum financial cost C_M, disk storage, D_S and a processing demand of G_f Gflops are defined. Similarly, each VM type $p \in P$ has a financial cost c_p (per period of time) and a set of characteristics such as storage capacity d_p, amount of memory,

Table 2.1 Clouds environment notations [10]

Notation	Description
P	The set of available VM types
C_M	The maximum user financial cost
T_M	The maximum user execution time
D_S	The disk storage required by the user
M_C	The amount of memory required by the user
G_f	The processing power required by the user
c_p	The financial cost of hiring the VM of type p for one period of time
d_p	The disk storage available in VM of type p
m_p	The amount of memory available in VM of type p
g_p	The processing power available in VM of type p
N_M	The limit of allocated VM that a single user can hire in each period of time

m_p and a processing power of g_p Gflop per period of time (Gflopt). Furthermore, cloud providers limit the number of VMs that each user can allocate per period of time. Table 2.1 describes the used notation for the problem.

A binary variable x_{pit} is defined for each $p \in P$, $i \in \{1, \ldots, N_M\}$ and $t \in T = \{1, \ldots, T_M\}$, such that $x_{pit} = 1$ if and only if VM i of type p is allocated (hired) at time t, otherwise $x_{pit} = 0$. Also, consider *makespan* variable t_m as the last time that a VM was allocated by the user. This scenario can be formulated as following:

$$\text{(CC-IP)} \quad \min \left(\alpha_1 \sum_{p \in P} \sum_{i=1}^{N_M} \sum_{t \in T} c_p x_{pit} + \alpha_2 t_m \right) \tag{2.1}$$

$$\text{subject to} \quad \sum_{p \in P} \sum_{i=1}^{N_M} \sum_{t \in T} c_p x_{pit} \leq C_M \tag{2.2}$$

$$\sum_{p \in P} \sum_{i=1}^{N_M} d_p \, x_{pit} \geq D_S \, x_{p'i't}, \qquad \forall t \in T, \forall p' \in P,$$

$$\forall i' \in \{1, \ldots, N_M\} \tag{2.3}$$

$$\sum_{p \in P} \sum_{i=1}^{N_M} m_p \, x_{pit} \geq M_C \, x_{p'i't}, \qquad \forall t \in T, \forall p' \in P,$$

$$\forall i' \in \{1, \ldots, N_M\} \tag{2.4}$$

$$\sum_{p \in P} \sum_{i=1}^{N_M} \sum_{t \in T} g_p x_{pit} \geq G_f \tag{2.5}$$

$$\sum_{p \in P} \sum_{i=1}^{N_M} x_{pit} \leq N_M, \qquad \forall t \in T \tag{2.6}$$

$$t_m \geq t \, x_{pit}, \qquad \forall t \in T, \forall p \in P,$$
$$\forall i \in \{1, \ldots, N_M\} \tag{2.7}$$

$$x_{pit+1} \leq x_{pit}, \qquad \forall t \in T, \forall p \in P,$$
$$\forall i \in \{1, \ldots, N_M\} \tag{2.8}$$

$$x_{pi+1t} \leq x_{pit}, \qquad \forall t \in T, \forall p \in P,$$
$$\forall i \in \{1, \ldots, N_M - 1\} \tag{2.9}$$

$$x_{pit} \in \{0, 1\}, \qquad \forall t \in T, \forall p \in P,$$
$$\forall i \in \{1, \ldots, N_M\} \tag{2.10}$$

$$t_m \in \mathbb{Z} \tag{2.11}$$

where $(\alpha_1 + \alpha_2) = 1$.

The objective function (2.1) pursues both the minimization of financial costs and total execution time (makespan). The parameters α_1 and α_2 define the weight of each one of the objectives (defined by the user). Constraints (2.2) express that the maximum user financial cost should not be exceeded. Inequalities (2.3) and (2.4) state that there is enough memory and disk storage to meet the user requirements in each time quantum. In a similar way, inequalities (2.5) enforce that the processing power of the hired VMs is large enough to satisfy the user application. Constraints (2.6) rule that the number of hired VMs is bound by the cloud providers limit while inequalities (2.7) ensure that *makespan* variable t_m is limited by the last time a VM was hired. Constraints (2.8) guarantee continuous hiring periods (i.e., if a VM is hired at time $t + 1$, then it must also be hired at time t). Furthermore, inequalities (2.9) are responsible to eliminate symmetrical solutions. Finally, inequalities (2.10) and (2.11) define the variables domain.

2.3.2 Federated Clouds Scenario

Besides executing stand-alone applications or workflows in single provider compute clouds, we can also explore federated cloud scenario. A federated cloud is a group of several clouds that are put together to meet the user needs. According to Buyya et al. [4], cloud providers have covered many regions of the planet with data centers in order to provide reliability and redundancy for the users. Especially for users interested in executing their applications in parallel, the scenario of federated clouds is interesting in at least three main points: (i) when the user reaches the limit of VMs that can be allocated in just one provider, (ii) to avoid costly data transfers between regions, and (iii) when the hired provider does not have any more available VMs and then needs to rent the resources from another provider.

In this new scenario, in order to take into account the execution of parallel applications in federated clouds, we extended formulation (CC-IP) to consider new characteristics such as communication costs between different providers. In order to represent this new scenario, some additional notation is needed.

Let q be the number of cloud providers and P_j be the set of available VM types by provider j, such $P = P_1 \cup P_2 \cup \ldots \cup P_q$ is the family of all VM types from all providers. In this new environment, each VM has a new communication cost $\overrightarrow{c}_{pip'i'}$ representing the transfer cost from VM i of type p to another VM i' of type p'. We consider that $\overrightarrow{c}_{pip'i'} = (uc_p + dc_{p'} + sc) * s$, if p and p' belong to different providers, or $\overrightarrow{c}_{pip'i'} = cs_p * sizedata$, otherwise, where uc_p is the cost to upload data from a VM of type p, $dc_{p'}$ is the cost to download data to a VM of type p', sc is the cost to store the transferred data, cs_p is the communication cost between VMs of the same type in the same provider, and s is the average size of the transmitted data. Furthermore, let N_M^j be the limit of VMs that a single user can hire in each provider j and in each quantum of time. We also define that $Pr(p)$ stands for the provider index of VM $p \in P$. Therefore, two new binary variables are presented: y_{pi} for each $p \in P$, $i \in \{1, \ldots, N_M^{Pr(p)}\}$, such that $y_{pi} = 1$ if and only if VM i of type p is hired, or $y_{pi} = 0$, otherwise, and $\overrightarrow{z}_{pip'i'}$ for each $p, p' \in P$, $i \in \{1, \ldots, N_M^{Pr(p)}\}$, $i' \in \{1, \ldots, N_M^{Pr(p')}\}$, such that $\overrightarrow{z}_{pip'i'} = 1$ if and only if $y_{pi} * y_{p'i'} = 1$, or $\overrightarrow{z}_{pip'i'} = 0$, otherwise. Table 2.2 expand the notation used in (CC-IP).

Table 2.2 Notations for federated clouds environment [10]

Notation	Description
P_j	The set of available VM types offered by provider j
P	$P = \{P_1 \cup P_2 \cup \ldots \cup P_q\}$
N_M^j	The limit of allocated VM that a single user can hire in each period of time in provider j
$Pr(p)$	Provider index of VM $p \in P$
$\overrightarrow{c}_{pip'i'}$	The communication cost from a VM i of type p. To another VM i' of type p'
uc_p	The upload cost from a VM p
dc_p	The download cost to a VM p
sc	The storage cost of the transmitted data
s	The average size of the transmitted data
cs_p	The communication cost of VM type p with other. VM types of the same cloud provider

Thus, we increase the previous formulation (CC-IP) by adding $\sum_{p \in P} \sum_{p' \in P} \sum_{i=1}^{N_M^{Pr(p)}} \sum_{i'=1}^{N_M^{Pr(p')}}$

$\overrightarrow{c}_{pip'i'} \overrightarrow{z}_{pip'i'}$ to the objective function (2.1), dropping constraint (2.6), and inserting the following inequalities to (CC-IP):

$$\sum_{p \in P_j} \sum_{i=1}^{N_M^{Pr(p)}} x_{pit} \leq N_M^{Pr(p)}, \ \forall j = 1 \ldots q, \forall t \in T \tag{2.12}$$

$$y_{pi} \geq \overrightarrow{z}_{pip'i'}, \ \forall p, p' \in P,$$
$$\forall i \in \left\{1, \ldots, N_M^{Pr(p)}\right\}, \text{ and } i' \in \left\{1, \ldots, N_M^{Pr(p')}\right\} \tag{2.13}$$

$$y_{p'i'} \geq \overrightarrow{z}_{pip'i'}, \ \forall p, p' \in P,$$
$$\forall i \in \left\{1, \ldots, N_M^{Pr(p)}\right\}, \text{ and } i' \in \left\{1, \ldots, N_M^{Pr(p')}\right\} \tag{2.14}$$

$$y_{pi} + y_{p'i'} - 1 \leq \overrightarrow{z}_{pip'i'}, \ \forall p, p' \in P,$$
$$\forall i \in \left\{1, \ldots, N_M^{Pr(p)}\right\}, \text{ and } i' \in \left\{1, \ldots, N_M^{Pr(p')}\right\} \tag{2.15}$$

$$\sum_{t \in T} x_{pit} \leq y_{pi}|T|, \ \forall p \in P,$$
$$\forall i \in \left\{1, \ldots, N_M^{Pr(p)}\right\} \tag{2.16}$$

In this generalized formulation, denoted as CC-IP-fed, inequalities (2.12) ensure that the number of hired VMs is bound by each cloud providers limit (equivalent to constraint (2.6)). The constraints (2.13), (2.14), (2.15), and (2.16) rule that the financial cost derive from the communication between different providers is considered. Note that by constraints (2.13), (2.14), and (2.15), whenever $x_{pit} = 1$ for some t, this means that $y_{pi} = 1$.

2.3.3 A Heuristic Approach

In [10], a greedy randomized adaptive search procedure (GRASP), named GraspCC [8], is introduced to tackle the problem of VM allocation in federated clouds. Each

GraspCC iteration consists of constructing an initial solution by method $coCC$ and then applying a local search procedure, denoted $lsCC$, to find a local optimum.

We define a *solution* $\{(p_1, i_1, t_1), (p_2, i_2, t_2), \ldots\}$ as a set of 3-tuples (p, i, t) indicating that VM i of type p was hired on period t. We denote S the set of all *feasible* solutions (i.e., solutions that respect the user's requirements). We also define $t_m(s) = \max_{(p,i,t) \in s} t$ as the last time period that a VM was hired in a feasible solution $s \in S$. Furthermore, we define a *cost function* $F : \mathbb{S} \to \mathbb{R}$, which define the solution quality. Note that function F tries to minimize financial and time costs (2.17), while (2.18) penalizes the infeasibility regarding maximum time and maximum financial cost. The terms λ_1 and λ_2 are coefficients of penalty related to the violation of time and cost requirements, respectively.

$$F(s) = \left(\alpha_1 \left(\sum_{(p,i,t) \in s} c_p + \sum_{(p,i,t) \in s} \sum_{(p',i',t') \in s} c_{pip'i'} \right) + \alpha_2 t_m(s) \right) \tag{2.17}$$

$$+ \lambda_1 (\max\{0, t_m(s) - T_M\}) + \lambda_2 \left(\max \left\{ 0, \sum_{(p,i,t) \in s} c_p - C_M \right\} \right) \tag{2.18}$$

Algorithm 1: *GraspCC*

1 **Input:** $P, C_M, T_M, D_S, M_C, G_f, \alpha_1, \alpha_2, \lambda_1, \lambda_2$
2 **Output:** solution s^*;
3 $s^* = \emptyset;\ F(s^*) = \infty;\ i = 0;$
4 **while** $i \leq iter$
5    $s = coCC(P, C_M, T_M, D_S, M_C, G_f, \alpha_1, \alpha_2, \lambda_1, \lambda_2);$
6    $s = lsCC(s, P, C_M, T_M, D_S, M_C, G_f, \alpha_1, \alpha_2, \lambda_1, \lambda_2);$
7   **if** $(F(s) < F(s^*))$ *and* $(s\ is\ feasible)$
8      $s^* = s;\ i = 0;$
9   **end if**
10   $i = i + 1;$
11 **end while**
12 **return** s^*;

The GraspCC algorithm is presented in algorithm 1. The value *iter* represents the maximum number of iterations without improvement. First, the construction phase is performed by algorithm $coCC$ in a random and greedy way (Algorithm 2). In this method, a solution is constructed by adding tuples, in each iteration, to the first period of time. The tuples are built from the ordered set L_P where VMs $p \in P$ appears in descending order of financial cost and processing power ($\alpha_1 c_p + \alpha_2 g_p$). The algorithm randomly chooses VM $\bar{p}$ from the β first VMs in L_P until the current solution satisfies the disk and memory requirements for $t = 1$. Furthermore, in lines (9)–(12), the solution is replicated in all remaining time periods until the demand for processing power is satisfied. Note that the maximum time and maximum financial cost requirements are not necessarily met in this initial solution, but this strategy is important to achieve diversity in the initial solution.

Algorithm 2: *coCC*

---

1 **Input:** $P, C_M, T_M, D_S, M_C, G_f, \alpha_1, \alpha_2, \lambda_1, \lambda_2$
2 **Output:** solution s;
3 $s = \emptyset$; $L_P = Order(P)$;
4 **while** $(\sum_{p|(p,i,1)\in s} d_p < D_S)$ or $(\sum_{p|(p,i,1)\in s} m_p < M_C)$
5   Choose VM $\bar{p}$ (index $\bar{i}$) randomly among the first β elements of L_P
6     $s = s \cup \{(\bar{p}, \bar{i}, 1)\}$;
7 **end while**
8 $\bar{i} = 2$;
9 **while** $(\sum_{p|(p,i,t)\in s} g_p < G_f)$
10    $s = \bigcup_{(p,i,1)\in s} (p, i, \bar{i}) \cup s$;
11    $\bar{i} = \bar{i} + 1$;
12 **end while**
13 **return** s

The initial solution s, provided by *coCC*, may be improved by a local search procedure denoted *lsCC* (Algorithm 3). First, we define neighborhood $N_r(s)$ as the set of solutions reached by exchanging r tuples in solution s by another r tuples that does not belong to s. These *movements* are executed extensively with the first improvement strategy. The *lsCC* method, at each iteration, replaces the current solution s by that with minimum cost function F in its neighborhood $N_r(s)$. This improving phase leads to a sequence of movements toward a local optimum solution, until no better solution is reached by the neighborhood. A neighborhood of $r \leq 2$ was used in this work, since the complexity of neighborhoods for values of $r > 2$ is impractical.

Algorithm 3: *lsCC*

---

1 **Input:** $s, P, C_M, T_M, D_S, M_C, G_f, \alpha_1, \alpha_2, \lambda_1, \lambda_2$
2 **Output:** solution s;
3 **while** (s improving)
4   **for all** $\bar{s} \in (N_1(s) \cup N_2(s))$
5   **if** $F(\bar{s}) < F(s)$
6        $s = \bar{s}$
7   **end if**
8   **end for**
9 **end while**

2.3.4   Experimental Results for Static Cloud Dimensioning

Coutinho et al. [10] previously compared the GraspCC-fed and the CC-IP-fed in terms of quality of the solution and total execution time using simulation. In these experiments, CPLEX 12.4 [29] was the chosen optimization software package to solve the CC-IP-fed formulation. The input data of the experiments was real performance data from a large range of applications as stated in [10] and VM types available in commercial clouds such as Amazon EC2, Google Cloud Platform, and Microsoft Azure (small, medium, large, xlarge, and 2xlarge [10]).

All results are presented in Table 2.3. In this experiment we used the following parameter values: $\lambda_1 = 1000$ and $\lambda_2 = 1000$, $\beta = \max_{p \in P}(N_M^j)$, and $iter = 40$. The chosen α_1 and α_2 represent the cases where variables are removed from the objective function ($\alpha_1 = 0$ or $\alpha_2 = 0$) and when all variables are considered ($\alpha_1 \neq 0$ and $\alpha_2 \neq 0$). The maximum number of VMs N_M^j in each provider j is the same defined by Amazon EC2.[8] The values of other parameters β, λ_1, λ_2, and $iter$ were empirically obtained as it is usually done in the parameter settings of metaheuristics. Both objectives of the cost function were normalized due to their distinct range values. In Table 2.3, the first column represents the application name. The next four columns represent the best feasible solution found by CC-IP-fed and its associated costs (not normalized): financial costs for VM deployment and communication and its execution time, respectively. The sixth column presents the execution time in seconds for CC-IP-fed to solve the problem. Analogously, the next five columns represent the same characteristics for the best solution found by GraspCC-fed. Finally, the last two columns present the chosen values for α_1 and α_2 in the cost function.

For some instances, a considerable time for CC-IP-fed to prove the optimality of the solution was necessary. It is worth noticing that in these experiments, we set a maximum execution time restriction of 24 h. The exact method was not able to find the optimal solution in instances marked with (*) in Table 2.3 following this time restriction. Note that GraspCC-fed presented an improvement of the execution time, in average 99.35% less than the execution time of CC-IP-fed. Furthermore, the GraspCC-fed heuristic found a better or equal solution than the CC-IP-fed formulation in most instances (which are highlighted in the Table 2.3), presenting a percentage difference from the best feasible solution found by CC-IP-fed of 5.43%, in average.

Despite the GraspCC-fed does not find a better solution than the CC-IP-fed for some instances, the needed time to execute it is always smaller than presented by the CC-IP-fed. For example, in terms of quality of the solution, GraspCC-fed found a solution 46.67% far from the formulation for the instance *cms-1000* with $\alpha_1 = 0$ and $\alpha_2 = 1$. However, in terms of execution time, GraspCC-fed needed only 57 s to obtain this solution, while the formulation needed 7.7 h. If this execution time was

---

[8]https://aws.amazon.com/ec2/faqs/

Table 2.3 Results of GraspCC-fed metaheuristic and CC-IP-fed mathematical formulation using CPLEX [10]

Instances	CC-IP-fed					GraspCC-fed						
	Function Cost	Solution value		Time	Total time (s)	Function Cost	Solution value		Time	Total time(s)	α_1	α_2
		Financial costs					Financial costs					
		Hiring	Communication				Hiring	Communication				
nug22-sbb	0.0041	3.52	0.21	1	825.00	**0.0041**	3.52	0.21	1	62.52	1	0
nug24-sbb	*0.0030	9.73	1.06	1	86,445.00	**0.0030**	9.67	1.06	1	255.97	1	0
nug25-sbb	0.0039	17.10	0.15	1	21,509.00	**0.0039**	17.10	0.15	1	532.68	1	0
nug28-sbb	*0.0085	38.75	6.46	1	86,493.00	**0.0078**	40.80	0.60	1	592.98	1	0
nug30-sbb	*0.0150	81.08	11.86	2	86,469.00	**0.0150**	81.83	10.86	2	466.43	1	0
cms-1000	0.0962	169.56	0.00	3	10,594.00	0.1316	232.02	0.00	4	120.92	1	0
cms-1250	0.1782	314.02	0.00	5	80,472.00	0.2078	366.34	0.00	6	100.16	1	0
cms-1500	*0.4519	796.58	0.00	11	86,438.00	0.3876	683.20	0.00	10	14.61	1	0
modgen-real	0.0028	1.98	0.01	3	44.00	**0.0028**	1.98	0.01	2	6.03	1	0
raxml-real	0.0028	1.98	0.00	4	44.00	**0.0028**	1.98	0.00	4	7.07	1	0
nug24-sbb	0.0208	37.17	18.91	1	3637.00	**0.0208**	16.83	6.65	1	122.69	0	1
nug25-sbb	0.0167	36.12	28.97	1	4920.00	0.0200	24.71	9.62	1	182.51	0	1
nug28-sbb	0.0139	49.14	2762.95	1	72,359.00	**0.0139**	42.58	4.88	1	224.87	0	1
nug30-sbb	0.0238	104.24	23.72	2	72,428.00	**0.0238**	102.20	11.72	2	239.63	0	1
cms-1000	0.1250	182.22	0.00	3	27,558.00	0.1833	256.61	0.00	4	56.97	0	1
cms-1250	0.2083	343.42	0.00	5	20,081.00	0.2417	371.83	0.00	6	52.32	0	1
cms-1500	0.4167	683.20	0.00	10	31,815.00	**0.4167**	683.20	0.00	10	14.54	0	1
modgen-real	0.0417	2.88	0.05	1	61.00	**0.0417**	2.49	0.09	1	3.24	0	1
raxml-real	0.0417	5.76	45.70	1	61.00	**0.0417**	2.54	0.05	1	3.26	0	1

nug22-sbb	0.0437	3.52	0.21	1	621.00	0.0437	3.52	0.21	1	74.60	0.5	0.5
nug24-sbb	0.0119	9.67	1.06	1	909.00	0.0119	9.67	1.06	1	308.15	0.5	0.5
nug25-sbb	0.0103	17.10	0.15	1	818.00	0.0103	17.10	0.15	1	709.39	0.5	0.5
nug28-sbb	0.0108	40.80	0.60	1	12,525.00	0.0108	40.80	0.60	1	988.12	0.5	0.5
nug30-sbb	*0.0193	81.08	11.06	2	86,523.00	0.0195	84.06	10.25	2	857.82	0.5	0.5
cms-1000	0.1106	169.56	0.00	3	56,879.00	0.1413	211.65	0.00	4	200.12	0.5	0.5
cms-1250	*0.1975	329.00	0.00	5	86,422.00	0.2281	363.34	0.00	6	108.70	0.5	0.5
cms-1500	0.4021	683.20	0.00	10	64,928.00	0.4021	683.20	0.00	10	14.69	0.5	0.5
modgen-real	0.0222	1.98	0.01	1	72.00	0.0222	1.98	0.01	1	7.37	0.5	0.5
raxml-real	0.0222	1.98	0.01	1	80.00	0.0222	1.98	0.01	1	7.66	0.5	0.5
Average	0.0778	121.81	83.42	2.66	28,720.63	0.0823	125.20	1.70	3.01	186.90		

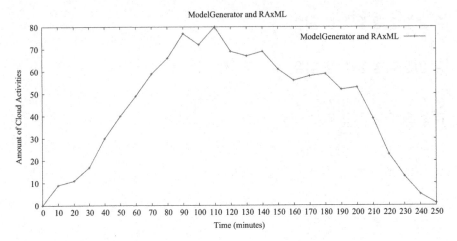

Fig. 2.2 Execution of ModelGenerator and RAxML (from SciPhylomics) in the Amazon EC2 and the Microsoft Azure using VMs given by the GraspCC-fed [10]

added to the overall needed time to find a solution, the total time using GraspCC-fed and CC-IP-fed would be 4.02 and 10.7 h, respectively. Thus, even when GraspCC-fed does not find the optimal solution, it can be considered an attractive alternative to solve the VM allocation problem in federated clouds.

Next, we present the results of a real execution of a workflow in a federated cloud scenario dimensioned using GraspCC-fed. In order to study the feasibility of this approach in federated cloud scenarios, we consider two commercial clouds (Amazon EC2 and Microsoft Azure) in the execution of the bioinformatics work-flow SciPhylomics [46]. We also use the scientific workflow system SciCumulus [16], adapted to work with federated clouds (SciCumulus-fed [10]).

Figure 2.2 presents the SciPhylomics executions using the GraspCC-fed solutions of the instances *modgen-real* and *raxml-real* of the Table 2.3 with $\alpha_1 = 0.5$ and $\alpha_2 = 0.5$. These values were used because it is more fair to define the same weights for time and financial costs. These executions suggested that 1 xlarge VM and 1 2xlarge VM from Amazon and 1 xlarge VM from Azure should be allocated per 1 h for each application, Model Generator and RAxML. Figure 2.2 presents the amount of tasks (axis Y) executing in a given period of time (X axis). We can state that GraspCC-fed indicated that three VMs are needed (47 virtual cores) for 1 h with financial cost of $1.99 for each application, totaling 2 h and a financial cost of $3.98, but the real execution using 3 VMs lasted for around 4 h (100% more) with an approximated financial cost of $7.96. This behavior was due to problems identified in the adapted version of the workflow engine (SciCumulus-fed). Although we have 47 virtual cores available for execution, SciCumulus was not able to benefit from the entire set of available VMs during the entire execution course of the workflow. This happened because we are using S3fs[9], and we face a severe delay when the

---

[9]https://github.com/s3fs-fuse/s3fs-fuse

data files are being synchronized among all VMs in the virtual cluster. This way, in the beginning of the workflow execution, several tasks were not ready to be executed since input data files were not available to be processed. SciCumulus-fed then waits until each data file is available in all VMs before starting a specific task.

This way, the number of tasks that are executing until 80 min is reduced, and many cores remain idle. Another problem was related to the scheduling mechanism of SciCumulus. SciCumulus is based on a cost model to distribute tasks in the several VMs. This cost model considers performance issues, financial cost, and reliability, but it was designed for a single-provider cloud. Since we are executing in different clouds, communication issues impact more than execution time of the task for several tasks. This way, SciCumulus scheduled tasks without taking into account the locality of these VMs, which requested more messages to be exchanged and impacted on the overall performance.

2.4   Dynamic Cloud Dimensioning

Static dimensioning of VMs may provide good estimations of the types and number of VMs to be used, but, in some cases, the corresponding estimated execution time and memory usage are not close to the real ones. Some applications may demand different computing power and memory usage along their executions, and the *a priori* estimation of the amount of VMs can be not suitable for them. Generally, the static dimensioning considers only the total demand of the application, not treating those usual variations during its execution. Moreover, clouds can be considered changing environments, where processing capacity and network speed, for example, can suffer performance variations along the application execution. Thus, the estimated amount of VMs may be not suitable when those performance and can lead to efficiency losses of applications. Then, it is important that the VM dimensioning approach monitors all those changes in the cloud environment and adapts it when necessary.

In order to solve that problem, several works propose the dynamic dimensioning of cloud computing. Dynamic dimensioning involves typically two phases. The first one is the monitoring of VMs, when data related to VM usage are collected. In the second phase, if the application or the environment suffers changes, that can impact application performance negatively or result in VM time waste; some actions are triggered to improve the application efficiency with the best usage of VMs. Those actions include the *redimensioning* of the number (or types) of VMs and the balancing of tasks not yet executed in that new scenario. In case of redimensioning, new VMs can be instantiated or eliminated, considering the demands of the application and the attendance quality given by the current cloud configuration.

In the last section, it was shown that the static dimensioning GraspCC provided good estimations of VMs and the corresponding time executions in average. However, in some cases, the obtained real execution time was not close to the estimated one. Particularly, the SciPhylomics workflow presented a real execution time 100% higher than the estimated one. In this case, the estimation was not suitable for the entire workflow because the number of parallel activities varied a lot and there was a particular activity that has to be executed before several others, limiting the parallelism during the execution a lot.

In [11], an extension of the previously proposed static approach is introduced. That approach, named dynamic dimensioning of cloud computing framework (DDC-F), is composed by two modules: (i) a monitoring module and (ii) a virtual machine dimensioning module. The first one monitors the VM, collecting data related to CPU and memory usage. The second module recalculates the number of VMs necessary to attend the workflow demand satisfactorily. DDC-F interacts with the workflow engine through a provenance repository that acts as a communication bridge between them. The workflow engine is responsible for instantiating VMs for the workflow execution and balancing of tasks among VMs, according to the obtained information from a provenance repository.

After the instantiation of VMs executed by the workflow engine, DDC-F is initiated to monitor the deployed VMs. Remark that, at this moment, the workflow engine can deploy a minimum number of VMs or the number of VMs estimated statically by GraspCC. The monitoring module executes in a distributed manner, being composed by a monitor process at each VM. The monitor process records local data about the CPU and memory usages, periodically, and sends out a message to all instantiated VMs whenever a significant change of performance occurs locally, in its own VM. In addition, when the monitor process identifies those changes or receives a message from another monitor in that state, it sends the last collected data about VM usage to the virtual machine dimensioning module. This module has a unique process running on a dedicated VM. It evaluates the need of *redimensioning* VMs or executing a load balance procedure, by running GraspCC and considering data received from all monitor processes. That decision can result in redistributing the remaining tasks among the already deployed VMs, instantiating or eliminating VMs, whether the current scenario is not suitable for the new demands of the workflow.

In order to evaluate the efficiency of the dynamic approach, a comparison with the static dimensioning, previously introduced, was accomplished considering two workflows: SciPhy, a well-behaved workflow with no choke point tasks, and SciPhylomics, the critical case in the static approach, that presented a poor estimation. Amazon EC2 was adopted as cloud environment with five types of VMs: small, medium, large, xlarge, and 2xlarge. Programs used in these workflows were executed with default parameters, but executed over larger input datasets. A redimensioning was considered in case of CPU or RAM memory usage exceeded 80% or dropped to 20% of the total capacity.

Results of the executions in Amazon EC2 for the SciPhy workflow are presented in Table 2.4, where the set of used VMs are shown for each time, the initial time t_0, and the others t_1, t_2 and t_3, when DDC-F changed the set of used VMs.

Table 2.4 Results of SciPhy execution [11]

Approach	Static GraspCC	Dynamic DDC-F
Set of VMs	2 small	t_0: 1 small
	8 xlarge	t_1: 10 xlarge, 1 large, 1 small
		t_2: 10 xlarge, 1 large, 6 small
		t_3: 13 xlarge, 1 large, 6 small
Execution time	107 min	55 min
Financial cost	U$4.86	U$4.04

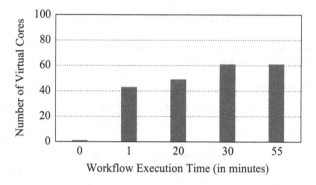

Fig. 2.3 The number of virtual cores in each period of time during the SciPhy workflow execution initiated with a VM [11]

Dynamic dimensioning is more suitable when there are performance variations in clouds, as occurred aforementioned. As GraspCC considered that VMs would present fixed processing capacity, and in this case it did not occur, the number of VMs to execute SciPhy was sub-estimated. Note that with the static dimensioning, two *quanta* of 1 h were required to execute the application, resulting in a financial cost of $4.86, against $4.04 with dynamic dimensioning. The number of virtual cores at each time along the execution can be seen in Fig. 2.3, and the number of VMs and their types are shown in Fig. 2.4.

A second experiment was accomplished with the workflow SciPhylomics that had presented a poor result with GraspCC. SciPhylomics was executed in two different scenarios. In one of them, the execution started with a virtual cluster estimated statically by GraspCC: 13 VMs xlarge and 1 VM large for 1 h. In the other, it started with a minimum quantity of VMs, i.e., 1 large.

Results of the executions are shown in Table 2.5, where the set of used VMs are also shown for each time, the initial time t_0, and the others t_1, t_2, and t_3, when DDC-F changed the set of used VMs.

In the experiment with SciPhylomics, DDC-F managed to reduce the financial cost when compared with GraspCC approach, because it adapted the number of

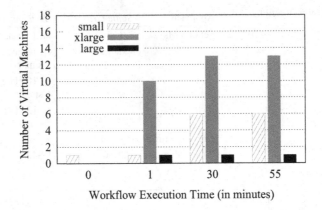

Fig. 2.4 The number of VMs according to each type of VMs instantiated during of the SciPhy workflow execution initiated with a VM [11]

Table 2.5 SciPhylomonics execution [11]

Approach	Static GraspCC	Dynamic DDC-F
Set of VMs	13 xlarge	t_0: 1 large
	1 large	t_1: 11 large, 2 small
		t_2: 6 xlarge, 1 large
Execution time	137 min	151 min
Financial cost	U$10.56	U$5.12

instantiated VMs in accordance with the demand of the moment. By using the static GraspCC, the large number of VMs initially instantiated remained available even when they stayed idle for more than 1 h time *quantum*. GraspCC overestimated the amount of VMs for this workflow because it assumed that the entire workflow could be parallelized and executed in 1 h. DDC-F did not manage to improve the execution time of that workflow, because of the overhead imposed to remove VMs and instantiate new ones in this case. On the other hand, the financial cost was better, around 52% less than GraspCC.

The number of virtual cores in each period of time along the execution can be seen in Fig. 2.5, and the number of VMs and their types can be seen in Fig. 2.6. In this execution, the total execution time of SciPhylomics was 2:31 h with a financial cost of U$5.12.

Finally, note that efficient dynamic dimensioning in a federated environment remains a challenge. Monitoring a federated cloud is not a trivial task because of high overheads necessary to obtain consistent data of the entire environment. As seen in this section, collecting consistent data from VMs requires that they communicate among themselves, what usually is much more expensive in a federated cloud than in regular cloud environments. So, it remains an open problem to be investigated in future works.

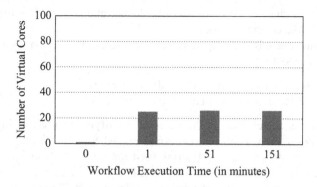

Fig. 2.5 The number of virtual cores in each period of time during the SciPhylomics workflow execution using DDC-F initiated with 1 m3.large VM [11]

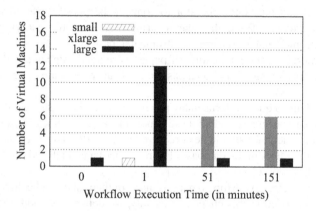

Fig. 2.6 The number of VMs according to each type of VMs instantiated during of the SciPhylomics workflow execution using DDC-F initiated with 1 m3.large VM [11]

2.5 Survey on Existing Approaches for Cloud Dimensioning

In the previous sections of this chapter, we presented the problem of cloud dimensioning (static and dynamic) and possible solutions. However, this is a fruitful research area, and many papers have already been proposed. This section aims at surveying existing works in the literature. Thus, this section presents a simplified version of a systematic review of the literature (SRL) in the topic of resource dimensioning for clouds. It is inspired in the SRL presented in [31].

A SRL is one of the possible ways for designing reviews, since we are focused at identifying, evaluating, and comparing available published papers associated to a particular topic area of interest for answering a specific scientific question. As proposed by Kitchenham et al. [34], a SRL has three main phases: (i) planning, (ii) conduction, and (iii) analysis of results. In the planning phase, we must have a clear goal of our research since a protocol must be defined at this stage. This protocol will be followed in the conduction phase.

In the context of this chapter, we defined two research questions that should be answered in our SRL:

1. RQ1: What approaches provide cloud dimensioning?
2. RQ2: Which techniques are used in these approaches?

Therefore, our search strategy consisted of identifying approaches in published papers that cover main concepts (or terms) related to cloud dimensioning techniques. Here, we define the search string used for conducting our search strategy in three electronic databases (ACM Digital Library, IEEEXPlore, and Scopus) for the scientific literature search: "(Cloud Dimensioning OR Cloud Provisioning OR Cloud Deployment) AND (Static OR Dynamic)."

The logical operator "AND" was used to connect the key terms (i.e., cloud dimensioning) and the "OR" operator to connect the possible variations derived from any key terms. Then, the search string was used for querying a set of existing electronic databases. Three electronic databases were selected based on the following criteria: (i) the publication of papers is regularly updated, (ii) all papers are available for download and analysis, and (iii) all papers are reviewed using a peer-review process.

Since the defined query returns many papers (in some databases, more than 3,000 papers), it is not feasible to read all these papers in a suitable time. Thus, we defined that the most impact ones should be considered in this SRL. This way, we sorted the papers using the filters in the databases (by relevance) and analyzed only the top 20 papers in each database.

Although we selected the top 20 papers, many of them may not be directly related to the topic discussed in this chapter. This way, we defined two additional criteria (inclusion/exclusion) to include papers in our research. The inclusion criterion refers to the study presented in the paper, which must involve both dimensioning and clouds. If two papers present the same research, only the latest published paper would be considered. For excluding papers (at the exclusion criterion), we consider the following topics: (i) papers must be available for downloading on the Internet, (ii) papers must be presented in electronic format, and (iii) papers should be written in English.

We conducted the simplified SRL between July and August 2016. Twenty-two papers were selected by our simplified SRL, as presented following. Interestingly, we observed that those papers were published in the last 7 years (since 2009) as presented in Fig. 2.7. Following we discuss each of these papers.

Endo et al. [20] highlight the main challenges of the VM provisioning problem in clouds, offering a detailed view of this problem which comprises from the initial modeling phase to the optimization phase. These challenges are discussed on four fundamental points: resource modeling, resource offering and treatment, resource discovery and monitoring, and resource selection. Although they present special challenges requiring new research, clouds are promising and may grow to be seen in various contexts.

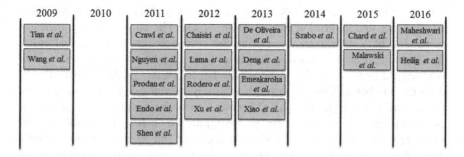

Fig. 2.7 Survey timeline

Several existing approaches focus on optimizing VM allocation statically or dynamically in terms of application execution time and financial costs [5, 6, 18, 19, 27, 35, 55] while others focus on energy-efficient VM allocation [50, 53, 64]. Some of these approaches can consider or not the concept of scientific workflow in the moment of cloud dimensioning, and, most of them, performed experiments by theoretical studies and simulation.

For example, Shen et al. [53], Xu et al. [64], and Rodero et al. [50] treat the VM allocation problem from the energy savings perspective. Usually they use virtualization technology, which is a fundamental technique widely employed in cloud computing for resource sharing. In this context, VM migration is one of the most common techniques used to alleviate anomalies and reduce load and server utilization in cloud datacenter. Shen et al. [53] automate the elastic resource scaling for multi-tenant cloud computing infrastructures through of a system called CloudScale. This system employs online resource demand prediction without any a priori knowledge about the applications running inside the cloud. It resolves scaling conflicts between applications using migration and integrates dynamic CPU voltage/frequency scaling to save energy with minimal impact on application. However, CloudScale does not adjust resource pressure threshold dynamically according to the workload type and only dimension isolated applications in clouds, not considering the concept of scientific workflow neither data dependencies among programs. Xu et al. [64] model the energy efficiency virtual resource allocation for clouds as a multi-objective optimization problem. The problem was solved by one of the existing evolutionary multi-objective optimization algorithms, non-dominated sorting genetic algorithm II (NSGA-II). They present through simulations that the NSGA-II can produce schedules of different numbers of server VMs with various characteristics in an acceptable time, thus decreasing the total operating energy of data center. Rodero et al. [50] introduce an autonomic energy-efficient thermal management while ensuring the QoS delivered to the users in the cloud infrastructure. They also proposed an application-centric energy-aware strategy for the problem of VM allocation that arises during VM migrations. The proposed approach was evaluated through simulations with real production HPC workload traces.

In addition to the concern of saving energy, researchers have been interested in optimizing the application executions in clouds. The purpose is to dimension the number of VMs aiming at reducing the execution time and financial costs. Thus, some approaches consider data of previous executions to make decisions about static dimensioning. The static approaches [5, 18, 27, 55] do not dynamically adjust the number of VMs; however they already provide good solutions in terms of time and costs. Chaisiri et al. [5] present an optimal algorithm to provision resources offered by multiple cloud providers, named OCRP. The OCRP solution is obtained by formulating and solving a stochastic integer programming model. The OCRP algorithm considers multiple provisioning stages with demand and price uncertainties. Different approaches such as deterministic equivalent formulation, sample-average approximation, and Benders decomposition are considered. The performance evaluation of the OCRP algorithm has been made only by numerical studies and simulations. Oliveira et al. [18] aim to optimize VM allocations in clouds using jointly a multi-objective cost function with genetic algorithms in a service called SciDim. The SciDim also uses provenance data to set an initial configuration for the VM allocation respecting budget and deadline constraints given by the users. Szabo et al. [55] introduce a multi-objective evolutionary algorithm that optimizes both the workflow runtime and size of transferred data of data-intensive scientific workflows. The proposed approach was validated using simulations and real experiments on the Amazon EC2. However, they did not consider heterogeneous cloud VM types, the optimization of the number of VMs, and the dynamic allocation of VMs. Heilig et al. [27] propose an efficient biased random-key genetic algorithm for the VM dimensioning problem in multi-cloud environments that aim to reduce the financial cost and the runtime of user applications using IaaS of several cloud providers. The algorithm is based on cloud brokerage mechanism and provides high-quality solutions. It assists users to select a suitable set of cloud resources from multiple cloud providers.

The dynamic approaches [6, 19, 35] are capable of adjusting cloud resources during the application execution. Therefore, they may use monitoring techniques for capturing data about cloud resources and then to make decisions about the amount of resources to be instantiated for the application for the completion of the execution. For example, Lama et al. [35] present a system that enables automated VM allocation for MapReduce environment in clouds, named AROMA. Even though MapReduce-like approaches are not similar to SWfMS, they can be used to model workflows as presented by Nguyen and Halem [44], Wang et al. [60], and Crawl et al. [12], which applied these approaches in the workflow domain. AROMA uses vector machines and genetic algorithms to obtain the appropriate resources and then allocate the VMs. This system shows effectiveness in providing performance guarantee of diverse Hadoop jobs, but it does not consider financial issues. Emeakaroha et al. [19] propose a management infrastructure that scales scientific workflow executions in the cloud while ensuring performance goals and successful workflow completion. They make decisions on how to dynamically allocate the necessary amount of resources to complete the workflow execution according to data originated from monitoring and a knowledge management strategy. However, they also do not consider financial issues that are fundamental in commercial clouds. Chard et al. [6] introduce an approach that elastically provisions cloud resources on demand in workflows. It monitors a job submission queue and provisions VMs based on predefined policies. The provisioner is able to appropriately choose VM types to execute a given application based on application profiles, select the most cost-effective VM type across availability zones using on-demand and spot prices, over-provision resources when VMs are highly disputed, and change to stable on-demand VMs when spot prices are volatile or requests are delayed. They evaluated the approach using realistic conditions in simulation of execution traces.

Several approaches also provide solutions for resource dynamic dimensioning in cloud data centers [57, 63]. Tian et al. [57] implement adaptive dimensioning procedures for cloud data centers that allocate computing resources for variable workloads meeting QoS requirements. Xiao et al. [63] design a system that uses virtualization techniques to dynamically allocate resources in data center based on application requirements. The system supports green computing since the number of servers in use is optimized. They introduce the concept of "skewness" to measure the variation in the utilization of server resource. Thus, different types of workloads can be combined nicely, and the resources utilization can be improved by minimizing skewness. The experiment results were performed only by trace-driven simulation.

Concerning the scheduling problem in clouds, Prodan et al. [49] present a scientific applications scheduler and a resource manager for heterogeneous computing infrastructures such as grids and clouds. They identify general behavior patterns that can be applied by a scheduler to minimize the cost of application execution. However, they do not consider the impact of time and budget limitations, and the experiments were performed using only a simulator. Deng et al. [15] propose an algorithm that selects the best policy from a scheduling policy portfolio. They studied an abstract algorithm selection model for portfolio scheduling and introduced a portfolio scheduling framework with various configuration parameters. The scheduler was evaluated only by trace-based simulation. Malawski et al. [39] develop several adaptive scheduling algorithms for scientific workflows that dimension and vertically scale the workflow execution to satisfy the users' constraints. They presented experimental results based on simulations of workflow executions. Although this approach is an important step, it does not optimize the initial VM configuration, i.e., it does not adjust the number of VMs before the execution of scientific workflow according to the user's constraints. If this VM allocation was optimized before the workflow execution, the performance of these adaptive VM configurations could be improved. Maheshwari et al. [38] use a multisite workflow scheduling technique to predict the execution time on resources and to identify the achievable network throughput between sites. In the experimental evaluation of the approach, real applications were used on multisite environments: traditional clusters and clouds. However, they did not consider more than one type of VMs in each cloud.

Table 2.6 presents several characteristics of the surveyed approaches. Table 2.6 allows for producing a higher level conclusion about the research and identifying missing research opportunities. We classified the approaches according to the

Table 2.6 Related works characteristics

Author	Approach	Scenario	Criteria	Evaluation	Kind of application
Endo et al. [20]	Survey	–	–	–	–
Shen et al. [53]	Static	Private cloud	QoS	Real testbed	Standalone application
Xu et al. [64]	Static	Data center	Energy	Simulation	Standalone application
Rodero et al. [50]	Dynamic	Data center	Energy	Simulation	Standalone application
Chaisiri et al. [5]	Static	Federated cloud	Cost	Simulation	Standalone application
Oliveira et al. [18]	Static	Public cloud	Cost, time	Real test	Workflow
Szabo et al. [55]	Static	Public cloud	Time, data transfer	Simulation, real test	Workflow
Heilig et al. [27]	Static	Federated cloud	Cost, time	Simulation	Standalone application
Lama et al. [35]	Dynamic	Private cloud	Time	Real testbed	Standalone application
Nguyen and Halem [44]	Dynamic	Private cloud	Time	Real testbed	Workflow
Wang et al. [60]	Dynamic	Private cloud	Time	Real testbed	workflow
Crawl et al. [12]	Dynamic	Private cloud	Time	Real testbed	workflow
Emeakaroha et al. [19]	Dynamic	Private cloud	Workflow completion, QoS	Real testbed	Workflow
Chard et al. [6]	Static, dynamic	Public cloud	Cost	Simulation	Workflow
Tian et al. [57]	Dynamic	Federated cloud	QoS	Simulation	Standalone application
Xiao et al. [63]	Dynamic	Private cloud	Skewness metric	Real testbed	Standalone application
Prodan et al. [49]	Dynamic	Grid	Cost, time	Simulation	Workflow
Deng et al. [15]	Dynamic	Public cloud	Time	Simulation	Standalone application
Malawski et al. [39]	Dynamic	Public cloud	Time	Simulation	Workflow
Maheshwari et al. [38]	Static	Federated cloud	Time, network throughput	Real test	Workflow

type of approach (dynamic or static), the type of cloud environment they are designed for (private, public, federated, etc.), the criteria used to dimension the cloud environment, the type of evaluation used in the paper, and the target kind of application. Most of the surveyed approaches provide dynamic mechanisms, which is intuitive since clouds are dynamic environments and performance variations are common. One missing opportunity can be identified when we analyze the target type of cloud of the proposed approaches. Most approaches focus on private and public cloud. However, just a few provide solutions for federated and multisite clouds, which are a reality. This way, new approaches for this type of clouds are needed. In terms of criteria used for dimensioning the cloud, most of the approaches optimize the environment for time and financial cost. However, just a few focus on reliability and energy criteria, which are very important nowadays. In addition, a multi-criteria approach would be very interesting for this problem. Most of the surveyed approaches were evaluated using simulations of small-scale environments (real testbed). Just a few evaluated the proposed approaches in real environments. Finally, most approaches focus on standalone applications. However, many HPC-based scientific experiments are modeled as scientific workflows, and solutions for this type of experiments are needed. Thus, dimensioning approaches for scientific workflows are still an open, yet important, issue and a research opportunity.

2.6 Conclusions and Open Problems

This chapter tackled the cloud dimensioning problem for parallel scientific applications. The problem consists in estimating the amount and types of virtual machines to execute an application, typically aiming at the reduction of its execution time, and sometimes considering also other objectives, such as reduction of financial costs when using a cloud provider and power saving, for example.

In that context, an integer mathematical formulation, called CC-IP, and a GRASP metaheuristic, GraspCC, proposed to reduce not only the execution time of the application but also the financial cost, were presented in detail. Experimental results on several instances of real parallel applications indicated that the presented method is an important decision tool to aid cloud users.

The extension of that proposal that takes into account the execution of parallel applications in federated clouds was also presented. That more general scenario considered new issues such as communication between providers. Tests on a real federated cloud environment, that used two commercial clouds (Amazon EC2 and Microsoft Azure), were then shown. In those real tests, scientific workflows were adopted as case study, since they are frequently used in large-scale parallel experiments.

Although that a priori estimation, called static dimensioning, usually provides good estimations, sometimes due to changes in the cloud environment or in the parallel application demands, it presents a poor performance. In those cases, a

VM dimensioning approach, aware at runtime of all those changes, is imperative. Thus, that chapter presented also a framework for dynamic dimensioning of cloud environments for scientific workflow execution, named DDC-F. The dynamic dimensioning approach presented advantages when executing scientific workflows in a real commercial cloud. It could compensate the performance loss by acquiring more powerful VMs to meet the scientists' deadline [8–11].

In addition, it can be difficult to execute some scientific application in only one cloud location due to the geographical distribution of scientists, data, and computing resources. For example, the data accessed by a HPC application may be in different databases of different research groups, or a parallel execution can require more resource than one location can offer. Thus, scientific applications often have to be partitioned and run in a multisite environment, i.e., a cloud with multiple distributed data centers.

We also surveyed several existing works in Sect. 2.5. This survey allowed us to produce a comparative table. Table 2.6 was used to produce a higher level conclusion about the research and identifying missing research opportunities. We classified the approaches according to the type of approach (dynamic or static), the type of cloud environment they are designed for (private, public, federated, etc.), the criteria used to dimension the cloud environment (time, financial costs, energy), the type of evaluation used in the paper, and the target kind of application. We concluded that there are some missing opportunities. For example, there are few papers that focus on scientific workflow dimensioning. Most approaches focus on stand-alone applications, but workflows are gaining much importance in the last years. In addition, most of existing approaches are focused on single-site (private and public) clouds. Just a few focus on federated and multisite clouds. Since these types of clouds are evolving in a fast pace, it is a hot topic in cloud dimensioning area. Finally, most of the existing approaches focus on time and financial costs. But, today, there are other costs involved such as energy and reliability, which may be an important research opportunity.

Acknowledgements Authors would like to thank CNPq and FAPERJ for partially sponsoring this research.

References

1. Altschul SF, Gish W, Miller W, Myers EW, Lipman DJ (1990) Basic local alignment search tool. J Mol Biol 215(3):403–410. citeseer.nj.nec.com/akutsu99identification.html
2. Alvares de Oliveira F, Sharrock R, Ledoux T (2012) Synchronization of multiple autonomic control loops: application to cloud computing. In: Proceedings of the 14th international conference on coordination models and languages, COORDINATION 2012. Springer, Berlin/Heidelberg, pp 29–43
3. Blom J, Albaum SP, Doppmeier D, Puhler A, Vorholter FJ, Zakrzewski M, Goesmann A (2009) EDGAR: a software framework for the comparative analysis of prokaryotic genomes. BMC Bioinform 10(1):154. doi:10.1186/1471-2105-10-154, http://www.biomedcentral.com/1471-2105/10/154

4. Buyya R, Ranjan R, Calheiros R (2010) InterCloud: utility-oriented federation of cloud computing environments for scaling of application services. In: Hsu CH, Yang L, Park J, Yeo SS (eds) Algorithms and architectures for parallel processing. Lecture notes in computer science, vol 6081. Springer, Berlin/Heidelberg, pp 13–31
5. Chaisiri S, Lee BS, Niyato D (2012) Optimization of resource provisioning cost in cloud computing. IEEE Trans Serv Comput 5(2):164–177
6. Chard R, Chard K, Bubendorfer K, Lacinski L, Madduri R, Foster I (2015) Cost-aware elastic cloud provisioning for scientific workloads. In: 2015 IEEE 8th international conference on cloud computing (CLOUD), pp 971–974
7. Collela P (2004) Defining software requirements for scientific computing. In: DARPA reports, pp 315–320
8. Coutinho R, Drummond L, Frota Y (2014) Optimization of a cloud resource management problem from a consumer perspective. In: Euro-Par 2013: parallel processing workshops. Lecture notes in computer science, vol 8374. Springer, Berlin/Heidelberg, pp 218–227
9. Coutinho R, Drummond L, Frota Y, de Oliveira D, Ocaña K (2014) Evaluating grasp-based cloud dimensioning for comparative genomics: a practical approach. In: IEEE international conference on cluster computing (CLUSTER), pp 371–379
10. Coutinho R, Drummond L, Frota Y, de Oliveira D (2015) Optimizing virtual machine allocation for parallel scientific workflows in federated clouds. Future Gener Comput Syst 46(0):51–68
11. Coutinho R, Frota Y, Ocaña K, de Oliveira D, Drummond LMA (2016) A dynamic cloud dimensioning approach for parallel scientific workflows: a case study in the comparative genomics domain. J Grid Comput 1–19
12. Crawl D, Wang J, Altintas I (2011) Provenance for MapReduce-based data-intensive workflows. In: Proceedings of the 6th workshop on workflows in support of large-scale science, WORKS '11. ACM, New York, pp 21–30
13. Dean J, Ghemawat S (2004) MapReduce: simplified data processing on large clusters. In: Proceedings of the 6th conference on symposium on opearting systems design & implementation, OSDI'04, vol 6. USENIX Association, Berkeley, pp 10–10
14. Deelman E, Singh G, Su MH, Blythe J, Gil Y, Kesselman C, Mehta G, Vahi K, Berriman GB, Good J, Laity AC, Jacob JC, Katz DS (2005) Pegasus: a framework for mapping complex scientific workflows onto distributed systems. Sci Program 13(3):219–237
15. Deng K, Song J, Ren K, Iosup A (2013) Exploring portfolio scheduling forlong-term execution of scientific workloads in IaaS clouds. In: Proceedings of SC13: international conference for high performance computing, networking, storage and analysis, SC '13. ACM, New York, pp 55:1–55:12
16. de Oliveira D, Ogasawara E, Baião F, Mattoso M: Scicumulus: a lightweight cloud middleware to explore many task computing paradigm in scientific workflows. In: 3rd international conference on cloud computing (2010), pp 378–385
17. de Oliveira D, Ocaña KA, Ogasawara E, Dias J, Gonçalves J, Baião F, Mattoso M (2013) Performance evaluation of parallel strategies in public clouds: a study with phylogenomic workflows. Future Gener Comput Syst 29(7):1816–1825
18. de Oliveira D, Viana V, Ogasawara E, Ocaña K, Mattoso M (2013) Dimensioning the virtual cluster for parallel scientific workflows in clouds. In: Proceedings of the 4th ACM workshop on scientific cloud computing, science cloud '13. ACM, New York, pp 5–12
19. Emeakaroha V, Maurer M, Stern P, Łabaj P, Brandic I, Kreil D (2013) Managing and optimizing bioinformatics workflows for data analysis in clouds. J Grid Comput 11(3):407–428
20. Endo PT, de Almeida Palhares AV, Pereira NN, Goncalves GE, Sadok D, Kelner J, Melander B, Mangs J (2011) Resource allocation for distributed cloud: concepts and research challenges. IEEE Network 25(4):42–46
21. Engen V, Papay J, Phillips SC, Boniface M (2012) Predicting application performance for multi-vendor clouds using dwarf benchmarks. In: Proceedings of the 13th international conference on web information systems engineering, WISE'12. Springer, Berlin/Heidelberg, pp 659–665. doi:10.1007/978-3-642-35063-4_50, http://dx.doi.org/10.1007/978-3-642-35063-4_50

22. Fadika Z, Dede E, Hartog J, Govindaraju M (2012) Marla: mapreduce for heterogeneous clusters. In: Proceedings of the 2012 12th IEEE/ACM international symposium on cluster, cloud and grid computing (Ccgrid 2012), CCGRID '12. IEEE Computer Society, Washington, DC, pp 49–56. doi:10.1109/CCGrid.2012.135, http://dx.doi.org/10.1109/CCGrid.2012.135

23. Feng H, Misra V, Rubenstein D (2007) Pbs: a unified priority-based scheduler. In: Proceedings of the 2007 ACM SIGMETRICS international conference on measurement and modeling of computer systems, SIGMETRICS '07. ACM, New York, pp 203–214. doi:10.1145/1254882.1254906, http://doi.acm.org/10.1145/1254882.1254906

24. Foster I, Kesselman C (2003) The grid 2: blueprint for a new computing infrastructure. The Elsevier series in grid computing, 2nd edn. Morgan Kaufmann, San Francisco

25. Freire J, Koop D, Santos E, Silva CT (2008) Provenance for computational tasks: a survey. Comput Sci Eng 10(3):11–21

26. Habib I (2006) Getting started with condor. Linux J 2006(149):2–. http://dl.acm.org/citation.cfm?id=1152899.1152901

27. Heilig L, Lalla-Ruiz E, Voß S (2016) A cloud brokerage approach for solving the resource management problem in multi-cloud environments. Comput Ind Eng 95:16–26

28. Hey T, Tansley S, Tolle K (eds) (2009): The fourth paradigm: data-intensive scientific discovery. Microsoft Research, Redmond

29. ILOG SA (2008) Cplex 11 user's manual

30. Jackson KR, Ramakrishnan L, Runge KJ, Thomas RC (2010) Seeking supernovae in the clouds: a performance study. In: Proceedings of the 19th ACM international symposium on high performance distributed computing, HPDC '10. ACM, New York, pp 421–429

31. Jamshidi P, Ahmad A, Pahl C (2013) Cloud migration research: a systematic review. IEEE Trans Cloud Comput 1(2):142–157. doi:10.1109/TCC.2013.10

32. Joshi SB (2012) Apache hadoop performance-tuning methodologies and best practices. In: Proceedings of the 3rd ACM/SPEC international conference on performance engineering, ICPE '12. ACM, New York, pp 241–242. doi:10.1145/2188286.2188323, http://doi.acm.org/10.1145/2188286.2188323

33. Juve G, Deelman E (2010) Scientific workflows and clouds. Crossroads 16(3):14–18. doi:10.1145/1734160.1734166, http://doi.acm.org/10.1145/1734160.1734166

34. Kitchenham B, Brereton P, Turner M, Niazi M, Linkman S, Pretorius R, Budgen D (2009) The impact of limited search procedures for systematic literature reviews #x2014; a participant-observer case study. In: 2009 3rd international symposium on empirical software engineering and measurement, pp 336–345. doi:10.1109/ESEM.2009.5314238

35. Lama P, Zhou X (2012) AROMA: automated resource allocation and configuration of MapReduce environment in the cloud. In: Proceedings of the 9th international conference on autonomic computing, ICAC '12. ACM, New York, pp 63–72

36. Lord E, Leclercq M, Boc A, Diallo AB, Makarenkov V (2012) Armadillo 1.1: an original workflow platform for designing and conducting phylogenetic analysis and simulations. PLoS ONE 7(1):e29903. doi:10.1371/journal.pone.0029903, http://dx.plos.org/10.1371/journal.pone.0029903

37. Ludäscher B, Altintas I, Berkley C, Higgins D, Jaeger E, Jones MB, Lee EA, Tao J, Zhao Y (2006) Scientific workflow management and the Kepler system. Concurr Comput: Pract Exp 18(10):1039–1065. doi:10.1002/cpe.994, http://dx.doi.org/10.1002/cpe.994

38. Maheshwari K, Jung ES, Meng J, Morozov V, Vishwanath V, Kettimuthu R (2016) Workflow performance improvement using model-based scheduling over multiple clusters and clouds. Future Gener Comput Syst 54:206–218

39. Malawski M, Juve G, Deelman E, Nabrzyski J (2015) Algorithms for cost- and deadline-constrained provisioning for scientific workflow ensembles in IaaS clouds. Future Gener Comput Syst 48:1–18. Special Section: Business and Industry Specific Cloud

40. Manfroi LF, Ferro M, Yokoyama AM, Mury AR, Schulze B (2013) A walking dwarf on the clouds. In: 2013 IEEE/ACM 6th international conference on utility and cloud computing (UCC), pp 399–404. doi:10.1109/UCC.2013.80

41. Matsunaga A, Tsugawa M, Fortes J (2008) Cloudblast: combining mapreduce and virtualization on distributed resources for bioinformatics applications. In: IEEE fourth international conference on eScience, eScience '08, pp 222–229. doi:10.1109/eScience.2008.62

42. Mattoso M, Werner C, Travassos GH, Braganholo V, Ogasawara E, Oliveira DD, Cruz SM, Martinho W, Murta L (2010) Towards supporting the life cycle of large scale scientific experiments. Int J Bus Process Integr Manag 5(1):79+

43. Moustafa A, Bhattacharya D, Allen AE (2010) iTree: a high-throughput phylogenomic pipeline. IEEE, Cairo, pp 103–107. doi:10.1109/CIBEC.2010.5716071, http://ieeexplore. ieee.org/lpdocs/epic03/wrapper.htm?arnumber=5716071

44. Nguyen P, Halem M (2011) A MapReduce workflow system for architecting scientific data intensive applications. In: Proceedings of the 2nd international workshop on software engineering for cloud computing, SECLOUD '11. ACM, New York, pp 57–63

45. Niemenmaa M, Kallio A, Schumacher A, Klemela P, Korpelainen E, Heljanko K (2012) Hadoop-BAM: directly manipulating next generation sequencing data in the cloud. Bioinformatics 28(6):876–877. doi:10.1093/bioinformatics/bts054, http://bioinformatics. oxfordjournals.org/cgi/doi/10.1093/bioinformatics/bts054

46. Ocaña K, de Oliveira D, Ogasawara ES, Dávila AMR, Lima AAB, Mattoso M (2011) SciPhy: a cloud-based workflow for phylogenetic analysis of drug targets in protozoan genomes. In: de Souza ON, Telles GP, Palakal MJ (eds) BSB. Lecture notes in computer science, vol 6832. Springer, pp 66–70

47. Paranjape K, Hebert S, Masson B (2012) Heterogeneous computing in the cloud: crunching big data and democratizing HPC access for the life sciences. Technical report, Intel Corporation

48. Phillips SC, Engen V, Papay J (2011) Snow white clouds and the seven dwarfs. In: 2011 IEEE third international conference on cloud computing technology and science (CloudCom), pp 738–745 doi:10.1109/CloudCom.2011.114

49. Prodan R, Wieczorek M, Fard H (2011) Double auction-based scheduling of scientific applications in distributed grid and cloud environments. J Grid Comput 9(4):531–548

50. Rodero I, Viswanathan H, Lee EK, Gamell M, Pompili D, Parashar M (2012) Energy-efficient thermal-aware autonomic management of virtualized HPC cloud infrastructure. J Grid Comput 10(3):447–473

51. Severin J, Beal K, Vilella AJ, Fitzgerald S, Schuster M, Gordon L, Ureta-Vidal A, Flicek P, Herrero J (2010) eHive: an artificial intelligence workflow system for genomic analysis. BMC Bioinform 11(1):240. doi:10.1186/1471-2105-11-240, http://bmcbioinformatics. biomedcentral.com/articles/10.1186/1471-2105-11-240

52. Shanahan JG, Dai L (2015) Large scale distributed data science using apache spark. In: Proceedings of the 21th ACM SIGKDD international conference on knowledge discovery and data mining, KDD '15. ACM, New York, pp 2323–2324 doi:10.1145/2783258.2789993, http:// doi.acm.org/10.1145/2783258.2789993

53. Shen Z, Subbiah S, Gu X, Wilkes J (2011) Cloudscale: elastic resource scaling for multi-tenant cloud systems. In: Proceedings of the 2nd ACM symposium on cloud computing, SOCC '11. ACM, New York, pp 5:1–5:14

54. Singh A, Chen C, Liu W, Mitchell W, Schmidt B: A hybrid computational grid architecture for comparative genomics. IEEE Trans Inf Technol Biomed 12(2):218–225 (2008). doi:10.1109/TITB.2007.908462, http://ieeexplore.ieee.org/lpdocs/epic03/wrapper. htm?arnumber=4358919

55. Szabo C, Sheng Q, Kroeger T, Zhang Y, Yu J (2014) Science in the cloud: allocation and execution of data-intensive scientific workflows. J Grid Comput 12(2):245–264

56. Taylor IJ, Deelman E, Gannon DB (2007) Workflows for e-science: scientific workflows for grids. Springer, London

57. Tian W (2009) adaptive dimensioning of cloud data centers. In: Proceedings of the 8th international conference on dependable, autonomic and secure computing, DASC '09. IEEE Computer Society, Washington, pp 5–10

58. Vaquero LM, Rodero-Merino L, Caceres J, Lindner M (2008) A break in the clouds: towards a cloud definition. SIGCOMM Comput Commun Rev 39(1):50–55
59. Wall DP, Kudtarkar P, Fusaro VA, Pivovarov R, Patil P, Tonellato PJ (2010) Cloud computing for comparative genomics. BMC Bioinform 11(1):259. doi:10.1186/1471-2105-11-259, http://bmcbioinformatics.biomedcentral.com/articles/10.1186/1471-2105-11-259
60. Wang J, Crawl D, Altintas I (2009) Kepler + Hadoop: a general architecture facilitating data-intensive applications in scientific workflow systems. In: Proceedings of the 4th workshop on workflows in support of large-scale science, WORKS '09. ACM, New York, pp 12:1–12:8
61. Wolstencroft K, Haines R, Fellows D, Williams AR, Withers D, Owen S, Soiland-Reyes S, Dunlop I, Nenadic A, Fisher P, Bhagat J, Belhajjame K, Bacall F, Hardisty A, de la Hidalga AN, Vargas MPB, Sufi S, Goble CA (2013) The Taverna workflow suite: designing and executing workflows of web services on the desktop, web or in the cloud. Nucleic Acids Res 41(Webserver-Issue):557–561. doi:10.1093/nar/gkt328, http://dx.doi.org/10.1093/nar/gkt328
62. Wozniak JM, Armstrong TG, Maheshwari K, Lusk EL, Katz DS, Wilde M, Foster IT (2013) Turbine: a distributed memory dataflow engine for high performance many-task applications. Fundamenta Informaticae Journal 128(3):337–366
63. Xiao Z, Song W, Chen Q (2013) dynamic resource allocation using virtual machines for cloud computing environment. IEEE Trans Parallel Distrib Syst 24(6):1107–1117
64. Xu L, Zeng Z, Ye X (2012) Multi-objective optimization based virtual resource allocation strategy for cloud computing. In: Proceedings of the 11th international conference on computer and information science, ICIS '12. IEEE Computer Society, Washington, DC, pp 56–61

Chapter 3
A Taxonomy of Adaptive Resource Management Mechanisms in Virtual Machines: Recent Progress and Challenges

José Simão and Luís Veiga

3.1 Introduction

Cloud computing infrastructures make extensive use of virtualization technologies, either at the system or programming language level, providing a flexible allocation of hardware resources and applying the necessary resource scheduling to run multi-tenant data centers [19, 96, 108]. Both system-level VMs (Sys-VM) and high-level language VMs (HLL-VM) are designed to promote isolation [86]. All these features are essential to consolidate applications into a smaller amount of physical servers, saving operational costs and reducing the carbon footprint of data centers [13, 30, 94].

Dynamic allocation of resources use different strategies, either aiming to maximize fairness in the distribution of resources or deliberately favor a given guest based on past resource consumption and prediction on future resource demand. Among all resources, CPU [35, 40, 110] and memory [3, 60, 100] are the two for which a larger body of work can be found. Nevertheless, other resources, such as the access to I/O operations, have also been analyzed [36, 51, 62].

Most HLL-VMs have only one guest at each time – the application. As a consequence, in most cases, some resources are monitored not to be partitioned but for the runtime to adapt its algorithms to the available environment. For example, a memory outage could force some of the already compiled methods to be unloaded, freeing memory to maintain more data resident. Several systems have been proposed to control system resources usage in HLL-VMs, most of them targeting the Java

J. Simão (✉)
INESC-ID Lisboa, Instituto Superior de Engenharia de Lisboa (ISEL/IPL), Lisbon, Portugal
e-mail: jsimao@gsd.inesc-id.pt

L. Veiga
INESC-ID Lisboa, Universidade de Lisboa – Instituto Superior Técnico, Lisbon, Portugal
e-mail: luis.veiga@inesc-id.pt

© Springer International Publishing AG 2017
N. Antonopoulos, L. Gillam (eds.), *Cloud Computing*, Computer Communications and Networks, DOI 10.1007/978-3-319-54645-2_3

runtime (e.g., [14, 17, 25, 83]). They use different approaches: from making modifications to a standard VM, or even proposing a new implementation from scratch, to modifications in the byte codes and hybrid solutions.

In each work, different compromises are made, putting more emphasis either on the portability of the solution (i.e., not requiring changes to the VM) or on the portability of the guests (i.e., not requiring changes to the application source code). In order to do so, VMs, or middlewares augmenting their services, can be framed into the well-known adaptation loop [68], where systems monitor themselves and their context, analyze the incoming values and detect significant changes, decide how to react, and act to execute such decisions. In this chapter, we group these steps in three distinct phases, similarly to the adaptability loop of other works in the context of autonomic systems [7, 57]: (i) monitoring, (ii) decision, and (iii) actuation. Monitoring determines which components of the system (e.g., hardware, VM, application) are observed. Control and decision take these observations and use them in some decision strategy to decide what has to be changed. Enforcement deals with applying the decision to a given component/mechanism of the VM.

However, existing surveys of virtualization technologies (e.g., [9, 53]) tend to focus on a wide variety of approaches which sometimes results only in an extensive catalog. One of the first published surveys of research in virtual machines was presented in 1974 [34]. Goldberg's work was focused on the principles, performance, and practical issues regarding the design and development of system-level virtual machines that, at the time, were developed by IBM, the Massachusetts Institute of Technology (MIT), and few others. Arnold et al. [9] focus only on HLL-VMs and particularly on the techniques that are used to control the optimizations employed by the just-in-time (JIT) compiler, taking advantage of runtime profiling information.

This chapter surveys several techniques used by virtual machines, and systems that depend on them, to make an adaptive resource management, extending previous preliminary work [73, 76]. Here we fully describe the adaptation loop of virtual machines discussing their principles, algorithms, mechanisms, and techniques. We then detail a way to qualitatively classify each of those according to their responsiveness, i.e., how fast it can react to change their comprehensiveness, i.e., the scope of the mechanisms involved; and their intricateness, i.e., the complexity of the modifications to the code base or to the underlying systems. These metrics are used to classify the mechanisms and scheduling policies. The goal is not to find the best system, as this depends on the scenario where the system is going to be used, but instead it aims to identity the tradeoffs underpinning each system.

Section 3.2 presents the architecture of high-level and system-level VMs, depicting the building blocks that are used in research concerning resource usage. Section 3.3 presents several adaptation techniques found in the literature and frames them into the adaptation loop. In Sect. 3.4, the classification framework is presented. For each of the resource management components of VMs, and for each of the three steps of the adaptation loop, we propose the use of a quantitative classification regarding the impact of the mechanisms used by each system. We then use this framework to classify 18 state-of-the-art systems in Sect. 3.5, aiming to compare and better understand the benefits and limitations of each one.

3.2 From Virtual Machines Fundamentals to Recent Trends

Virtualization technologies have been used since the primordials of multiuser systems. The idea of having better isolation among different users in a multiuser system was first explored by IBM [5]. In these systems, each user was assigned a *virtual machine* which executed in the context of a so called *control program* (CP).

In the last two decades, this idea was extended and further explored to support the execution of commodity operating systems in each virtual machine, without losing performance. Resource isolation was further enforced so that badly behaving virtual machines cannot disrupt the service of other instances [12]. This is due not only to the software but also to new hardware support that enhances the performance of VMs running on a multi-tenant server [29].

System-level virtual machines execute under the control of a virtual machine monitor (VMM) to control the access of the guest operating system running in each virtual machine to the physical resources, virtualizing processors, memory, and I/O. Recently, operating systems extended the process-level isolation mechanisms with further virtualization of the file system, name spaces, and drivers (e.g., network) [55, 107]. Furthermore, the integration of resource consumption controls made it possible to run workloads on a new kind of execution environment, called *container*, under the same OS.

High-level language VMs, which are highly influenced by the Smalltalk virtual machine [28], also provide a machine abstraction to their guest, which is an end-user application. The just-in-time (JIT) compiler is responsible for this translation and is, in itself, a source of adaptation driven by the dynamics in the flow of execution (e.g., hot methods are compiled using more sophisticated optimizations) [9]. Memory management has a high impact on the use of memory and CPU. After more than three decades of research work focusing on tunning garbage collection algorithms [50], recent research work is made toward the selection of application-specific algorithms and parameters, in particular, heap size and the moment of triggering memory collection [43, 59, 89].

Figures 3.1, 3.2, 3.3, and 3.4 depicts four types of deployments. The first is a traditional configuration where an operating system (OS) regulates the access of native applications (i.e., the ones that use the services of the OS) to the hardware. The second, Fig. 3.2, represents a configuration where a hypervisor, known as virtual

Fig. 3.1 Non virtualized system

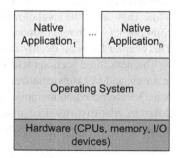

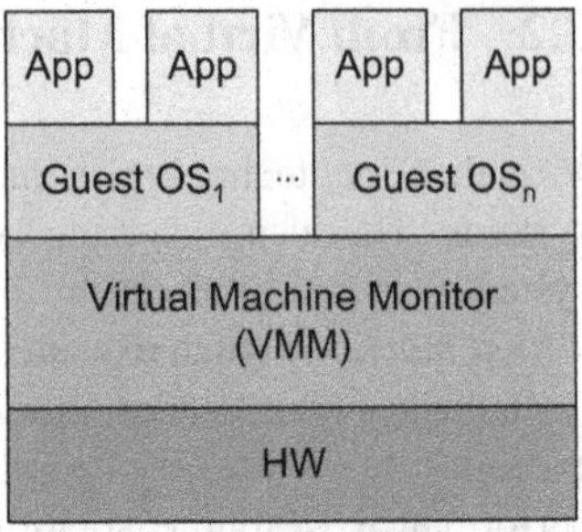

Fig. 3.2 System-level VM

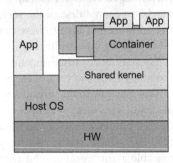

Fig. 3.3 Container type VM

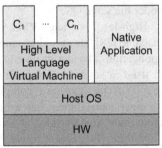

Fig. 3.4 High-level language
VM

machine monitor, takes control of the hardware, making it possible to host several system-level virtual machine on top of the same physical resources. Each virtual machine runs a possibly different operating systems instance. Figure 3.3 shows the position of containers. These execution environments share the kernel with the host OS and allow applications to run with an extra level of isolation from the remaining user-level processes. Finally, Fig. 3.4 depicts the position of high-level language VMs. They are at the level of native applications but support the hosting of *managed* components which rely (almost exclusively) on the services provided by these VMs. This chapter focus on deployments Figs. 3.2 and 3.4.

The next three sections will briefly describe how fundamental resources, CPU, memory, and I/O are virtualized by the two types of VMs. The systems presented in Sect. 3.5 are based on the building blocks presented here, using them to implement different adaptive resource management strategies. We conclude with a section about recent trends on the mechanism available on these two types of VMs.

3.2.1 Computation as a Resource

The virtualization of the CPU concerns two distinct aspects: (i) the translation of instructions and (ii) the scheduling of virtual CPUs to a physical CPU. In this chapter, we focus on the scheduling problem. Although an efficient binary translation is of utmost importance, and several techniques are used [86], this is done in a way that is dependent on the execution requirement of a given tenant. In Sys-VMs, the VMM must decide the mapping between the real CPUs and each running VM [12, 21]. In the case of HLL-VMs, they rely on the underlying OS to schedule their threads of execution. In spite of this portability aspect, the specification of HLL-VMs is supported by a memory model [58] making it possible to reason about the program behavior.

The VMM scheduler, where each guest VM is assigned to one or more virtual CPUs (VCPU), has different requirements from the schedulers used in operating systems [92]. Typically, the OS uses a priority-based approach which is different from the family of schedulers used by the VMM. The VM monitor scheduling is ruled by a *proportional share* assigned to each VM of the system, based on its *share* (or *weight*) [21, 90].

Cherkasova et al. [21] further classify schedulers as (i) work conservative or nonwork conservative and (ii) preemptive or non-preemptive. Work conservative schedulers take the *share* as a minimum allocation of CPU to the VM. If there are available CPUs, VCPUs will be assigned to them, regardless the VM's share. In nonwork conservative, even if there are available CPUs, VCPUs will not be assigned above a given previously defined value (known as *cap* or *cpu limit*). A preemptive scheduler can interrupt running VCPUs if a ready to run VCPU has a higher priority.

In Sect. 3.5, we present different systems that dynamically change the scheduler's parameters to give guest VMs the capacity that best fits their needs.

3.2.2 Memory as a Resource

The design of memory management system is inherently complex, regardless of the target environment. Virtual machines (VMs) are no exception, and they add an extra level to the system stack.

As pointed out by Smith et al. [86], the VMM extra level of indirection generalizes the virtual memory mechanisms of operating systems. To maintain isolation, the guest OS continues to see a real address (i.e., machine address) but this address can in fact change during the activation of the VM. So, the VMM must establish a *virtual* → *real* → *physical* mapping for each guest OS and VM.

When an OS kernel, running on an active VM, uses a *real* address to perform an operation (e.g., I/O), the VMM must intercept this address and change it to the correspondent physical one. On the other hand, user level applications use a *virtual* address to accomplish their operations. To avoid a twofold conversion, the VMM keeps *shadow pages* for each process running on each VM, mapping *virtual* → *physical* addresses. Access to the page table pointer is virtualized by the VMM, trapping read or write attempts and returning the corresponding table pointer of the running VM. The translation lookaside buffer (TLB) continues to play its accelerating role because it will still keep in cache the *virtual* → *physical* addresses.

To effectively manage the allocation of physical memory, the VMM must reassign pages between VMs. The decision about which specific pages are to be relinquished is actually made by the guest OS running on the VM that is selected by the VMM to give away memory. This is done by interacting with a kernel driver at the OS, known as the *balloon* driver [12, 100].

The balloon driver is controlled by memory management policies which will be introduced in Sect. 3.3. When the balloon is instructed to inflate, it will make the guest OS swap memory to secondary storage. When the balloon is instructed to deflate, the guest OS can use more physical pages, reducing the need to swap memory. Another issue related to memory management in the VMM is the sharing of machine pages between different VMs. If these pages have code or read-only data, they can be shared avoiding redundant copies.

The goal of memory's virtualization in high-language VMs is to free the application from explicit dealing with memory deallocation, giving the perception of an unlimited address space. This avoids keeping track of references to data structures (i.e., objects), promoting easier extensibility of functionalities because the bookkeeping code that must be written in non-virtualized environment is no longer needed [86, 106].

Different strategies have been researched and used during the last decades. Simple *mark and sweep*, *compacting*, or *copying collectors* all identify live objects starting from a root set (i.e., the initial set of references from which live objects can be found, containing thread stacks and globals). All these approaches strive for a balance between the time the program needs to stop and the frequency the collecting process needs to execute. This is mostly influenced by the heap dimension, and, in practice, some kind of nursery space is used to avoid searching all the heap.

As parallel hardware becomes ubiquitous and GC pause time reduction becomes essential, the stop-the-world approach has been questioned, resulting in the design of concurrent and incremental collectors [23, 95]. However, recent studies show that the base approach has no fundamental scalability problem [31] and that the GC impact can be diminished with parallel techniques, which still need to stop the program, but that explore the root set in parallel.

Researchers have analyzed garbage collection performance and found it to be application dependent [88] and even input dependent [59, 93]. Based on these observations, several adaptation strategies have been proposed [9], ranging from parameters adjustments (e.g., the current size of the managed heap [38, 83]) to changing the algorithm itself before the first execution [85] or at runtime [88].

3.2.3 Input/Output as a Resource

In both types of VMs, virtualization of input/output deals with the emulation, accounting, and constraining of using available physical devices. In spite of these similar goals, virtualization occurs with different impacts. In a VMM, the access to device drivers can be para-virtualized or fully virtualized. In the first scenario, a cooperative guest OS is expected to call a virtual API in the VMM [12]. In the second scenario (a fully virtualized environment), the VMM can either intercept the I/O operation, at the device driver or system call level [86]. The typical option is to virtualize at the device driver level, installing virtual device drivers at each guest, which, from the guest operating system standpoint, are regular drivers.

The main challenge in I/O virtualization for fully virtualized systems, such as the ESX [100] or the KVM [54] hypervisors, is to avoid the extra context switches between the guest and the host to handle interrupts generated by I/O devices [2, 36]. The interrupts are, by nature, asynchronous and sent to the CPU to signal the completion of I/O operations. So, the overhead comes from the extra CPU cycles necessary to exit the guest, run the host interrupt handler, and inject the virtual interrupt in the guest.

The performance of I/O-intensive applications in a virtualized environment is also affected by the CPU scheduling and memory sharing mechanisms [20, 21, 62, 67]. The CPU scheduling strategy of each physical core to the virtual cores has impact in the I/O performance of the applications running on top of virtual machines. A detailed analysis of the scheduler's impact on VM's performance is available in the literature [21, 62]. The main observations were related to the domain driver's preemption during the dispatch of multiple network events and the order of VMs in the run queue.

High-level language VMs rely on the operating system API to accomplish input/output operations as disk and network read and writes. Depending on the address space isolation supported by the VM, accounting and regulation have different levels of granularity. In a classic JVM implementation, accountability can be done globally at the VM or on a per-thread basis [91]. In HLL-VMs supporting the abstraction of different address spaces (e.g., isolates in multitask VM [25], application domains in the Common Language Runtime) accounting is made independently for each of these spaces.

In summary, although the interaction with I/O devices has a major role in the design of virtual machines, the subsystems responsible for this task do not have to make regular scheduling or allocation decisions. So, this chapter will not focus on these works but on adaptive techniques related to the virtualization of CPU and memory (which indirectly contribute to the performance of I/O-intensive applications).

3.2.4   Research Trends

The ACM library [1] shows that articles with the terms "VM" and "virtual machine" continues to increase. Extrapolating the total number of publications up to 2016 to the end of the decade, the number will more than double the results of the previous decade, the 2000s. Because of their strategic role in cloud deployments, they will certainly continue to be analyzed and enhanced.

Regarding Sys-VMs, major research efforts continue in memory virtualization techniques. For example, Amit et al. propose VSwapper [6], which substitutes the classic balloon driver in the common case of uncooperative guests. Although this situation is known for its poor performance, VSwapper uses a combination of intricate techniques to overcome the problem, monitoring host disk blocks and establishing a relation to guest memory pages in order to detect page writes and reads that hinder performance.

When looking to HLL-VMs, research in resource management is currently driven by the need to incorporate further mechanisms to regulate memory usage when running manage runtimes in clusters. Although this has been a topic of research for more than a decade now [26], new challenges were introduced by cloud deployments, namely, the execution on top of Sys-VMs and big-data applications.

Manage runtimes are the basis of modern processing and storage framework widely used by cloud-enabled applications. However, because many times they execute on top of Sys-VMs, there is the need to externally instruct the HLL-VM to relinquish some memory so that the VMM can deliver it to other tenants [45, 69].

Considering a single node running instance, some improvements for big-data workloads are also being explored to avoid the problems introduced by object churn and very large heap sizes [33], including in NUMA-based architectures [32]. But because typically the workloads run on top of multiple physical nodes, researchers are looking for ways to coordinate resource management, in particular GC operations [56, 74].

3.3   Adaptation Techniques

In a software system, adaptation is regulated by monitoring, analyzing, deciding, and acting [68]. Monitoring is fed by sensors, and actions are accomplished by actuators, forming a process known as the *adaptation loop*, as depicted in Fig. 3.5. Virtual machines, regardless of their type, are no exception. The two intermediate phases, analysis and decision, are in many cases seen as one [57]. An example is the observe, decide, and act loop proposed by IBM for autonomic systems [7]. This chapter follows the same approach and resumes the adaptation loop to three major phases: monitor, analysis/decision, action.

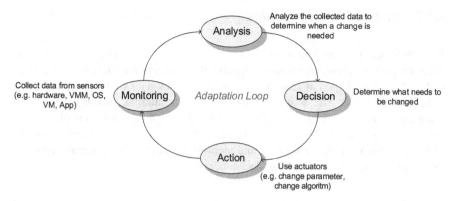

Fig. 3.5 Adaptation loop

In a broad sense, virtual machines have an important property of autonomic systems which is self-optimization [7]. An example is the adaptive JIT compilation techniques of HLL-VMs [9] or GC algorithms that use feedback-directed online techniques to avoid page faults [37]. Furthermore, virtual machines export adaptability mechanisms that are used by outside decision systems to reconfigure VM's parameters or algorithms.

There is a broad range of strategies regarding the analysis and decision processes. Many solutions that augment system VMs use control theory elements, such as the proportional-integral-derivative controller, and additive-increase/multiplicative-decrease (AIMD) rules, to regulate one or more VM parameters. Typically, when the analysis and decision are done in the critical execution path (e.g., scheduling, JIT, GC), the choice must be done as fast as possible, and so, a simpler logic is used.

In our previous work, we have addressed adaptation with strategies based on economic models and awareness of the workloads. Regarding system VMs, we have addressed adaptation of VM allocation [72] and resizing mechanisms [79, 81]. Regarding high-level language VMs (Java VM), we have studied the economics of enforcing resource (CPU and memory) throttling [78], taking into account application performance [80], and the tradeoffs between resource savings and performance degradation/improvement, when aggressively transferring resources among applications [77]. At the middleware level, federating several VMs, adaptation concerns memory management in object caching/replication aggressiveness [97], driven by declarative policies [98], and adapting the number of VMs/nodes dynamically allocated to multi-threaded Java applications, running on top of multi-tenant clustered runtimes [75].

Next we will present and discuss the state of the art regarding the three major steps of the adaptation loop for each type of VM and their internal resource management mechanisms.

3.3.1 System Virtual Machine

The VMM has built-in parameters to regulate how resources are shared by their different guests. These parameters regulate the allocation of resources to each VM and can be adapted at runtime to improve the behavior of applications given a specific workload. The adaptation process can be internal, driven by profiling made exclusively inside of the VMM, or external, which depends on application's events such as the number of pending requests. In this section, the two major VMM subsystems, CPU scheduling and memory manager, will be framed into the adaptation processes – monitoring, decision, and acting.

3.3.1.1 CPU Management

CPU management relates to activities that can be done exclusively inside the hypervisor or both inside and outside. An example of an exclusively inside activity is the CPU scheduling algorithm. To enforce the weight assigned to each VM, the hypervisor has to monitor the time of CPU assigned to each VCPUs of a VM, decide which VCPU will run next, and assign it to a CPU [21, 70]. An example of an inside and outside management strategy is the one employed by systems that monitor events outside the hypervisor (e.g., operating systems load queue, application level events) but then use its internal actuators to adjust parameters. For example, monitoring the waiting time inside the spin-lock synchronization primitive (in the kernel of the guest operating system) may be necessary to inform the hypervisor's scheduler about the best co-scheduling [64] decisions of VCPUs [103].

Decision strategies can be simple, like the proportional share-based that enforces predefined *shares* defined by high-level policies in a multi-tenant environment. More complex decisions, made outside the hypervisor, include (i) control theory using a PID controller [66, 110], (ii) linear optimization [65], and (iii) signal processing and statistical learning algorithms [35].

The actions taken by the CPU scheduler inside the hypervisor include (i) number of VCPUs [70], (ii) co-scheduling [99, 103, 104], (iii) VCPU migration [99], and (iv) number of threads and sleep time [110]. Systems where decisions are made outside the hypervisor use the available actuators, namely, (i) VCPU share and (ii) VCPU *cap* [35, 42, 65].

3.3.1.2 Memory Management

In this step of the control loop, the VMM needs to determine how pages (or parts of it) are being used by each VM. To do so, it must collect information regarding (i) page utilization [61, 100, 102] and (ii) page (and sub-page) contents equality or similarity [39, 100]. Some systems also propose to monitor application performance, either by instrumentation or external monitoring, in order to collect information closer to the application's semantics [45, 69].

The VMM supports overcommit, that is, the total memory configured to the overall VMs can be higher than the one that is physically available. When pages of memory need to be transferred between VMs (and their guest OS), different types of decisions are made based on (i) shares [100], (ii) feedback control [42], (iii) LRU reference histogram [102], and (iv) linear programming [45].

To change the system state regarding its memory use, there are three main approaches: (i) page sharing, (ii) page transfer between VMs, and (iii) compress page contents. While page sharing and transfer relies on intrinsic mechanisms of the VMM, as presented in Sect. 3.2.2, page compression is an extension to these base mechanisms.

3.3.2 High-Level Language Virtual Machine

In this section, the three major language VM subsystems, JIT compiler, GC, and resource manager, will be framed into the adaptation processes. HLL-VMs monitor events inside their runtime services or in the underlying platform. As always, there is a trade-off between deciding fast but poorly or deciding well (or even optimally) but spending too much resource and time in the process of doing so. Most systems base their decision on a heuristic, that is, some kind of adjustment function or criterion that although it cannot be fully formally reasoned about, it still gives good results when properly used. Nevertheless, some do have a mathematical model guiding their behavior [93]. Next we will analyze the most common strategies.

3.3.2.1 Just in Time Compilation

The JIT is mostly self-contained in the sense that the monitoring process (also known as profiling in this context) collects data only inside the VM. Modern JIT compilers are consumers of a significant amount of data collected during the compilation and execution of code.[1] Hot method information is acquired using (i) sampling and (ii) instrumentation. In the first case, the execution stacks are periodically observed to determine hot methods. In the second case, method code is instrumented so that its execution will fill the appropriate runtime profiling structures. Sampling is known to be more efficient [9] despite its partial view of events.

To determine which methods should be compiled or further optimized, there are two distinct groups of techniques: (i) counter-based and (ii) model-based. Counter-based systems look at different counters (e.g., method entry, loop execution) to

---

[1]The adaptive optimization system (AOS) in Jikes RVM [4] produces a log with approximately 700 kB of information regarding call graphs, edge counters and compilation advice when running and JIT compiling 'bloat', one of DaCapo's benchmarks [15].

determine if a method should be further optimized. The threshold values are typically found by experimenting with different programs [9]. In a model-driven system, optimization decisions are made based on a mathematical model which can be reasoned about. Examples include a cost-benefit model where the recompilation cost is weighted against further execution with the current optimization level [4, 52].

Adaptability techniques in the JIT compiler are used to produce native optimized code while minimizing impact in application's execution time overhead. Because native takes more memory than intermediate representations, some early VMs discarded native code compilations when memory became scarce. With the growth of hardware capacity, this technique is less used. Thus, the actions that can complete the adaptation loop are (i) partial or total method recompilation, (ii) inlining, or (iii) deoptimization.

3.3.2.2 Garbage Collection

Although the way garbage collection is made usually does not change during program's execution, managed runtimes incorporate some form of memory adaptation strategy [9]. In the literature, several sensors are used to guide the decision process, both from the managed runtime and operating system, including: (i) memory structure dimensions (e.g., heap in use) [84, 85], (ii) GC statistics (e.g., GC load, GC frequency) [88], (iii) relevant events in the operating systems (e.g., page faults, allocation stalls) [37, 44], and (iv) working set size [109].

Improvements to overall system performance are made by reducing time spent in GC operations. Heap-related structures are adapted both before and during program execution. Adjusting before program execution is made after a previous analysis of several executions, varying relevant parameters. While there are some mathematical models of objects' lifetimes, they are essentially used to explain the GC behavior and not to drive a decision process [11]. The techniques used in the decision phase range from heuristics to more formal processes: (i) simple heuristics, (ii) machine learning, (iii) PID controller, and (iv) microeconomic theories such as the elasticity of demand curves.

Actions regarding GC adaptability range from simply triggering the GC in a specific situation to the hot-swap of the algorithm itself (e.g., to avoid memory exhaustion [88]), as described next: (i) GC parameters [85], (ii) heap size [84], and (iii) GC algorithm [88].

3.3.2.3 Resource Management

Monitoring resources, that is, collecting usage or consumption information about different kinds of resources at runtime (e.g., state of threads, loaded classes) can be done through (i) a service exposed by the runtime [10, 25] and (ii) byte code instrumentation [49]. In the former, it is possible to collect more information, both from a quantitative and qualitative perspective. A well-known example is the Java Management Extensions (JMX) [63]. Because HLL-VMs do not necessarily expose this kind of service, instrumentation allows some accounting in a portable way. Accounted resources usually include CPU usage, allocated memory, and relevant system objects such as threads or files.

This subsystem has to decide whether a given action (e.g., consumption) over a resource can be done or not. This is accomplished with a policy, which can be classified as (i) internal or (ii) external. In an internal policy, the reasoning is hard-coded in the runtime, possibly only giving the chance to vary a parameter (e.g., number of allowed opened files). An external policy is defined outside the scope of the runtime, and thus, it can change for each execution or even during execution.

This subsystem is particularly important in VMs that support several independent processes running in a single instance of the runtime. Research and commercial systems apply resource management actions to (i) limit resource usage and (ii) perform resource reservation. Limiting resource usage aims to avoid denial of service or to ensure that the (possibly paid) resource quota is not overused. The last scenario is less explored in the literature [25]. Resource reservation ensures that when multiple processes are running in the same runtime, it is possible to ensure a minimum amount of resources to a given process.

3.3.3 Summary of Techniques

In this section, we summarize several techniques identified in the literature. Figure 3.6 presents the techniques used in the adaptation loop of Sys-VMs. They are grouped by the two major adaptation targets, CPU and memory, and then into the three major phases of the adaptation loop. The CPU management sub-tree is the one that has more elements (i.e., more adaptation techniques). This reflects the emphasis given by researchers to this component of Sys-VMs. Regarding memory, early work of Waldspurger [100] and Barham et al. in [12] laid solid techniques for virtualizing and managing this resource. Recent work shows that to improve performance of workloads regarding their use of memory, it is crucial to have more application-level information [45, 102].

Figure 3.7 presents the techniques used in the adaptation loop of systems using HLL-VMs. They are grouped into the three major adaptation targets: (i) JIT compiler, (ii) garbage collection, and (iii) resource management. Each adaptation target is then divided into the three phases of the adaptation loop. The garbage collection sub-tree has a higher number of elements when compared with any of the other two. This reflects different research paths but also a higher dependency of the garbage collection process on the workloads and on the context of execution (i.e., shared environment, limited memory, etc.).

The techniques used in the monitoring and action phase are domain-specific. For example, there are sensors related to the utilization of memory pages or actuators

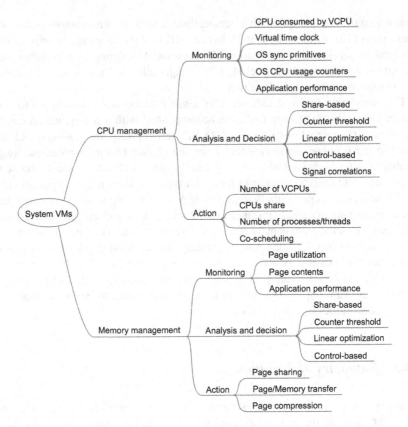

Fig. 3.6 Techniques used by System VMs in the monitoring, decision and action phases

that change a parameter in the garbage collection algorithm. On the contrary, the strategies used in the decision phase can be found in other adaptability works and, in general, in autonomic computing systems [7, 57].

Maggio et al. [57] have focused attention on the characterization of decision techniques. They divide them into three broad categories: heuristics, control-based, and machine learning. In fact, we can also see these categories when we look to the techniques identified in this section. Figures 3.6 and 3.7 show that the decision strategies are either heuristic (e.g., microeconomics, share-based), control-based (e.g., PID controller), based on signal processing techniques (e.g., correlation of different windows of samples), and machine learning (e.g., reinforcement learning). Regarding strategies that use linear programming, they are used only to make a general model of the scheduling variables. In practice, these approaches use integer linear programming which is known to be NP-hard. Thus, they use some kind of greedy approach to solve it.

Based on the survey of these different techniques, the next section will present a classification framework that aims to compare complete adaptive systems.

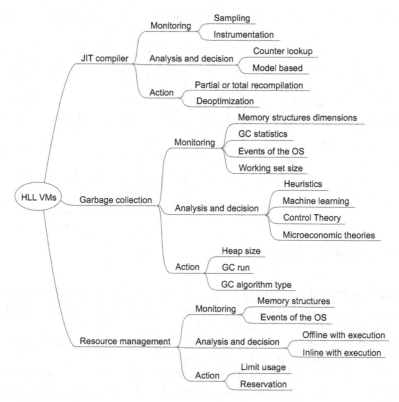

Fig. 3.7 Techniques used by HLL-VMs in the monitoring, decision and action phases

3.4 The RCI Taxonomy

To understand and compare different adaptation processes, we now introduce a framework for classification of VM adaptation techniques. The classification is based on the different techniques described earlier and depicted in Figs. 3.6 and 3.7. The analysis and classification of the techniques and the way they are used in each of the adaptation loops revolve around three fundamental criteria: *Responsiveness*, *Comprehensiveness*, and *Intricateness*. We call it RCI taxonomy. Our goal is to put each system in perspective and compare them regarding three criteria. The final RCI values of a given system depend on the techniques the system uses for monitoring, decision, and acting.

These aspects were chosen, not only because they encompass many of the relevant goals and challenges in VM adaptability research but also because they seem to embody a fundamental underlying tension: *to achieve improvements in two of these aspects the system must do so at the expense of the other*. System design is always a trade-off between different choices. A well-known example is the

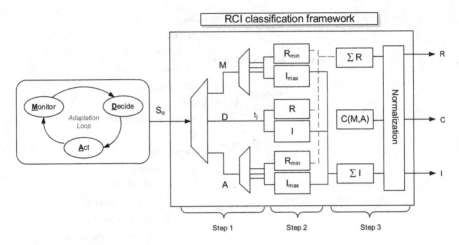

Fig. 3.8 A step-by-step classification process

CAP theorem [18], showing the tension existing in the general design of distributed systems. In the particular case of peer-to-peer systems, high availability, scalability, and support for dynamic populations are other kind of tensions [16].

The framework starts by taking the input system and decomposing it into the adaptation techniques used in the monitoring, decision, and acting phase. This is represented in step 1 of Fig. 3.8. Then, for each technique, a value for R and I is determined (step 2). The metric C is determined in step 3 by taking into account the order of magnitude of the number of sensors and actuators. Also in step 3, the previous values are aggregated and normalized, determining the final RCI tuple for the system.

Decomposing the system into the previously mentioned parts (step 1) is simply done by analyzing the reported techniques, both in their nature and cardinality. To proceed with the classification process, the framework must determine

 (i) which quantitative value is assigned to each technique in the monitoring, decision or acting phase and
 (ii) how these values are aggregated to reach a final RCI tuple.

These two steps are detailed in the following sections. First, Sect. 3.4.1 discusses a quantitative criteria, where design options, representing groups/classes of techniques, are assigned a single value. Next, Sect. 3.4.2 maps the set of specific techniques presented in Sect. 3.3 to these classes, so that each technique is assigned a unique value of R and I. This completes step 2 of the classification process. Finally, Sect. 3.4.3 explains the rationale of step 3, showing how the previous values are aggregated with the C metric to determine a system's RCI.

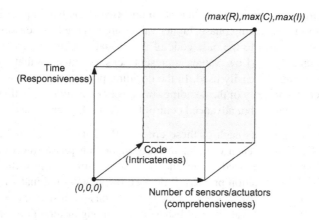

Fig. 3.9 Systems design interval

3.4.1 Quantitative Criteria of the RCI Taxonomy

We think the three metrics are able to capture a *design interval* as presented in Fig. 3.9. They are a proxy for time, space, and complexity-related characteristics. Our conjecture is that we will see systems that are away from the minimum and the maximum of the cube, that is, neither too simple (e.g., near the base of the coordinates) nor excelling in the three metrics (e.g., near or coincident with the maximum point in the design space). The following list points the exact meaning of the three criteria, regarding each of the adaptation phases. Next, we will detail how they are mapped to a numeric scale, in each phase, which will be used to determine the RCI of systems.

- **Responsiveness**. It captures time-related characteristics of the techniques. Regarding the monitoring phase, it depends on the latency of reading a value. Higher values are assigned to sensors immediately available on the VM code base, where higher values represent external sensors (operating system or application specific). For the decision phase, responsiveness is lower in those techniques that take longer to reach a given adaptation target. Regarding the action phase, high values indicate that the effect is (almost) immediate, while a low value represents actuators that will take some time to produce effects.
- **Comprehensiveness**. It captures quantity-related characteristics of the techniques. Regarding the monitoring and deciding phases, it gets higher as the quantity of the monitored sensors increases. Regarding the acting phase, the comprehensiveness value grows with the quantity of actuators that the system can engage.

- **Intricateness**. It captures the inherent complexity of the techniques. Regarding the monitoring and acting phase, higher values are reserved for sensors/actuators that had to be added to the base code of the virtual machine, operating system, or application layer. Low values represent sensors/actuators that are already available and can be easily used. In the deciding phase, intricateness represents the inherent complexity of the deciding strategy. For example, an if-then-else rule has low intricateness but advanced control theory has higher values.

Figure 3.10 represents each of these criteria (R, C, I) for the three adaptation phases (M, D, A). For each criteria, in each adaptation phase, the figure shows several options there are used during the classification of a given technique, used in step 2 of the classification process. It does so by showing the mapping between a design option (e.g., use a sensor that is an extension inside the VM) and a quantitative value. These values establish an order among different options.

It is important so stress that these design options do not represent a specific technique but a class of techniques. For example, "direct reading" in the criterion I of the phase M is to be selected when the sensor is available in the original code

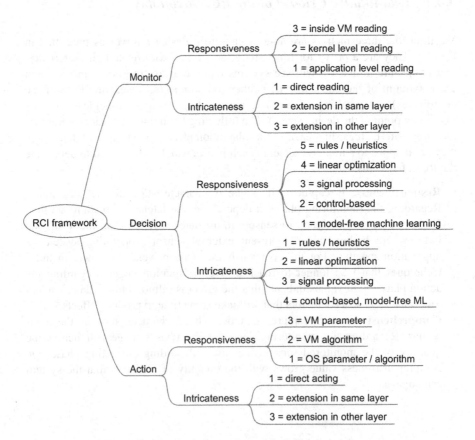

Fig. 3.10 Quantitative values for the design options of the RCI framework

base or in another level of the system stack, without the necessity of building further extensions. This indirection makes the classification system generic because the number of techniques, sensors, and actuators can grow in the future while being accommodated by the taxonomy in one of the existing classes. Even so, we think these classes are expressive and distinctive enough to characterize different levels of responsiveness, comprehensiveness, and intricateness.

The mapping between classes and specific techniques will be presented next, in Sect. 3.4.2. Note also that the scale of the values is not important (they typically represent different orders of magnitude) as long as the values are positive and monotonically increasing or decreasing, in accordance with the corresponding criteria.

Across all the adaptation phases, comprehensiveness is directly represented by the number of sensors or actuators, as explained previously. This is represented by n, which is a positive quantity (between 1 and 3) corresponding to the number of sensors or actuators that are used. This means that the comprehensiveness increases as this number grows. The other two criteria have more distinctive characterizations in each of the adaptation phases, which we elaborate next:

- **Monitoring**. The responsiveness of the monitoring phase depends on the cost of reading. The cost of reading relates to the time spent in reading a single value, that is, how fast can a single value be collected. This depends on the layer where the sensor is in relation to where the decision is made. For example, some systems use application-level monitors which require inter-process communication to read them (e.g., number of completed SQL transactions [45]). Others depend only on values collected inside the virtual machine monitor or the HLL-VM context. A middle-ground approach is that of systems that depend on sensors from other layers, such as the OS, but, reading them has a low cost (e.g., the /proc virtual file system).

  The intricateness of the monitoring phase is a measurement of how complex is the code for reading sensors. Value 1 is assigned to systems that use preexisting sensors of the virtual machine or in the execution environment, which have a direct access. Value 2 is for extensions made inside the virtual machine, and value 3 is assigned when extensions were made in the underlying system and/or hardware (e.g., operating system, in the case of HLL-VMs).

- **Deciding**. The responsiveness and intricateness of the deciding phase is in a large part inspired by the study of Maggio et al. [57]. They discuss how feedback control mechanisms compare to each other in the context of a benchmark suite composed of multi-threaded programs, instrumented with the Application Heartbeat framework [46]. Taking into account the analyzed techniques, our classification framework is based on five decision types (i) rules/heuristics, (ii) linear optimization, (iii) control-based solutions, (iv) signal processing techniques, and (v) model-free machine learning solutions.

  We have classified these five types of decision strategies as decreasingly responsive, because they take an increasing amount of time to reach a certain target point. They are increasingly intricate with the exception of control-based solutions which we consider more intricate than signal processing. This is so because of the panoply of parameters that usually have to be tuned. A model-free solution has also the highest intricateness value because the tuning of assigning credits to each possible action and the balance between exploitation and exploration (i.e., balancing between making the best decision given current information or explore more system states) [57].

- **Acting**. In this phase, responsiveness reflects the capacity of the actuator to produce an observable and measurable consequence. Any throttle to the processing capacity will have almost immediate effect and so a value of 1 is assigned to this type of actuator. Regarding memory, tweaking the set of pages assigned to a VM will have a quicker impact than simply changing its memory share. Changing heap parameters is, in comparison with the other techniques, the least responsive one, and so it gets a value of 3. Intricateness has, in this phase, a similar characterization to the one made in the monitoring phase.

In the following section, we map the previous analyzed techniques to this tree of design options.

3.4.2   Classification of Techniques

Based on the quantitative values of the taxonomy described in the previous section, we now focus on mapping of the techniques described in Sect. 3.3 to a value, so that a final RCI of each system can be determined and different systems can be compared.

Tables 3.1, 3.2, and 3.3 refer to system-level virtual machines and map a specific sensor, actuator, or decision technique to a particular value. For each line, the first column identifies a technique (as presented in Figs. 3.6 and 3.7) while the second and third columns contain a design class and the corresponding value, for

Table 3.1 System VMs: sensors monitored

Sensor	*R* option	Value	*I* option	Value
Page utilization	Inside VM	3	Direct reading	1
Page contents	Inside VM	3	Extension same layer	2
Page faults	Kernel	2	Direct reading	1
Memory demand	Kernel	2	Direct reading	1
Application's performance	Outside	1	Direct reading	1
Virtual time clock	Inside VM	3	Direct reading	1
CPU consumed by each VCPU	Inside VM	3	Direct reading	1
Xen CPU/Mem consumed	Kernel reading	2	Direct reading	1
OS sync primitives	Kernel	2	Extension other layer	3
OS CPU usage counter	Kernel	2	Direct reading	1

Table 3.2 System VMs: decision techniques

Control technique	R option	Value	I option	Value
Share based	Rule/heuristic	5	Rule/heuristic	1
Counter threshold	Rule/heuristic	5	Rule/heuristic	1
Integer linear programming	Linear optimization	4	Linear optimization	2
PID controller	Control-based	2	Control-based	4
Resource usage samples correlation	Signal processing	3	Signal processing	3
LRU histogram	Rule/heuristic	5	Rule/heuristic	1

Table 3.3 System VMs: actuators used in the action phase

Actuator	R option	Value	I option	Value
Page sharing	VM parameter	3	Extension in same	2
Page compression	VM algorithm	2	Extension in same	2
Page/memory transfer	VM parameter	3	Direct acting	1
Co-scheduling	VM parameter	3	Extension in same	2
Number of VCPUs assigned to CPU	VM parameter	3	Direct acting	1
Change shares or caps	VM parameter	3	Direct acting	1
Number of processes/threads	VM parameter	3	Direct acting	1

Table 3.4 HLL VMs: sensors monitored

Sensor	R option	Value	I option	Value
Memory structures dimensions	Inside	3	Direct	1
Events of the operative system	Kernel	2	Direct	1
Working set size	Kernel	2	Extension other layer	3
GC load	Inside	3	Direct	1
Frequency of GC	Inside	3	Direct	1
Memory usage patterns	App	3	Extension same layer	2

Table 3.5 HLL VMs: decision techniques

Control technique	R option	Value	I option	Value
If-then-rule	Rule/heuristic	5	Rule/heuristic	1
Generic condition	Rule/heuristic	5	Rule/heuristic	1
Reinforcement learning	Model-free ML	1	Model-free ML	4
PID controller	Control-based	2	Control-based	4
Elasticity (micro-economy)	Rule/heuristic	5	Rule/heuristic	1

responsiveness (second column) and intricateness (third column). Tables 3.4, 3.5, and 3.6 are the ones corresponding to the high-level language virtual machines and follow the same logic.

Looking at the techniques used in the monitor phase, Tables 3.1 and 3.4 show us that only two techniques have the minimum responsiveness. This is so because most

Table 3.6 HLL VMs: actuators used in the action phase

Actuator	R option	Value	I option	Value
Heap size	VM parameter	3	Direct	1
Run GC	VM parameter	3	Direct	1
Change GC algorithm	VM algorithm	2	Extension same layer	2
Limit usage	VM algorithm	2	Extension same layer	2
Reservation	VM algorithm	2	Extension same layer	2

of the sensors are *near* the VM execution space (either in a subsystem of the VM or in the operating system). Low intricateness also is dominant as most sensors are already available.

Regarding the decision phase, analyzed in Tables 3.2 and 3.5, a majority of techniques have high responsiveness values. As a consequence, they are less intricate. In HLL-VMs, techniques are usually either very simple or have maximum complexity.

Finally, regarding the action phase, we note that all actuators are either already available in the VM code base or are extensions to the VM code base. Contrary to sensors, no new actuators are proposed for other layers of the execution stack. This leads to not having, in practice, actuators with the maximum intricateness.

3.4.3 Aggregation of Quantities

In this section, we give the details about the implementation of the final stage of step 2 and how step 3 operates, as depicted in Fig. 3.8.

Regarding the final stage of step 2, because a given system may use more than one sensor, in the monitoring phase, and more than one actuator, in the acting phase, the framework must determine a single R and I value for these two phases (i.e., R_M, R_A, I_M, I_A). Regarding responsiveness, we consider the technique with the lowest responsiveness, as presented in Equation 3.1. This was so because the monitor or the action phase will be as responsive as the least responsive technique the system uses. Regarding the intricateness metric, we use the technique with the highest value as a representative of the phase's intricateness. Finally, note that this is not an issue for the decision phase because specific systems only use one strategy.

$$R_\pi = minimum \ of \ techniques' \ responsiveness, \ where \ \pi \ \in \ \{M,A\} \qquad (3.1)$$

For a given system, S_α, the three metrics of the framework, responsiveness, comprehensiveness, and intricateness are represented by $R(S_\alpha)$, $C(S_\alpha)$, and $I(S_\alpha)$, respectively. Each of these metrics depends on the specific values of the techniques used by the system. So, to determine $R(S_\alpha)$, the framework adds the responsiveness of each phase of the adaptation loop (**Monitor**, **Decision**, **Action**), as presented in

Table 3.7 Example of the aggregations made in step 2 for system S_α

System	Monitor	R	I	Decision	R	I	Action	R	I
S_α	T_a	2	3	T_d	2	3	T_e	1	2
	T_b	3	2				T_f	2	1
	T_c	1	2						
		1	**3**		**2**	**3**		**1**	**2**

Table 3.8 Example of the arithmetic operations in step 2 for system S_α

System	R	C	I
S_α	1+2+1	#sensors+#actuators	3+3+2

Equation 3.2. A similar operation is done to determine the intricateness metric.

$$R(S_\alpha) = \sum_{\pi \in \{M,D,A\}} R_\pi(S_\alpha) \tag{3.2}$$

To determine comprehensiveness, $C(S_\alpha)$, the framework takes into account the number of sensors used in the monitoring phase, the number of actuators used in the acting phase, and adds them to reach a single value. This is the operation identified as $C(M,A)$ in step 3 of Fig. 3.8.

As an example, consider system S_α, which uses several hypothetical techniques for each phase of the adaptation loop. Step 1 of the framework determines that the techniques must be identified (e.g., $T_{a..f}$). Then, for each technique, a quantitative value is assigned regarding its responsiveness and intricateness for the three phases of the adaptation loop.

The last line of Table 3.7 shows the result of the *aggregation* operations used to determine, for each of the three phases, the **R** and **I** values. The aggregate function *minimum* is used for responsiveness, while the aggregate function *maximum* is used for intricateness.

Table 3.8 completes the example, showing the *arithmetic* operations necessary to determine the overall **R**, **C**, and **I** values of the hypothetical system S_α. The values from the last line of Table 3.7 are the ones used to determine **R** and **I** in Table 3.8, following the Equation 3.2.

3.4.4 Critical Analysis of the Taxonomy

The RCI taxonomy aims to show trade-offs in the design of adaptive systems in the context of virtual machines. Its critical point is the design options tree, presented in Fig. 3.10, and the corresponding quantitative values. It can be the case that either the design options do not represent the entire design space or that the quantitative values are not correctly assigned. We tried to minimize this by designing the taxonomy after examining several systems to better understand the scope of the design space. However, we are still to collect the opinions of other researchers in the area on using the taxonomy, and possibly improving it based on their feedback.

In the next section, relevant works are analyzed regarding monitoring and adaptability in virtual machines, both at system as well as managed language level. The RCI taxonomy is used to compare different systems and better understand how virtual machine researchers have explored the tension between responsiveness, comprehensiveness, and intricateness.

3.5 VM Systems and Their Classification

In this section, we start by surveying several state of the art systems, regarding system-level VMs, Sect. 3.5.1, and high-level language VMs, Sect. 3.5.2. In each case, we frame the analyzed systems into the classification framework presented in Sect. 3.4, describing each of the techniques used, resulting in the classification and comparison of complete systems.

3.5.1 System Virtual Machine

The following are succinct descriptions of system-level VMs and systems that extend them. We start by presenting a well-known open-source hypervisor. A list of systems that extend this or other similar hypervisors follows. Most of them are centered either on CPU or memory. At the end of the section, Table 3.9 summarizes the techniques used in each system. This process was identified as step 1 in Fig. 3.8. This is the base for determining each system's RCI.

3.5.1.1 Friendly Virtual Machines (FVM)

This VMM aims to neither overused or underused resources. The responsibility for adjusting the demand of the underlying resources is delegated to each guest, resulting in a distributed adaptation system [110]. The decision phase is regulated by feedback control rules such as additive-increase/multiplicative-decrease (AIMD), typically used in network congestion avoidance [22]. A VM runs inside a hosted virtual machine, the user-mode Linux. The FVM's daemon installed at each guest controls the number of processes and threads that are effectively running at each VM. When only a single thread of execution exists, FVM will adapt the rate of execution forcing the VM to periodically sleep.

Table 3.9 Sys-VM Systems

System	Dominant resource	Monitor	Decision	Action	Modified VMM/VM
FVM	CPU	VTC	PID Controller AIMD	Number of threads, periodic sleep	Yes
Auto control	CPU, I/O	CPU, I/O usage, Average response time	Model predictive, Quadratic solver	Cap, disk share	No
Press	CPU	CPU, Mem, I/O usage	Pearson correlation	CPU cap	No
HPC	CPU	VCPU utilization rate, System Parallel level	Rules with AISD	Number of VCPUs	No
ASMan	CPU	Spin locks utilization and waiting time	Thresholding rules	Co-scheduling	Yes
Ginko	Mem	Average time per URL request, #SQL transactions, response time	Linear programming	Balloon	No
Overbooking	CPU, Mem	CPU, Mem, Average time per URL request	PID controller	CPU cap, balloon	No
VMMB	Mem	Page faults, swap operations	LRU histogram	Balloon, VMM swapping	Yes
Difference engine	Mem	(sub-)Page contents	Not recently used	Page sharing, patching, compression	Yes

3.5.1.2 ASMan

The Adaptive Scheduling Manager (ASMan) [103] is an extension to Xen's scheduler. It adds the capacity to co-schedule virtual CPUs (VCPU) of VMs where there are threads holding a blocking synchronization mechanism, such as spin locks. In non-virtualized systems, threads holding spin locks are not preempted. In a virtualized system, the VCPU continues to be held by the thread but, because the hypervisor sees the VCPU as being idle, the VCPU is taken from execution and placed on the waiting queue. Using the concept of VCPU-related degree (VCRD), the ASMan system determines the degree of relationship between the VCPUs in a VM. The system dynamically determines this metric by monitoring, in each guest OS, the time spent in spin locks. The VM is then classified with a low or high VCRD if it is below or above a certain threshold. When the VCRD is high, the VCPUs of that VM are co-scheduled.

3.5.1.3   HPC Computing

Shao et al. [70] adapt the VCPU mapping of Xen [12] for high-performance computing applications, based on runtime information collected by a monitor that must be running inside each guest's operating system. They adjust the number of VCPUs to meet the real needs of each guest. Decisions are made based on two metrics: the average VCPU utilization rate and the *parallel level*. The *parallel level* mainly depends on the length of each VCPU's run queue. The adaptation process uses an additive increase and subtractive decrease (AISD) strategy. Shao et al. focus their work on benchmarks used to represent the common operations of high-performance computing applications. It acts on number of VCPUs assigned to each VM.

3.5.1.4   Auto Control

The Auto Control system [65] uses a control theory model to regulate resource allocation, based on multiple inputs and driving multiple outputs. Inputs include CPU and I/O usage, together with application specific metrics. It acts on the allocation of caps for CPU and disk I/O. For each application, there is an application controller which collects the application's performance metrics (e.g., application throughput or average response time) and, based on the application's performance target, determines the new requested allocation. The model is adjusted automatically, and so it can adapt to different operating points and workloads.

3.5.1.5   PRESS

PRedictive Elastic ReSource Scaling for cloud systems (PRESS) [35] tries to allocate just enough resources to avoid service level violations while minimizing resource waste. To handle both cyclic and noncyclic workloads, PRESS tracks resource usage and predicts how resource demands will evolve in the near future. The decision phase (which includes the analysis of observed values) uses signal processing techniques (i.e., fast Fourier Transform and the Pearson correlation). PRESS tries to look for a similar pattern (i.e., a signature) in the resource usage history. If this fails, PRESS uses a discrete-time Markov chain. The prediction scheme is used to regulate the CPU cap of the target VM.

3.5.1.6   Overbooking and Consolidation

Heo et al. [42] focus on monitoring memory usage (including page faults) and application performance. They show that allocating memory in such an overcommitted environment, without taking also into account the CPU, results in significant service level violations. The system uses a PID controller to dynamically change the allocating of memory (using the ballon driver) and the CPU cap.

3.5.1.7 Difference Engine

Differently from other system, Gupta et al. [39] share page content at the sub-page level, using a technique named page patching, which is made by observing the difference relative to a reference page. Based on a not recently used policy, difference engine also uses memory compression for pages that are not significantly similar to other pages in memory. Both techniques extends the more traditional mechanisms of copy-on-write full page sharing, already present at the Xen VMM.

3.5.1.8 VMMB

In [61], Min et al. present VMMB, a virtual machine memory balancer for unmodified operating systems. VMMB monitors the memory demand (i.e., nested page faults and to guest swapping) and reallocates memory based on the QoS requirement of each VM. It uses the LRU histogram as input for their decision algorithm that determines the memory allocation size of each VM while globally minimizing the page miss ratio. Similar to other works, they use balloon driver to enforce each VM's new memory size. When this is not enough, a VMM-level swapping is used to select a set of victim pages and immediately allocate memory to a selected VM.

3.5.1.9 Overall System Analysis

Table 3.9 summarizes the systems analyzed in this section. After the system name, the second column identifies the dominant resource, that is, the resource over which the system is monitoring but also acting. From the third to the fourth column, we present the techniques used in each of the adaptation phases. The last column allows us to quickly determine if the system proposes extensions to the code base of the VM or not.

Figure 3.11 depicts the overall RCI of each system that uses or augments a system-level VM. It presents a visual, quantitative, and comparative analysis, which completes Table 3.9. Overall, systems tend to favor responsiveness design options (as this metric prevails in every system).

When looking for memory-dominant systems (difference engine, VMMB, Ober-booking, Ginko) we see that Overbooking is less responsive because it tries to embrace a large number of sensors and actuators. In the CPU-dominated systems, HPC is the one classified as the most responsiveness but uses simpler techniques (low intricateness) and a minimum number of sensors and actuators. ASMan is more intricate, basically because it needs extensions for the monitoring and action phase, but it had to give up on some responsiveness.

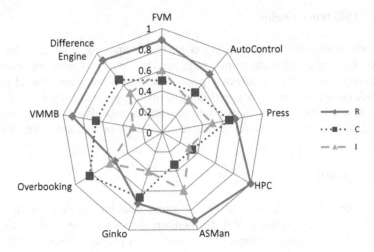

Fig. 3.11 RCI of Sys-VMs

3.5.2 High-Level Language Virtual Machines

This section will present and discuss different systems that monitor resource usage, resulting in either imposing limitations or changing the policies of the JIT, GC, or resource manager subsystems. Adaptation in high-language virtual machines is made by changing their building block parameters (e.g., JIT level of optimization, GC heap size) or the actual algorithm used to perform certain operations. This section starts by presenting classic work on Java Virtual Machines (JVMs) whose goal was to incorporate resource usage constraints on regular VMs. It then surveys more recent systems where the focus was to diminish the impact of GC in program execution. At the end of the section, Table 3.10 summarizes the techniques used in each system. As in the case of system-level VMs, this process is the implementation of step 1 in Fig. 3.8, which is the base for determining each system RCI.

3.5.2.1 KaffeOS

Built on top of Kaffe virtual machine [10], KaffeOS [10] provides the ability to run Java applications isolated from each other and also to limit their resource consumption. KaffeOS, adds a process model to Java that allows a JVM to run multiple untrusted programs safely. The runtime system is able to account for and control all of the CPU and memory resources consumed on behalf of any process. Consumption of individual processes can be separately accounted for, because the allocation and garbage collection activities of different processes are separated. To

Table 3.10 HLL-VM systems

System	Dominant resource	Monitor	Decision	Action	Modifications
JRES	Mix	CPU, heap, I/O	Rules	Limitation (CPU, heap, I/O)	VM
Isla vista	Mem	Allocation stalls in OS	Rules	Heap rezise	VM
Resource-driven	Mem	Page faults, resident set size	3 types of rules	Whole heap collection	VM
Control	Mem	GC overhead	PID controller	Heap resize	Yes
PAMM	Mem	Heap size, page faults	Threshold	Run GC	Program
CRAMM	Mem	WSS via virtual memory manager, heap utilization	Fixed rule	Heap resize	VM/OS
Elasticity curve	Mem	Number of GCs, heap size	Elasticity threshold	Heap resize	VM
Switch	Mem	Heap size, GC load, GC frequency	Threshold rule	GC algorithm	VM
Learning	Mem	Available memory (current and variation between observations)	Reinforcement learning	Run GC	VM

account for memory, KaffeOS uses a hierarchical structure where each process is assigned a hard and a soft limit. Hard limits relate to reserved memory. Soft limits acts as guard limit not assuring that the process can effectively use that memory. Children tasks can have, globally, a soft limit bigger than their parent, but only some of them will be able to reach that limit.

3.5.2.2   JRES

The work of Czajkowski et al. [24] uses native code, library rewriting, and byte code transformations to account and control resource usage. JRES was the first work to specify an interface to account for heap memory, CPU time, and network consumed by individual threads or groups of threads. The proposed interface allows for the registration of callbacks, used when resource consumption exceeds some limits and when new threads are created.

3.5.2.3 Multitask Virtual Machine (MVM)

The MVM [25] extends the Sun Hotspot JVM to support *isolates* and resource management. *Isolates* are similar to processes in KaffeOS. The distinguishing difference of MVM is in its generic Resource Management (RM) API, which uses three abstractions: resource attributes, resource domain, and dispenser. Each resource is characterized by a set of attributes (e.g., memory granularity of consumption, reservable, disposable). In [25] the MVM is able to manage the number of open sockets, the amount of data sent over the network, the CPU usage, and heap memory size. When the code running on an isolate wants to consume a resource, it will use a library (e.g., send data to the network) or runtime service (e.g., memory allocation). In these places, the resource domain to which the isolate is bound will be retrieved. Then, a call to the dispenser of the resource is made, which will interrogate all registered user-defined policies to know if the operation can continue. A dispenser controls the quantity of a resource available to resource domains.

3.5.2.4 Isla Vista

Grzegorczyk et al. [37] takes into account a phenomenon known as *allocation stalls*, which happens during memory allocation when the system has only a few free pages. If this is so, one or more resident pages must be evicted to disk before any new page can be assigned to the requesting process. *Isla vista* implements an algorithm inspired by the exponential backoff model for TCP congestion control to avoid the stall, where transmission rate relates to heap size, and packet loss relates to page faults. Doing so, the heap size increases linearly when there are no allocation stalls. Otherwise, the heap shrinks and the growth factor for successive heap growth decisions is reduced. This is an heuristic to balance between inevitable paging operations and time spent in GC operations.

3.5.2.5 GC Switch

Soman et al. [88] adds to the memory management system the capacity of changing the GC algorithm during program execution. The system monitors application behavior (i.e., GC load versus the time used by application's threads) and resource availability, in order to decide when to dynamically switch the GC strategy. Their decision in based on heuristics so that when the GC load is *high*, they switch from a Semi-Space (which performs better when more memory is available) to a Generational Mark-Sweep collector (which performs better when memory is more constrained).

3.5.2.6 Paging-Aware GC

Hertz et al. [44] developed a GC triggering system that takes into account the overall state of the system where the VM is running and not its single process. Two approaches were considered. VMs use a whiteboard area to know if a GC is taking place in the system. If so, they defer their collection to avoid clustering the environment with simultaneous collection. The other is called *selfish*, and the VM only takes in consideration the heap size and page faults. Based on simple heuristics like the difference in sizes of the resident set and the evolution of page faults, the GC is triggered.

CRAMM [109], on the other hand, dynamically builds the working set size (WSS) as the application progresses, monitoring minor and major page faults. It then acts on the heap size to improve application performance. The system extends the virtual memory manager of the operating system so that the WSS is dynamically built as the application progresses, monitoring minor and major page faults. After each heap collection, the system requests a WSS estimate. It then considers this value to resize the heap. After each GC run, the histogram is also reset since the new heap size will produce a new reference histogram pattern.

3.5.2.7 GC Economics

In [83], Singer et al. relates the heap size and number of garbage collections with the price and demand law of microeconomics – with bigger heaps, there will be less collections. Their decision strategy is an heuristic based on the concepts of *memory elasticity* to find a tradeoff between heap size and execution time, driven by a user-supplied elasticity target. Actions are made over the heap size, to shrink or keep.

3.5.2.8 Control Theory

Heap sizing was also researched as a control theory problem [105]. In Whites et al.'s work, a PID controller is used where the control variable is the heap resize ratio, and the measurement variable is the GC overhead. To determine the new heap size, the controller, after each collection cycle, measures the error between the current GC overhead and the target GC overhead, specified by the user. The goal is to achieve and maintain the user-defined target GC overhead. The controller's parameters, such as the gain and the oscillatory period, were manually fine-tuned for a set of benchmarks. They have only tested their system under a full-heap collector.

3.5.2.9 Machine Learning for Memory Management

Machine learning techniques have been used to dynamically learn which is the best moment to garbage collect [8] and to choose, a-priori, the best GC configuration (algorithm, serial, parallel) [82, 84] given an profile run of the application. In the first case, a reinforcement learning algorithm is used. A binary action is to be taken in each step leading to the decision to run the GC or not. The reinforcement learning algorithm accumulates penalties based on its decisions, and, as time passes, it *learns* which are the best situations to run the GC. In the second group of papers, an offline machine learning algorithm, based on decision trees, is used to generate a classifier that, given a profile run of a *new* program (i.e., not used to build the model), can predict a GC algorithm that minimizes the execution time.

3.5.2.10 Overall Systems Analysis

Table 3.10 summarizes the systems analyzed in this section. The majority of them are focused on the management of the heap size and use simple heuristics to guide this process. Exceptions are the ones using a PID controller [105] and a machine learning algorithm. However, these two systems either have to be fine-tuned manually or impose limitations on the type of garbage collector. Only one work takes into account the collocation of VMs and the need to transfer memory between them [44]. Even so, it is focused on the individual performance of each instance and not the distribution of memory based on the progress of each workload.

Figure 3.12 depicts the overall RCI of each system that augments a high-level language VM, complementing the analysis of Table 3.10. As in the case

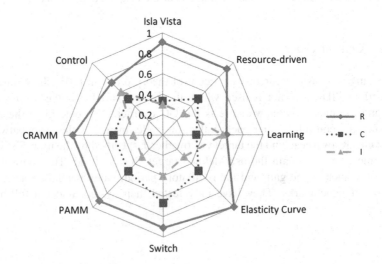

Fig. 3.12 RCI of HLL-VMs

of system-level VMs, systems have design options that favor responsiveness. The system taking into account the elasticity curve of microeconomics has the highest level of responsiveness perhaps because of its low overall intricateness of sensors, decision process, and actuators. We also see that the extra intricateness of the decision phase in "Control" and "Learning" had a cost. In the first case, it was the overall responsiveness, while in the second, the system had to be designed with a smaller number of sensors, reducing comprehensiveness. Further research is needed to determine if other unexplored techniques in these two fields can bring more advantage.

3.6 Summary and Open Research Issues

In this chapter, we reviewed the main approaches for adaptation and monitoring in virtual machines, their tradeoffs, and their main mechanisms for resource management. We framed them into the adaptation loop model (monitoring, decision, and actuation). Furthermore, we proposed a novel taxonomy and classification framework that, when applied to a group of systems, can help visually in determining their similarities and differences. Framed by this, we presented a comprehensive survey and analysis of relevant techniques and systems in the context of virtual machine monitoring and adaptability.

This taxonomy was inspired by two conjectures that arise from the analysis of existing relevant work in monitoring and adaptability of virtual machines. We presented the RCI conjecture on monitoring and adaptability in systems, identifying the fundamental tension among responsiveness, comprehensiveness, and intricateness, and how a given adaptation technique aiming at achieving improvements on two of these aspects can only do so at the cost of the remaining one.

In last years, the widespread use of management systems for containerized applications, like Docker [48] and Kubernetes [47], resurrected the interest of container-based operating system (COS) [87]. Sys-VMs allow for each guest to have a complete stack of the operating system and applications running in isolation from other guests. In contrast to this, containers lose some of the CPU and I/O isolation and share the same kernel OS, promising close to bare metal performance [71]. A container-based approach can give high-performance computing applications an easy and light way to transport jobs and a comprehensive resource scheduling environment [101].

An approach that is also becoming popular is the use of containers inside Sys-VMs. Doing so, data center providers can reuse their current virtualization infrastructure while going toward the need of more users. Also from a desktop environment point of view, having containers inside Sys-VMs allows the for non-Linux users to enjoy this technology and benefit from an extra degree of isolation when running their sensitive workloads [27, 101].

With managed runtimes dominating the landscape of systems to process big data, research will continue to reduce the impact of platforms in workload's performance,

especially regarding automatic memory management and the interface between
HLL-VMs and the underlying execution stack. Regarding memory management,
the generational principle is well suited for most general applications, but in big-
data deployments, either related to storage or stream processing, this assumption
is not always beneficial, and new segmenting options have to be considered [33].
Regarding the deployments of managed runtimes, further efforts are necessary to
explore how to reduce the cost of interfacing with operating services (especially
I/O) as this is also a cause of performance bottleneck. A research opportunity is
hybrid runtimes that run in kernel mode and take direct advantage of the available
hardware [41].

Acknowledgements This work was supported by national funds through Fundação para a Ciência
e a Tecnologia with reference PTDC/EEI-SCR/6945/2014, and by the ERDF through COMPETE
2020 Programme, within project POCI-01-0145-FEDER-016883, the Engineering School of the
Polytechnic Institute of Lisbon (ISEL/IPL).

References

1. ACM Digital Library. http://dl.acm.org/. Visited Nov 2016
2. Adams K, Agesen O (2006) A comparison of software and hardware techniques for x86
   virtualization. In: Proceedings of the 12th international conference on architectural support
   for programming languages and operating systems, ASPLOS XII. ACM, New York, pp 2–13
3. Agmon Ben-Yehuda O, Posener E, Ben-Yehuda M, Schuster A, Mu'alem A (2014) Ginseng:
   market-driven memory allocation. In: Proceedings of the 10th ACM SIGPLAN/SIGOPS
   international conference on virtual execution environments, VEE'14. ACM, New York,
   pp 41–52
4. Alpern B, Augart S, Blackburn SM, Butrico M, Cocchi A, Cheng P, Dolby J, Fink S, Grove
   D, Hind M, McKinley KS, Mergen M, Moss JEB, Ngo T, Sarkar V (2005) The Jikes research
   virtual machine project: building an open-source research community. IBM Syst J 44:399–
   417. doi:http://dx.doi.org/10.1147/sj.442.0399
5. Amdahl GM, Blaauw GA, Brooks FP (1964) Architecture of the IBM system/360. IBM J Res
   Dev 8:87–101. doi:http://dx.doi.org/10.1147/rd.82.0087
6. Amit N, Tsafrir D, Schuster A (2014) Vswapper: a memory swapper for virtualized
   environments. In: Proceedings of the 19th international conference on architectural support
   for programming languages and operating systems, ASPLOS'14. ACM, New York, pp 349–
   366. doi:10.1145/2541940.2541969
7. An architectural blueprint for autonomic computing. Technical report, IBM (2005)
8. Andreasson E, Hoffmann F, Lindholm O (2002) To collect or not to collect? Machine learning
   for memory management. In: Proceedings of the 2nd java virtual machine research and
   technology symposium. USENIX Association, Berkeley, pp 27–39
9. Arnold M, Fink SJ, Grove D, Hind M, Sweeney PF (2005) A survey of adaptive optimization
   in virtual machines. Proc IEEE 93(2):449–466. Special issue on program generation,
   optimization, ans adaptation
10. Back G, Hsieh WC (2005) The KaffeOS java runtime system. ACM Trans Prog Lang Syst
    27:583–630. doi:http://doi.acm.org/10.1145/1075382.1075383
11. Baker HG (1994) Thermodynamics and garbage collection. SIGPLAN Not 29:58–63.
    doi:http://doi.acm.org/10.1145/181761.181770
12. Barham P, Dragovic B, Fraser K, Hand S, Harris T, Ho A, Neugebauer R, Pratt I,
    Warfield A (2003) Xen and the art of virtualization. SIGOPS Oper Syst Rev 37:164–177.
    doi:http://doi.acm.org/10.1145/1165389.945462

13. Beloglazov A, Buyya R (2010) Energy efficient resource management in virtualized cloud data centers. In: 10th IEEE/ACM international conference on cluster, cloud and grid computing (CCGrid), 2010, Melbourne, pp 826–831
14. Binder W, Hulaas J, Moret P, Villazón A (2009) Platform-independent profiling in a virtual execution environment. Softw Pract Exper 39:47–79. doi:10.1002/spe.v39:1. http://portal. acm.org/citation.cfm?id=1464245.1464249
15. Blackburn SM, Garner R, Hoffmann C, Khang AM, McKinley KS, Bentzur R, Diwan A, Feinberg D, Frampton D, Guyer SZ, Hirzel M, Hosking A, Jump M, Lee H, Moss JEB, Moss B, Phansalkar A, Stefanović D, VanDrunen T, von Dincklage D, Wiedermann B (2006) The DaCapo benchmarks: java benchmarking development and analysis. In: OOPSLA'06: Proceedings of the 21st annual ACM SIGPLAN conference on object-oriented programming systems, languages, and applications. ACM, New York, pp 169–190. doi:http://doi.acm.org/10.1145/1167473.1167488
16. Blake C, Rodrigues R (2003) High availability, scalable storage, dynamic peer networks: pick two. In: Jones MB (ed) HotOS, Lihue. USENIX, pp 1–6
17. Bobroff N, Westerink P, Fong L (2014) Active control of memory for java virtual machines and applications. In: 11th international conference on autonomic computing (ICAC 14). USENIX Association, Philadelphia, pp 97–103. https://www.usenix.org/conference/icac14/technical-sessions/presentation/bobroff
18. Brewer EA (2010) A certain freedom: thoughts on the CAP theorem. In: Richa AW, Guerraoui R (eds) PODC. ACM, p 335
19. Buyya R, Yeo CS, Venugopal S, Broberg J, Brandic I (2009) Cloud computing and emerging it platforms: vision, hype, and reality for delivering computing as the 5th utility. Future Gener Comput Syst 25(6):599–616
20. Cheng L, Wang CL (2012) vbalance: using interrupt load balance to improve i/o performance for SMP virtual machines. In: Proceedings of the third ACM symposium on cloud computing, SoCC'12. ACM, New York, pp 2:1–2:14
21. Cherkasova L, Gupta D, Vahdat A (2007) Comparison of the three cpu schedulers in XEN. SIGMETRICS Perform Eval Rev 35:42–51. doi:http://doi.acm.org/10.1145/1330555.1330556
22. Chiu DM, Jain R (1989) Analysis of the increase and decrease algorithms for congestion avoidance in computer networks. Comput Netw ISDN Syst 17(1):1–14
23. Click C, Tene G, Wolf M (2005) The pauseless gc algorithm. In: Proceedings of the 1st ACM/USENIX international conference on virtual execution environments, VEE'05. ACM, New York, pp 46–56. doi:http://doi.acm.org/10.1145/1064979.1064988
24. Czajkowski G, von Eicken T (1998) Jres: a resource accounting interface for java. In: Proceedings of the 13th ACM SIGPLAN conference on Object-oriented programming, systems, languages, and applications, OOPSLA'98. ACM, New York, pp 21–35. doi:http://doi.acm.org/10.1145/286936.286944
25. Czajkowski G, Hahn S, Skinner G, Soper P, Bryce C (2005) A resource management interface for the java platform. Softw Pract Exper 35:123–157. doi:10.1002/spe.v35:2. http://portal. acm.org/citation.cfm?id=1055953.1055955
26. Czajkowski G, Wegiel M, Daynes L, Palacz K, Jordan M, Skinner G, Bryce C (2005) Resource management for clusters of virtual machines. In: Proceedings of the fifth IEEE international symposium on cluster computing and the grid – volume 01, CCGRID'05. IEEE Computer Society, Washington, DC, pp 382–389. http://portal.acm.org/citation.cfm?id=1169222.1169492
27. Dantas B, Fleitas C, Francisco AP, Simão J, Vaz C (2016) Beyond NGS data sharing and toward open science. doi:10.5281/zenodo.190489
28. Deutsch LP, Schiffman AM (1984) Efficient implementation of the smalltalk-80 system. In: Proceedings of the 11th ACM SIGACT-SIGPLAN symposium on principles of programming languages, POPL'84. ACM, New York, pp 297–302. doi:http://doi.acm.org/10.1145/800017.800542
29. Enabling intel virtualization technology features and benefits. http://www.intel.com/content/dam/www/public/us/en/documents/white-papers/virtualization-enabling-intel-virtualization-technology-features-and-benefits-paper.pdf. Visited Nov 2016

30. Farahnakian F, Pahikkala T, Liljeberg P, Plosila J, Hieu NT, Tenhunen H (2016) Energy-aware VM consolidation in cloud data centers using utilization prediction model. IEEE Trans Cloud Comput 99:1–1. doi:10.1109/TCC.2016.2617374
31. Gidra L, Thomas G, Sopena J, Shapiro M (2013) A study of the scalability of stop-the-world garbage collectors on multicores. In: Proceedings of the eighteenth international conference on architectural support for programming languages and operating systems, ASPLOS'13. ACM, New York, pp 229–240
32. Gidra L, Thomas G, Sopena J, Shapiro M, Nguyen N (2015) Numagic: a garbage collector for big data on big NUMA machines. In: Proceedings of the twentieth international conference on architectural support for programming languages and operating systems, ASPLOS'15. ACM, New York, pp 661–673. doi:10.1145/2694344.2694361
33. Gog I, Giceva J, Schwarzkopf M, Vaswani K, Vytiniotis D, Ramalingan G, Murray D, Hand S, Isard M (2015) Broom: sweeping out garbage collection from big data systems. In: Proceedings of the 15th USENIX conference on hot topics in operating systems, HOTOS'15. USENIX Association, Berkeley, pp 2–2. http://dl.acm.org/citation.cfm?id=2831090.2831092
34. Goldberg RP (1974) Survey of virtual machine research. Computer 7(9):34–45
35. Gong Z, Gu X, Wilkes J (2010) Press: predictive elastic resource scaling for cloud systems. In: International conference on network and service management (CNSM), 2010, Niagara Falls, pp 9–16
36. Gordon A, Amit N, Har'El N, Ben-Yehuda M, Landau A, Schuster A, Tsafrir D (2012) ELI: bare-metal performance for I/O virtualization. In: Proceedings of the seventeenth international conference on architectural support for programming languages and operating systems, ASPLOS XVII. ACM, New York, pp 411–422
37. Grzegorczyk C, Soman S, Krintz C, Wolski R (2007) Isla vista heap sizing: using feedback to avoid paging. In: Proceedings of the international symposium on code generation and optimization, CGO'07. IEEE Computer Society, Washington, DC, pp 325–340. doi:http://dx.doi.org/10.1109/CGO.2007.20
38. Guan X, Srisa-an W, Jia C (2009) Investigating the effects of using different nursery sizing policies on performance. In: Proceedings of the 2009 international symposium on memory management, ISMM'09. ACM, New York, pp 59–68. doi:http://doi.acm.org/10.1145/1542431.1542441
39. Gupta D, Lee S, Vrable M, Savage S, Snoeren AC, Varghese G, Voelker GM, Vahdat A (2008) Difference engine: harnessing memory redundancy in virtual machines. In: Proceedings of the 8th USENIX conference on operating systems design and implementation, OSDI'08. USENIX Association, Berkeley, pp 309–322. http://dl.acm.org/citation.cfm?id=1855741.1855763
40. Hagimont D, Mayap Kamga C, Broto L, Tchana A, Palma N (2013) DVFS aware CPU credit enforcement in a virtualized system. In: Middleware 2013. Lecture notes in computer science, vol 8275. Springer, Berlin/Heidelberg, pp 123–142
41. Hale KC, Dinda PA (2016) Enabling hybrid parallel runtimes through kernel and virtualization support. In: Proceedings of the 12th ACM SIGPLAN/SIGOPS international conference on virtual execution environments, VEE'16. ACM, New York, pp 161–175. doi:10.1145/2892242.2892255
42. Heo J, Zhu X, Padala P, Wang Z (2009) Memory overbooking and dynamic control of XEN virtual machines in consolidated environments. In: Proceedings of the 11th IFIP/IEEE international conference on symposium on integrated network management, IM'09. IEEE Press, Piscataway, pp 630–637. http://dl.acm.org/citation.cfm?id=1688933.1689025
43. Hertz M, Bard J, Kane S, Keudel E, Bai T, Kelsey K, Ding C (2009) Waste not, want not: resource-based garbage collection in a shared environment. Technical report TR-2006-908, University of Rochester
44. Hertz M, Kane S, Keudel E, Bai T, Ding C, Gu X, Bard JE (2011) Waste not, want not resource-based garbage collection in a shared environment. In: Proceedings of the international symposium on Memory management, ISMM'11. ACM, New York, pp 65–76. doi:http://doi.acm.org/10.1145/1993478.1993487

45. Hinesa M, Gordon A, Silva M, Silva DD, Ryu KD, Ben-Yehuda M (2011) Applications know best: performance-driven memory overcommit with ginkgo. In: CloudCom'11: 3rd IEEE international conference on cloud computing technology and science, Athens, pp 130–137

46. Hoffmann H, Eastep J, Santambrogio MD, Miller JE, Agarwal A (2010) Application heartbeats: a generic interface for specifying program performance and goals in autonomous computing environments. In: Proceedings of the 7th international conference on autonomic computing, ICAC'10, Washington, DC, pp 79–88

47. http://kubernetes.io. Visited Nov 2016

48. https://www.docker.com/. Visited Nov 2016

49. Hulaas J, Binder W (2008) Program transformations for light-weight cpu accounting and control in the java virtual machine. High. Order Symbol. Comput. 21:119–146. doi:10.1007/s10990-008-9026-4

50. Jones R, Hosking A, Moss E (2011) The garbage collection handbook: the art of automatic memory management, 1st edn. Chapman & Hall/CRC, Boca Raton

51. Kesavan M, Gavrilovska A, Schwan K (2010) On disk i/o scheduling in virtual machines. In: Proceedings of the 2nd conference on I/O virtualization, WIOV'10. USENIX Association, Berkeley, pp 6–6. http://portal.acm.org/citation.cfm?id=1863181.1863187

52. Kulkarni S, Cavazos J (2012) Mitigating the compiler optimization phase-ordering problem using machine learning. In: Proceedings of the ACM international conference on object oriented programming systems languages and applications, OOPSLA'12. ACM, New York, pp 147–162

53. Liu H, Jin H, Liao X, Deng W, He B, Xu CZ (2015) Hotplug or ballooning: a comparative study on dynamic memory management techniques for virtual machines. IEEE Trans Parallel Distrib Syst 26(5):1350–1363. doi:10.1109/TPDS.2014.2320915

54. Lublin U, Kamay Y, Laor D, Liguori A (2007) KVM: the Linux virtual machine monitor. In: Ottawa Linux Symposium, Ottawa

55. Lxc. https://linuxcontainers.org/. Visited Nov 2016

56. Maas M, Asanović, K., Harris T, Kubiatowicz J (2016) Taurus: a holistic language runtime system for coordinating distributed managed-language applications. In: Proceedings of the twenty-first international conference on architectural support for programming languages and operating systems, ASPLOS'16, Atlanta, pp 457–471

57. Maggio M, Hoffmann H, Papadopoulos AV, Panerai J, Santambrogio MD, Agarwal A, Leva A (2012) Comparison of decision-making strategies for self-optimization in autonomic computing systems. ACM Trans Auton Adapt Syst 7(4):36:1–36:32. doi:10.1145/2382570.2382572

58. Manson J, Pugh W, Adve SV (2005) The java memory model. SIGPLAN Not. 40:378–391. doi:http://doi.acm.org/10.1145/1047659.1040336

59. Mao F, Zhang EZ, Shen X (2009) Influence of program inputs on the selection of garbage collectors. In: Proceedings of the 2009 ACM SIGPLAN/SIGOPS international conference on virtual execution environments, VEE'09, pp 91–100. ACM, New York. doi:http://doi.acm.org/10.1145/1508293.1508307

60. Mian R, Martin P, Zulkernine F, Vazquez-Poletti JL (2012) Estimating resource costs of data-intensive workloads in public clouds. In: Proceedings of the 10th international workshop on middleware for grids, clouds and e-science, MGC'12. ACM, New York, pp 3:1–3:6

61. Min C, Kim I, Kim T, Eom YI (2012) VMMB: virtual machine memory balancing for unmodified operating systems. J Grid Comput 10(1):69–84. doi:10.1007/s10723-012-9209-4

62. Ongaro D, Cox AL, Rixner S (2008) Scheduling I/O in virtual machine monitors. In: Proceedings of the fourth ACM SIGPLAN/SIGOPS international conference on Virtual execution environments, VEE'08. ACM, New York, pp 1–10. doi:http://doi.acm.org/10.1145/1346256.1346258

63. Oracle (2016) Java management extensions (JMX) technology, visited 28-11-2016

64. Ousterhout JK (1982) Scheduling techniques for concurrent systems. In: ICDCS, Miami. IEEE Computer Society, pp 22–30

65. Padala P, Hou KY, Shin KG, Zhu X, Uysal M, Wang Z, Singhal S, Merchant A (2009) Automated control of multiple virtualized resources. In: Proceedings of the 4th ACM European conference on Computer systems, EuroSys'09. ACM, New York, pp 13–26. doi:http://doi.acm.org/10.1145/1519065.1519068

66. Park SM, Humphrey M (2009) Self-tuning virtual machines for predictable escience. In: Proceedings of the 2009 9th IEEE/ACM international symposium on cluster computing and the grid, CCGRID'09. IEEE Computer Society, Washington, DC, pp 356–363. doi:http://dx.doi.org/10.1109/CCGRID.2009.84

67. Ram KK, Santos JR, Turner Y (2010) Redesigning Xen's memory sharing mechanism for safe and efficient I/O virtualization. In: Proceedings of the 2nd conference on I/O virtualization, WIOV'10. USENIX Association, Berkeley

68. Salehie   M,   Tahvildari   L   (2009)   Self-adaptive   software: landscape   and research   challenges.   ACM   Trans   Auton   Adapt   Syst   4:14:1–14:42. doi:http://doi.acm.org/10.1145/1516533.1516538

69. Salomie TI, Alonso G, Roscoe T, Elphinstone K (2013) Application level ballooning for efficient server consolidation. In: Proceedings of the 8th ACM European conference on computer systems, EuroSys'13. ACM, New York, pp 337–350. doi:10.1145/2465351.2465384

70. Shao Z, Jin H, Li Y (2009) Virtual machine resource management for high performance computing applications. In: International symposium on parallel and distributed processing with applications, pp 137–144. doi:http://doi.ieeecomputersociety.org/10.1109/ISPA.2009.52

71. Sharma P, Chaufournier L, Shenoy P, Tay YC (2016) Containers and virtual machines at scale: a comparative study. In: Proceedings of the 17th international Middleware conference, Middleware'16. ACM, New York, pp 1:1–1:13. doi:10.1145/2988336.2988337

72. Silva JN, Veiga L, Ferreira P (2011) A^2HA – Automatic and adaptive host allocation in utility computing for bag-of-tasks. J Internet Services Appl 2(2):171–185

73. Simão J, Veiga L (2012) A classification of middleware to support virtual machines adaptability in IAAS. In: Proceedings of the 11th international workshop on adaptive and reflective middleware, ARM'12. ACM, New York, pp 5:1–5:6

74. Simão J, Lemos J, Veiga L (2011) A^2-VM a cooperative java VM with support for resource-awareness and cluster-wide thread scheduling. In: 19th international conference on cooperative information systems (COOPIS 2011), Crete. LNCS. Springer

75. Simao J, Rameshan N, Veiga L (2013) Resource-aware scaling of multi-threaded java applications in multi-tenancy scenarios. In: IEEE 5th international conference on cloud computing technology and science (CloudCom), 2013, Bristol, vol 1, pp 445–451. IEEE

76. Simão J, Singer J, Veiga L (2013) A comparative look at adaptive memory management in virtual machines. In: IEEE CloudCom 2013, Bristol. IEEE

77. Simão J, Veiga L (2012) Qoe-JVM: an adaptive and resource-aware java runtime for cloud computing. In: OTM confederated international conferences "On the Move to Meaningful Internet Systems". Springer, Berlin/Heidelberg, pp 566–583

78. Simao J, Veiga L (2012) VM economics for java cloud computing: an adaptive and resource-aware java runtime with quality-of-execution. In: Proceedings of the 2012 12th IEEE/ACM international symposium on cluster, cloud and grid computing (CCGrid 2012), Ottawa. IEEE Computer Society, pp 723–728

79. Simão J, Veiga L (2013) Flexible SLAs in the cloud with a partial utility-driven scheduling architecture. In: IEEE 5th international conference on cloud computing technology and science, CloudCom 2013, Bristol, 2-5 Dec 2013, vol 1, pp 274–281. IEEE Computer Society. doi:10.1109/CloudCom.2013.43

80. Simão J, Veiga L (2013) A progress and profile-driven cloud-vm for resource-efficiency and fairness in e-science environments. In: Proceedings of the 28th annual ACM symposium on applied computing, Coimbra. ACM, pp 357–362

81. Simão J, Veiga L (2014) Partial utility-driven scheduling for flexible SLA and pricing arbitration in cloud. IEEE Trans Cloud Comput 99:467–480. https://www.computer.org/csdl/trans/cc/2016/04/06963452-abs.html

82. Singer J, Brown G, Watson I, Cavazos J (2007) Intelligent selection of application-specific garbage collectors. In: Proceedings of the 6th international symposium on memory management, ISMM'07. ACM, New York, pp 91–102. doi:10.1145/1296907.1296920
83. Singer J, Jones R (2011) Economic utility theory for memory management optimization. In: Rogers I (ed) Proceedings of the workshop on implementation, compilation, optimization of object-oriented languages and programming systems. ACM, p 4. http://www.cs.kent.ac.uk/pubs/2011/3156. Position paper
84. Singer J, Jones RE, Brown G, Luján M (2010) The economics of garbage collection. SIGPLAN Not 45:103–112. doi:http://doi.acm.org/10.1145/1837855.1806669
85. Singer J, Kovoor G, Brown G, Luján M (2011) Garbage collection auto-tuning for java mapreduce on multi-cores. In: Proceedings of the international symposium on memory management, ISMM'11. ACM, New York, pp 109–118
86. Smith J, Nair R (2005) Virtual machines: versatile platforms for systems and processes. Morgan Kaufmann, San Francisco
87. Soltesz S, Pötzl H, Fiuczynski ME, Bavier A, Peterson L (2007) Container-based operating system virtualization: a scalable, high-performance alternative to hypervisors. In: Proceedings of the 2Nd ACM SIGOPS/EuroSys European conference on computer systems 2007, EuroSys'07. ACM, New York, pp 275–287. doi:10.1145/1272996.1273025
88. Soman S, Krintz C (2007) Application-specific garbage collection. J Syst Softw 80:1037–1056. doi:http://dx.doi.org/10.1016/j.jss.2006.12.566
89. Soman S, Krintz C, Bacon DF (2004) Dynamic selection of application-specific garbage collectors. In: Proceedings of the 4th international symposium on Memory management, ISMM'04. ACM, New York, pp 49–60. doi:http://doi.acm.org/10.1145/1029873.1029880
90. Stoica I, Abdel-Wahab H, Jeffay K (1996) On the duality between resource reservation and proportional share resource allocation. Technical report, Old Dominion University, Norfolk
91. Suri N, Bradshaw JM, Breedy MR, Groth PT, Hill GA, Saavedra R (2001) State capture and resource control for java: the design and implementation of the aroma virtual machine. In: Proceedings of the symposium on JavaTM virtual machine research and technology symposium, JVM'01. USENIX Association, Berkeley, pp 11–11. http://portal.acm.org/citation.cfm?id=1267847.1267858
92. Tanenbaum AS (2007) Modern operating systems, 3rd edn. Prentice Hall Press, Upper Saddle River
93. Tay YC, Zong X, He X (2013) An equation-based heap sizing rule. Perform Eval 70(11): 948–964
94. Tchana A, Palma ND, Safieddine I, Hagimont D, Diot B, Vuillerme N (2015) Software consolidation as an efficient energy and cost saving solution for a SaaS/PaaS cloud model. Springer, Berlin/Heidelberg, pp 305–316
95. Tene G, Iyengar B, Wolf M (2011) C4: the continuously concurrent compacting collector. SIGPLAN Not 46(11):79–88
96. Vaquero LM, Rodero-Merino L, Caceres J, Lindner M (2008) A break in the clouds: toward a cloud definition. SIGCOMM Comput Commun Rev 39(1):50–55
97. Veiga L, Ferreira P (2002) Incremental replication for mobility support in obiwan. In: 22nd international conference on distributed computing systems, 2002 proceedings, Vienna. IEEE, pp 249–256
98. Veiga L, Ferreira P (2004) Poliper: policies for mobile and pervasive environments. In: Kon F, Costa FM, Wang N, Cerqueira R (eds) Proceedings of the 3rd workshop on adaptive and reflective middleware, ARM 2003, Toronto, 19 Oct 2004. ACM, pp 238–243. doi:10.1145/1028613.1028623
99. VMware (2009) VMware vSpher 4: the CPU scheduler in VMware ESX 4
100. Waldspurger CA (2002) Memory resource management in VMware ESX server. SIGOPS Oper Syst Rev 36:181–194. doi:http://doi.acm.org/10.1145/844128.844146

101. Weidner O, Atkinson M, Barker A, Filgueira Vicente R (2016) Rethinking high performance computing platforms: challenges, opportunities and recommendations. In: Proceedings of the ACM international workshop on data-intensive distributed computing, DIDC'16. ACM, New York, pp 19–26. doi:10.1145/2912152.2912155
102. Weiming Z, Zhenlin W (2009) Dynamic memory balancing for virtual machines. In: Proceedings of the 2009 ACM SIGPLAN/SIGOPS international conference on virtual execution environments, VEE'09, Washington, DC, pp 21–30
103. Weng C, Liu Q, Yu L, Li M (2011) Dynamic adaptive scheduling for virtual machines. In: Proceedings of the 20th international symposium on high performance distributed computing, HPDC'11. ACM, New York, pp 239–250
104. Weng C, Wang Z, Li M, Lu X (2009) The hybrid scheduling framework for virtual machine systems. In: Proceedings of the 2009 ACM SIGPLAN/SIGOPS international conference on virtual execution environments, VEE'09. ACM, New York, pp 111–120. doi:http://doi.acm.org/10.1145/1508293.1508309
105. White DR, Singer J, Aitken JM, Jones RE (2013) Control theory for principled heap sizing. In: Proceedings of the 2013 international symposium on memory management, ISMM'13. ACM, New York, pp 27–38
106. Wilson PR (1992) Uniprocessor garbage collection techniques. In: Proceedings of the international workshop on memory management, IWMM'92. Springer, London, pp 1–42. http://portal.acm.org/citation.cfm?id=645648.664824
107. Windows server containers. https://msdn.microsoft.com/en-us/virtualization/windowscontainers/about/index. Visited Nov 2016
108. Xu F, Liu F, Jin H, Vasilakos A (2014) Managing performance overhead of virtual machines in cloud computing: a survey, state of the art, and future directions. Proc IEEE 102(1):11–31
109. Yang T, Berger ED, Kaplan SF, Moss JEB (2006) Cramm: virtual memory support for garbage-collected applications. In: Proceedings of the 7th symposium on operating systems design and implementation, OSDI'06. USENIX Association, Berkeley, pp 103–116
110. Zhang Y, Bestavros A, Guirguis M, Matta I, West R (2005) Friendly virtual machines: leveraging a feedback-control model for application adaptation. In: Proceedings of the 1st ACM/USENIX international conference on virtual execution environments, VEE'05. ACM, New York, pp 2–12. doi:http://doi.acm.org/10.1145/1064979.1064983

Part II
Science Cloud

Chapter 4
Exploring Cloud Elasticity in Scientific Applications

Guilherme Galante and Rodrigo da Rosa Righi

4.1 Introduction

Scientific computing is the key to solving "grand challenge" applications in many domains and has provided advances and new knowledge in diverse fields of science. It can be seen as a combination of engineering, natural science, computer science, and mathematics, making scientific computing a demanding field for all participating parties: engineers contribute with challenging applications and technical knowledge; physicists and other natural scientists build the models; mathematicians provide numerical methods and algorithms for the simulation of complex processes; and computer scientists contribute with the construction of infrastructures, data structures, and algorithms.

Running large and accurate simulations requires a huge number of computing resources, often demanding the use of supercomputers, computer clusters, or grids. Scientific computing has historically been dependent on the advances of high performance computing (HPC) and parallel processing. In general, supercomputers, clusters, and grids have a fixed number of resources that must be maintained in terms of infrastructure configuration, scheduling (where tools such as PBS,[1] OAR,[2]

---

[1]http://www.pbsworks.com
[2]https://oar.imag.fr

G. Galante (✉)
Computer Science Department, Western Parana State University (Unioeste), Cascavel-PR, Brazil
e-mail: guilherme.galante@unioeste.br

R.R. Righi
Applied Computing Graduate Program, Universidade do Vale do Rio dos Sinos (Unisinos), São Leopoldo-RS, Brazil
e-mail: rrrighi@unisinos.br

© Springer International Publishing AG 2017
N. Antonopoulos, L. Gillam (eds.), *Cloud Computing*, Computer Communications and Networks, DOI 10.1007/978-3-319-54645-2_4

OGS[3] are usually employed for resource reservation and job scheduling), and energy consumption. In addition, tuning the number of processes to execute a HPC application can be a hard procedure: (i) a short or a large value for this parameter will not explore the distributed system in an efficient way and (ii) a fixed value cannot fit irregular applications, where the workload varies along the execution or sometimes is not predictable in advance.

In addition to these computing infrastructures, cloud computing has proved itself as a new way to acquire computing resources on demand [38]. According to Simmhan et al. [33], the use of a cloud computing environment can be attractive to the scientific community in many ways, benefiting not only users that own small applications but also those who run their experiments in supercomputing centers. In fact, several authors in the technical literature share this opinion and present advantages and benefits of using cloud computing to execute scientific experiments [30, 37]. Cloud computing offers to end users a variety of resources ranging from hardware to application levels, by charging them on a pay-as-you-go basis, allowing immediate access to required resources without the need to purchase additional infrastructure. In addition, an important characteristic, not available on traditional architectures (e.g., clusters and grids) emerged on cloud computing: *elasticity*. Elasticity can be defined as the ability of a system to dynamically add or remove computational resources used by an application or user to match the current demand as closely as possible [15].

Cloud elasticity abstracts the infrastructure configuration and technical details about resource scheduling from users, who pay for resources, and energy consequently, in accordance with the application's demands. The use of elasticity in scientific applications is a subject that is starting to receive attention from research groups [11]. This interest is related to the benefits it can provide that include improvements in applications performance, cost reduction, and better resource utilization. Improvements in the performance of applications can be achieved through dynamic allocation of additional processing, memory, network, and storage resources. Examples of using elasticity in scientific applications include: (i) the dynamic storage space allocation when data exceeds the capacity allocated for the hosted environment in the cloud [27]; (ii) applications that use the MapReduce paradigm, where it is possible to increase the number of working nodes during the Map and consequently to scale down the resources during the Reduce phase [18]; and (iii) workflows execution, in which we can dynamically adjust the pool of nodes required to resolve a given workflow step [22].

Considering the importance of elasticity to the concept of cloud computing, as well as the possibilities of using it in scientific computing, we present in this chapter the state of the art and an analysis of the current elasticity solutions, aiming at pointing out some research opportunities in the area. In addition to

---

[3]http://gridscheduler.sourceforge.net

fundamental concepts and research opportunities, we present two different elasticity approaches, both developed by our research group, to support the construction of elastic scientific applications in IaaS and PaaS cloud models.

4.2   Basic Concepts and State of the Art

Elasticity is defined as the ability of a system to dynamically add or remove computational resources used by an application or user to match the current demand as closely as possible [15]. Resources can include everything from single virtual processors (VCPU) to a complete virtual cluster. The concept could also be extended to applications. An elastic application is able to adapt itself to handle changes in resources or to request or release resources according to demands.

In this context, several elasticity solutions have been developed by public providers and by academy. In this section, we present a classification of existing solutions and establish the state of the art of elasticity in computational clouds. In addition, we present some initiatives of using elasticity in scientific applications.

4.2.1   Taxonomy and Classification

Aiming at providing a classification of the existing approaches to cloud elasticity, we present a taxonomy that enables to differentiate aspects of the proposed elasticity solutions. The taxonomy is summarized in Fig. 4.1.

To be able to take advantage of elasticity, it is necessary that both architecture and application support this feature in some form. Thus, at the first level, the solutions are separated into two groups: (1) *elastic architectures* and (2) *elasticity support mechanisms*.

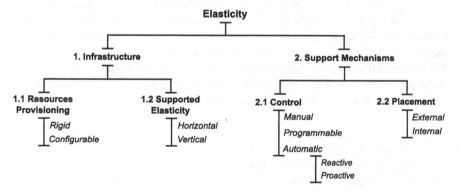

Fig. 4.1 Elasticity mechanism classification

The elasticity provided by cloud infrastructures is inherent to the use of virtualization techniques and to the availability of a large amount of physical resources. However, the manner it is provided to the user varies for each cloud platform according to how resources are offered and which elasticity type is supported. Resources can be provided in two different modes: *fixed* or *configurable*. In fixed mode, virtual machines (VMs) are offered with a predefined configuration of CPU, memory, and I/O (e.g., *instance types* by Amazon[4] and *server sizes* in GoGrid[5] and Rackspace[6]). The problem in providing resources in such way occurs when users cannot map their specific demands into one of the configurations offered by the provider. In configurable mode users can customize VM resources according to their needs. Although this model is the more appropriate to the cloud concept, the configurable mode is available in few cloud providers, such as ProfitBricks[7] and CloudSigma.[8]

Depending on how the cloud implements the provisioning of resources, we can classify its elasticity as horizontal or vertical [36]. In the horizontal approach, the number of instances (VMs) is increased or decreased. On the other hand, the vertical approach adjusts the VM attributes, such as CPU, memory, disk bandwidth, or storage. In some cases, requirements extend beyond the capacity of its hosting node, so that it needs to be migrated to another node that has the required capacity. Migration can also be used to reduce power consumption, by consolidating VMs into fewer nodes and enabling some nodes to be switched off [16]. Horizontal elasticity is the method supported by the clouds that provide fixed allocation, considering the impossibility of changing the VM configurations. In turn, vertical elasticity may be supported to allow the fine grain elasticity in configurable providers.

Different classes of scientific applications have different workload patterns and characteristics, and, therefore, their elasticity requirements may vary accordingly. Ideally, highest levels of economic elasticity may be achieved by enabling cloud consumers to customize any combination of resource capacity and as much as their application workloads require [19]. Ben-Yehuda et al. [4] propose the Resource-as-a-Service (RaaS) model, where compute, memory, and I/O resources could be rented and charged for in dynamic amounts and not in fixed bundles. Clients rent VMs with some minimal amount of resources, and other resources needed are continuously rented in a fine-grained fashion. The resources available for rent include processing, memory, and I/O resources, as well as emerging resources such as accelerators, FPGAs and GPUs. Processing capacity is sold on a hardware-thread basis, or as number of cycles per unit of time; memory is sold by frames; and I/O is sold on the basis of I/O devices with bandwidth and latency guarantees.

---

[4]https://aws.amazon.com/ec2/instance-types/

[5]https://wiki.gogrid.com/index.php/Cloud_Servers

[6]https://www.rackspace.com/cloud/servers

[7]https://www.profitbricks.com/

[8]http://www.cloudsigma.com/

Scientific applications have almost always been designed to use a fixed number of resources and cannot explore elasticity without appropriate support [31]. The simple addition of instances and the use of load balancers have no effect for these applications since they are not able to detect and use these resources. In addition, the fact of either a premature death of a process or a consolidation of a VM that hosts one or more processes from a tightly coupled parallel code can imply performance penalties or termination of the application.

Thus, to take full advantage of the elasticity provided by the cloud, needs more than an elastic infrastructure. We also need support mechanisms to enable applications to adapt the resources or be adjusted according to changes in available environment. Elasticity mechanisms differ from each other in the techniques and means they use for performing these tasks and can be classified according to the *control* and *placement*.

The control is the form of interaction necessary for the execution of elasticity actions. Manual control means that the user is responsible for monitoring the virtual environment and applications and performs all relevant elasticity actions using an interface for cloud-user interaction. In the programmable control, the elasticity actions are performed through API (application programming interface) calls. Most cloud providers offer an API for allocation and deallocation of elastic resources. Generally, the APIs are available for web-friendly languages such as, Java, PHP, and Ruby. In automatic control, all the actions are taken by an elasticity controller based in a set of rules, user settings, workload patterns, and service level agreements (SLA). The elasticity controller uses information about the workload, CPU and memory usage, network traffic, etc., to take decisions when and how to scale the resources. These information are collected by a monitoring system or by the application itself.

According to the technique used by the controller to trigger elasticity actions, we can subclassify the automatic control in *reactive* or *proactive* [16, 36]. Reactive approaches (Fig. 4.2a) typically use rules-condition-action statements and prede-

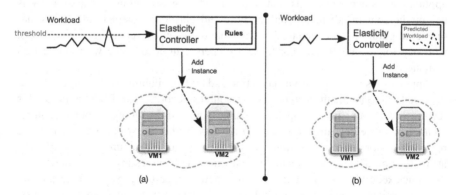

Fig. 4.2 Thresholds- and if-condition-then-based reactive elasticity (**a**) and prediction-based proactive elasticity (**b**)

fined thresholds for elasticity management. Most commercial cloud providers offer purely reactive approaches using threshold-based rules, in which the scaling decisions are triggered based on some performance metrics and predefined thresholds. Proactive mechanisms (Fig. 4.2b) are typically time series based, where a sequence of events at defined intervals is analyzed to find patterns that can be used to forecast future values. The general strategy is to use a workload predictor and then use a performance model to determine the amount of resources required to service the predicted demand. A variety of performance models have been proposed and are presented in the work of Lorido-Botran et al. [24].

The *placement* of an elasticity mechanism is, from application point of view, *external* or *internal*. External mechanisms are those implemented as a separate service and generally uses a monitoring system to collect information about the environment in which the application is running. Such information includes the number of requests received, CPU and memory usage, number of connected clients, and response time. In turn, internal mechanisms are implemented within the application and, in addition to environmental information, can also trigger actions based on internal events.

4.2.2   Elasticity in Scientific Applications

Elasticity is an important feature that can be explored by scientific applications. Traditionally, these applications are executed on parallel architectures, such as cluster or grid architectures. Overall, both have a fixed number of resources that must be maintained in terms of infrastructure configuration, scheduling, and energy consumption. In addition, tuning the number of processes to execute a parallel application can be a difficult procedure: (i) a small or a large amount of processing resources will not efficiently explore the distributed system, causing under- or over-provisioning of resources, and (ii) a fixed value cannot fit irregular applications, since workloads that may vary during execution or occasionally is not predictable in advance. Conversely, cloud elasticity abstracts the infrastructure configuration and technical details about resource scheduling from users, who pay for resources, and consequently energy, in accordance with application demands.

Applications make use of virtualization and high availability of resources offered by clouds to dynamically acquire new resources according to demands [11]. This feature is specially interesting for dynamic applications whose resource requirements cannot be determined exactly in advance, either due to changes in runtime requirements or due to interesting changes in application structure. The use of these attributes could lead to applications with new and interesting usage modes and dynamic execution on clouds and therefore new application capabilities [20].

Some scientific applications could natively take advantage from elasticity on clouds or be easily adapted to it. Particularly, these applications are characterized by having data locality, loosely coupling, high throughput, or fault tolerance, fitting better the current cloud model. Examples are those applications developed using the MapReduce paradigm [34]. This application model can scale incrementally in the number of computing nodes, allowing users not only to launch many servers at the beginning but also to increase the number of servers in the middle of computation [9, 18]. New servers can automatically figure out the current job progress and poll the queues for work to process. Some cloud providers support MapReduce (e.g., Amazon Elastic MapReduce[9]) enabling running this type of application directly on the public cloud without worrying about installing and configuring a MapReduce cluster.

Workflows are other examples of approaches that can benefit from elasticity [28]. They can use the cloud capability to increase or reduce the pool of resources according to the needs of the workflow at any given time of processing [5]. Cloud providers have recognized the importance of workflow applications to science and provide their own native solutions, such as the Amazon Simple Workflow Service (SWF).[10] Platforms and frameworks for elastic execution of workflows were also proposed in academy [10, 22, 23, 41].

Other scientific applications (e.g., MPI, multithreaded) rely on IaaS cloud services and solely use static execution modes, in which an instance of VM is perceived as a cluster node [20]. For those applications, moving them to the cloud is usually not sufficient to take advantage of elasticity and must be adapted to be suitable for the cloud. For example, tightly coupled applications will need to be re-engineered to realize the full benefits of elasticity. Thus, to efficiently support elastic execution across cloud infrastructures, tools and frameworks are required. Trying to address this issue, a couple of academic researchers have developed solutions to enable the development of elastic scientific applications in different models.

ElasticMPI offers elasticity for MPI applications by stopping and relaunching the application with a newer resource configuration [31]. The system assumes that the user knows in advance the expected conclusion time for each phase of the program. The monitoring system can detect that the current configuration cannot fulfill the given deadline and adds more virtual instances. Vectors and data structures are redistributed, and the execution continues from the last iteration. Applications that do not have an iterative loop cannot be adapted by the framework, since it uses the iteration index as execution restarting point. Furthermore, the approach of ElasticMPI imposes changes in the application source code by inserting monitoring directives. And if programming with MPI, the SpotMPI toolkit can be used to facilitate the execution of real MPI applications on volatile auction-based cloud platforms (spot instances) [35]. The toolkit provides optimal checkpointing intervals and restarting of applications after out-of-bid situations through calculations of the density of out-of-bid failures from price history.

---

[9]https://aws.amazon.com/emr/

[10]https://aws.amazon.com/swf/

Rajan et al. [29] presented Work Queue, a framework for the development of elastic master-slave applications. Applications developed using Work Queue allow adding slave replicas at runtime. The slaves are implemented as executable files that can be instantiated by the user on different machines. When executed, the slaves communicate with the master that on demand coordinates the task execution and the data exchange.

Ali-Eldin et al. [1] describe an autonomous elasticity controller for bursty workloads. The proposed controller changes the number of virtual machines allocated to a service based on both monitored load changes and predictions of future load. The cloud infrastructure is modeled as a closed loop control system, and queuing models are used to design a feedback elasticity controller. This model is used to construct a hybrid reactive-adaptive controller that quickly reacts to sudden load changes, prevents premature release of resources, and takes into account the heterogeneity of the workload, avoiding oscillations and decreasing total resource usage.

Wottrich et al. [40] propose OpenMR, an execution model based on OpenMP and MapReduce that enables the usage of highly parallel, distributed machine clusters while automatically providing fault tolerance and workload balancing. Since OpenMR is built upon MapReduce, the elasticity solutions developed for MapReduce are also available to OpenMR.

Galante and Bona [12] also propose a solution to provide elasticity for OpenMP. In this solution, the OpenMP directives are extended to support the automatic adjustment of the number of VCPUs according to the amount of threads in execution. These elasticity-aware directives can automatically control elasticity, hiding the complexity of writing and executing elasticity strategies from the user. In addition, some routines were added to user-level library, targeting to provide a more precise control over the elastic execution. The solution also includes support for elastic memory allocation, taking advantage of the ballooning technique available in most modern hypervisors.

Moltó et al. [26] developed an architecture for dynamic memory allocation for scientific applications. The authors focused on dynamic memory management to automatically fit at runtime the underlying computing infrastructure to the application, thus adapting the memory size of the VM to the memory consumption pattern of the application. The architecture uses the VM memory usage information to decide when to scale up or scale down.

A more generic platform is proposed by Caballer et al. [6]. The CodeCloud platform supports the execution of scientific applications in different programming models (such as master-slave, MPI, MapReduce, and workflows) on cloud infrastructures. The elasticity is automatically reactive and is enabled by a set of rules that define the elasticity modes of the infrastructure during the execution of the application.

Table 4.1 summarizes the characteristics of the frameworks and platforms developed to provide elasticity to scientific applications.

Table 4.1 Elasticity mechanisms and features

Proposed by	App. type	Supported elasticity
Chohan et al. [9]	MapReduce	Manual horizontal
Iordache et al. [18]	MapReduce	Manual horizontal
Yu et al. [41]	Workflows	Manual horizontal
Byun et al. [5]	Workflows	Manual horizontal
Raveendran et al. [31]	MPI	Programmable horizontal
Taifi et al.[35]	MPI	Programmable horizontal (spot instances)
Rajan et al. [29]	Master-slave	Manual horizontal
Ali-Eldin et al. [1]	Bursty	Automatic-reactive-proactive horizontal
Moltó et al. [26]	Many	Automatic-reactive vertical (memory)
Wottrich et al. [40]	OpenMP/MapReduce	Manual horizontal
Galante and Bona [12]	OpenMP	Programmable vertical
Caballer et al. [6]	Master-slave/MPI/ MapReduce/Workflow	Automatic-reactive horizontal and vertical

4.3 Developing Elastic Scientific Applications

This section presents two approaches to offer cloud elasticity for scientific applications, both developed in the research group of the authors.

4.3.1 Programming Level Elasticity

In this section, we describe an approach to explore cloud elasticity, in which the control is performed at programming level, i.e., the elasticity controller is embedded in the application source code, allowing the allocation and deallocation of resources by the application itself without needing external mechanisms or user interaction [13].

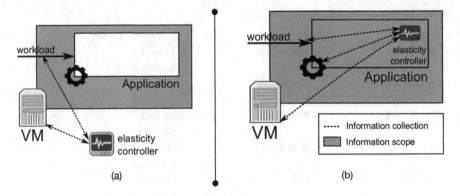

Fig. 4.3 Monitoring system approach (**a**) versus embedded elasticity control (**b**)

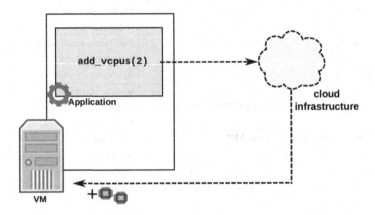

Fig. 4.4 Dynamic resource allocation using elasticity primitives

As shown in Fig. 4.3, moving the elasticity controller to the application code allows access to all internal information, while monitoring-based mechanisms collect only information about workloads and state of the virtual machines. Thus, the control logic can also consider internal events, configuration parameters, input data, and more. For example, you can add new VCPUs when new threads are created or allocate more memory to a new allocated data structure.

In the proposed approach, the collection of information and the elasticity actions are part of the application source code; thus, an appropriate mechanism should be offered to enable such tasks. In this chapter, we propose the use of elasticity primitives, corresponding to a set of basic functions that allow communication with the underlying cloud infrastructure for the request or release of resources and collection of information from the virtual environment.

Figure 4.4 illustrates the operation of the primitives for dynamic resource allocation. When the primitive is executed, a request is sent to the cloud asking for new features. If resources are available, these are allocated to the virtual environment. In this example, the addition of two VCPUs is requested, which are allocated to the virtual machine where the application is running.

The primitive set must provide horizontal and vertical elasticity, enabling the allocation of complete virtual machines and the reconfiguration of virtual machines by the addition of components such as VCPUs, memory, and storage. We must also consider primitives to collect information from the virtual environment and cloud infrastructure. Such information is essential for the development of elasticity controllers, since it helps to determine the need for new resources and if there is availability for allocation.

The possibility of considering the resources allocation as a part of the program logic creates a new paradigm for the design and development of applications. In this paradigm, the resources are a variable element of the program and can be instantiated and modified on the fly. This feature allows programmers to develop and to integrate the elasticity control considering particular characteristics of applications such as programming model, internal events, input data, and configuration parameters.

As a consequence, novel features (not provided for in general purpose elastic mechanisms) can be aggregated to scientific applications. We can develop dynamic and flexible applications that adapt their own execution environment according to its logical structure and demands to achieve performance gains, improve the use of resources, reduce the cost of implementation, or even take advantage of idle or low-cost resources. We can also modify legacy applications, libraries, and parallel programming frameworks (originally designed to support a fixed number of resources during the execution) for supporting the elasticity provided by cloud environments. An example is the elastic OpenMP [12] presented in Sect. 4.2.2.

To offer support for the development of scientific applications using programming level elasticity control, we developed the Cloudine framework. The framework focuses on parallel and distributed applications that runs directly over the VM operating system of IaaS clouds. Cloudine supports C/C++ languages and provides a set of primitives for dynamic allocation of VCPUs, memory, and virtual machines.

4.3.1.1 Architecture

The framework architecture comprises two main components: runtime environment and elasticity API, as illustrated in Fig. 4.5. The runtime environment manages the provisioning of resources using cloud infrastructure, and the API provides a set of primitives to enable applications, to interact with the underlying layers.

The Runtime environment is the component that manages the dynamic provisioning of resources and performs all interaction between the elastic applications (via API) and cloud infrastructure. All elasticity actions are processed by the runtime environment and sent to the underlying cloud.

The elasticity API provides the set of primitives that enable the construction of elastic applications for the Cloudine platform. To date, the API supports C/C++

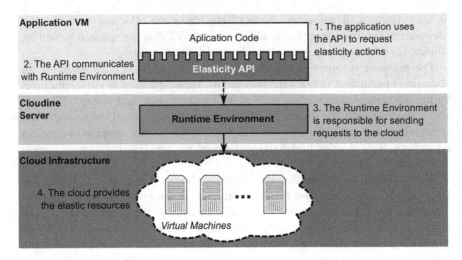

Fig. 4.5 Cloudine architecture

languages and offers 12 primitives, providing dynamic allocation of VCPUs, memory, and virtual machines. VCPU and memory information are also provided. All primitives are implemented in the dynamic shared library `libclne.so`. Table 4.2 shows the functions implemented so far and its description.

Cloudine can be used in two ways in the construction of elastic applications. In the first, we use directly the elasticity API in the implementation of the application, leaving to the programmer the job of creating the control logic. The second way is to use the API to include elasticity features to frameworks already consolidated, enabling the construction of elastic applications transparently through modified middleware.

Some clouds may not support all types of primitives. For example, Amazon EC2 does not support the dynamic allocation of memory or VCPUs, only supporting the allocation and deallocation of complete instances. Thus, the set of primitives which can be effectively used for an application depends on the underlying cloud characteristics. Examples of using Cloudine in scientific applications could be found in previous works [12–14].

4.3.2 Middleware Level Elasticity

This section describes the AutoElastic model, which analyzes alternatives for the following problem statements [32]:

1. *Which mechanisms are needed to provide cloud elasticity transparently at both user and application levels?*
2. *Considering resource monitoring and VM management procedures, how can we model the elasticity as a viable capability on HPC applications?*

Table 4.2 Cloudine API functions

Function	Description
`int clne_add_vcpu(int N)`	Add N VCPUs to the current VM
`int clne_rem_vcpu(int N)`	Remove N VCPUs from the current VM
`int clne_add_node(int N)`	Add N nodes to the virtual environment (cluster). This function also creates (or updates) a file in the VM containing the IP addresses of the cluster machines
`int clne_rem_node(int N)`	Remove the actual node from the virtual environment (cluster)
`int clne_add_memory(long int N)`	Add N megabytes of memory to the current VM
`int clne_rem_memory(long int N)`	Remove N megabytes of memory from the current VM
`int clne_get_freemem()`	Returns the free memory amount of the VM host machine
`int clne_get_maxmem()`	Returns the total memory amount of the VM host machine
`int clne_get_mem()`	Returns the total memory amount of the current VM
`int clne_get_freecpu()`	Returns the free CPU amount of the VM host machine
`int clne_get_maxcpu()`	Returns the total CPU amount of the VM host machine
`int clne_get_vcpus()`	Returns the VCPU amount of the current VM

Our idea is to provide reactive elasticity in a transparent and effortless way to the user, who does not need to write rules and actions for resource reconfiguration. In addition, users must not need to change their parallel application, not inserting elasticity calls from a particular library nor modifying the application to add/remove resources by themselves. Considering the second aforementioned question, AutoElastic should be aware of the overhead to instantiate a VM, taking this knowledge to offer this feature without prohibitive costs. Figure 4.6a illustrates the traditional approaches of providing cloud elasticity to HPC applications, while Fig. 4.6b highlights AutoElastic's idea. AutoElastic allows users to compile and submit an HPC nonelastic aware application to the cloud. So, the middleware at PaaS level transforms a nonelastic application in an elastic one and manages resource (and also application processes, consequently) reorganization through automatic VM allocation and consolidation procedures.

The first AutoElastic ideas were published in a previous work [32], in which our idea was to present a deep analysis of the state of the art in the cloud elasticity area, presenting the gaps in the HPC landscape. The mentioned article considered only a pair of thresholds (one upper threshold and one lower threshold), besides not explaining the interaction between the application processes and the AutoElastic Manager. Here we present a novel prediction function (see Equations 4.1 and 4.2),

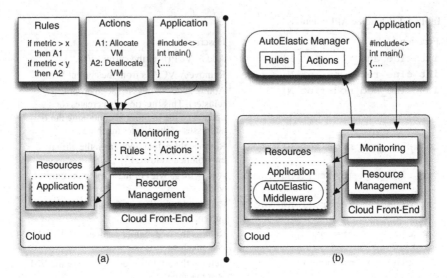

Fig. 4.6 General ideas on using elasticity: (**a**) standard approach adopted by Amazon AWS and Windows Azure, in which the user must pre-configure a set of elasticity rules and actions; (**b**) AutoElastic idea, contemplating a Manager that coordinates the elasticity actions and configurations on behalf of the user

a graphical demonstration about how an application talks with the Manager and extensive details about the application used in the tests. Moreover, we also present novel types of graphs, exploring the impact of the thresholds in the application performance, the relationship between CPU load and allocated CPU cores, and energy consumption profiles.

4.3.2.1 Architecture

AutoElastic is a cloud elasticity model that operates at the PaaS level of a cloud platform, acting as a middleware that enables the transformation of a nonelastic parallel application in an elastic one. The model works with both automatic and reactive elasticity in their horizontal (managing VM replicas) and vertical modes (resizing computational infrastructure), providing allocation and consolidation of compute nodes and virtual machines. As PaaS model, AutoElastic proposes a middleware to compile an iterative-based master-slave application, besides an elasticity Manager. Figure 4.7a depicts user interaction with the cloud, who needs to concentrate their efforts only on the application coding. The Manager hides the details from the user on writing elasticity rules and actions. Figure 4.7b illustrates the relationships among processes, virtual machines, and computational nodes. In our scope, an AutoElastic cloud can be defined as follows:

- **AutoElastic cloud**: a cloud modeled with m homogeneous and distributed computational resources, where at least one of them (Node0) is always active.

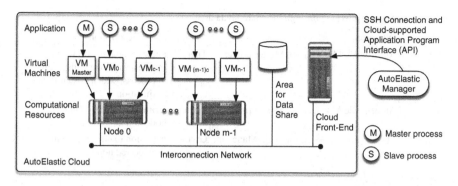

Fig. 4.7 AutoElastic architecture, highlighting the distribution of nodes, VMs, and processes. Each VM encompasses a single application process, and each node runs c processing VMs, where c denotes the number of processing cores in the node

This node is in charge of running a VM with the master process and other c VMs with slave processes, where c means the number of processing units (cores or CPUs) inside a particular node. The elasticity grain for each scaling up or down action refers to a single node and, consequently, its VMs and processes. Lastly, at any time, the number of VMs running slave processes is equal to $n = c \times m$.

Here, we are presenting the AutoElastic Manager as an application outside the cloud, but it could be mapped to the first node, for example. This flexibility is achieved by using the API of the cloud software packages. Taking into account that HPC applications are commonly CPU intensive [2], we opted for creating a single process per VM and c VMs per compute node to explore its fully potential. This approach is based on the work of Lee et al. [21], where they seek to explore a better efficiency in parallel applications.

The user can enter an SLA with the minimum and maximum number of allowed VMs. If this file is not provided, it is assumed that this maximum is twice the number of VMs observed at the application launch. The fact that the Manager, and not the application itself, increases or decreases the number of resources provides the benefit of asynchronous elasticity. Here, asynchronous elasticity means that process execution and elasticity actions occur concomitantly, not penalizing the application because of resource overhead (node and VM) reconfiguration (allocation and deallocation). However, this asynchronism leads to the following question: How can we notify the application about resource reconfiguration? To accomplish this, AutoElastic communicates among the VMs and the Manager using a shared memory area. Other options of communication should also be possible, including using NFS, message-oriented middleware (such as JMS or AMQP), or tuple spaces (JavaSpaces, for instance). The use of a shared area for data interaction among VM instances is a common approach in private clouds [7, 25, 39]. AutoElastic uses this idea to trigger actions as presented in Table 4.3.

Based on Action 1, the current processes may start working with the new set of resources (a single node with c VMs, each one with a new process). Figure 4.8

Table 4.3 Actions provided through the shared data area

Action	Direction	Description
Action 1	AutoElastic Manager → Master process	There is a new compute node with c virtual machines, each one with a new application process, which has an IP and a unique identification
Action 2	AutoElastic Manager → Master process	Request permission to consolidate a compute node and its VMs
Action 3	Master process → AutoElastic Manager	Giving permission to consolidate the previously requested node

illustrates the functioning of the AutoElastic Manager when creating a new slave, so launching Action 1 afterward. Action 2 is relevant for the following reasons: (i) not stopping a process executing while either communication or computation procedures take place and (ii) ensuring that application will not be aborted with the sudden interruption of one or more processes. In particular, the second reason is important for MPI applications that run over TCP/IP networks, since they commonly crash with a premature termination of any process. Action 3 is normally taken by a master process, which ensures that the application has a consistent global state where processes may be disconnected properly. Afterward, the remaining processes do not exchange any message to the given node. We are working with a shared area because it makes easier the notification of all processes about resource addition or dropping and then performing communication channel reconfigurations in a simple way.

AutoElastic offers cloud elasticity using the replication technique. In the activity of enlarging the infrastructure, the Manager allocates a new compute node and launches new virtual machines on it using an application template. The bootstrap of a VM is ended with the execution of a slave process which will do requests to the master. The instantiation of VMs is controlled by the Manager, and only after they are running, the Manager notifies the other processes through Action 1. The consolidation procedure increases the efficiency on resource utilization (not partially using the available cores) and also provides a better management of energy consumption. Particularly, Baliga et al. [3] claim that the number of VMs in a node is not an influential factor for energy consumption, but the fact of a node is turned on or not.

As presented in the works of Chiu and Agrawal [8] and Imai et al. [17], data monitoring is given periodically. Hence, AutoElastic Manager obtains the CPU metric, applies time series based on past values, and compares the final metric with the maximum and minimum thresholds. More precisely, we are employing moving average in accordance with Equations 4.2 and 4.1. $LP(i)$ returns a CPU load prediction when considering the execution of the n slave VMs in the Manager intervention number i. To accomplish this, $MM(i,j)$ informs the CPU load of a virtual machine j in the observation i. Equation 4.2 uses moving average by considering the last z observations of the CPU load $Load(k,j)$ over the VM j, where

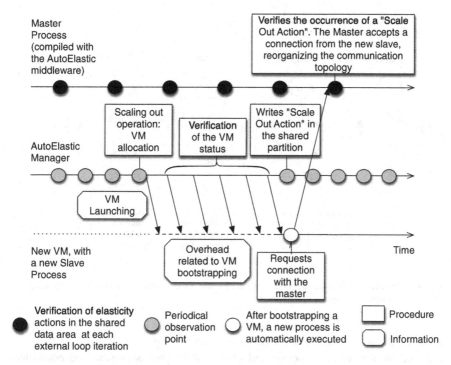

Fig. 4.8 Functioning of the master, the new slave and the AutoElastic Manager to enable the asynchronous elasticity

$i - z \leq k \leq i$. Finally, Action 1 is triggered if LP is greater than the maximum threshold, while Action 2 is thrown when LP is lower than the minimum threshold:

$$LP(i) = \frac{1}{n} \cdot \sum_{i=0}^{n-1} MM(i,j) \tag{4.1}$$

where

$$MM(i,j) = \frac{\sum_{k=i-z+1}^{i} Load(k,j)}{z} \tag{4.2}$$

for $i \geq z$.

4.3.2.2 Model of Parallel Application

AutoElastic exploits data parallelism on iterative-based message passing parallel applications. Figure 4.9 shows an iterative application supported by AutoElastic where each iteration is composed by three steps: (a) the process master distributes

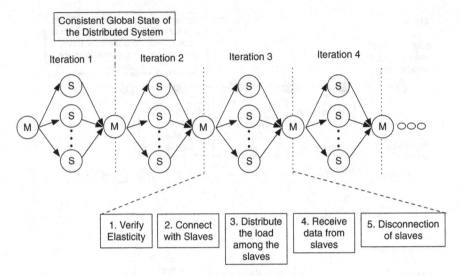

Fig. 4.9 Iterative application supported by AutoElastic. Process reorganization takes place before starting each new iteration

the load among the active slave processes; (b) slave processes compute the load received by the master process; and (c) the slave processes send the computed results to the master process. The elasticity occurs always in between each iteration where the computation has a consistent global state, allowing changes in the number of processes. In particular, the current version of the model still has the restriction to operate with applications in the master-slave programming style. Although trivial, this style is used in several areas, such as genetic algorithms, Monte Carlo techniques, geometric transformations in computer graphics, cryptography algorithms, and applications that follow the embarrassingly parallel computing model [31]. However, the Action 1 allows existing processes to know the identifiers of the new ones allowing an all-to-all communication channel reorganization eventually. Another characteristic is that AutoElastic deals with applications that do not use specific deadlines for concluding the subparts.

As AutoElastic project decision, elasticity feature must be offered to programmers without changing their application. Thus, we modeled the communication framework by analyzing the traditional interfaces from MPI 1.x and MPI 2.x. The first creates processes statically, where a program begins and ends with the same number of processes. On the other hand, MPI 2.0 has support for elasticity, since it offers the possibility of creating processes dynamically, with transparent connections to the existing ones. AutoElastic follows the MPMD (multiple program multiple data) approach from MPI 2.x, where the master has an executable and the slaves another.

Based on the MPI 2.0, AutoElastic works with the following directives: (i) publication of connection ports, (ii) finding the server based on a particular port, (iii) accepting a connection, (iv) requesting a connection, and (v) making a disconnection. Different from the approach in which the master process launches the slaves using a spawn-like directive, the proposed model operates according to another approach of MPI 2.0 for dynamic process management: connection-oriented communication using point to point, as sockets do. The launching of a VM automatically occurs in the execution of a slave process, which requests a connection with the master afterward. Here, we emphasize that an application with AutoElastic does not need to follow the MPI 2.0 interface but the semantic of each aforementioned directive.

Figure 4.10a presents a pseudo-code of the master process. The master performs a series of tasks, sequentially capturing a task and dividing it before sending for processing on slaves. Concerning the code, the method in the line 4 of Fig. 4.10a checks the distributed environment and publishes a set of ports (disjoint set of numbers, names, or a combination of them) to receive a connection from each slave process. Data communication happens in an asynchronous model, where sending data to the slaves is non-blocking and receiving data from them is blocking. The occurrence of an external loop is convenient for elasticity, since the beginning of each iteration is a possible point for resource and process reconfiguration, including communication channel reorganizations. Still, the beginning of a new loop implies in a consistent global state for the distributed system.

The transformation of a nonelastic into an elastic application can be offered in different ways:

(i) Implementation of an object-oriented program using polymorphism to override the method to manage the elasticity

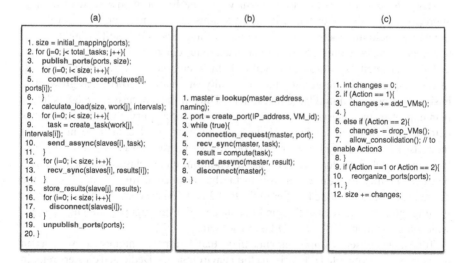

```
(a)
1. size = initial_mapping(ports);
2. for (j=0; j< total_tasks; j++){
3.   publish_ports(ports, size);
4.   for (i=0; i< size; i++){
5.     connection_accept(slaves[i],
ports[i]);
6.   }
7.   calculate_load(size, work[j], intervals);
8.   for (i=0; i< size; i++){
9.     task = create_task(work[j],
intervals[i]);
10.    send_assync(slaves[i], task);
11.  }
12.  for (i=0; i< size; i++){
13.    recv_sync(slaves[i], results[i]);
14.  }
15.  store_results(slave[j], results);
16.  for (i=0; i< size; i++){
17.    disconnect(slaves[i]);
18.  }
19.  unpublish_ports(ports);
20. }
```

```
(b)
1. master = lookup(master_address,
naming);
2. port = create_port(IP_address, VM_id);
3. while (true){
4.   connection_request(master, port);
5.   recv_sync(master, task);
6.   result = compute(task);
7.   send_assync(master, result);
8.   disconnect(master);
9. }
```

```
(c)
1. int changes = 0;
2. if (Action == 1){
3.   changes += add_VMs();
4. }
5. else if (Action == 2){
6.   changes -= drop_VMs();
7.   allow_consolidation(); // to
enable Action3
8. }
9. if (Action ==1 or Action == 2){
10.   reorganize_ports(ports);
11. }
12. size += changes;
```

Fig. 4.10 Application model in pseudo-language: (**a**) Master process; (**b**) slave process; (**c**) and elasticity code to be inserted in the Master process at PaaS level by using either method overriding, source-to-source translation, or wrapper technique

(ii) Using a source-to-source translator to insert code between lines 4 and 5 of the master code
(iii) Development of a wrapper for procedural languages in order to change the function in line 4 of Fig. 4.10a. Regardless of the technique, the elasticity code is simple and shown in Fig. 4.10c. A region of additional code checks the shared directory if there is a new action for AutoElastic. For example, this part of code can be inserted as an extension of the function publish_ports() following the technique number (iii) above.

Although the initial focus of AutoElastic is on master-slave, the use of the socket-like MPI 2.0 ideas eases the inclusion of processes and the reestablishment of connections to compose a new totally arbitrary topology. At implementation level, it is possible to optimize connections and disconnections if the process persists in the list of active processes. This behavior is especially pertinent over TCP/IP connections, since this suite uses an onerous three-way handshake protocol for connection establishment.

4.4 Elasticity Analysis and Research Opportunities

Section 4.3 presented two proposals to explore elasticity for HPC scientific applications. Table 4.4 shows a comparison analysis between the two approaches, highlighting advantages and disadvantages. A relevant question here to choose one of the elasticity approach is: what is the abstraction level required by the user to enable cloud elasticity in his/her application? If the user wants to use this cloud capacity in an effortless and transparent way, AutoElastic model seems the most appropriate. On the other hand, if the user aims at obtaining total control of the execution, including metric values, parameters, and places to insert elasticity calls, Cloudine is the best approach to support such requirements.

Cloud elasticity is a desirable facility both in commercial and academic areas. In the first, elasticity represents the possibility of small enterprises to grow their business without an initial large investment. Thus, if the enterprise success is lower than expected, the enterprise does not have to pay for acquiring physical resources beforehand. On the other hand, if the core business receives a large number of requests, here elasticity has a crucial role to expand the processing infrastructure to support such new demand patterns. In addition, cloud elasticity is known as a pertinent facility to reduce a metric in the business area: time to market. In the academic area, as discussed earlier in Sects. 4.2 and 4.3, we observe that elasticity is gaining more and more attention on big data and high-throughput computing areas, which address many CPU- or I/O-bound activities.

Today, we observe improvements in virtualization techniques, as well as in network setup, to enable HPC-driven cloud environments. Dedicated clusters remain as the main option to run HPC applications; however, on the other hand, public and private cloud providers are also more and more focusing on offering facilities

Table 4.4 Comparing elasticity approaches for scientific applications

	Autoelastic	Cloudine
Objective	To reduce the time of a parallel application	To provide elasticity support in such a way the users can tune application parameters
Target machine	Cloud computing, particularly composed of homogeneous computational nodes	Cloud computing
Target application	Iterative master-slave MPI applications	Parallel applications written in any of the five parallel programming models (master-slave, Bag-of-tasks, Divide-and-Conquer, Pipeline, and Bulk-Synchronous Parallel
Differential approach	Presents the concept of asynchronous elasticity, where processes are not blocked when scaling in or scaling out actions take place	Programming level elasticity, which is offered through a set of elasticity programming directives
Impact in the infrastructure	Horizontal elasticity, with the addition or drop of a single node with c virtual machines. Here, c denotes the number of processing cores (each VM executes a new slave process)	The effectiveness of the solution depends on the target cloud provider, if it supports horizontal or vertical elasticity or not. In addition, the effectiveness also depends on the monitoring API offered by the cloud provider.
Advantages	The user does not need to insert elasticity directives in his/her application. He/she only launches the application to the cloud, so the elasticity Manager on the fly manages the right number of resources and processes to execute the application.	Unprecedented functionalities can be integrated in the application code. In this way, it is possible to develop dynamic and flexible applications that adapt their own executing environment in accordance with the incoming demands
Limitations	The elasticity grain always refers to a single compute node. This strategy can incur a lack of reactiveness on resource allocation and deallocation procedures, so penalizing the application time and the use of resources.	The effort at the programmer viewpoint, since he/she is in charge of considering elasticity issues at both application design and implementation times
Solution complexity	AutoElastic acts at the PaaS level of a cloud; thus, the users only need to compile the application with the AutoElastic middleware. In particular, AutoElastic has a wrapper that transforms a nonelastic application into an elastic one.	Both the application design and implementation (or adaptation) must consider the control of the elasticity in the application source code. In this way, the user must implement dynamic process creation by himself/herself using an appropriate set of elasticity directives

and flexible configurations to reduce the performance gap between the two parallel machines (cluster and cloud resources). Sections 4.2 and 4.3 discussed about how to employ cloud elasticity over HPC-like scientific applications. Below, we are compiling some issues that could be further explored to disseminate the use of elasticity, as well as to understand its capacities and limitations.

- Cloudine represents an initiative of a programming library, which can be used to write elastic applications. However, we observe that there is a gap in providing a *de facto* standard interface for such role as either web services are for web-based transactional applications or MPI (message passing interface) is for high performance computing. An idea could be to explore elasticity directives, for example, in the next version of MPI so approaching such an interface to the cloud panorama.
- In scientific application plethora, today we observe the use of cloud elasticity to execute workflow-based, Bag-of-Tasks, and Master-Slave HPC applications. Nevertheless, the challenge is to visualize performance gains that could be explored with resource reorganization over other parallel programming models, including Divide-and-Conquer and Bulk-Synchronous parallel.
- The use of lower and upper thresholds is a problem to enable reactive elasticity, mainly for two reasons: (i) a good pair of thresholds for a particular set of application and infrastructure could present collateral effects like VM thrashing when at least one element of the aforesaid set is changed. ProActive elasticity could be a solution; however this technique normally comprises large warm-up periods to train the prediction algorithms, and it is often associated as a time-consuming operation. Thus, hybrid approaches could be explored to extract the better of the two approaches: simplicity and intuitivity from the reactive elasticity and predictability and thresholdless character from proactive elasticity.
- Today, services offered at SaaS (software-as-a-service) level such as Google Docs and Google Mail are very diffused worldwide, so abstracting infrastructure, localization, and technical details from users properly. Thus, we expect the development of elasticity policies on public cloud providers to adapt the mentioned services in accordance with the demands, since we observe that often performance and response time are put away in particular parts of the day.
- Definition of metrics to evaluate how effective an elasticity system is. At least, we envision three metrics: time, resource consumption, and cost [32]. Time refers to the execution time to conclude an HPC application, so being a pertinent metric mainly when comparing elastic and inelastic systems. Resource consumption refers to a sum when considering each VM deployment and its time as active. For example, consider the situation: 20s with 2VMs, 120s with 4VMs, 100s with 6VMs, and 80s with 4VMs; here we have resource consumption $= 20.2 + (120.4 + 80.4) + 100.6 = 1440$. The cost, in turn, is used to analyze how viable is the execution, with or without elasticity. Based on the standard notion of cost in the parallel computing area, which considers time $\times$ processors, here we can use time and the previously computed resource consumption metric.

4.5 Conclusion

Demand for HPC continues to grow, driven in large part by ever-increasing demands for more accurate and faster simulations to meet new regulatory requirements, to increase safety, or to reduce financial risks. In this context, this chapter presented the possibility to explore cloud elasticity in this scope. In our understanding, elasticity is pertinent to provide resource configuration adaptivity mainly for irregular and dynamic applications, where unpredictable workloads and nondeterministic inter-process communication take place. In addition, non-dedicated and heterogeneous execution environments can also extract the advantages of such facility to on-the-fly adapt the resources in accordance with the application demands and infrastructure modifications. The benefits of cloud elasticity are clear to the HPC community; what remains unsolved concerns which is the best alternative to provide it for HPC applications. This chapter detailed two alternatives: one at programming level and another at middleware level. They represent a good start to rethink adaptivity and resource allocation, but the authors agree that the use of standard elasticity mechanisms and interfaces is crucial to disseminate the use of this promising facility in the HPC landscape.

Acknowledgements This work was partially supported by the following Brazilian Agencies: FAPERGS, CAPES, and CNPq (grants 457501/2014-6 and 305531/2015-8).

References

1. Ali-Eldin A, Kihl M, Tordsson J, Elmroth E (2012) Efficient provisioning of bursty scientific workloads on the cloud using adaptive elasticity control. In: Proceedings of the 3rd workshop on scientific cloud computing date, ScienceCloud'12. ACM, New York, pp 31–40
2. Azmandian F, Moffie M, Dy JG, Aslam JA, Kaeli DR (2011) Workload characterization at the virtualization layer. In: Proceedings of the 19th international symposium on modeling, analysis simulation of computer and telecommunication systems, MASCOTS'11. IEEE Computer Society, Washington, DC, pp 63–72
3. Baliga J, Ayre RWA, Hintony K, Tucker RS (2011) Green cloud computing: balancing energy in processing, storage, and transport. Proc IEEE 99(1):149–167
4. Ben-Yehuda AO, Ben-Yehuda M, Schuster A, Tsafrir D (2012) The resource-as-a-service (RAAS) cloud. In: Proceedings of the 4th USENIX conference on hot topics in cloud computing, HotCloud'12. USENIX, pp 1–5
5. Byun E, Kee Y, Kim J, Maeng S (2011) Cost optimized provisioning of elastic resources for application workflows. Future Gen Comput Syst 27(8):1011–1026
6. Caballer M, de Alfonso C, Moltó G, Romero E, Blanquer I, García A (2014) Codecloud: a platform to enable execution of programming models on the clouds. J Syst Softw 93(0):187–198
7. Cai B, Xu F, Ye F, Zhou W (2012) Research and application of migrating legacy systems to the private cloud platform with cloudstack. In: Proceedings of the international conference on automation and logistics, ICAL'12. IEEE, pp 400–404

8. Chiu D, Agrawal G (2010) Evaluating caching and storage options on the Amazon web services cloud. In: Proceedings of the 11th international conference on grid computing, GRID'10. IEEE, pp 17–24

9. Chohan N, Castillo C, Spreitzer M, Steinder M, Tantawi A, Krintz C (2010) See spot run: using spot instances for mapreduce workflows. In: Proceedings of the 2nd USENIX conference on hot topics in cloud computing, HotCloud'10. USENIX, pp 1–7

10. de Oliveira D, Viana V, Ogasawara E, Ocana K, Mattoso M (2013) Dimensioning the virtual cluster for parallel scientific workflows in clouds. In: Proceedings of the 4th ACM workshop on scientific cloud computing, ScienceCloud'13. ACM, New York, pp 5–12

11. Galante G, Bona LCE (2012) A survey on cloud computing elasticity. In: Proceedings of the international workshop on clouds and eScience applications management, CloudAM'12. IEEE, pp 263–270

12. Galante G, Bona LCE (2014) Supporting elasticity in openmp applications. In: Proceedings of the 22nd Euromicro conference on parallel, distributed and network-based processing, PDP'14. Euromicro, pp 188–195

13. Galante G, Bona LCE (2015) A programming-level approach for elasticizing parallel scientific applications. J Syst Softw 110(C):239–252

14. Galante G, Bona LCE, Claudio Schepke (2014) Improving olam with cloud elasticity. In: Murgante B, Misra S, Rocha AMAC, Torre C, Rocha JG, Falcão MI, Taniar D, Apduhan BO, Gervasi O (eds) Computational science and its applications – ICCSA 2014: 14th international conference, Guimarães, June 30–July 3, 2014, Proceedings, Part VI. Springer, pp 46–60

15. Herbst NR, Kounev S, Reussner R (2013) Elasticity in cloud computing: what it is, and what it is not. In: Proceedings of 10th international conference on autonomic computing, ICAC'13. USENIX, San Jose, pp 23–27

16. Hummaida AR, Paton NW, Sakellariou R (2016) Adaptation in cloud resource configuration: a survey. J Cloud Comput 5(1):57:1–57:16

17. Imai S, Chestna T, Varela CA (2012) Elastic scalable cloud computing using application-level migration. In: Proceedings of the 5th international conference on utility and cloud computing, UCC'12. IEEE, pp 91–98

18. Iordache A, Morin C, Parlavantzas N, Feller E, Riteau P (2013) Resilin: elastic mapreduce over multiple clouds. In: Proceedings of 12th international symposium on cluster, cloud and grid computing, CCGRID'13. IEEE, pp 261–268

19. Islam S, Lee K, Fekete A, Liu A (2012) How a consumer can measure elasticity for cloud platforms. In: Proceedings of the 3rd international conference on performance engineering, ICPE'12. ACM, pp 85–96

20. Jha S, Katz DS, Luckow A, Merzky A, Stamou K (2011) Understanding scientific applications for cloud environments. In: Buyya R, Broberg J, Goscinski AM (eds) Cloud computing: principles and paradigms, chapter 13. John Wiley & Sons, pp 345–371

21. Lee Y, Avizienis R, Bishara A, Xia R, Lockhart D, Batten C, Asanovic K (2011) Exploring the tradeoffs between programmability and efficiency in data-parallel accelerators. In: Proceedings of the 38th annual international symposium on computer architecture, ISCA'11, pp 129–140

22. Leslie LM, Sato C, Lee YC, Jiang Q, Zomaya AY (2015) DEWE: a framework for distributed elastic scientific workflow execution. In: Proceedings of the 13th Australasian symposium on parallel and distributed computing, AusPDC'15. ACS, Sydney, pp 3–10

23. Lin C, Lu S (2011) SCPOR: an elastic workflow scheduling algorithm for services computing. In: Proceedings of the 5th IEEE international conference on service-oriented computing and applications, SOCA'11. IEEE Computer Society, Washington, DC, pp 1–8

24. Lorido-Botran T, Miguel-Alonso J, Lozano JA (2014) A review of auto-scaling techniques for elastic applications in cloud environments. J Grid Comput 12(4):559–592

25. Milojicic D, Llorente IM, Montero RS (2011) Opennebula: a cloud management tool. IEEE Internet Comput 15(2):11–14

26. Moltó G, Caballer M, Romero E, de Alfonso C (2013) Elastic memory management of virtualized infrastructures for applications with dynamic memory requirements. In: International conference on computational science, ICCS'13; Procedia Comput Sci 18:159–168

27. Nicolae B, Riteau P, Keahey K (2014) Bursting the cloud data bubble: towards transparent storage elasticity in IaaS clouds. In: Proceedings of the 28th international parallel and distributed processing symposium, IPDPS'14. IEEE, pp 135–144

28. Pandey S, Karunamoorthy D, Buyya R (2011) Workflow engine for clouds. In: Buyya R, Broberg J, Goscinski A.M. (eds) Cloud computing: principles and paradigms, chapter 12. John Wiley & Sons, pp 321–344

29. Rajan D, Canino A, Izaguirre JA, Thain D (2011) Converting a high performance application to an elastic cloud application. In: Proceedings of the 3rd international conference on cloud computing technology and science, CLOUDCOM'11. IEEE, pp 383–390

30. Ramakrishnan L, Jackson KR, Canon S, Cholia S, Shalf J (2010) Defining future platform requirements for e-science clouds. In: Proceedings of the 1st symposium on cloud computing, SoCC'10. ACM, New York, pp 101–106

31. Raveendran A, Bicer T, Agrawal G (2011) A framework for elastic execution of existing MPI programs. In: Proceedings of the international symposium on parallel and distributed processing workshops and PhD forum, IPDPSW'11. IEEE, pp 940–947

32. Righi RdR, Rodrigues VF, da Costa CA, Galante G, de Bona LCE, Ferreto T (2016) Autoelastic: automatic resource elasticity for high performance applications in the cloud. IEEE Trans Cloud Comput 4(1):6–19

33. Simmhan Y, van Ingen C, Subramanian G, Li J (2010) Bridging the gap between desktop and the cloud for escience applications. In: Proceedings of the 3rd international conference on cloud computing, CLOUD'10. IEEE, pp 474–481

34. Srirama SN, Jakovits P, Vainikko E (2012) Adapting scientific computing problems to clouds using MapReduce. Future Gen Comput Syst 28(1):184–192

35. Taifi M, Shi JY, Khreishah A (2011) SpotMPI: a framework for auction-based HPC computing using Amazon spot instances. In: Proceedings of the 11th international conference on algorithms and architectures for parallel processing, ICA3PP'11. Springer, pp 109–120

36. Vaquero LM, Rodero-Merino L, Buyya R (2011) Dynamically scaling applications in the cloud. ACM Comput Commun Rev 41:45–52

37. Vecchiola C, Pandey S, Buyya R (2009) High-performance cloud computing: a view of scientific applications. In: Proceedings of the 10th international symposium on pervasive systems, algorithms, and networks, ISPAN'09. IEEE, pp 4–16

38. Villamizar M, Castro H, Mendez D (2012) E-clouds: a saas marketplace for scientific computing. In: Proceedings of the 5th international conference on utility and cloud computing, UCC'12. IEEE, pp 13–20

39. Wen X, Gu G, Li Q, Gao Y, Zhang X (2012) Comparison of open-source cloud management platforms: openstack and opennebula. In: Proceedings of the 9th international conference on fuzzy systems and knowledge discovery, FSKD'12, pp 2457–2461

40. Wottrich R, Azevedo R, Araujo G (2014) Cloud-based OpenMP parallelization using a mapreduce runtime. In: 26th IEEE international symposium on computer architecture and high performance computing, SBAC-PAD'14. IEEE, pp 334–341

41. Yu L, Thain D (2012) Resource management for elastic cloud workflows. In: Proceedings of the 2012 12th IEEE/ACM international symposium on cluster, cloud and grid computing, CCGRID'12. IEEE, pp 775–780

Chapter 5
Clouds and Reproducibility: A Way to Go to Scientific Experiments?

Ary H. M. de Oliveira, Daniel de Oliveira, and Marta Mattoso

5.1 Introduction

Computational scientific experiments use computing techniques integrated to methodologies and scientific programs to support the development of science. Experiments in different domains of knowledge are often dependent of data-oriented computational methods [30, 33]. e-Science [56] emerged as a data-oriented science that is based on computational scientific experiments. The goal is to make science evolution more efficient and productive [24]. Among the challenges of e-Science development, there is the processing and analysis of large scientific datasets that currently produce a range of several terabytes to petabytes of data [5, 34, 35, 55]. As computers become more powerful, the complexity of analyzing scientific data also grows at the same pace due to the volume, complexity, and variety of data that is generated [16, 30, 57]. Scientific development involves a massive production of data and must be accompanied by approaches that allow for the reproducibility of experiments, making it possible to verify and validate the results produced by these simulations.

For a scientific experiment to be considered "scientific" it must be reproducible [19]. To reach the same conclusions as a previous experiment, scientists have to analyze and compare data products (we use the term data product or dataset to

A.H.M. de Oliveira (✉)
Federal University of Tocantins, Palmas, Brazil
e-mail: aryhenrique@mail.uft.edu.br

D. de Oliveira
Fluminense Federal University, Niterói, Brazil
e-mail: danielcmo@ic.uff.br

M. Mattoso
Federal University of Rio de Janeiro (COPPE/UFRJ), Rio de Janeiro, Brazil
e-mail: marta@cos.ufrj.br

© Springer International Publishing AG 2017
N. Antonopoulos, L. Gillam (eds.), *Cloud Computing*, Computer Communications and Networks, DOI 10.1007/978-3-319-54645-2_5

refer to data in any form, such as files, tables, and virtual collections) and metadata related to the experiment execution. Metadata allows for scientists to check if the experiment followed the same procedure of previous executions [32]. It is defined as the basic principle of the scientific method, which assists in the comparison process and methods and validation of results [23]. This is the evidence used to test and sustain the adopted methods and obtained results. Reproducibility is a way to certify that the results are correct and the method is convincing and reproducible [23]. The science progress depends on the effective dissemination and reproducibility of existing research [47]. Nevertheless, it is necessary to access the material used in the production of the results to analyze and evaluate it [6]. Science advances faster when it is possible to build on existing results and when new ideas can be easily measured against the state of the art [38].

The reproducibility of a scientific experiment with rigor, transparency, and verification is a decisive factor when assessing quality [41]. The American Physical Society (APS)[1] emphasizes the importance of reproducibility. According to APS, science is the systematic use of knowledge gathering about the universe and the organization and condensation of that knowledge in laws and theories testable. They complement that a way to maintain the credibility and success of science is to anchor it in the scientist's disposition to expose ideas and results of their studies to independent tests and replication of these tests by other scientists. Reproducibility is a way to allow the published knowledge to become available to the general public [15]. A scientific contribution is considered valuable if, among other things, other researchers are able to reproduce its results with success [52].

However, it is far from trivial to achieve reproducibility in computer-based scientific experiments. Many of these experiments are composed by several activities that invoke computing and data-intensive programs. Several experiments execute for weeks or months in parallel even in high-performance computing (HPC) environments such as clusters, grids, and clouds. In order to be reproduced by third-party scientists or teams, several existing approaches [7, 10, 40, 58] collect provenance data [11] related to executions of these experiments to foster reproducibility. Provenance, or lineage, of a scientific experiment is related to metadata associated to the data products generated by a specific experiment execution. Simmhan et al. [50] define provenance as the "information that helps determine the derivation history of a data product, starting from its original sources." The main goal of provenance is to give credibility and confidence to the results and methods [23]. Although provenance plays a very important role, it is not sufficient to reproduce scientific experiments. A scientific experiment may have several software and hardware dependencies that must be preserved in the moment of reproduction. One problem that arises is how to reproduce these dependencies since software may be discontinued, computer architectures may be not supported anymore, etc.

---

[1]http://www.aps.org/policy/statements/99_6.cfm

Clouds can play a fundamental role in e-Science reproducibility [22]. Clouds are strongly based on the concept of virtualization in which virtual machines (VM) are a key issue. The entire environment used to execute the experiment (programs, data, etc.) can be packed in an image (e.g., an ISO), and VMs can be deployed based on this image. This fosters the ability to encapsulate the entire context of the experiment in a VM, which may virtually reproduce the same environment used to execute the experiment. However, just having the technology infrastructure is not enough, there are issues on how to pack the experiments, what to register, how to help on reproducing it with different parameters, etc.

Despite the vast literature on reproducibility of experiments, the terms used in the papers are quite diverse and do not help in mapping the field. In addition, there lacks a reference architecture to compare the state-of-the-art solutions. Also, the potential of cloud computing seems underutilized in reproducing experiments. Given this context, this chapter discusses how clouds can foster reproducibility and has three main contributions: a taxonomy on reproducibility of experiments, a reference architecture for reproducibility support using clouds, and an evaluation of current approaches for cloud-based reproducibility. The taxonomy organizes the concepts and terminology of reproducibility independent of the scientific domain area. The goal is to provide a common definition and classification for e-Science research reproducibility. This taxonomy can be used to guide researchers among the innumerous possibilities. The second contribution presents the basic functional requirements to guide the construction and analysis of a reproducible infrastructure in clouds. The proposed reference architecture helps on the characterization of tools for the reproducibility of experiments. Then, as a third contribution, current available tools are evaluated based on a set of properties and functionalities presented on this taxonomy and reference architecture.

This chapter is organized in five sections besides this introduction. Section 5.2 presents the proposed taxonomy with an organization of concepts and terminology related to reproducibility. Section 5.3 discusses about how clouds can foster reproducibility following the classes of the taxonomy. Section 5.4 proposes a reference architecture that makes an experiment reproducible. Section 5.5 presents a survey on reproducibility approaches that are based on clouds, and, finally, Sect. 5.6 concludes this chapter.

5.2 A Taxonomy on Reproducibility of Experiments

The amount of published papers and proposed approaches evidences that reproducible science has emerged as an important concept in the last years according to Freire et al. [20]. Several technologies, platforms, applications, infrastructure, and standards have been already proposed. However, the concepts involved need clear definitions and classifications. Considering the huge interest on reproducible science and the difficulty in finding organized definitions of concepts associated to this field, we present in this chapter a taxonomy for reproducibility approaches in e-Science.

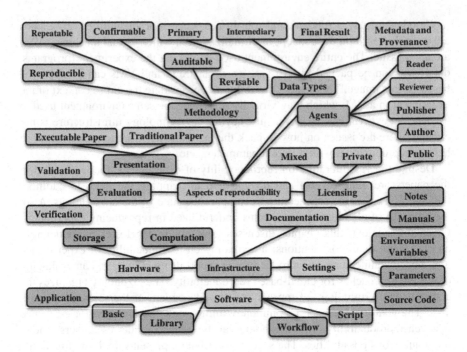

Fig. 5.1 The proposed taxonomy for reproducible science

Taxonomies are a particular classification structure where the concepts are arranged in a hierarchical way. The proposed taxonomy provides an understanding of the domain and aims at helping the scientist to compare different approaches for reproducible science, particularly when using clouds.

We believe that this taxonomy will be useful to the scientific community to compare different proposed approaches. By analyzing this taxonomy, scientists may consider which features meet their needs, and depending on the scientific experiment, these needs may vary. The taxonomy considers a broad view of reproducible science and aims at exploring its major aspects. Using the taxonomy as a common vocabulary may help scientists to find common characteristics of existing approaches and aid into choosing the most adequate one. This section describes several sub-taxonomies that compose a general taxonomy. For the sake of simplicity, the proposed taxonomy, presented in Fig. 5.1, classifies the characteristics of reproducible science in terms of authors, reproduction type, access/use license and copyrights, content presentation form, evaluation methods, and research objects. The term "research objects" is used to define an abstraction for communication, sharing, and reuse of scientific experiment results [4]. The research objects are composed of different artifacts used or generated by a scientific experiment [4], like papers (manuscripts), notes, datasets, documentation, hardware and software infrastructure, and configuration parameters. Following, we discuss each sub-taxonomy in detail.

Agent. A reproducible science is influenced by the action of four actors as discussed by Koop et al. [37]: (1) the author that designs and implements experiments to generate the results used in the scientific paper; (2) publishers that receive and publish papers so that readers in general may have access to the contents; (3) reviewers that evaluate the content and other materials, check results, and validate the methodology; and (4) readers that access the paper to get access to its contents to analyze the results, rerun the experiment, and reuse research elements.

Methodology. The methodology to be followed to reproduce an experiment's findings depends on the extent of reproducibility level desired. A report generated after the reproducibility workshop in computer science and mathematics organized by ICERM (Institute for Computational and Experimental Research in Mathematics[2]) suggested a classification of levels for reproducible science based on the access to documents and materials used for the scientific experiment. This workshop report presents five levels of reproducible science [53]: reviewable, replicable, confirmable, auditable, and reproducible. These five levels have also been described in [18] as (1) a review allows for results to be achieved independently through a complete description of the algorithms and methodology without the need of using software provided by the author; (2) a repetition defines that research results can be reproduced only in the infrastructure that they were originally obtained; (3) a confirmation allows for accessing objects used in the experiment execution; however, it does not support the experiment re-execution; (4) the auditable level has records of materials used in the experiment; however, they aim to be presented to a reviewer when requested; and (5) reproduction requires a robust methodology which allows for reproducing the results in an operational environment different from the one it was originally obtained.

Licensing. The license to access or use the results of a reproducible science can be defined in three different ways: public, private, or mixed [9]. When the scientific result is defined as public, the paper and research objects are widely accessible to the general public, that is, anyone can get the objects used in the experiment and reproduce the results and methodology. When the scientific result is defined as private, the scientific paper and the research objects have controlled access to a specific audience, through an access control and distribution of research subjects. The mixed license has access restrictions and concession policies for each research object, which can be public or private according to the adopted license. Reproducibility involves reproducing research objects such as configuration parameters, final results, and a set of elements used for the derivation of these results.

Presentation. A scientific paper is the way for presenting research objects used to produce a result. Currently, a paper can be written using a traditional form or by creating an executable paper. Traditional papers present static content, allowing

---

[2]http://icerm.brown.edu/home/index.php

for the inclusion of URLs for access to research objects related to a published result. Executable papers have dynamic content, allowing for readers to inform values and parameters to test the methodology and check the published result. They may contain code fragments or mechanisms that set actions for the experiment re-execution. The main goal of the executable paper is to improve the understanding and reproducibility of electronic publications allowing for readers and reviewers to interact, explore, and validate the experiments [32].

Evaluation. To verify the computational results of an experiment, it is necessary to recreate the conditions in which the experiment was performed right from the beginning [49]. Reproducible science supporting solutions aim at providing mechanisms that allow for reproducing an experiment and its conclusions based on measures and metrics established for the evaluation of results [2]. A reproducible experiment should provide mechanisms for validation and verification of the methodology and experimental results. Verification evaluates whether the results generated by the experiment are in agreement with the methodologies or observations of the phenomenon being studied. Validation evaluates whether the methodology proposed by the research properly resolves what it was designed to solve. Validation can be obtained by analyzing workflow execution trails from workflow systems using log records or provenance [12, 42].

Data. Many e-Science experiments are supported by data-oriented techniques and tools. The input data used by a simulation program is processed to produce results (output data). Tools like worfklow systems are used in e-Science to orchestrate the processing of data in a coherent flow of activities [3, 56]. This introduces the concept of intermediate data, when one activity produces a portion of data that should be available to start the execution of the next activity in the flow. Thus, reproducible experiment data may be classified as primary, intermediate, final results, metadata, and data provenance. Primary data is used as input data of the experiments. In general, data is obtained from measurements or environment monitoring, in which an instrument or sensor is deployed. Intermediate data, also called derivatives, is produced during the execution and is the result of the application of algorithms and analysis techniques for deriving information from input data. It is subject to an arrangement or structure for the production of the final results. The final results represent the final product of an experiment execution (following a methodology). Metadata and provenance data are, respectively, additional information about the three classes of data. Metadata are data descriptors that give meaning to the data. One of the broader definitions, Greenberg [26] defines metadata as data that describes the objects' structure and the features associated with this object. Provenance is defined as the origin or an object derivation history from its original source [12]. These information can be used to evaluate quality, reliability, or trust of an object [43]. Provenance describes steps in which the data were derived, adding significant value to the data [50].

Infrastructure. Freire et al. [19] present *two* formal concepts to define computational infrastructure reproducibility: (1) an experiment made by a laboratory L in a time t is considered reproducible if it can be replicated in a different laboratory L' in a posterior time t', and (2) a computational experiment developed in a time t in a hardware/operational system s using data d is reproducible if it can be executed in a time t' in a system s' with data d', which are similar or identical to d. This definition highlights the need to preserve the operational environment in which the experiment was deployed. Hence, the infrastructure refers to all the computation resources used during the process of planning, designing, building, and executing a reproducible experiment. The infrastructure is further categorized in four classes: documentation, settings, hardware, and software, detailed as follows.

Documentation. The documentation is an indispensable element to assist other scientists to understand the research. An algorithm configuration, the parameter lists, and their values used for the experiment must be clearly indicated. An available URL containing the software that implements the algorithm with information about the used datasets helps to obtain the necessary elements to redeploy the research objects used in the experiment. The documentation consists of registering the digital material used. The goal is to assist other scientists to deploy the research objects that are required to reproduce the experiment. Documentation also serves as a guide to understand the reasoning of the researchers while designing each element and the research as a whole. The concept of notes from Guo and Seltzer [29] emphasizes the importance to include notes in the data products used and generated in the experiment execution to allow accurate retrieval of files referenced in the notes. Documentation is formed, in general, by the instruction manual, research author notes, and other supporting materials.

Settings. Settings refer to the data settings and operational information responsible for creating and configuring the operational computational environment. The goal is to deploy and run the software under the same hardware used for executing the original experiment. Settings are formed by environment variables, which should be set in the operational system where the research objects will be deployed and the software will run.

Hardware. All equipments used for computations of scientific experiments must be registered as part of the infrastructure. The hardware is represented by machines, computer networks, and storage, that is, the computer environment. A machine is represented by two types of resources: processor and main memory. The computer network provides information about the logical and physical organization, such as the IP address and latency. The storage is the mechanism for data persistence in a secondary memory structure. The architecture organizes the previous elements to reflect the experiment performance and storage, taking into account characteristics such as the use of physical computers or virtual environment.

Software. Elements that perform the instructions and algorithms of an experiment are represented by registering the corresponding software. They are classified into six groups: basic, application, libraries, source code, script, and workflow. Basic software are formed by operational systems, virtualization software (hypervisors), and compilers, responsible for generating an executable from a source code provided by the scientist. Application software is a program (executable file) used to perform a specific activity. Libraries are formed by subprograms set with code and auxiliary data that provide some services to basic software and applications. Libraries are invoked during compilation and execution. The source codes are files written in a programming language ready to be compiled and used for activity execution. Since the reproduction of a certain result through its source code can be affected by the compiler used in the code compilation process, it is necessary to inform which compiler was used to generate the experiment results and which were the parameters applied. A script is a file with instructions set in code used by the operational system for control programs. A workflow is an abstraction that allows for the composition of programs, thus creating a coherent flow of activities [56]. It is executed by an engine called scientific workflow management system (SWfMS) to automate the activities involved in the workflow.

5.3 How Clouds Can Foster Reproducibility in Science?

Cloud computing has emerged as a computing model where web-based services allow for different kinds of users to obtain a large variety of resources, such as software and hardware. Cloud computing has demonstrated applicability to a wide range of problems in several domains, including scientific ones such as astronomy and bioinformatics. In fact, several scientists have adopted this computing model and moved their experiments (programs and data) from local environments such as clusters and grids to the cloud [13, 34]. One intuitive advantage provided by clouds is that scientists are not required to assemble expensive computational infrastructure to execute their experiments or even configure many pieces of software each time the experiment is executed. An average scientist is able to run experiments just by allocating the necessary resources in a cloud.

In addition to offering an adequate infrastructure for executing experiments, clouds can also foster the reproducibility of experiments, even if these experiments were not originally executed in clouds. As highlighted in the taxonomy presented in Sect. 5.2, clouds are natural providers of important requirements for reproducibility. The first requirement is the need of an infrastructure that is able to encapsulate characteristics of computational environments used in the execution of experiments. This requirement is natively addressed by clouds, since clouds are based on the concept of virtualization. Clouds allow for scientists to create virtual machines that act like a real computer with a specific operating system. All software executed on these virtual machines are separated from the underlying hardware resources. It allows, for example, that a computer that is running Linux 64 bits hosts a virtual machine that runs Microsoft Windows 32 bits. In addition, full virtualization can be applied, which allows for simulating the hardware and software originally used to execute the scientific experiment to run unmodified.

Another requirement is to gather and store intermediate and final results of the experiments for achieving reproducibility. Several experiments can produce many terabytes of data that should be preserved for long-term analysis. Cloud-based storage such as Amazon S3[3] can address this requirement. Online storage is an integral part of life now, and this is not different in the scientific domain. Besides specialized services such as S3, other general purpose cloud storage services can be used to store scientific data, including Google Drive,[4] Dropbox,[5] and OneDrive.[6]

Storing metadata and provenance data is also an issue in reproducibility. Provenance data is commonly stored in a structured way. For example, provenance data can be stored in a relational database, in a graph database, using JSON files, etc. The database as a service cloud paradigm delivers databases similar to what is found in relational database management systems (RDBMSs) and NoSQL DBMS. Provenance and metadata can be managed in this type of service since it offers flexibility in the data model, scalability, security, and reliability.

Another requirement is how to manage application's source codes that have to be recompiled to reproduce an experiment. Version control services such as GitHub[7] and BitBucket[8] already provide this service in the cloud. In addition, providers such as Amazon AWS already have services such as Amazon AWS CodeCommit,[9] which is a version control service that is associated with Amazon S3 to store versions of documents, source code, and binary files. The advantage of using version control services in comparison with storage services (such as Amazon S3) is that version control services are designed for team software development, i.e., it to merge source code from two or more users.

All these features make clouds a suitable environment to foster reproducibility in scientific experiments. However, just having the technology infrastructure is not enough, there are issues on how to pack the experiments, what to register, how to help on reproducing with different parameters, etc. This way, approaches for reproducibility have to be developed on top of clouds to benefit from these characteristics. The following section presents a reference architecture for reproducibility. The goal of this architecture is to help in comparing current solutions on reproducibility as well as to highlight open issues and directions that can be followed when developing a new approach.

---

[3]https://aws.amazon.com/s3

[4]https://apps.google.com/products/drive/

[5]https://www.dropbox.com/

[6]https://onedrive.live.com/

[7]https://github.com/

[8]https://bitbucket.org/

[9]http://docs.aws.amazon.com/codecommit/latest/userguide/welcome.html

5.4   Reproducible Research Architecture

In the previous sections, we discussed several features, factors, and requirements of
a reproducible science. In this section we present our design of an architecture to
represent a generic reproducible science support solution. Different authors point
out important reproducible features, while others discuss new insights, identifying
new opportunities and challenges. Each paper presents its own solution, making it
difficult to have a generic view of a reproducible experiment and compare solutions
to analyze open issues. Our proposed reference architecture aims to fill this gap. It
shows how these several features have been combined into a reference architecture
for the reproducibility of experiments. Figure 5.2 presents the architecture with its
components and how they can benefit from clouds.

The architecture is divided into four main tiers: (1) interface, which performs
the interaction of the service internal elements with external entities; (2) controller,
which controls the elements provided by the interface; (3) research object manager,
which manages all research objects involved in the experiment; and (4) storage
engine, which manages devices and storage mechanisms for files and data search.
Following we describe each module of each tier in the architecture.

Reproducible Experiment Content Viewer (Interface Tier). It is a communication interface with external entities. It provides the mechanism for visually
presenting elements and allows for external infrastructure, such as conference

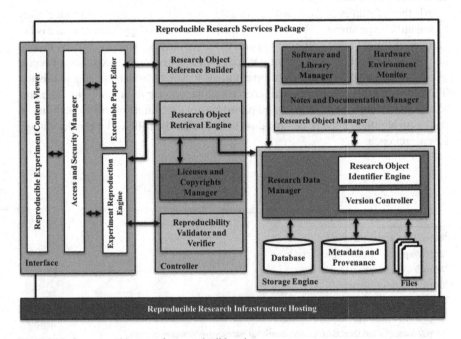

Fig. 5.2 Reference architecture for reproducible science

management systems to create links with the objects and the experiment. By using this interface, components are accessible for interaction with users, platforms, and external infrastructures. This interface can be implemented by a cloud app. A cloud app is an evolution of a web app. Similarly to web apps, they are used to access online services over the Internet, but they are not dependent on web browsers to work.

Access and Security Manager (Interface Tier). It controls user access and external entities to research objects. This control considers the types of actors that interact with the experiment, which by default are composed of authors, reviewers, journals, and readers. It interacts with the reproducible experiment content viewer module to register stakeholders in accessing research objects. It communicates with the research object retrieval engine module to identify and filter which research objects must be presented. The filter uses the guidelines established in the licenses and copyrights manager to select the research objects that can be displayed.

Executable Paper Editor (Interface Tier). It allows for including references to research objects in the manuscript, creating a link to an object in a paper. Many of the existing approaches are based on libraries and mechanisms for annotation in HTML documents and in the text body in LaTeX to reference research objects. These references can be included in a paper in the traditional way, i.e., using links to static content, or an executable paper, thus creating elements that allow for inclusion, execution, and updates dynamically.

Experiment Reproduction Engine (Interface Tier). It provides a means for the re-execution and reproduction of an experiment by executing code fragments inserted in the manuscripts in digital format The experiment reproduction engine makes reproducible science more dynamic, since users can monitor the use and execution of each research object embedded in the experiment. It interacts with the reproducibility verifier and the validator modules. This engine allows for users to access experiment validation and verification forms using search parameters and input data already reported by the experiment author. The engine also allows for testing of new values to evaluate the experiment robustness.

Reproducibility Validator and Verifier (Controller Tier). This module contemplates the verification and validation activities to evaluate the experiment reproduction. Verification evaluates whether the produced results are correct, checking if they are equivalent or whether the differences between the produced data are values within an acceptable statistical margin. The validation mechanism evaluates if the methodology for obtaining the results was reproduced.

Research Object Reference Builder (Controller Tier). It links the textual elements of a scientific paper to research objects stored in files or databases. It receives a link request to an object through the executable paper editor and then requests the registration of this link to the experiment data manager. This association produces records that are stored in the provenance database. Some studies link the manuscript to research objects through annotation mechanisms in LaTeX documents to do the element association at runtime. Other studies present dynamic mechanisms for the re-execution of codes within the executable papers.

Research Objects Retrieval Engine (Controller Tier). It retrieves the elements that have to be exhibited by the reproducible experiment content viewer, based on the actors' requests and the selection rules. To display contents it is necessary to identify the license type related to each research object, as well as restrictions and rules associated with them. This engine aims at checking what distribution type of the research object is permitted (visualization, distribution, use, etc.) and also identifies what license type applies to each type of actor.

Licenses and Copyrights Manager (Controller Tier). This module identifies the license restrictions and copyrights related to the research objects. It can be invoked by the research object retrieval engine or the research object reference builder to present, respectively, a research object according to the license guidelines and copyright. It also records the correct authorship and license to an object when it is added to a reproducible experiment.

Software and Library Manager (Research Object Manager Tier). There are six software groups: basic, application, libraries, source code, script, and workflow. Each class has characteristics that are different from the others, and some are dependent on other software classes. All these classes need information about the hardware environment in which they were deployed, that is, which operational base was used to host it. Therefore, the first feature to be controlled by the software and library manager is the infrastructure information of the software deployment. In addition, it must identify the software and library dependencies, environment variables, and configuration parameters required for the software to run properly.

Hardware Environment Monitor (Research Object Manager Tier). This monitor identifies the architecture behind a reproducible experiment. Such information is generally related to the computer system and the storage infrastructure. E-Science experiments perform analyses on platforms that range from workstations to specialized high-performance computing infrastructures, such as clusters, grids, and clouds. Some experiments are based on physical computer system architectures, while other approaches use hardware virtualization, where the resource usage is managed by a hypervisor. The hardware environment monitor must collect information regarding processing (CPU), memory, hardware architecture (32, 64 bits), as well as data about network and connectivity. Furthermore, it should monitor issues related to data storage such as storage capacity, since scientific experiments can produce large amounts of data.

Notes and Documentation Manager (Research Object Manager Tier). It allows for the insertion of notes in research objects, thus allowing the scientist to associate reasoning and an interpretation regarding the use or production of a research object. In addition, it also allows for the inclusion of documents describing each infrastructure element and how they should be deployed and used. The notes and documents can be stored in files through the file system, and the links with research objects are registered in the database component.

Research Data Manager (Storage Tier). Stores the data used and produced during the experiment execution. There are four data types in the scientific environment, and each of these data should be stored at the most appropriate form based on its data structure requirements. As defined in the taxonomy, reproducible experiment data may be classified as primary, intermediate, final results, metadata, and data provenance. Research data is stored in databases or file systems, as well as in the provenance and metadata databases. The choice of the storage mechanism is oriented by the data characteristics to be stored, considering factors such as data size and the purpose of its use. It receives data of all the elements of the research object: manager, builder, retrieval engine, and identifier engine. The research data manager can be deployed in the cloud and benefit from cloud storage and DbaaS solutions.

Reference Builder (Storage Tier). For each research object type, there should be an association of a unique identification through interaction with the module research object identifier engine and should also be associated to a use license and authorship information, using the support of licenses and copyrights manager module. Identification can be based on established standards such as the digital object identifier (DOI) system [46]. The DOI represents the digital content identification on the network identifying abstract and digital and physical entities, managed by the federation of register agencies under policies and infrastructure provided by the DOI International Foundation [46]. This control helps in the correct identification of materials used to produce a result.

Reproducible Experiment Hosting Infrastructure (Storage Tier). The reproducible experiment with its research objects should be shared to the public through an accessible repository on the Internet, allowing for authors to centralize information about their research, interacting more efficiently with users interested in the published contents.

5.5 Survey on Approaches for Reproducible Science

There are several approaches to support experiment reproducibility. Depending on the level of reproducibility support, they may benefit from scientific workflows, provenance data gathering, and executable scientific papers. Many of these approaches are designed to use virtual machines, thus being suitable for their deployment in cloud computing environments, which is the focus of this chapter. Simmhan, Antoniu, and Goble [51] mention that clouds can play an important role in data-driven science and in special for reproducibility. In a talk on reproducibility of experiments in life sciences, Goble [25] explores issues involved in the development of technical and social infrastructures for reproducibility. In this talk, she also mentions that developing approaches for reproducibility is hard, high cost, and unrewarded blue-collared labor, and not every experiment is reproducible in the long term. Many experiments become less reproducible over time, even if using cloud environments.

In this section we survey some existing approaches to help in making an experiment reproducible. We group these approaches based on their reproducibility support level. The first group encompasses executable papers, which are mostly focused on reviewable experiments that might be also replicable, confirmed, and audited, but not necessarily fully reproducible. Executable papers are defined as a single published digital object that has both manuscript and all the code required to reproduce the results [32]. The main objective of an executable paper is to increase understanding and reproduction of electronic publications, allowing for readers and reviewers to interact, explore, and validate the experiments. The main approach examples are collage [44], SHARE [48], and paper-mache [6]. These last two are detailed in the following subsections.

The second group focuses on supporting reproducing the results in an operational environment different from the one it was originally obtained. They obtain environment information at a low level of execution, collecting data at the operating system level, e.g., the file system and program calls from the operating system. They provide for information and resources to enable the reproduction of experiments. CDE (*code, data, and environment*) [27], ReproZip [8], SciCumulus [45], and PASS (*provenance aware storage systems*) [39] are examples that gather data at the OS level.

The third group, similar to the second, also aims at reproducing experiments, but go one step further and use virtualization concepts to deploy an environment in the cloud that is equivalent to the environment where the experiment was originally executed. Systems from these three groups are detailed as following.

5.5.1 SHARE: Sharing Hosted Autonomous Research Environments

SHARE is a web application that enables the creation and sharing of executable scientific papers. The main motivations for developing SHARE were:

- Reduce installation or configuration difficulty to perform the computations on the input data;
- Minimize problems in obtaining software versions for implementation of all functions;
- Optimize process of downloading, installation, and configuration of each software used in scientific research, and
- Register and control properly the software license distribution adopted in the research.

SHARE claims that it is important that readers access the environment used to develop a research and all research objects (software, data, infrastructure, and operating environment) properly installed and configured. The approach proposes to link a digital product with a VM that is created, configured, and stored within the infrastructure where SHARE was deployed. SHARE supports *three* types of users [48]: authors, publishers, and readers. The authors create SHARE VMs with all elements used in the experiment within. Then, it associates the VM elements to a paper. A scientific paper is submitted to publishers and readers through a web browser. Each reproducible element is associated with a link that grants access to a VM.

SHARE gives the user the ability to interactively explore the equations, tables, and graphs of a paper. The VM is executed as the paper information is requested by the user. The SHARE VM infrastructure enables the experiments design that use high-performance computing strategies. In addition, SHARE stores incoming sessions of VMs through the *log* files.

5.5.2 Paper Mâché

Paper mâché is a management system that allows for exploring scientific papers in an interactive way, reproducing, and validating the results to test hypotheses [6]. It allows for creating a paper and submitting it to the reviewers, so they can explore and assess the content of experiments before publication. Once published, it allows for exploring, discussing, and commenting the authors' paper. Paper Mâché has three main elements in its architecture:

- Executable paper with textual content, images, audio, and movies;
- Comments containing the review and discussion on material published and shared; and
- The VM with the source code, executables, data, libraries, and encapsulated dependencies.

Using paper mâché, the paper content is created in traditional text editors, in formats *.doc or *.tex. The VM associated with the scientific paper is created according to hypervisor adopted by paper mâché. Therefore, the author must create a script to link the paper content published with the encapsulated components in the VM. This association allows for recovering and reproducing executable elements.

In paper mâché, the environment is encapsulated within the VM. The hypervisor used by the approach should ensure the VM retrieve, redeploy, and reproduce. This allows for reproducing and testing new values in the paper executable components and verifying that the expected results were produced. Paper mâché also allows for deploying experiments on VMs in cloud providers. Paper mâché authors' emphasize that cloud computing can provide the ability to test and interact with a range of supercomputer experiments, which is not possible with the current version.

5.5.3 CDE: Code, Data, and Environment

The CDE development (code, data, and environment) was motivated by scientific code distribution technical barriers that hindered scientific applications sharing. The CDE is an automatic deployment mechanism of source code, data, and computational environments used for execution of a program on x86-Linux in other machines x86-Linux. The CDE eliminates the need to install software from a source environment to a destination [28]. The CDE monitor system calls on files, code, data, and environment variables while running a program using the debugging tool called *ptrace*.[10,11]

The *ptrace* is a monitoring mechanism that creates a process called *tracer*. The *tracer* process monitors and controls the execution of another process called *tracee*. The *tracer* process monitors and analyzes the system call trail in the *tracee* execution capturing information about the process, registers, and memory uses of the *tracee* process. Monitoring is based on the PID number (OS process identifier) of tracee through the ptrace command. Hence, CDE encapsulates the ptrace tool in its implementation to allow the package creation with all elements raised during the execution of an application or command on a Linux operating system.

Figure 5.3 shows CDE architecture. In this context, a call is made to execute an application in Python[12] called *analise.py*. It is passed *seq1.fasta* as a parameter. The application call must be made through the command *cde* preceding the execution command. In this step, CDE is invoked to capture and encapsulate the elements used in the execution. It store the elements and dependencies identified by *ptrace* in a directory. Each element is copied to the CDE package directory (*CDE package*) like a unit to be shared.

To reproduce a research, users just need to acquire the CDE package of the experiment and run command *cde − exec* to unpack the experiment directory with

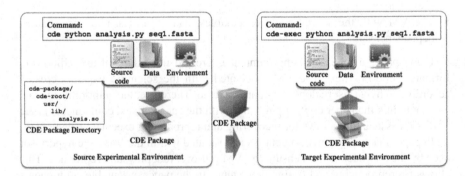

Fig. 5.3 Operation scheme CDE approach [28]

---

[10]http://linux.die.net/man/2/ptrace

[11]http://www.linuxjournal.com/article/6100

[12]https://www.python.org/

all elements used in original execution. The scientist can browse the experiment and reproduce it according to the original script [27]. The CDE is a good solution for experiment encapsulation allowing computer environment's portability and thus enabling scientific applications reproduction.

5.5.4   Reprozip

The Reprozip is a tool that packages necessary elements to reproduce the scientific research results oriented by provenance data [8]. The main objective is to share the experiment with reviewers and readers so that they can unpack it and reproduce it without the need to install additional software. The Reprozip combines CDE approach and virtual machines to generate computer system snapshots. It encapsulates only the elements used in the experiment execution. ReproZip is built on top of the VisTrails workflow system [37] to make workflows portable and reproducible in third-party infrastructure.

The Reprozip performs two main stages, the packaging of the computing environment and the subsequent unpack on a target computer. The packaging consisting of *three* steps: (1) capturing provenance data, (2) provenance analysis, and (3) packages generation. In the first step, the Reprozip uses *system trap* to get provenance. It orchestrates and captures the system call track execution of the execution process. The provenance is stored in a database managed by MongoDB.[13] In the analysis step, the Reprozip creates an experiment provenance tree. Each node of the tree represents an operating system process, and the edges between nodes represent the link of the parent process with child processes. This link allows to identify the resource dependencies with executable programs, input and output files. Finally, it creates a package with workflow, software, and input and output files used in the result derivation.

The Reprozip's deployment for reproduction consists of unpacking process that extracts the experiment package in a given directory and makes the configuration of programs, datasets, configuration parameters, and environment variable workflow [8]. The result of this process is the original environment recovery ready for experiment reproduction.

5.5.5   PASS: Provenance Aware Storage Systems

PASS [39] *provenance aware storage systems* is an approach for provenance processing and gathering in a VM with the Xen hypervisor. A PASS experiment is deployed and run on a set of guest virtual machines running under an operating system host. The PASS provenance mechanism is implemented on host system. It

---

[13]http://www.mongodb.org/

intercepts system calls made by guest virtual machines to the host [39], monitoring changes in the virtual machine file systems and storing this information in a provenance database.

The PASS environment consists of multiple virtual machines called domain (Dom). One of the virtual machines, called Dom0, has the controller function. It is responsible for virtual machine reporting and booting. The other virtual machines, called visitors, are named like DomU. Applications that make up the experiment are deployed on guest systems called DomU.

The system calls made from the guest virtual machine are intercepted by the interceptor module. It extracts information from the kernel data structures and moves on to the observer module. The observer module translates calls to provenance records, creating dependency relationships between files and processes. Then, the analyzer module eliminates duplicate records. The distributor module stores the object provenance in a log file within the file system, called Lasagna. The last component, called Waldo, gets the provenance records and stores in provenance base for future reference and information retrieval.

PASS is used for provenance query on low-level details and execution trails obtained during the execution. It is a good solution for applications requiring low-level details for validation and reproduction.

5.5.6 SciCumulus Workflow System

Workflow systems assist scientists to orchestrate a set of activities in a coherent flow. Most of the workflow system capture provenance data (metadata), but fail to store all produced data and programs used in the experiment. Provenance data alone is insufficient to allow for experiment reproduction. One advantage of SciCumulus (or simply SCC) [14] is that it is designed to execute in the cloud, i.e., all programs and data are deployed in the cloud to run the workflow. SCC orchestrates scientific workflow activity execution in a distributed set of virtual machines. Each virtual machine is associated with an image that contains all programs and data and can be deployed for reproduction in the future. The SCC offers a computing infrastructure to support parallel workflows with provenance capture in the cloud environment. Although SCC is not designed to be a scientific reproduction approach, it allows for encapsulating the computing infrastructure storage in a virtual machine in the cloud. This allows the computing environment sharing for other scientists interested in experiment results.

5.5.7 Reproducible Research in the Cloud

Several authors [1, 13, 33, 36] discuss the benefits of migrating experiments from workstations, clusters, and computational grid to the cloud. Cloud-computing features and resources may allow for fostering reproduction and motivating the approach development based on this paradigm. WSSE [17], Chef [36], and AMOS [54] are the most representative proposed approaches.

5.5.7.1 WSSE: Whole System Snapshot Exchange

The whole system snapshot exchange (WSSE) approach is a concept designed to treat reproductive problems related to computing infrastructure and storage of research objects. The WSSE proposes to generate digital data and source code snapshots to be produced and distributed within a cloud-computing provider [17]. The WSSE proposal is to use the cloud-based implementation of scientific experiment advantages with reproduction support through the definition of three layers: data, systems, and services.

In the data layer, the cloud can store and share large datasets with resources needed to process computations on this data. Generally, the size of datasets of scientific data may vary from gigabytes to several terabytes or more. In many cases it is not possible to copy these large file data from one computer to another easily and efficiently [17]. To avoid this problem, it is proposed to exchange data only within the cloud-computing environment.

In system layer, the computers used in the result production are copied in their entirety, including the operating system, software, and database, for VM to be exchanged with other researchers [17]. This process allows the researchers to get exact replicas of the computer used for the result production. The service layer allows computations deployed in the cloud that can be accessed by external applications generating reproduction solution-oriented services. The data and systems associated with scientific experiments can be stored in the cloud VM preserving the environment used in the original experiment execution.

5.5.7.2 Chef

Klinginsmith et al. [36] propose an approach called Chef to deploy virtual clusters for reproducibility in clouds. In the approach, the computational resources are divided into two layers: (1) infrastructure and (2) software. The first layer manages the IaaS (Infrastructure as a Service), communicating with the cloud provider's API to instantiate VMs, configure the network, and allocate storage space. The second layer manages the software on the VM. Both layers are managed by Chef configuration management tool. Chef is used to automate the virtual cluster configuration and the necessary software installation to experiment reproduction in the similar environment.

Chef was implemented in AMIs (Amazon machine image) on Amazon EC2 (elastic cloud compute) and EMIs (eucalyptus machine image) on FutureGrid Eucalyptus Clouds.[14] It is necessary to instantiate, configure, and register the VM

---

[14]https://www.eucalyptus.com/eucalyptus-cloud/iaas

manually and also install a Chef client to assist VM setup process. The result is the possibility of virtual cluster replication on different cloud providers using a software layer in common [36].

According to Chef designers, cloud computing can be used to reproduce experiments and applications of e-Science researchers in a simple way. This is due to the cloud providing the necessary infrastructure for the data storage and management, as well as computing power to transform data in scientific knowledge.

5.5.7.3 Reproducibility with AMOS

Strijkers et al. [54] presents an e-Science tool that can be used to pack codes, software, and scientific experiment parameters to design electronic papers. The authors proposed to preserve the dependencies in an executable paper to enable the experiment reproduction. The AMOS use scientific workflow as a way to define the experiment execution and cloud-computing IaaS as a platform to encapsulate the code dependencies and software in VMs.

The AMOS system proposed by Strijkers et al. uses a VM containing a set of tools previously installed to implement a mechanism which initializes and configures VMs on demand [54]. The goal is that VMs templates can be recreated or cloned for experiment reproduction. Thus researchers can create various templates and store them in an executable paper database. Data and application execution management process VMs are instrumented by a workflow agent (WFA) or a workflow system.

AMOS' developers argue that code and data encapsulation in VMs preserves the experimental environment, however, emphasize that this compatibility is dependent on the virtualization software. They highlighted that still there is no effective solution based on metadata and source data to increase the executable papers capacity; therefore, the key would be the infrastructure virtualization.

5.5.7.4 PDIFF: Using Provenance and Data Differencing for Workflow Reproducibility

Missier et al. [42] propose PDIFF, an algorithm that uses a comparison of workflow provenance traces collected from workflows executed in virtual machines to check if an experiment has been reproduced. PDIFF runs on top of e-Science Central [31] that is a workflow system that can be deployed on clouds. e-Science central stores all provenance data in a VM with a non-relational graph database, called Neo4j (www. neo4j.org). The provenance database used by e-Science Central contains both traces and the provenance for other items of e-Science Central. PDIFF then transverses the graph in Neo4J and checks if there is a divergence between two workflow executions by comparing their associated provenance traces. By using PDIFF along with e-Science Central, scientists may have the perception that the challenges in reproducibility of results can be easily overcome.

5.5.8   Final Considerations

The taxonomy presented in Sect. 5.2 provides several important classes to describe the terms involved with reproducible science. In this subsection, we classify each of the surveyed approaches following the proposed taxonomy classes. Table 5.1 presents the main characteristics of each approach. In general, the surveyed approaches focus on a reduced set of features from each group of reproducibility levels to address a specific aspect. For example, some approaches focus on validation and verification methods for the evaluation; agent support, reproduction methodology, etc. It is worth noticing that all approaches surveyed in this section support the computing and storage infrastructure architectural features. All of them provide some support for the hardware infrastructure aspects as computing and storage.

5.6   Conclusions

As discussed in this chapter, computing has become fundamental for science development in various scientific application domains. It helps science to become reproducible accelerating the productivity of scientists and new discoveries. However, reproducible science is an important, yet open, problem, despite current efforts found in the literature.

Clouds can play an important role to achieve reproducibility in science. However, just having the technology infrastructure is not enough, there are issues on how to pack the experiments, what to register, how to help on reproducing with different parameters, etc.

Therefore, an important step toward reproducible science is to define terminology standards and a framework to guide the construction of new solutions. Taxonomies are already used in several domains to classify information considering some preestablished aspects. This can be applied in several knowledge areas to assist in the classification of concepts in a domain. This chapter presents a compilation of concepts related to reproducibility in e-Science, which were used to guide the comparison of existing systems for reproducible research using clouds. This compilation evolved into designing a taxonomy, proposed in Sect. 5.2, which drove the design of a reference architecture that was used to evaluate the state-of-the-art approaches in supporting reproducible science.

The reference architecture, proposed in this chapter, represents a generic representation that can be adopted to guide the construction of new reproducibility approaches benefiting from clouds. The architecture is divided into tiers that can be deployed in the cloud. The architecture reflects functions of particular classes from the taxonomy. Therefore, the architecture helps in identifying a list of functions and points out possible interactions and interfaces between modules.

Table 5.1 Comparison of surveyed approaches

Approach	Agent	Data	Evaluation	Methodology	Setting	Software
SHARE	Author, reader, reviewer	Primary, final, intermediary, metadata	Verification, validation	Repeatability	Environment, variable	Application, basic, library, script, source code
Paper Mache	Author, reader, reviewer	Primary, final, intermediary	Verification	Reproducibility	Environment, variable	Application, basic, library, script, source code
CDE	Author, reader	Primary, final, intermediary	Verification	Reproducibility	Environment, variable	Application, basic, library
ReproZip	Author, publisher, reader, reviewer	Primary, final, intermediary, metadata, provenance	Verification, validation	Reproducibility	Environment, variable, parameter	Application, basic, library, script, source code, workflow
PASS	Author, reader	Primary, final, intermediary, metadata	Verification, validation	Reproducibility	Environment, variable	Application, basic, library
SciCumulus	Author, reader	Primary, final, intermediary, metadata, provenance	Verification, validation	Reproducibility	Environment, variable, parameter	Application, basic, library, script, source code, workflow
WSSE	Author, reader	Primary, final, intermediary	Verification	Reproducibility	Environment, variable	Application, basic, library, script, source code
Chef	Author, reader	Primary, final, intermediary	Verification	Reproducibility	Environment, variable	Application, basic, library, script, source code
AMOS	Author, reader	Primary, final, intermediary, metadata, provenance	Verification, validation	Reproducibility	Environment, variable, parameter	Application, basic, library, script, source code, workflow
PDIFF	Author, reader	Primary, final, intermediary, metadata, provenance	Verification, validation	Reproducibility	Environment, variable, parameter	Application, basic, library, script, source code, workflow

Despite the current solutions that address making an experiment reproducible in clouds, there are still several open problems. It is necessary to consider issues of presentation and hosting of executable papers, references, edition and construction of research objects, authorship management, licensing, rights of copying and distribution of research objects, version control, unique identification, documentation and annotation management, as well as obtaining the necessary infrastructure for the reproduction.

Therefore, this chapter is an important step to organize the involved concepts in a taxonomy and discuss how clouds can foster reproducibility based on an architectural framework to guide the construction of new cloud-based solutions.

Acknowledgements This work was partially funded by Brazilian agencies CAPES, FAPERJ, and CNPq.

References

1. Armbrust M, Armando F, Rean G et al (2010) A view of cloud computing. Commun ACM 53(4):50–58
2. Baggerly KA, Berry DA (2012) Reproducible research, Amstatnews: The Membership Magazine of the American Statistical Association
3. Barga R, Gannon D (2006) Scientific versus business workflows. In: Workflows for e-Science: scientific workflows for grids. Springer, pp 09–16
4. Belhajjame K, Roure DD (2012) Goble CA research object management: opportunities and challenges. In: Proceedings of the 2012 ACM conference on computer supported cooperative work – CSCW'2012. ACM, New York
5. Berriman GB, Groom SL (2013) (2011) How will astronomy archieves survive the data tsunami? ACM Queue 9:1–8
6. Brammer GR, Crosby RW, Matthews SJ et al (2011) Paper Mâché: creating dynamic reproducible science. Proc Comput Sci 4:658–667
7. Cao B, Plale B, Subramanian G, Robertson Ed, Simmhan YL (2009) Provenance information model of Karma version 3. SERVICES I 2009:348–351
8. Chirigati F, Shasha D, Freire J (2013) Packing experiments for sharing and publication. In: Proceedings of the 2013 ACM SIGMOD international conference on management of data – SIGMOD '13, pp 977–980
9. Cooper MH (2010) Charting a course for software licensing and distribution. SIGUCCS 2010:153–156
10. da Cruz SMS, Barros PM, Bisch PM, Machado Campos ML, Mattoso M (2008) Provenance services for distributed workflows. CCGRID 2008:526–533
11. Davidson SB, Freire J (2008) Provenance and scientific workfows: challenges and opportunities. In: Proceedings of the 2008 ACM SIGMOD international conference on management of data – SIGMOD '08. pp 1345–1350
12. Deelman E, Berriman B, Chervenak A et al (2010) Metadata and provenance management. In: Shoshani A, Rotem D (eds) Scientific data management: challenges, technology and deployment. Chapman & Hall/CRC, BocaRaton
13. Deelman E, Singh G, Livny M, et al (2008) The cost of doing science on the cloud: the montage example. In: Proceedings of the 2008 ACM/IEEE conference on supercomputing, SC '08, pp 1–12

14. de Oliveira D, Ocaña KACS, Baião FA, Mattoso M (2012) A provenance-based adaptive scheduling heuristic for parallel scientific workflows in clouds. J Grid Comput 10(3): 521–552
15. Donoho DL (2010) An invitation to reproducible computational research. Biostatistics 3:376–388
16. Donoho D, Maleki A, Rahman NI et al (2009) Reproducible research in computational harmonic analysis. Comput Sci Eng 11:8–18
17. Dudley JT, Butte AJ (2010) In silico research in the era of cloud computing. Nat Biotechnol 28:1181–185
18. Firtina C, Alkan C (2016) On genomic repeats and reproducibility. Bioinformatics 32(15):2243–2247
19. Freire J, Bonnet P, Shasha D (2012) Computational reproducibility: state-of-the-art, challenges, and database research opportunities. In: Proceedings of the 2012 ACM SIGMOD international conference on management of data – SIGMOD'12. ACM, New York, pp 593–596
20. Freire J, Fuhr N, Rauber A (2016) Reproducibility of data-oriented experiments in e-Science (Dagstuhl Seminar 16041). Dagstuhl Rep 6(1):108–159
21. Gavish M, Donoho D (2011) A universal identifier for computational results. In: International conference on computational science, vol 4, pp 637–647
22. Gillam L, Antonopoulos N (2010) Cloud computing: principles, systems and applications. Springer, London
23. Goble C (2012) The reality of reproducibility in computational science: reproduce? repeat? rerun? and does it matter. Keynotes and panels. In: 8th IEEE international conference on e-Science, vol 327, pp 415–416
24. Gray J (2009) Jim Gray on eScience: a transformed scientific method. In: Hey T, Tansley S, Tolle K (ed) The fourth paradigm data-intensive scientific discovery. Microsoft Research, Redmond
25. Goble CA (2013) Results may vary: reproducibility, open science and all that Jazz. LISC@ISWC 2013:1
26. Greenberg J (2002) Metadata and the world wide web. Encycl Libr Inf Sci 72:244–261
27. Guo P (2012) CDE: a tool for creating portable experimental software packages. Comput Sci Eng 14:32–35
28. Guo PJ, Engler D (2011) CDE: using system call interposition to automatically create portable software packages. In: Proceedings of the 2011 USENIX conference on USENIX annual technical conference, USENIXATC'11, pp 21–21
29. Guo PJ, Seltzer M (2012) BURRITO: wrapping your lab notebook in computational infrastructure. In: Proceedings of 4th USENIX workshop on the theory and practice of provenance (TaPP'12)
30. Hanson B, Sugden A, Alberts B (2011) Making data maximally available. Science 331:649
31. Hiden H, Woodman S, Watson P, Cala J (2013) Developing cloud applications using the e-science central platform. R Soc Lond Philos Trans A Math Phys Eng Sci
32. Hinsen K (2011) A data and code model for reproducible research and executable. Proc Comput Sci 4:579–588
33. Howe B (2012) Virtual appliances, cloud computing, and reproducible research. Comput Sci Eng 14:36–41
34. Juve G et al (2013) Comparing futuregrid, Amazon EC2, and open science grid for scientific workflows. Comput Sci Eng 15:20–29
35. Karpathiotakis M, Branco M, Alagiannis I, Ailamaki (2014) A adaptive query processing on RAW data. Proc VLDB Endow 7:1119–1130
36. Klinginsmith J, Mahoui M, Wu YM (2011) Towards reproducible escience in the cloud. In: IEEE third international conference on cloud computing technology and science (CloudCom). pp 582–586
37. Koop D, Santos E, Mates P et al. (2011) Provenance-based infrastructure to support the life cycle of executable papers. Procedia Computer Science 4:648–657

38. Krishnamurthi S, Vitek J (2015) The real software crisis: repeatability as a core value. Communications da ACM 58:34–36
39. Macko P, Chiarini M, Seltzer M (2011) Collecting provenance via the Xen hypervisor. In: Proceedings of 3rd USENIX workshop on the theory and practice of provenance (TaPP '11), pp 1–15
40. Marinho A, Murta L, Werner C, Braganholo V, da Cruz SMS, Ogasawara ES, Mattoso M (2012) ProvManager: a provenance management system for scientific workflows. Concurr Comput Pract Exp 24(13):1513–1530
41. Mcnutt M (2014) Journals unite for reproducibility. Science 346:679
42. Missier P, Woodman S et al (2013) Provenance and data differencing for workflow reproducibility analysis. Concurr Comput Pract Exp 28:995–1015
43. Moreau L, Groth P (2013) Provenance: an introduction to PROV. Synthesis lectures on the semantic web: theory and technology. Morgan & Claypool, San Rafael
44. Nowakowski P, Ciepiela E, Harezlak D et al (2011) The collage authoring environment. In: Executable paper grand challenge international conference on computational science, ICCS 2011, vol 4, pp 608–617
45. Oliveira D, Ogasawara E, Baião F, Mattoso M (2010) SciCumulus: a lightweigh cloud middleware to explore many task computing paradigm in scientific workflows. In: IEEE 3rd international conference on cloud computing
46. Paskin N (2010) Digital Object Identifier (DOI) system. In: Bates MJ, Maack MN (eds) Encyclopedia of library and information sciences, 3rd edn, chap. 157. Taylor & Francis, pp 1586–1592
47. Peng R (2009) Reproducible research and biostatistic. Biostatistics 3:405–408
48. Pieter Van Gorp SM (2011) SHARE: a web portal for creating and sharing executable research papers. Int Conf Comput Sci 4:1–9
49. Schwab M, Karrenbach M, Claerbout J (2000) Making scientific computations reproducible. Comput Sci Eng 2:61–67
50. Simmhan YL, Plale B, Gannon D (2005) A survey of data provenance in e-Science. SIGMOD Rec 34:31–36
51. Simmhan Y, Ramakrishnan L, Antoniu G, Goble CA (2016) Cloud computing for data-driven science and engineering. Concur Comput Pract Exp 28(4):947–949
52. Stodden V (2009) The legal framework for reproducible scientific research: licensing and copyright. Comput Sci Eng 11:35–40
53. Stodden V, Bailey DH, Borwein J et al (2013) Setting the default to reproducible: reproducibility in computational and experimental mathematics. Technical report, ICERM workshop reproducibility in computational and experimental mathematics
54. Strijkers R, Cushin R, Vasyunin D (2011) Toward executable scientific publications. Proc Comput Sci 4:707–715
55. Szalay AS, Blakeley JA (2009) Gray's laws: database-centric computing in science. In: Hey T, Tansley S, Tolle KM (ed) The fourth paradigm. Microsoft research, Redmond, pp 5–11
56. Taylor I, Deelman E, Gannon DB et al (2006) Workfows for e-Science: scientific workfows for grids. Springer, New York/Secaucus
57. Vitek J, Kalibera T (2012) R3: repeatability, reproducibility and rigor. SIGPLAN 47:30–36
58. Yogesh L. Simmhan, Beth Plale, Gannon D (2008) Karma2: provenance management for data-driven workflows. Int J Web Serv Res 5(2):1–22

Chapter 6
Big Data Analytics in Healthcare: A Cloud-Based Framework for Generating Insights

Ashiq Anjum, Sanna Aizad, Bilal Arshad, Moeez Subhani, Dominic Davies-Tagg, Tariq Abdullah, and Nikolaos Antonopoulos

6.1 Introduction

With exabytes of data being generated from genome sequencing, a whole new science behind genomics big data has emerged. Adding to that, the recent advances in storage and processing technologies have enabled the generation, storage, retrieval, and processing of exabytes of genomics and healthcare data in electronic form. As technology improves, the cost of sequencing a human genome is going down considerably, and, in turn has increased the number of genomes being sequenced. Handling huge amounts of genomics data along with a vast variety of clinical data using existing frameworks and techniques has become a challenge.

There is a wide interest in genomics data because it can allow meaningful insights to be generated. These insights could range from a variety of things including genomics research as well as more practical uses such as personalized medicine for a particular genome. Genomics is producing data sizes of 2–40 EB/year [43] which is stored in local databases or in cloud storage. Cloud computing is used for storage, distribution, and processing of this data so that applications can run on remote machines that already have access to data ([43]).

A data platform that integrates genomics/healthcare data while enabling quick and efficient analysis would allow extraction of practical insights in a short frame of time. Developing such a platform poses a number of challenges on its own.

A. Anjum (✉) • S. Aizad • B. Arshad • M. Subhani • D. Davies-Tagg • T. Abdullah
N. Antonopoulos
College of Engineering and Technology, University of Derby, Kedleston Road, DE22 1GB,
Derby, UK
e-mail: A.Anjum@derby.ac.uk; S.Aizad@derby.ac.uk; B.Arshad@derby.ac.uk;
M.Subhani@derby.ac.uk; D.Davies-Tagg@derby.ac.uk; T.Abdullah@derby.ac.uk;
N.Antonopoulos@derby.ac.uk

© Springer International Publishing AG 2017   153
N. Antonopoulos, L. Gillam (eds.), *Cloud Computing*, Computer Communications
and Networks, DOI 10.1007/978-3-319-54645-2_6

These challenges relate to integrating genomics and clinical data sources, ensuring consistency of the integrated data, and developing a big data platform that stores and manages the integrated data. An overview of these challenges and a brief description of the proposed framework are provided in the remainder of this section.

With respect to integration of big data, it is imperative to maintain the consistency of data between the data sources and the data warehouse. Since the data is in the magnitude of exabytes, the issue converges to big data analytics. Infrastructures such as that provided over cloud are required to ensure that the consistency is maintained between the data sources and the warehouse. In a clinical information management environment, data consists of heterogeneous data sources with multitude of data types at distributed locations. Clinicians and scientists generate data which is individually captured at disparate locations and brought together to a warehouse for reporting, decision support, and data analysis. This data needs to be correctly integrated in order to ensure the consistency and coherence of the system at large. Any inconsistency may result in breaking the data warehouse, which in turn would affect the reports being generated (examples include quarterly comparisons and trends to daily data analysis) and biostatistical analysis among other things. Therefore, there is a need for structured migration and integration of data between the sources and the data warehouse to ensure that the integrity of the warehouse can be maintained. In such an environment, coherence and consistency of data is imperative in order to protect the integrity of the warehouse. Since the data from heterogeneous sources is in exabytes, it is essential to provide a scalable environment for clinical analytics. A possible solution is the provision of a scalable environment for clinical data integration and system integrity based on graphs. The infrastructure provided for such an environment needs to take the frequent use of data into account. Large-scale graph processing systems such as Giraph [7] and GraphLab [25] provide support for data consistency by providing configurable consistency models.

The infrastructure of the system should be such that it should allow frequently used data to be quickly retrieved when required, whereas the data which is not in much use should be allowed to reside in the system. Technologies such as Hadoop make storing a large scale of data trivial, but Hadoop by itself is often not an ideal platform for working with data and performing the levels of complex analysis and interactive querying often afforded to data warehouses [10, 42]. Thus, in order to store huge amounts of data in a cost-effective and time-efficient manner and deliver a high standard of analytics performance, Hadoop's scalability may be used to accommodate storing data. On the other hand, there is a need to maintain existing scale-up data warehouses and analytics environments to provide the fast and efficient analysis people expect. But using both technologies can only work if we move data between environments when required.

Generating insights from the integrated data is only possible after developing suitable infrastructure for storing and retrieving the data. Analyzing this data is a user-driven and iterative nontrivial task. In a lot of cases, the data needs to be revisited several times in order to get the required insights. Different challenges and their solutions are discussed.

This chapter proposes a cloud-based framework for integrating genomics/healthcare data in a big data platform which would enable users to generate meaningful insights in their domain. The platform provides a solution to the challenges discussed above. The rest of the chapter is organized as follows: Section 6.2 introduces genomics and clinical data sets. Section 6.3 explains the integration of these data sets. An approach for maintaining data consistency during and after the integration is explained in Sect. 6.4. The infrastructure for storing the data is explained in Sect. 6.5, whereas Sect. 6.6 explains the data analytics approaches for generating insights from the data, and Sect. 6.7 concludes the chapter.

6.2 Genomics and Clinical Data

The cloud-based data analytics platform focuses on integrating the genomics and clinical data sets and on generating insights from the integrated data. It is important to understand these data sets before introducing the cloud-based data analytics platform.

6.2.1 Genomics Data

The genetic makeup of an organism is responsible for coding its different characteristics. A complete set of genetic information is contained in the genome, which consist of genes. The genes are a sequence of four different molecules known as nucleotide bases: adenine (A), guanine (G), thymine (T), and cytosine (C). Different combinations and frequency of these nucleotides generate a huge variety of genes within a genome. Understanding the constitution of these genes was a mystery until development of sequencing methods. The 1970s and 1980s saw manual DNA sequencing methods such as Maxam-Gilbert sequencing [28] and Sanger sequencing [39]. Automated sequencing methods such as shotgun sequencing were introduced in the 1990s. Over the next decade, scientists were able to sequence unicellular and multicellular organisms using these methods. It wasn't until 2001 that the human genome was completely sequenced. By 2005, next-generation sequence (NGS) technologies [30] were introduced.

Before sequencing, other techniques such as genome-wide association studies between thousands of individuals were used because genome sequencing was an unthinkable thing to do. However, as technologies advanced, the sequencing market has become very competitive in recent years. Many platforms, such as Illumina [1], 454 Life Sciences [2], and Complete Genomics [3], to name a few, are available commercially for research and clinical use.

Sequencing is now the first step for research investigating the genome at the basic level. Genome sequencing technology takes a sample of the genetic material in a test

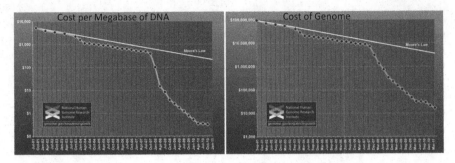

Fig. 6.1 Cost per raw megabase of DNA sequence and genome over the years. Published by National Human Genome Research Institute (NHGRI) (National Human Genome Research Institute [31])

tube and converts it to a string of As, Gs, Ts, and Cs representing the genome and stores it as a text file. A human genome consists of three billion bases. The size of a text file containing these is, on average, 6×10^9 bits.

As the cost of sequencing is decreasing (Fig. 6.1.), more and more genomics data is becoming readily available sparking several initiatives such as 1000 Genomes Project (1000 Genomes Project Consortium [4]) and the 100,000 Genome Project [11]. One of the aims of initiatives like these is to discover medical insights especially for more serious diseases such as cancer.

6.2.2 Clinical Data

Clinical data sets are generated during the course of ongoing patient care or as part of a clinical trial program. Major sources include electronic health records, claims data, disease registries, health surveys, clinical trials data, and administrative data. These are a vital source for health and medical research.

6.3 Data Integration

Data integration is the first challenge while developing a cloud-based data analytics platform. The data sources in clinical research domain are diversified, such as health records, clinical trials, disease records, etc. On the other hand, the genomics data sets are generally very data intensive such as genome sequences, variants, annotations and gene expressions data sets, etc. Due to the massive size of genomics data sets, the problem of integration enters into the domain of big data problems. Integrating these data intensive genomics sources with a set of diversified clinical sources is a considerable challenge that chiefly implies building storage capable of containing heterogeneous data types.

The clinical data ranges from patients' health records, diagnostic test results including laboratory reports and imaging scans, disease history, to hospital administration, and finance data. These data sets are captured in different repositories, such as health records maintained by each hospital or clinical trials conducted by state or different pharma or nonprofit organizations. The clinical data sets within these repositories are comprised of a large variety of parameters within a single study, and then there are further variations among parameters across different studies, as per the requirement of underlined research. Integrating this large variety of parameters of various data types across multiple studies is a challenging problem in itself because the integrated clinical data should have an intuitional output.

The next challenge is to integrate these parameters with genomics data sets. Traditionally, the information about genomics is not captured in the clinical data sets. Therefore, the genomics data is only available from separate genomics sources, mainly the repositories such as NCBI, Ensembl, or 1000 Genomes Project [4]. These data types are, therefore, different from those of clinical data sets. Hence, in order to integrate them with clinical data sets, the challenge is to make the data types compatible with each other so that they can be consolidated within a single warehouse.

Combining data sets from different clinical sources with genomics data can help understanding a clinical problem at a deeper level by empowering it with genomics background information. This big data integration may help to delve into genetic background of clinical problems, which will ultimately aid various users of these data sets. The major benefit, that can be foreseen from clinical and genomics data integration, will be to design personalized treatments for patients. Pharmacogenomics industry can also gain the advantage to provide more personalized solutions to healthcare, such as designing drugs with improved efficacy. Researchers from both clinical and genomics domains can also use the integrated data to discover the insights of complicated biological problems, such as finding new biomarkers. Hence, it can be estimated that data integration could help every academic or industrial institution related to these dimensions of medical science.

There exist some clinical data integration solutions, such as those provided by SAS [40], Edifecs [13], Lumeris [26], etc., but they are only focused on data management and administration purposes and are not targeted for clinical research. These solutions target combining various clinical data sets from different sources and providing them from a single platform. However, there are no solutions for clinical and genomics data integration available hitherto. Due to the absence of any data model that can accommodate both clinical and genomics data sets, there is a need to design and construct such a data model which provides a single platform access to both domains.

In the last decade, increasing trend has been observed in this direction of research. Researchers have studied and proposed various integration models for integrating multi-omics data. The two most common approaches that can be found in literature are multistage analysis and meta-dimensional analysis.

Multistage analysis is a stepwise or hierarchical analysis method. It helps to reduce search space by stage-wise analysis [35]. It essentially analyzes and integrates only two data types at a time while analyzing across the data space. Triangle method is the most common method under this approach which has been widely used for association studies. This method is more commonly used for SNP (single nucleotide polymorphism) associations with expression data and genes themselves [21, 35]. Some clinical phenotypes can be a result of interaction between different genes and multiple clinical parameters. Due to step-wise analysis, this approach cannot capture those phenotypes which are determined by factors acting from various sources. It is a robust and rather simple approach; however, it is not recommended when multiple different sources are required to be integrated [16, 35].

Meta-dimensional studies involve simultaneous analysis of all the data sources to produce complex models [35]. There are various methods under this approach, each of which is based on a different data model. The approach can be selected according to the underlining research goals. Either the multiple data sets are integrated prior to building a common model on them, or an individual model is built on each data set before integrating them as illustrated in Fig. 6.2. Bayesian networks and neural networks have been more commonly observed in the integration-based research [8, 14]. Meta-dimensional approach facilitates the capability to search across various data types among multiple data sets. This vast search capability aids to detect those phenotypic traits which are caused by mutual interaction of multiple factors from different clinical and genomics sources. Although this integration using meta-

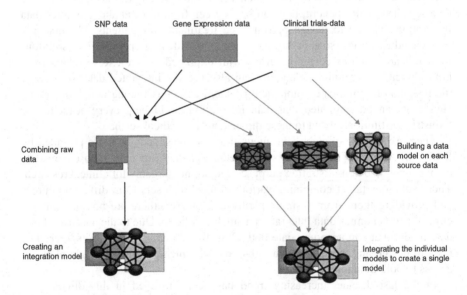

Fig. 6.2 An illustration of meta-dimensional approach

dimensional approach leads to rather complex and less robust models, it helps to search across a wider spectrum of data types [16, 35].

Due to the huge size of genomics data sets, and large variability of clinical parameters, it is not viable to integrate all parameters. Only those parameters should be integrated which may provide deeper intuition after integration. Most researchers have identified gene expression data and SNP data sets to be most relevant to integrate with the clinical data. Since determining the gene expression of SNPs can help to find out ultimate effects of a gene on a phenotype, therefore, these parameters have been widely seen to be integrated with clinical data in research [21, 24, 32, 35]. For future prospects, the research can be further extended to incorporate additional genomics parameters for integration, such as annotations data.

A promising solution to integrate the clinical and genomics data will be to design a relational data model based on meta-dimensional approach and implement it within a data warehouse. Since meta-dimensional approach provides a wider search spectrum, therefore, this approach seems more promising to be implemented for clinical and genomics data integration where a wide variety of parameters and large data sets are required to be integrated. Out of various meta-dimensional approaches, graph-based models seem more promising such as Bayesian networks [14, 18]. A probabilistic schema can be designed to implement on this data model. Some previous work shows that star-based schema can be designed for biomedical data [38, 46]. These schema designs can be adopted and modified to meet the requirements of the data sets and data warehouse under consideration. The performance and scalability of the integration model will be a critical factor to be controlled in this case. If the model is not capable of scaling to larger data sets, or it fails to provide same performance with larger data sets, then such a model will not be sustainable for a futuristic model.

6.4   Data Consistency

Ensuring consistency of integrated data is a crucial part of the big data analytics platform. Data coming from heterogeneous sources requires to be effectively integrated to ensure the coherence of the source data and the warehouse [38]. A change in one of the data sources not only affects the data in that data source but also affects the interrelationships between the multiple data sources. As the structure of the data warehouse is defined based on the structure of the individual data sources and based on the interrelationships between the sources, a single change has the potential to significantly impact the warehouse. More importantly, the data in the warehouse may not be consistent with the data in the data sources when a change occurs in the data source. This in turn means that the inconsistent changes might result in breaking the data warehouse. Evolution of clinical data results is one such example of inconsistent source change that needs to be reflected in the data warehouse. Since the data from these sources is of the magnitude of petabytes, the challenge of data consistency emerges as a part of the big data domain. Furthermore in context of big data applications, it is imperative to maintain data consistency across the entire spectrum of application to ensure correct results and traceability of individual elements in the system.

One of the prime issues in an evolving data warehouse environment is the dynamic nature of sources. The evolving nature of sources can lead to breaking the data warehouse which is a major issue in maintaining data consistency. Inconsistent changes can lead to generation of inaccurate reports such as those based on personalized patient analysis further leading to incorrect diagnosis. In order to prevent the system from breaking due to inconsistent changes, this endeavor aims to explain a possible solution to ensure consistency between the heterogeneous data sources and the clinical data warehouse. As explained in the previous section, once the data has been integrated, consistency mechanisms need to ensure that the sources and data warehouse are consistent and reflects the evolving data from clinical data sources.

In order to prevent the breaking of data warehouse from the evolving changes in the data sources, a possible solution is the use of graphs to ensure the coherence and consistency of data between the sources and the warehouse. Graphs can scale well to represent millions of entities in a clinical domain [36] thus allowing to ensure the scalability of the system. This is of particular interest in the domain of clinical data since integrating data from disparate sources will be of a much higher magnitude compared to the data coming from sources. Graphs are governed by graph models that allow a flexible and uniform representation of data originating from heterogeneous sources. This study aims to investigate suitable graph data models for accurate representation of data both at the source and data warehouse level. Furthermore, graph models provide the ability to predict functional relationships between heterogeneous data sources in order to ensure the correctness of source data with respect to the data warehouse. Thus, the need for a scalable environment for clinical analytics arises to ensure the integrity of a data warehouse without compromising the integrity of the clinical data warehouse. Existing state-of-the-art graph analytical systems do not fully encompass the needs for such a system.

In conjunction with source data, another key component in a data warehouse environment is metadata [17]. Metadata describes the context in which the data was collected and hence means to query the sources. Since the data comes from distributed sources, a lot of research deals with capturing metadata at the source level. Any change occurring at the source needs to be reflected in the metadata repository by updating it, leading to generation of new metadata. Both the updated and prior metadata are essential to aid in the replication and integration of sources. For the purpose of our research work, we will be looking at the metadata repository known as Semantics Manager [5] by Akana. Semantics Manager enables enterprises to define, understand, use, and exchange data by managing standards and metadata as organizational assets.

Several approaches have been investigated for clinical data integration that help to ensure data consistency such as integration engines [19, 45] or ontology-based data integration [20]. Integration engines provide a useful way of solving the basic communication problems between systems, but they do nothing to address true integration of information particularly in the context of data consistency [19, 45]. This approach works well and has been effective, but when the number of possible interactions between systems increases, the limitations of scalability become apparent. The use of graph-based integration of data being generated from multiple data sources is a viable option to address this issue [36].

Graphs [34, 36] are particularly useful for the description and analysis of interactions and relationships in a clinical domain. Graphs provide useful features such as analytical flexibility, in particular to evaluate relationships, integration of data, and comparison of results, to name a few. Graphs are currently being used to analyze social networks, knowledge bases, biological networks and protein synthesis, etc. [36]. A graph consists of a set of nodes and a set of edges that connect the nodes. The nodes are the entities of interest, and the edges represent relationships between the entities. Edges can be assigned weights, directions, and types. This is particularly useful in a clinical domain, the directions in edges help to represent causality between nodes, while the edges themselves can be annotated to represent the relationship between entities.

In order to ensure that the changes have been integrated consistently, source graphs need to be correctly replicated. This leads to the need to investigate and implement models that allow quick generation, integration, and replication of graphs so that the source data can be quickly and effectively integrated. Furthermore, in order to replicate and integrate graphs, powerful graph models such as the property graph model [6], Bayesian networks [33], or Markov models [33] are required. These graph models allow efficient inference of clinical data [33] essential to determine relationships between disparate clinical data sources. Graph models can be divided into two classes: undirected and directed graph models. Markov models [33] are an example of undirected graph model, while property graph model is an example of directed graph model. Bayesian networks can accommodate a variety of knowledge sources and data types; they are computationally expensive and difficult to explore previously unknown network. Bayesian networks do not have feedback loops due to the acyclic nature of Bayesian network graphs. In contrast to Bayesian networks, property graph model [6] represents data as a directed multigraph consisting of finite (and mutable) set of nodes and edges. Both vertices and edges can have assigned properties (attributes) which can be understood as simple name-value pairs, shown in Fig. 6.3. A dedicated property can serve as a unique identifier for vertices and edges. In addition to this, a type property can be used to represent the semantic type of the respective vertex or edge. Properties of vertices and edges are not necessarily determined by the assigned type and can therefore vary between vertices or edges of the same type. Vertices can be connected via different edges as long as they have different types or identifiers. The Property graph model [6] not only offers schema flexibility but also permits managing and processing data and metadata jointly. Graphs are generated by the graph engine based on the graph models.

Fig. 6.3 Property graph
model (Property Graph
Model [6])

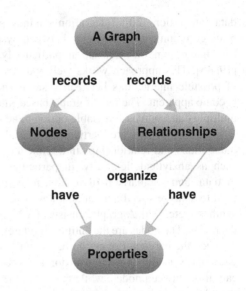

The property graph model provides the following key characteristics that differ from the classical relational data model:

- Relationships as first-class citizens – With the property graph model, relationships between entities are promoted as first-class citizens of the model with unique identity, semantic type, and possibly additional attributes.
- Increased schema flexibility – In a property graph model, edges are specified at the instance and not at the class level, i.e., they relate two specific vertices, and vertices of the same semantic types can be related via different edges.
- No strict separation between data and metadata – Vertices and edges in a graph can have assigned semantic types to indicate their intended meaning. These types can be naturally represented as a tree (taxonomy) or graph themselves. This allows their retrieval and processing as either type definitions, i.e., metadata or (possibly in combination with other vertices) as data.

In order to process large graphs such as those generated in clinical domain, there is a need for systems that can scale well over hundreds and thousands of nodes and edges at a single point in time. To ensure that this requirement can be achieved, several large-scale graph processing systems have been designed such as Apache Giraph [7], GraphLab [25], and Pregel [27]. Apache Giraph is an iterative graph processing framework, built on top of Apache Hadoop [9]. The input to a Giraph computation is a graph composed of vertices and directed edges. GraphLab is a graph-based, high-performance, distributed framework written in C++. The GraphLab framework is a parallel programming abstraction targeted for sparse iterative graph algorithms. It provides a high-level programming interface, allowing a rapid deployment of distributed machine learning algorithms. Pregel is Google's scalable and fault tolerant API that is sufficiently flexible to express arbitrary graph

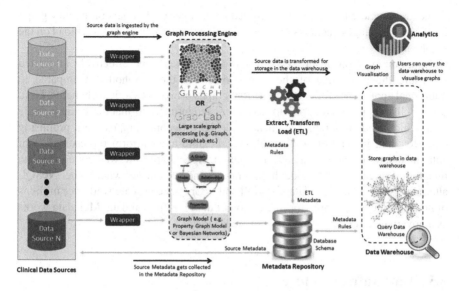

Fig. 6.4 Proposed solution architecture to maintain data consistency in a big data environment

algorithms. Giraph is a suitable choice for applications where scalability is essential [7]; in contrast to that, GraphLab is effective in applications where processing time is critical [25]. In order for the system to scale well, these systems can be deployed over cloud to ensure the scalability of the system at large.

A proposed solution (Fig. 6.4) is a graph-based system that ensures coherent integration of data from heterogeneous clinical data sources for consistency and scalable analytics. In order to ensure consistency in the disparate clinical data sources and data warehouse, graphs can be used based on the property graph model. In order to accommodate the overarching requirement of the amount of data, large-scale graph processing engines such as Giraph [7] can be used since it is based on the property graph model. The proposed system can be designed based on the gather-apply-scatter (GAS) programming paradigm [25]. This will allow an incremental graph problem to be reduced to a subproblem that operates on a portion, or subgraph, of the entire evolving graph. This subgraph abstraction will aim for the solution to substantially outperform the traditional static processing techniques. There are multiple heterogeneous clinical data sources with varying data (clinical trials data, genomics data, EHR data, etc.). The proposed solution shall incorporate a metadata repository that ingests the metadata from the disparate clinical data sources in order to ensure the correctness of the data once it resides in the clinical data warehouse. The wrapper ingests the clinical source data and passes it on to the graph processing engine that will generate a graph and then allows it to push into the clinical data warehouse. If the source data changes/evolves, e.g., over the course of the clinical trial, metadata repository detects the change and automatically alerts the data warehouse to update the graph in it, the changes are then made to the subset of the graph where the source has evolved so the overhead of generating new graph every time a changes occurs is omitted, reducing the computational workload on the graph engine.

Data coming from heterogeneous sources requires to be effectively integrated to ensure the coherence of the source data and the warehouse. Compared to traditional approaches for data integration, graphs promise significant benefits. First, a graph- like representation provides a natural and intuitive format for the underlying data, which leads to simpler application designs. Second, graphs are a promising basis for data integration as they allow a flexible and uniform representation of data, metadata, instance objects, and relationships. Graphs are well suited for data integration since they can model highly interconnected entities where other NoSQL alternatives and relational databases fall short. Graphs can scale well over millions of nodes hence are suitable for integration of data for clinical data. Metadata works as a governance framework in such an environment.

6.5   Data Infrastructure

Data integrated from diverse genomics and clinical sources requires a cloud-based platform for storage and retrieval. We explain the infrastructure for data storage, retrieval, and data movement on an on-demand basis.

When planning a multi-storage data warehouse environment, the data needs to be understood and evaluated to determine whether a specific data set needs storing within a high-performance legacy warehouse or on a commodity Hadoop cluster. A method to accomplish this is through assigning data with a "Data Temperature."

"Hot" represents the in-demand and mission critical data in direct need for quick decision making, through to "Frozen" data which is accessed very infrequently and often is represented as archived. In between these two extremes are "Warm" data which is commonly used but does not have a huge amount of urgency, and "Cold" data which is infrequently accessed [44].

The assigned temperature of data is used to determine its storage location. The frequently accessed "Hot" data is stored within fast storage such as high-performance main-memory systems (scale-up), and the infrequently accessed "Cold" is stored on the large amount of cheap commodity storage such as Hadoop (scale-out) [22].

To make informed decisions about the data and where it should be moved, it is vital to identify what data is hot, and what is cold. Factors that are commonly used to establish data temperature are the frequency of access and age, so the more frequent the access and the more recent the data then the hotter the data ranked. These factors can be used separately or collectively (Fig. 6.5).

In evaluating the data, certain workloads and data tasks may be identified that would be more suitable for batch-type work upon cold Hadoop storage. Usage and age are common factors for data temperature, but it is also important to consider

Fig. 6.5 Data temperatures
with age of data

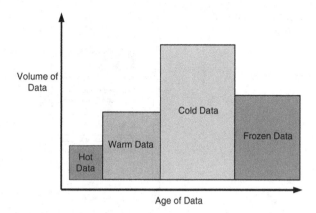

data that could have a priority based upon a specific task or alternatively based around a specific group of user requirements for the data, so it is important to consider business operations and other influencing factors when establishing a data temperature. Another example of this could be a set of data that remains unused for long periods of time but becomes incredibly important at a single point of the year, the age and usage values would not be able to account for this but incorporating business logic or machine-learned knowledge would.

Read and write operations are expensive, and are best avoided [23], but with "Hot" storage being in short supply and high demand, it is inevitable that data will be moving in and out (read and write) of this storage layer frequently. When planning to implement a multi-temperature storage environment, it is vital to plan how frequently and at what scale data will move. If it was based purely on the temperature, then you could potentially have data moving in and out of the hotter storage tiers constantly through the day which would be a considerable drain on resources and considerably impact system performance [12] (Fig. 6.6).

To prevent such a problem, movement operations to rebalance the temperature need to be scheduled at opportune times but also need to be relatively frequent to ensure the benefits of a multi-temperature system are maintained and so that you are not moving huge amounts of data at one time.

6.6 Data Analysis

The main aim of data analytics is to provide quick healthcare. The available genomics data and the new data that is being generated on almost a daily basis needs to be explored in a meaningful way. As a result, new insights, such as different relationships between disease and genome, may be identified. Furthermore, this could be a significant step toward personalized medicine based on an individual's genome. This is a very difficult challenge given the size of genomics data. Add to

Fig. 6.6 Multitiered data
storage

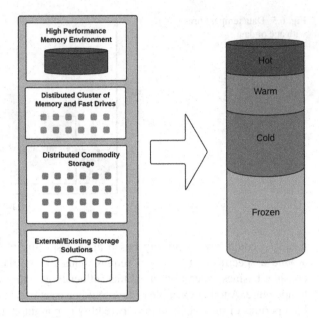

it the integrated clinical data and the complexity of the problem increases several folds. There are many challenges along the way starting with finding an effective way of storage and retrieval of this huge amount of data. Once the data can be accessed quickly, insights could be found by generating useful data models.

The existing frameworks and platforms carry out genomics data analysis using SQL, NoSQL, and high throughput approaches. For example, [37]) look at genome data-management by storing the data files and importing data into a relational database system for analysis using SQL. Another platform called Genome Analysis Toolkit integrates data access patterns with MapReduce to allow analysis [29]. The HIG platform makes use of in-memory technology and distributed computing to increase the speed of processing by intelligent scheduling [41]. The SQL approaches are not appropriate for scalable analytics. NoSQL approaches are not optimized in reading data. MapReduce approaches are scalable but do not support iterative analytics. Most of the time, data integration as well as storage is not taken into account.

One way to address the scale of data and latency of accessing integrated genomics data is to introduce an in-memory Warehouse. The genomics data can be analyzed on its own as well as in combination with clinical data. Genomics data can be pushed into the warehouse, but in order to store it efficiently, state-of-the-art approaches such as tiling may be used [15]. The tiling approach breaks down the genomics data into short overlapping segments called "tiles" and adds unique tags before and after each tile, along with a hash table of variants and its position in the genome. These tiles are then stored in a library. Gene variants are stored as a new tile in the library at the same position in the genome as the reference genome. The genome is represented by a file containing pointers to the tiles in the library, thus reducing the size of the genome file from around 200GB to a few kilobytes (KB). Tiling could be integrated with the warehouse so that genomics data is efficiently stored in the warehouse in parallel to clinical data.

For analysis, the stored data should be quickly retrievable by addressing the computational cost associated with genome data browsing. Traditional methods for searching genome databases compare a sequence from a query to all the sequences (i.e., several GBs of data) present within the database being searched, with thousands of queries being processed a day. This method is, however, computationally expensive. With exabytes of genomics data, this creates a limitation to query and browse data quickly. To address this, approaches which will allow genomics data to be browsed within the least possible time should be explored. The current warehouse architecture is not scalable, but it can browse finite amount of data very quickly. Efficient memory and storage management models and innovative algorithms for processing large amounts of data should be investigated to offer high-speed iterative analytics.

Analytics on genome data predicts disease risks, drug efficacy, and other outcomes. This requires integration of data from external sources. Several iterations of the data should sift through the data. To allow for fast and intelligent processing of data using the approaches such as machine learning, the stored genomics data could be represented as machine readable graphs (Fig. 6.7). Different graph models should be investigated, and a suitable one, which could support high-performance iterative analysis, should be selected. Previously, genome data has been represented as graphs [35]. This could be extended to exploit the graph model for newer ways of processing genomics data that is structured into the tiling approach. Using a graph model will overcome the problem of processing the data iteratively because a graph-like representation will offer opportunities to rapidly generate and compute graphs using emerging hardware architectures and computing platforms.

The information associated with a genome and its variants will be linked within the graph model. Graphs will ensure that the genomics data they are representing is functionally correct, and results being produced are consistent with stored data. Using a graph model will also ensure the correctness of the analytics being performed on the data because of their capabilities to be mathematically and

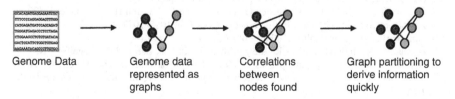

Genome Data   Genome data represented as graphs   Correlations between nodes found   Graph partitioning to derive information quickly

Fig. 6.7 Genomics data represented as graphs. Correlations are found between nodes, and useful information is extracted using algorithms such as graph partitioning

statistically verified. Hundreds of associations between genes and variants could be deduced by linking the nodes in the graph model (Fig. 6.7). However, not all the correlations deduced within the data sets would be of importance in different analytical studies of the genome. In order to extract the required information only, approaches and algorithms such as graph partitioning should be investigated (Fig. 6.7). In this way a few meaningful correlations from hundreds of associations could be extracted using several iterations.

Hosting the warehouse in a cloud environment will provide the infrastructure for scalable analytics. As the warehouse is based on distributed, in-memory architecture hosted on a cloud environment, both performance and scalability will be addressed in the resulting infrastructure.

6.7   Conclusions

In this chapter, we presented a cloud-based data analytics platform. It provides an infrastructure for integrating diverse sources of genomics and clinical data. The approaches for maintaining consistency of the integrated data are also explained. It is ensured that data is in consistent state before and after integration. Analytics approaches for generating insights from the integrated data are discussed toward the end of the chapter.

References

1. (n.d.) (Illumina) Retrieved October 2016, from http://www.illumina.com/
2. (n.d.) (454 Life Sciences) Retrieved October 2016, from http://www.454.com/
3. (n.d.)   (Complete   Genomics)   Retrieved   October   2016,   from   http://www. completegenomics.com/
4. 1000 Genomes Project Consortium (2010) A map of human genome variation from population-scale sequencing. Nature 467(7319):1061–1073
5. (2016, August) Retrieved from Akana: https://www.akana.com/products/semantics-manager
6. (2016, 09 01) Retrieved from Property Graph Model: https://github.com/tinkerpop/blueprints/wiki/Property-Graph-Model
7. (2016, September) Retrieved from Giraph: http://giraph.apache.org/
8. Akavia UD, Litvin O, Kim J, Sanchez-Garcia F, Kotliar D, Causton HC, . . . , Pe'er D (2010) An integrated approach to uncover drivers of cancer. Cell 1005–1017
9. Apache Hadoop Goes Realtime at Facebook (n.d.) Facebook
10. Borthakur D, Muthukkaruppan K, Ranganathan K, Rash S, Sarma JS, Spiegelberg N, . . . , Aiyer A (2011) Apache hadoop goes realtime at facebook proceedings of the 2011 ACM SIGMOD international conference on management of data. ACM, Athen, Greece, pp 1071–1080
11. Brierly C (2010) Press release for UK10K. Retrieved from http://www.wellcome.ac.uk/News/Media-office/Press-releases/2010/WTX060061.htm
12. Crago SP, Yeung D (2016) Reducing data movement with approximate computing techniques. 2016 IEEE International Conference on Rebooting Computing (ICRC), IEEE, pp 1–4

13. Edifecs CDI (n.d.) Retrieved from https://www.edifecs.com/downloads/Clinical_Data_Integration_Solution_Brief_2015.pdf
14. Fridley BL, Lund S, Genkins GD, Wang L (2012) A Bayesian integrative genomic model for pathway analysis of complex traits. Genet Epidemiol 36:352–359
15. Guthrie S, Connelly A, Amstutz P, Berrey AF, Cesar N, Chen J et al (2015) Tiling the genome into consistently named subsequences enables precision medicine and machine learning with millions of complex individual data-sets. PeerJ Preprints 3:e1780. doi:10.7287/peerj.preprints.1426v1
16. Hamid JS, Hu P, Roslin NM, Ling V, Greenwood CM, Beyene J (2009) Data integration in genetics and genomics: methods and challenges. Human Genomics and Proteomics
17. Harris PA, Taylor R, Thielke R, Payne J, Gonzalez N, Conde JG (2009) Research electronic data capture (REDCap) – a metadata-driven methodology and workflow process for providing translational research informatics support. J Biomed Inform 42:377–381
18. Holzinger ER, Ritchie MD (2012) Integrating heterogeneous high-throughput data for meta-dimensional pharmacogenomics and disease-related studies. Pharmacogenomics 13(2):213–222. Retrieved from https://www.ncbi.nlm.nih.gov/pmc/articles/PMC3350322/pdf/nihms357046.pdf
19. Karasawas K, Baldock R, Burger A (2004) Bioinformatics integration and agent technology. J Biomed Inform 37:205–219
20. Lapatas V, Stefanidakis M, Jimenez RC, Via A, Schneider MV (2015) Data integration in biological research – an overview. J Biol Res – Thessaloniki 22:1–16
21. Lee E, Cho S, Kim K, Park T (2009) An integrated approach to infer causal associations among gene expression, genotype variation, and disease. Genomics 94:269–277
22. Levandoski JJ, Larson P-A, Stoica R (2013) Identifying hot and cold data in main-memory databases. In: Proceedings of the 2013 IEEE International Conference on Data Engineering (ICDE 2013) IEEE Computer Society, Washington, DC, USA, pp 26–27
23. Lin H, Ma X, Chandramohan P, Geist A, Samatova N (2005) Efficient data access for parallel BLAST. In: 19th IEEE international parallel and distributed processing symposium, IEEE, pp 72–82
24. Louie B, Mork P, Martin-Sanchez F, Halevy A, TarczyHornoch P (2005) Data integration and genomic medicine. J Biomed Inform 40:5–16
25. Low Y, Gonzalez JE, Kyrola A, Bickson D, Guestrin CE, Hellerstein J (2014) Graphlab: a new framework for parallel machine learning arXiv preprint arXiv: 1408.2041
26. Lumeris CDI (n.d.) Retrieved from http://lumeris.com/wp-content/uploads/2014/05/Lumeris-SOL.CDI_.05-14.v1.pdf
27. Malewicz G, Austern MH, Bik AJ, Dehnert JC, Horn I, Leiser N, Czajkowski G (2010) Pregel: a system for large-scale graph processing. In: Proceedings of the 2010 ACM SIGMOD international conference on management of data, ACM, pp 135–146
28. Maxam AM, Gilbert W (1977) A new method for sequencing DNA. Proc Natl Acad Sci U S A 74(2):560–564
29. McKenna A, Hanna M, Banks E, Sivachenko A, Cibulskis K, Kernytsky A et al (2010) The genome analysis toolkit: a MapReduce framework for analyzing next-generation DNA sequencing data. Genome Res 20:1297–1303
30. Metzker ML (2010) Sequencing technologies – the next generation. Nat Rev Genet 11:31–46
31. National Human Genome Research Institute (2016) National Human Genome Research Institute. Retrieved from https://www.genome.gov/27565109/the-cost-of-sequencing-a-human-genome/
32. Nevins JR, Huang ES, Dressman H, Pittman J, Huang AT, West M (2003) Towards integrated clinico-genomic models for personalized medicine: combining gene expression signatures and clinical factors in breast cancer outcomes prediction. Human Mol Genet 12:R153–R157
33. Nielsen TD, Jensen FV (2009) Bayesian networks and decision graphs. Springer Science & Business Media, New York

34. Park Y, Shankar M, Park BH, Ghosh J (2014) Graph databases for large-scale healthcare systems: a framework for efficient data management and data services. In: Data Engineering Workshops (ICDEW), IEEE, pp 12–19
35. Ritchie MD, Holzinger ER, Li R, Pendergrass SA, Kim D (2015) Methods of integrating data to uncover genotype-phenotype interactions. Genetics 16:85–97
36. Rodriguez MA, Neubauer P (2010) Constructions from dots and lines. Bull Am Soc Inf Sci Technol 36:35–41
37. Rohm U, Blakeley JA (2009) Data management for high-throughput genomics. Conference on innovative data systems
38. Salem A, Ben-Abdallah H (2015) The design of valid multidimensional star schemas assisted by repair solutions. Vietnam J Comput Sci 2:169–179
39. Sanger F, Coulson AR (1975) A rapid method for determining sequences in DNA by primed synthesis with DNA polymerase. J Mol Biol 94(3):441–448
40. SAS CDI (n.d.) Retrieved from [24] Louie B, Mork P, Martin-Sanchez F, Halevy A, TarczyHornoch P (2005) Data integration and genomic medicine. J Biomed Inform 40:5–16
41. Schapranow M (2013) HIG – an in-memory database platform enabling real-time analyses of genome data. In: IEEE international conference on big data, pp 691–696. doi:10.1109/Big-Data.2013.6691638
42. Songting C (2010) Cheetah: a high performance, Custom data warehouse on top of MapReduce Proc VLDB Endow, pp 1459–1468
43. Stephens ZD, Lee SY, Faghri F, Campbell RH, Zhai C, Efron MJ et al (2015) Big data: astronomical or genomical? PLoS Biol 13:e1002195
44. Subramanyam R (2015) HDFS heterogeneous storage resource management based on data temperature. 2015 international conference on cloud and autonomic computing, ICCAC, pp 232–235
45. Sujasnsky W (2001) Heterogeneous database integration in biomedicine. J Biomed Inform 35:285–298
46. Wang L, Zhang A, Ramanathan M (2005) BioStar models of clinical and genomic data for biomedical data warehouse design. Int J Bioinform Res Appl 1:63–80

Part III
Data Cloud

Chapter 7
High-Performance Graph Data Management and Mining in Cloud Environments with X10

Miyuru Dayarathna and Toyotaro Suzumura

7.1 Introduction

X10 is a high-productivity, high-performance programming language aimed at large-scale distributed and shared-memory parallel applications [18, 75]. It is a strongly typed, garbage-collected, class-based, object-oriented language built on the Asynchronous Partitioned Global Address Space (APGAS) programming model. An X10 application runs over a collection of places which are possibly large and possibly heterogeneous [6].

While there have been multiple different applications of X10 language, graph processing implementations have been quite unique due to the inherent complexity and scalability issues associated with implementing the graph algorithms. Graph processing mainly has two flavors. First category is offline batch graph analytics. Second category is online graph query processing. In this chapter we discuss the implementation of both these types of applications with X10. We present how ScaleGraph [29, 30] has been implemented with X10 to solve the issues of large graph processing in HPC clusters. We present Acacia [28, 31] which is a distributed graph database engine developed using X10 to handle the online graph query processing. A significant challenge associated with implementation of online graph

M. Dayarathna (✉)
WSO2, Inc., Mountain View, CA, USA

University of Moratuwa, Moratuwa, Sri Lanka
e-mail: miyurud@wso2.com

T. Suzumura
T.J. Watson Research Center, IBM, New York, NY, USA

Barcelona Supercomputing Center, Barcelona, Spain

University of Tokyo, Tokyo, Japan
e-mail: suzumura@acm.org

© Springer International Publishing AG 2017
N. Antonopoulos, L. Gillam (eds.), *Cloud Computing*, Computer Communications and Networks, DOI 10.1007/978-3-319-54645-2_7

query processing systems is the lacking of suitable benchmarks for measuring their performance. While previous implementations focused on non-distributed benchmarking frameworks, we implement a distributed graph database benchmarking framework with X10 called XGDBench [25–27].

Through real-world implementations which ran on distributed large-scale compute clusters, we demonstrate the feasibility of use of X10 language for developing large-scale graph data processing applications. With scalability experiments conducted on Tsubame 2.0 supercomputer (also referred to as TSUBAME Cloud), we have shown the ability of scaling large-scale graph computing workloads with X10 applications. Furthermore, with XGDBench we have shown how realistic workloads could be generated with X10's collection of places. In this chapter we investigate various concepts and techniques which could be followed to implement large graph processing systems using X10.

The rest of the chapter is organized as follows: First, we describe the challenges involved with large graph processing and the technologies used to address these challenges in Sect. 7.2. Also we review previous work which has been conducted in this regard. Next, we provide an overview to the X10 language and describe its basic language constructs in Sect. 7.3. We present the details of implementing a large graph processing library with X10 in Sect. 7.4. Next, we discuss the implementation of Acacia distributed graph database server with X10 in Sect. 7.5. Then we describe the implementation of XGDBench graph database benchmarking framework in Sect. 7.6. We provide the conclusions in Sect. 7.7.

7.2 Challenges and Technologies: Review of Previous Work

In this section we look at how the large graph data processing has been conducted and how various PGAS techniques as well as non-PGAS techniques have been applied for HPC graph data mining.

7.2.1 HPC Graph Data Processing

Construction of graph processing libraries with support for variety of graph algorithms has been a widely studied area. One of the famous examples for such graph libraries is igraph [23]. Igraph has been heavily used by complex network analysis community. It has support for classic graph theory problems such as minimum spanning trees and network flow. Core of the igraph has been written in C. There are two extensions for igraph, one in R and another in Python. Lee et al. created Generic Graph Component Library (GGCL) [51] which is a library built on C++ STL. Graph algorithms on GGCL do not depend on the data structures on which they operate. Stanford Network Analysis Package (SNAP) [52] is a general purpose network analysis and graph mining library developed by Leskovec et al.. Version 2011-13-31 of SNAP supports maximum 250 million vertices and 2 billion edges [52]. The library calculates structural properties and generates regular and random graphs. Similar to ScaleGraph, SNAP supports attributes on nodes and edges and has been used to analyze large graphs with millions of nodes and billions of edges. However compared to ScaleGraph, one of the major limitations of all the abovementioned libraries is that they are made to run on workstations.

Boost Graph Library (BGL) is a C++ STL library for graph processing [12, 37]. Part of the BGL is a generic graph interface that allows access to the graph's structure while hiding the details of the implementation. A parallel version of the library (PBGL) [38] has been developed using MPI. However, if the user is not well versed in using C++ and STL, the learning curve of the BGL becomes very steep [50]. Hence BGL and PBGL might not be an acceptable solution for application programmers at large. Note that by using the term "application programmer" we represent not only high-end parallel application programmers but also application programmers on next-generation systems such as SMP-on-a-chip and tightly coupled blade servers [48]. ParGraph [43] is a generic parallel graph library which is comparable to PBGL. ParGraph is written in C++, and it has similar syntax to PBGL. Different from BGL, PBGL, and ParGraph, ScaleGraph requires less code for specifying a graph computation, requiring less programming effort. This way, ScaleGraph promotes productivity in HPC graph analysis. Furthermore, in contrast to ScaleGraph, BGL and PBGL do not support vertex and edge attributes.

Standard Template Adaptive Parallel Library (STAPL) [4] is a generic library with similar functionality to Boost. STAPL targets scientific and numerical applications, also intended for exploiting parallelism for graph algorithms. However like Boost libraries, STAPL does not define broadly applicable abstractions for graphs [67].

Java Universal Network/Graph (JUNG) is a comprehensive open-source graph library [65, 74]. It supports a variety of representations of graphs such as directed and undirected graphs, multimodal graphs, hypergraphs, and graphs with parallel edges (i.e., multi-edges). Since JUNG has been developed using Java, it offers the interoperability with rich third-party libraries written in Java. Current distribution of JUNG includes a number of graph algorithms related to data mining and social network analysis [74]. Current version of JUNG does not support distributed implementation of algorithms which is a limitation in applying it to distributed graph processing scenarios.

While there has been large-scale graph algorithm implementation on main stream parallel architectures such as distributed memory machines, there are some other studies focusing on specific machine architectures which are currently less popular. Examples include the works by Madduri et al. [55], Bader et al. [9, 33], and Berry et al. (Multithreaded Graph Library) [13], which describe the ability of using massively multithreaded machines to implement graph algorithms. While distributed memory application developers focus on maximization of locality to minimize interprocess communication, program developers for massively multithreaded machines having large shared memory (e.g., Cray MTA-2) do not focus on locality or data exchange [56]. Some of the works of this domain (e.g., Multithreaded Graph Library) have been extended to commodity processors yet with lesser performance [11]. Different from them, with ScaleGraph we concentrate on productivity of specifying graph computations in distributed settings while maintaining scalability aspects in commodity machines ranging from developer laptops to supercomputers.

There has been prior work on specifying graph computations on X10. Cong et al. worked on creating fast implementations of irregular graph problems on X10 [20, 21]. They also worked on creating an X10 work stealing framework (XWS) with the aim of solving the problem of present software systems not supporting irregular parallelism well. However, both these works do not focus on creating a Graph API with well-defined abstractions for representing graphs.

While ScaleGraph is a large graph analysis library on the domain of PGAS languages, Pregel [56] is a computational model for analyzing large graphs with billions of vertices and trillions of edges. Pregel focuses on building a scalable and fault-tolerant platform with an API that is flexible in expressing arbitrary graph algorithms using vertex-centric computations. Similar to PBGL, Pregel's C++ API requires more programming effort compared to ScaleGraph's API which is also targeted for users outside the HPC domain.

7.2.2 Graph Data Management

There are few notable distributed graph databases present in the state of the art. G^* is a distributed graph database server which manages collections of large graphs by distributing storage across multiple servers [49]. System G is another graph database server which provides a whole spectrum solution which includes graph storage, runtime, analytics, and visualization [83]. However, none of them have investigated RDF graph storage. Titan is a distributed graph database server. However, it does not have a native storage as Acacia-RDF. Instead it uses a third-party key-value store such as Cassandra, HBase, BerkeleyDB, etc., as its backend storage. SW-Store is an extension of a column-oriented DBMS that is designed for high-performance RDF data management [1]. Li-Yung Ho et al. [44] described a distributed graph database architecture for large social computing. But their focus was not on RDF graphs. Their underlying communication has been implemented using MPI, while Acacia-RDF uses the socket back end of Managed X10/Java sockets for communication.

DREAM is a distributed RDF engine with adaptive query planner and minimal communication [42]. Different from Acacia-RDF, DREAM does not partition RDF data sets. DREAM partitions only SPARQL queries. Although this eliminates the requirement of joining partitioned subgraphs during certain query execution, duplication of the same RDF data set across multiple computers consumes significant storage resources which is different from the objectives of Acacia-RDF. TriAD is a distributed RDF engine which is based on shared-nothing, main-memory architecture which uses an asynchronous message passing protocol [41]. However, in Acacia-RDF communication is done based on master-worker pattern.

Zeng et al. implemented Trinity.RDF, a distributed, memory-based graph engine for web scale RDF data [85]. Similar to Acacia-RDF which is built on top of Acacia, Trinity.RDF is based on Trinity graph engine. However, Trinity is a distributed in-memory key-value store, while Acacia-RDF persists the graph data sets across multiple compute nodes and systematically loads data into memory during query processing. g-Store is a graph-based RDF data management system which maintains the data as a directed multi-edge graph where each vertex corresponds to a subject or object [87]. However, g-Store is a non-distributed system. SemStore is a semantic-preserving distributed triple store [82]. Different from Acacia-RDF which follows vertex-cut paradigm, SemStore adopts a coarse-grained unit named rooted subgraph. TripleBit is a compact system for storing and accessing RDF data [84]. Papailiou et al. presented a system that addresses graph-based, workload-adaptive indexing of large RDF graphs by caching SPARQL query results [66]. RDF-3X engine is pursuing a RISC-style architecture with streamlined indexing and query processing [61]. However, RDF-3X is a non-distributed system.

7.2.3   HPC Graph Data Management Benchmarks

HPC Scalable Graph Analysis Benchmark represents a compact application with multiple analysis techniques that access a single data structure representing a weighted, directed graph. This benchmark is composed of four separated operations (graph construction, classification of large vertex sets, graph extraction with breadth-first search, graph analysis with betweenness centrality) on a graph that follows a power-law distribution [10]. However, this benchmark does not evaluate some features that are inherent to graph databases such as object labeling, attribute management, etc. [10], a feature that will dominate future graph database systems. Furthermore, HPC Scalable Graph Analysis Benchmark does not evaluate the OLTP features of graph DBMSs.

Recently, a benchmark for graph traversal operations on graph databases was described by Ciglan et al. [19]. They designed their graph database benchmark focusing on traversal operations in a memory-constrained environment where the whole graph cannot be loaded and processed in memory. Similar to them, XGDBench implements graph traversal as one of the workload items. However, XGDBench is a benchmarking framework rather than a benchmark specification.

There are popular benchmarks for graph data stores from the Semantic Web community such as Lehigh University Benchmark (LUBM) [40], Berlin [14], DBpedia [58], and SP2Bench [72]. None of these benchmarks employ statistical graph generator model which allows very large-scale, realistic synthetic graphs.

Vicknair et al. compared performance of Neo4j graph database and MySQL [78] for graph data storage. However, their study did not focus specifically on cloud environments. Rohloff et al. conducts an evaluation of triple-store technologies for large data stores [69]. Triple stores also have been used as graph database management systems on various occasions. We use AllegroGraph, a famous triple store (which is also popular as a graph database) for evaluation of XGDBench due to this reason. However, Rohloff et al.'s work was conducted using the LUBM, and their study focused on evaluating triple-store technologies. Another similar work on benchmarking RDF stores has been conducted by Thakker et al. [76]. However, they used the University Ontology Benchmark (UOBM) [54] for this purpose.

7.3   Overview of X10

X10 is an experimental PGAS language currently being developed by IBM Research in collaboration with academic partners [18, 46]. The project started in 2004 and tries to address the need for providing a programming model that can withstand architectural challenges posed by multiple cores, hardware accelerators, cluster, and supercomputers. The main role of X10 is to simplify the programming model in such a way that it leads to increases in programming productivity for future systems [48] such as extreme scale computing systems [32]. X10 has been developed from the beginning with the motivation of supporting hundreds of thousands of application programmers and scientists with providing ease of writing HPC code [18]. Previous programming models use two separate levels of abstraction for shared-memory thread-level parallelism (e.g., pthreads, Java threads, OpenMP) and distributed-memory communication (e.g., JMS, RMI, MPI) which results in considerable complexity when trying to create programs that follow both the approaches [2]. X10 addresses this problem by introducing the notion of places. Every activity in X10 runs in a place which is collection of non-migrating mutable data objects and the activities (similar to threads) that operate on the data [2]. Therefore, the notion of places includes both shared-memory thread-level parallelism as well as distributed-memory communication which makes the life of the programmer easier. Supporting both concurrency and distribution has been the first-class concern of the programming language's design [39]. X10 is available freely under open-source license.

X10 is a strongly typed, object-oriented language which emphasizes static-type checking and static expression of program invariants. The choice of static expression supports the motivation of improving programmer productivity and performance. X10 standard libraries are designed to support applications to extend and customize their functionality, which is a supporting factor for X10 library developers.

7.4   Large Graph Processing with X10

7.4.1   ScaleGraph Architecture

ScaleGraph library has been designed from the ground-up with the aim of defining solid abstractions for large-scale graph processing. The architecture of ScaleGraph

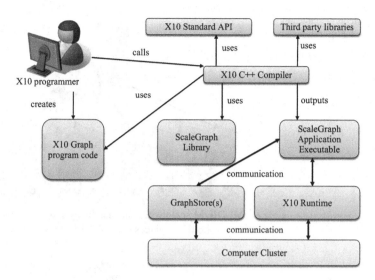

Fig. 7.1 ScaleGraph Architecture

is shown in Fig. 7.1. X10 application programmers can utilize our library to write graph applications for Native X10. ScaleGraph library depends on third-party C++ libraries such as Xerces-C++ XML Parser [68], numerical packages such as SCALAPACK [15], etc.

X10 applications which use ScaleGraph can be written to operate in three different scales called SMALL, MEDIUM, and LARGE. The SMALL scale represents a graph application that runs on a single place (Lets take the maximum supported graph size as $2^n (n : n > 0, n \in N)$). We created this configuration to support complex network analysis community at large, who might be interested of using our library in single machine settings. If an application which uses the library in SMALL scale is run in multiple places, the graph will be stored in the place designated by *home* (i.e., Place 0).

The second configuration type is MEDIUM scale in which the number of vertices stored in one place is $2^m (m : m > n, m \in N)$; however the total graph size equals to $(2^m * numberofplaces)$. For example, when the application is developed for MEDIUM scale size with $m = 25$ and is run on 32 places, the application can handle graphs up to 2^{30} (i.e., ≈ 1 billion) vertices (As shown in Fig. 7.2a).

The third category of applications is the LARGE scale (shown in Fig. 7.2b). This category has been created to support scenarios where the end user does not have enough compute resources to instantiate sufficient places to hold billion scale graphs. This type of application scenario will be frequent for users with small compute clusters with limited RAM or even in resource-full compute clusters such as supercomputers when the processed graph needs to be persisted on disks.

We have introduced such three scales of operations due to resource availability and performance trade-offs present in many graph analysis applications. While the

Fig. 7.2 Medium-scale and
large-scale configurations of
ScaleGraph

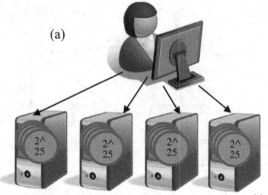

(a)

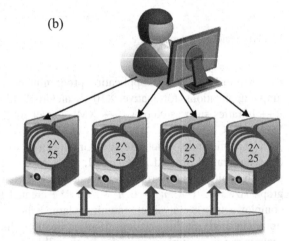

MEDIUM scale with four machines and each machine
holds 32 places (i.e., Total 128 places).

(b)

LARGE scale with four machines and each machine holds
32 places (i.e., Total 128 places). However only a
portion of the graph is loaded on to the machines.

library scales well with increasing numbers of machines, one cannot expect it to
process a very large graph that could not be kept on a single laptop's memory.
We believe the three scales of operation modes lead to a more simple yet robust
architecture of ScaleGraph.

The library has been modeled entirely using object-oriented software design
techniques. Current design of the library contains six main categories: graph, I/O,
generators, metrics, clustering, and communities. Package structure of ScaleGraph
is shown in Fig. 7.3.

The graph package holds all the classes related to graph representation. All
the graphs of ScaleGraph implement a single interface called *Graph*. ScaleGraph

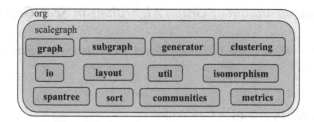

Fig. 7.3 Package structure of ScaleGraph

separates graph representation from the rest of the algorithms. A Graph in Scale-Graph is just a data structure, and it has no associated operations implementing specific analysis algorithms (e.g., degree, pagerank, centrality, etc.). Graph algorithms are coded in separate classes. We have developed two types of Graph classes named PlainGraph and AttributedGraph. The PlainGraph is used to store non-attributed graphs (i.e., Graphs without attributes for both vertices and edges), while AttributedGraphs can store attributes on both vertices and edges.

We use an adjacency list representation of graph data in our Graph interface. Most of the real-world graphs are sparse graphs which can be efficiently represented using an adjacency list compared to an adjacency matrix. While adjacency matrices provide a marginal advantage over adjacency lists for memory utilization for representing big graphs, and less time for edge insertion and deletion, it is a well-recognized fact that adjacency lists are better for most applications of graphs [73].

ScaleGraph contains a set of classes for reading and writing graph files located under org.scalegraph.io. All the readers implement *Reader* interface, while all the writers implement *Writer* interface both of which are located on org.scalegraph.io. There are many different types of graph file formats used by the complex network research community. Out of them, we support some frequently used file formats for attributed graphs such as GML, GEXF, GraphML, CSV, GDF, and GraphViz. For non-attributed graphs we support popular formats such as edgelist, CSV, DIMACS, LGL, and Pajek. Certain file formats have more than single file reader/writer classes. An example is ScatteredEdgeListReader which reads a collection of files created by partitioning an edgelist file in small pieces.

The generators package includes a collection of graph generators. We have already implemented an RMAT [17] generator and are working on other generators such as BarabasiAlbertGenerator, CitationgraphGenerator, ErdosRenyiGenerator, etc.

ScaleGraph contains a set of classes for obtaining the structural properties of graphs. ScaleGraph has implemented betweenness centrality and degree distribution structural property calculation. The planned other metrics include diameter, pagerank, density, complexity, cliques, KCores, Mincut, connected component, etc.

Currently the main interfaces of ScaleGraph include *Graph*, *Reader*, and *Writer* interfaces which are described above.

7.4.2   Implementation of Graph Algorithms in ScaleGraph

In this section we describe the metrics used for scalability evaluation study of ScaleGraph.

7.4.2.1   Degree Distribution Calculation

Degree distribution is one of the widely studied properties of a graph. Degree of a vertex in a graph is the number of edges connected to it [62]. If one denotes degree by k, then the degree distribution can be represented by p_k. Two types of degree distributions can be calculated for directed graphs such as World Wide Web graph and citation networks called in-degree and out-degree distributions. In the context of a web graph, in-degree of a vertex V is the number of vertices that link to V. Out-degree of V is the number vertices that V links to [62]. ScaleGraph supports calculation of both in-degree and out-degree for directed graphs. In ScaleGraph a Boolean flag has been used to determine the directedness of a graph. If the flag is set to true, the graph is treated as a directed graph.

7.4.2.2   Betweenness Centrality

Betweenness centrality (BC) [5, 35] is a graph metric which measures the extent to which a vertex lies on paths between other vertices [60]. It is one of the most frequently employed metrics in social network analysis [16]. We can define BC of a general network as follows. Let n_{st}^i be the number of geodesic paths (i.e., shortest paths) from s to t that pass through i (s,t, and i are vertices of the graph, s$\neq$t$\neq$i). Let s denote the total number of geodesic paths from s to t as g_{st}. Then the BC of vertex i (i.e., x_i) is given by

$$x_i = \sum_{st} n_{st}^i / g_{st} \qquad (7.1)$$

We implement a more efficient version of BC introduced by Brandes [16]. For a graph with n vertices and m edges, this algorithm requires O(n+m) space. The algorithm runs in O(nm) and O(nm+n^2log n) time on unweighted and weighted graphs, respectively [16]. Brandes algorithm traverses the vertices in nonincreasing order of their distance from source vertex (Brandes does not mandate use of a specific traversal algorithm for this purpose [16]). Once this is done, it backtracks through the frontiers to update sum of important values of each vertex [53]. However, it should be noted that in the case of AttributedGraph we use Dijkstra's algorithm instead of BFS in order to account for edge weights. We do not do any approximation of BC, rather we calculate exact BC scores on large graphs.

In our BC algorithm at the beginning, Place 0 instantiates `BetweennessCent‑rality` class objects in all the places. After construction of each object, it invokes the method for constructing neighbor map that includes information of the neighbor connectivity. Once each object constructs their own neighbor map, each object runs Brandes on assigned vertices on them and calculates BC in parallel. Finally, betweenness scores are scattered among each place via a distributed all reduce operation, which are then reported as an array object from Place 0. A code snippet of our BC implementation on `PlainGraph` is shown in Fig. 7.4. Note that important X10 language constructs are highlighted in bold italics font in Figs. 7.4 and 7.5.

```
val distVertexList:DistArray[Long] = this.plainGraph.getVertexList();
val localVertices = distVertexList.getLocalPortion();
val numParallelBfsTasks = Runtime.NTHREADS;

finish {
  for(taskId in 0..(numParallelBfsTasks -1 )) {
            async doBfsOnPlainGraph(taskId, numParallelBfsTasks,
                            this.numVertex, localVertices);
  }
}

// If undirected graph divide by 2
if(this.plainGraph.isDirected() == false) {
   if(this.isNormalize) {
      // Undirected and normalize
      betweennessScore.map(betweennessScore, (a: Double) => a /
                        (((numVertex - 1) * (numVertex - 2))) );
   } else {
      // Undirected only
       betweennessScore.map(betweennessScore, (a: Double) => a / 2 );
   }
} else {
   if(this.isNormalize) {
      // Directed and normalize
      betweennessScore.map(betweennessScore, (a: Double) => a /
                        ((numVertex -1) * (numVertex - 2)) );
   }
}

if(Place.ALL_PLACES > 1) {
            Team.WORLD.allreduce(here.id, betweennessScore, 0,
betweennessScore, 0, betweennessScore.size, Team.ADD);
}
```

Fig. 7.4 A code snippet of BC calculation on PlainGraph

```
makeCorrespondenceBetweenIDandIDX();

//Step 1: Make a degree matrix and a Laplacian matrix and solve a
generalized eigenvalue problem
val l:DenseMatrix = getEigenvectors();
if(l == null){
            return null;
}

//copy eigenvectors to DistArray
val nPoints = l.M;
val points = DistArray.make[Vector](Dist.makeBlock(0..(nPoints-1)),
(Point) => Vector.make(nClusters));
finish for(p in points.dist.places()) async at(p) {
            for([i] in points.dist.get(p)){
                        for(var j:Int = 0; j < nClusters; j++){
                                    points(i)(j) = l(i, l.N - j - 1);
                        }
            }
}

//Step 2: Apply K-Means algorithm to eigenvectors
val resultArray:DistArray[Int] = kmeans(nClusters, points);
val result:ClusteringResult = makeClusteringResult(nClusters,
resultArray);
```

Fig. 7.5 A code snippet of spectral clustering algorithm of ScaleGraph

7.4.2.3 Spectral Clustering

Graph clustering is the act of grouping the vertices of the graph into clusters considering the edge structure of the graph in such a way that there should be many edges within each cluster and relatively few edges between the clusters [71]. Graph clustering algorithms can be divided in to two categories called "node-clustering algorithms" and "graph-clustering algorithms" [3]. Spectral clustering is a node-clustering algorithm.

If there are n objects labeled x_1, x_1, x_2, ..., x_n with a pairwise similarity function F defined between them (F is symmetric and nonnegative), spectral clustering includes all methods and techniques that partition the set into clusters by using eigenvectors of matrices, like F itself or other matrices derived using it [34]. Spectral clustering algorithm includes two main steps as shown in Fig. 7.5. First, spectral clustering algorithm transforms the initial set of objects in to a set of points in space, whose coordinates are elements of eigenvectors. In spectral clustering an eigenvector or a combination of several eigenvectors is used as the vertex similarity measure for computing the clusters. Next, the set of points are clustered via standard techniques such as k-means clustering [57]. Spectral clustering has the ability of separating data points that could not be resolved by applying k-means clustering directly, which is a key advantage compared to other techniques. Spectral clustering has been applied for analysis of the network of the Internet autonomous-system domains, graph partitioning, etc. [71]. A code snippet depicting the spectral clustering implementation of ScaleGraph is shown in Fig. 7.5. Our spectral clustering code utilizes SCALAPACK [15] for solving eigenvalue problem [64].

7.5 X10-Based Distributed Graph Database Engine

Data in the form of linked/graph data have become prominent in recent computing applications. Examples for such applications are spread across multiple domains such as online social networks, Semantic Web (DBpedia), and major search engines (e.g., Google, Yahoo!, Bing, etc.). Facebook's Like button, BBC's wildlife, and music pages are some examples for use of linked data [81]. Linked data provides a set of techniques for interacting with structured data on the web. *Resource Description Framework (RDF)* is a standard model for data interchange on the web which supports this interaction [79]. A single RDF statement describes a relationship between two entities. These three elements are called *subject, predicate*, and *object* in the linked data terminology and are often referred to as a *triple*. RDF is the data model used by Semantic Web ontologies and knowledge bases such as DBpedia, Probase, YAGO, etc. A number of database systems have been developed in recent years by both academia and industry to cater the need of managing and mining large linked data sets. Some of the notable examples include Trinity [85], GraphChiDB, AllegroGraph, Titan [8], etc.

With Acacia-RDF we have made significant architecture changes to Acacia [28]. First, we introduced our own native store which eliminated the dependency with Neo4j. Second, we have enhanced Acacia to run not only on clusters but also on single computers such as laptops. Third, we have implemented a scalable SPARQL query processor in X10. Fourth, we have implemented a replication-based fault tolerance mechanism for Acacia-RDF. Finally, we have implemented several additional graph algorithms in Acacia's distributed data abstraction.

7.5.1 System Design

An overview of Acacia-RDF's system architecture is shown in Fig. 7.6. There are two key components of Acacia system: master and worker. Front end is a command-line user interface for Acacia's master. There are front-end commands to list the system statistics, to upload/delete graphs, to get system statistics, commands to run graph algorithms, etc.

Once an RDF graph is submitted to the system, RDF Partitioner extracts the vertices, edges, and their properties. The RDF graph is partitioned using Metis. Each partitioned subgraph is stored in the native graph store structures, and the native stores are distributed across X10 places.

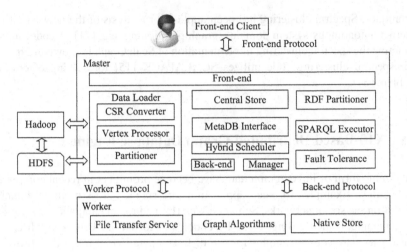

Fig. 7.6 Overview of Acacia

During the query execution, SPARQL query submitted by the user is parsed by SPARQL executor to identify triple patterns present within the query. The identified patterns are matched with the partitioned RDF graph data sets which are located in multiple X10 places. In order to optimize the query execution on Acacia-RDF, we have introduced query results caching mechanism which operates on each and every worker of Acacia-RDF. The query-caching mechanism checks to see if the query and the target graph (unmodified) are the same for a previous query execution session. If these parameters are the same, then already-cached results are sent to the master for aggregation rather than reloading the relevant subgraphs from the disk storage and executing the queries.

There are two main types of SPARQL query executions that happen in Acacia-RDF. These are *single-variable queries* and *multivariable queries*. In the case of single-variable queries, we merge the intermediate results at the workers and send the final results to the master. However, in the case of multivariable queries, we send the intermediate results from each and every worker to the master, and merging of the intermediate results is done at the master. This type of intermediate results aggregation has been followed to ensure the correctness of the results obtained from the SPARQL processor.

7.5.2 Implementation of Acacia

We implemented Acacia using X10 programming language. We used managed X10 when developing Acacia-RDF. In managed X10, the X10 application gets translated in to a pure Java application. We leverage the notion of places, language constructs

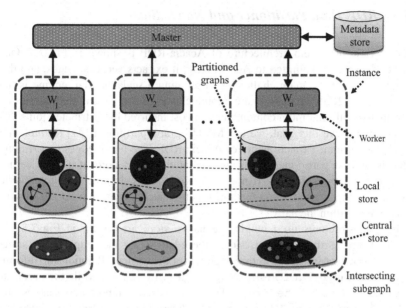

Fig. 7.7 System architecture of Acacia-RDF. Note that both local store and central store are of Acacia native store type

for asynchronous execution (i.e., `async`, `finish`, etc.) available in X10 when developing the Acacia system. Furthermore, we leverage the built-in fault tolerance mechanism of X10 when formulating Acacia's fault tolerance mechanism [24].

We have made several significant architectural changes with RDF extension for the initial Acacia system described in [28]. The most notable change is the elimination of the Neo4j instances and replacing them with a native store developed by us. Furthermore, we had observed that considerable amount of edges stored are for certain graphs in central store. With Acacia-RDF we have eliminated this bottleneck by distributing the central store across workers as and when required. Figure 7.7 shows how this is being done. We follow a random partitioning technique to equally divide the number of edges across central stores located on each instance. Furthermore, the previous version of Acacia's data loading phase depended on a sequence of MapReduce jobs. With Acacia-RDF we have eliminated this dependency and have introduced a *MetisPartitioner* which constructs METIS file format and conducts graph data partitioning. Therefore, the latest modifications allow the Acacia system to be run even in a single computer which allows the system to be used in multiple use cases compared to the previous system. Next, we describe how Acacia's RDF extension has been implemented on top of Acacia system.

7.5.3   RDF Data Partitioner and Native Store

Another view of system architecture of Acacia-RDF is shown in Fig. 7.7. Once an RDF data set is submitted to Acacia-RDF, it extracts vertices, edges, and their attributes. One of the main challenges in building a scalable RDF engine is how to partition the RDF data across a compute cluster in such a way that queries can be evaluated with minimum communication cost incurred by distributed joins [82]. In order to achieve this goal, we use METIS graph partitioner [47] to implement the graph partitioning functionality of Acacia-RDF. The list of edges is partitioned by Metis, and the partitioned edges are separated to local stores if the two vertices belong to the same subgraph. If not, the edge is stored in a central store. Vertex attributes, predicates, and other metainformation such as partition ID are stored in separate files within the native storage.

The data structures used within the native store are shown in Fig. 7.8. Out of them LocalSubGraphMap stores the edge list of the graph being stored. VertexPropertyMap stores the properties of the vertices. Relationship information are stored in RelationshipMapWithProperties, while the predicates are stored in PredicateStore. There are several important variables such as IsCentralStore, VertexCount, EdgeCount, PredicateCount, PartitionCount, etc. All these data structures are serialized using Kryo library when storeGraph() method of the native store is called. The stored data is loaded in to memory when loadGraph() is called. Since only objects can be serialized in Java, we transfer variables to a MetaInfo map when serialized and extract those values from the map when deserialized.

Acacia-RDF maintains all the operational information in a metadata store implemented using HSQLDB. Metainformation includes details such as IDs of graphs, hosts, IP addresses configured with Acacia, partition IDs, sizes of partitions, locations where they are stored, etc.

7.5.4   SPARQL Query Processor

SPARQL query processor executes SPARQL queries specified by the users on the partitioned RDF graphs of Acacia-RDF. User can either select to list maximum 100 lines of results on the front-end command line interface or store the entire results of query execution on a file. We use an ANTLR-based SPARQL grammar for parsing SPARQL queries [36]. The user-specified SPARQL query is transferred to each worker by the Acacia manager. Each worker runs the SPARQL query they received in parallel and returns back the result to master based on the abovementioned criteria. Since the RDF graphs are partitioned and stored across multiple places, the central stores are consulted when running SPARQL queries which require joining multiple subjects and objects. This is a common architectural feature present across all the graph algorithms implemented in Acacia.

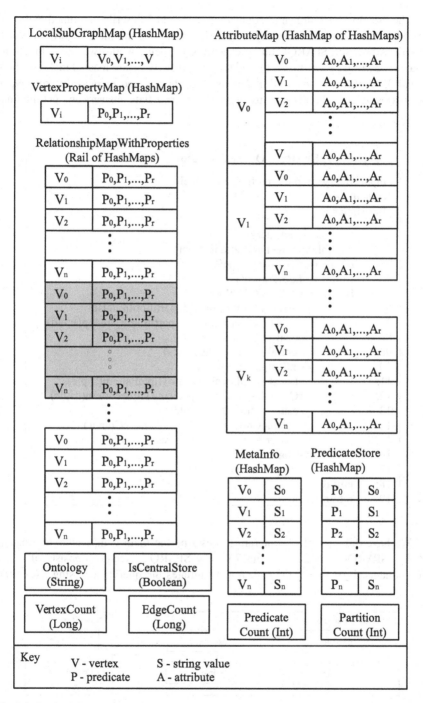

Fig. 7.8 Design of Acacia native store's data structures. Native store has been designed to store both plain graphs and RDF graphs. Data types of each of the data structure/variable are shown within parenthesis

The pseudo-codes shown in Algorithms 1, 2, and 3 describe the functionality of the SPARQL executor of Acacia-RDF. Algorithm 1 is the main algorithm which describes how the SPARQL query execution happens, while two of its functions `executeTriplePattern()` and `MergeAnswer()` are located in Algorithms 2 and 3, respectively. Algorithm 2 is used to identify and process different types of queries. Algorithm 3 is used to merge the intermediate answers and get the final result.

Algorithm 1: SPARQL Query Processor

Input : query, graphId, partitionId, placeId
Output : result
Description :

```
1:      t ← tokenizer(query)
2:      variableMap ← t.getVariableMap()
3:      qType ← t.getQueryType()
4:      triples ← t.getTriples()
5:      if qType = "SELECT" then
6:              ls ← NativeStore(graphId, partitionId, false)
7:              cs ← NativeStore(graphId, partitionId, true, placeId)
8:              tpLocal ← TriplePattern(ls)
9:              tpCentral ← TriplePattern(cs)
10:             for all triple in triples do
11:                 rLocal ← tpLocal.executeTriplePattern(triple)
12:                 rCentral ← tpCentral.executeTriplePattern(triple)
13:                 result ← rLocal + rCentral
14:                 variableCount ← triple.getVariableCount()
15:                 answer ← mergeAnswer(result, variableCount)
16:             end for
17:             result ← format(answer)
18:     end if
19:     return result
```

We have drawn a block diagram to describe the main components of Acacia-RDF's SPARQL processor in Fig. 7.9. The SPARQL executor consists of many components. First one is the executor. It initiates the query processing. Next one

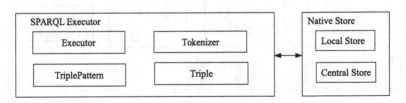

Fig. 7.9 SPARQL query processor

is the tokenizer. It breaks the query into tokens. TriplePattern represents different triple patterns. Triple represents the components of a triple in a query.

During the query execution, the executor initiates the query processing. Tokenizer breaks the query into tokens. Then, if the query type is SELECT, the Executor should return the matching result set to the user. After tokenization, data should be loaded. Data is loaded from native store. Next, each triple in the query should be matched with loaded data in order to find matching results for the triple. After that, intermediate results of each triple should be joined to get the final result set. Finally, executor will return the matching result set for the given query.

Algorithm 2: executeTriplePattern(triple)

Input : triple
Output : modifiedTriples
Description :

```
1:  pattern ← getPattern(tripple)
2:  if pattern = "?X:predicate:object" then
3:      pId ← predicateId(pattern)
4:      pMap ← getPredicateMap(pId)
5:      for all entry in pMap do
6:              if entry.value.contains(object) then
7:                  result.add(entry.key)
8:              end if
9:      end for
10: end if
11: if pattern = "subject:predicate:?X" then
12:     pId ← predicateId(pattern)
13:     pMap ← getPredicateMap(pId)
14:     for each entry in pMap do
15:         if entry.key = sbject then
16:                 result.add(entry.values)
17:         end if
18:     end for
19: end if
20: if pattern = ?X:predicate:?Y then
21:     pId ← predicateId(pattern)
22:     pMap ← getPredicateMap(pId)
23:     for all entry in pMap do
24:             for all value in entry.Values do
25:                     result.add(entry.key,value)
26:             end for
27:     end for
28: end if
```

```
Algorithm 3: mergeAnswer()

Input : interimResult, variablesCount, answerSet
Output : answerSet
Description :

1: if answerColumns = 1 then
2:      if column got results first time then
3:              natural join results and existing answers
4:      else
5:              reduce the answer set (AND results)
6:      end if
7: else if answerColumns = 2 then
8:      if both columns got results first time then
9:              natural join results and existing answers
10:     else if b is got the results and b is at first time then
11:             reduce by 'a' column and natural join by 'b' column
12:     else if a is got the results and a is at first time then
13:             reduce by 'b' column and natural join by 'a' column
14:     else if both are at first time then
15:             reduce by both a and b.
16:     end if
17: end if
```

7.5.5 Evaluation of Acacia's Performance

The experiments conducted on Acacia-RDF are threefold. In all these experiments, we set up Acacia-RDF in a cluster of four computers. The systems were running on Ubuntu Linux, X10 2.5.2, and JDK 1.7.

In the first experiment, Acacia-RDF was configured to run with max 8 GB heap, four places. The aim of the experiment was to compare performance of Acacia-RDF with Neo4j. We used four LUBM data sets of the sizes listed in Table 7.1 during the experiments. We used Neo4j 2.2.4 in this experiment and batch uploaded the LUBM data sets into separate Neo4j databases. We ran first and third LUBM queries (Q1 and Q3) on each of the systems. In the case of Neo4j, we formulated the two LUBM queries as Cypher queries. In the case of Acacia-RDF, we used the SPARQL syntax.

Table 7.1 RDF graph data sets

ID	Data set name	Vertices	Edges	File size
G_1	LUBM-5	0.10 M	0.83 M	51.9 MB
G_2	LUBM-10	0.21 M	1.70 M	105.9 MB
G_3	LUBM-20	0.44 M	3.59 M	224.8 MB
G_4	LUBM-40	0.86 M	7.10 M	445 MB
G_5	LUBM-80	1.7 M	14.33 M	862 MB
G_6	LUBM-160	3.6 M	28.50 M	1.7 GB

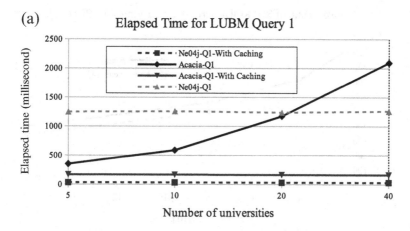

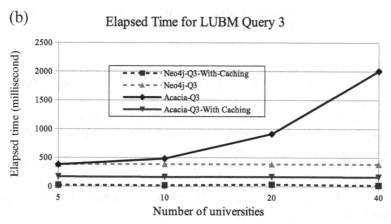

Fig. 7.10 Elapsed time for running LUBM queries 1 and 3

We have plotted the results in Fig. 7.10. Note that all the performance values listed in this chapter (except Neo4j non-cached scenarios) are three times averages taken after running multiple warm up runs of the same query. In the case of Neo4j non-cached scenario, when we obtain the performance numbers for the first query, we first ran third query ten times and then ran first query. This was to avoid Neo4j's query-caching feature which made third query to run without the effect of caching. This leads to fair comparison between the two systems when they do not employ any caching. The corresponding result is shown in the curve *Neo4j-Q1*. The results obtained by just running Neo4j three times without such technique are shown in *Neo4j-Q1-With-Caching*. We did similar experiment for LUBM Q3 scenario as well.

From the first category of the experiments, we observed that Acacia-RDF outperforms Neo4j in certain scenarios when both the systems operate without

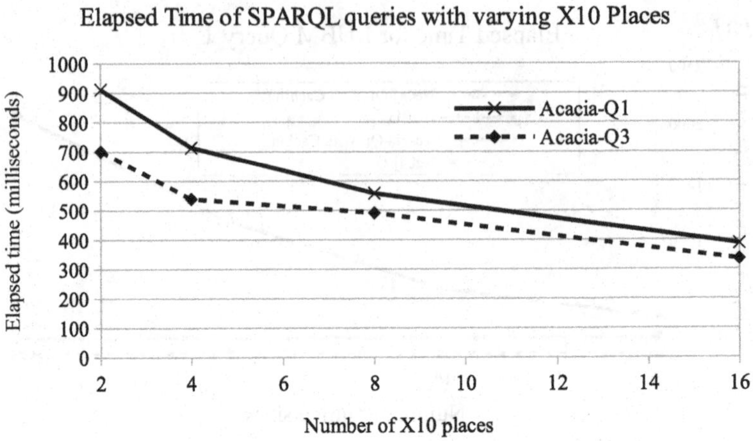

Elapsed Time of SPARQL queries with varying X10 Places

Fig. 7.11 Elapsed time for running LUBM query 1 (Q1) and query 3 (Q3) with variable numbers of X10 places on G_2. LUBM Q1 and Q3 are single-variable queries

caching mechanisms' help for graphs less than LUBM 20. However, Acacia-RDF's execution time rises along with the number of universities in the input LUBM data. We conducted Nmon [63]-based profiling of the experiments and observed that the communication between the master and worker increases with the size of the LUBM data set. We are currently working to reduce this communication overhead in order to speed up LUBM query execution.

In the second experiment we conducted a scalability experiment of LUBM queries with varying number of X10 places. The objective was to observe the scalability of LUBM query execution. The results are shown in Figs. 7.11 (single-variable queries) and 7.12 (multivariable query).

From the second category of experiments we observed that Acacia-RDF system scales with the increasing number of X10 places. Although it is not a linear speedup, we observe considerable performance gain when adding more X10 places. For example, for the LUBM query 1, on G_2 Acacia-RDF completed execution in 0.9 s with two places, while the same query ran in 0.4 s with 16 places.

Finally, we evaluated the fault tolerance mechanism of Acacia-RDF. For this we choose G_5 data set which is one of the two larger data sets used in our experiments. We observed the system characteristics when the system runs Q2 with 16 places and when the system runs Q2 with one place crashed (only having 15 alive places). The elapsed time (three times average) of nonfaulty execution was 51.2 s, while with one place killed it took 53.4 s of execution. In both the cases we receive the correct result for executing LUBM Q2.

Overall through these experiments we observed Acacia-RDF's scalability in a distributed environment with first and third LUBM queries running with 16 places on LUBM 10 data set with elapsed times of approximately 2 s. Furthermore, Acacia-RDF reported less than ten seconds elapsed times on 16 places for running the first three queries of the LUBM benchmark on G_6.

Elapsed Time of LUBM Q2 (multi-variable query) with varying X10 Places

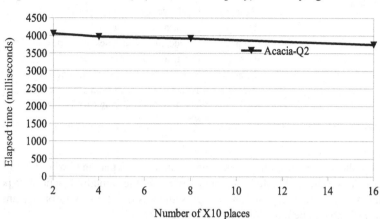

Fig. 7.12 Elapsed time for running LUBM query 2 (Q2) with variable numbers of X10 places on G_2. LUBM Q2 is a multivariable query

We have identified several areas which need further improvements. Although we have implemented a query results caching mechanism, its operation during continuously updated data sets needs to be evaluated. We have significantly improved the size of the data set which can be uploaded to the Acacia-RDF system by optimizing the RDF Partitioner. However, we hope to optimize RDF Partitioner to work with much larger data sets in future (beyond LUBM 160).

7.6   XGDBench Graph Database Benchmarking Framework on Clouds

7.6.1   Methodology of XGDBench

Almost every software benchmark has been developed around a real-world application scenario of the software system that it intends for benchmarking [45]. We developed XGDBench focusing on a graph database application for social networking services which fits for the theme of graph databases on exascale clouds. This is because online social networks (OSNs) are one of the rapidly growing areas that generates massive graphs and data storage, and analysis of such online social networks is conducted in cloud infrastructures [70].

It is a common phenomenon in social networks that people with similar interests (i.e., attributes) are more likely to become friends in the real world. For example, if person A and person B went to the same high school, and both of them graduated in the same year, there is a higher probability that they are friends in the real world, as

Table 7.2 Basic operations of graph databases

Operation	Description
Read	Read a vertex and its properties
Insert	Inserts a new vertex
Update	Update all the attributes of a vertex
Delete	Delete a vertex from the DB
Scan	Load the list of neighbors of a vertex
Traverse	Traverses the graph from a given vertex using BFS This represents finding friends of a person in social networks

well as in the social network service than compared to a person C who did not go to the same high school. The fact that people went to the same high school or people graduated in a particular year can be represented as questions with binary answers (yes/no) which can be represented as attribute vectors.

7.6.2 Requirements of XGDBench

In this section we describe the performance aspects that are specifically targeted by XGDBench. These performance aspects are represented by individual operations. These individual operations (which are listed in Table 7.2) get intermixed according to some predefined proportions to create workloads.

7.6.2.1 Attribute Read/Update

Graph databases in exascale clouds will have to handle massive graphs online, and they will partially load the graph into memory. The workloads will include both read/update operations. However, in most of the future exascale applications, the read operations will dominate the workload [72]; we included read-heavy (e.g., a workload with 0.95 probability of read operation and 0.05 probability of write operation [22]) and read-only (having only read operations) workloads with XGDBench.

Graphs need to be updated online. In a typical OSN, a node represents a user, and an edge represents friendship/relationship. Properties of nodes/edges include messages, photos, etc. The friendship graph of OSNs changes at a slower rate compared to their properties. Therefore, performance of attribute update operation is critical compared to node/edge update. We included an update-heavy workload with XGDBench due to this reason.

Moreover, the benchmarking platform needs to be scalable to store data in memory for update operations. This will eliminate unexpected delays involved in reading large data from secondary storage.

7.6.2.2   Graph Traversal

Unlike other database types, graph databases have the unique property of having data encoded in their graph structures. These information could only be obtained by traversing the graph. Therefore, the benchmark should have support for evaluating the performance of graph traversal operations. While there are a variety of graph traversal techniques, we decided to use an algorithm that will be most frequently executed against the graph database. This is because it is more important to check the performance of frequently used operations than operations that run infrequently which do not have requirements for real-time execution. We selected a scenario of listing friends of friends, which is one of the frequently used traversal operations in OSNs. This includes execution of BFS (breadth-first search) from a particular vertex for detecting the connected component of a graph. Breadth-first search traverses a graph in a level-wise manner. Before visiting the vertices at path length $(k + 1)$, the traverser first needs to visit all the vertices within path length k [80]. BFS can be also considered as layers or waves growing outward from a given vertex. The vertices in the first wave are the immediate neighbors of the starting vertex, and they have distance of 1. The neighbors of those neighbors have distance of 2, etc. [60].

Note that most real-world graphs are irregular data structures [77], and therefore it is possible for starting the traversal from a vertex that is heavily connected with the other vertices as well as starting the traversal from an unconnected vertex.

Based on the aforementioned requirements we define the following set of basic operations on a graph database (shown in Table 7.2). We believe that these basic operations are sufficient for defining many workloads that are frequently present in graph databases.

7.6.3   Implementation of XGDBench

Implementation details of XGDBench are shown in Fig. 7.13. XGDBench client is the software application that is used to execute the benchmark's workloads. Its main components are graph generator, graph data structure, workload executor, Graph DB Workload, and Graph DB Interface Layer. The XGDBench client is written in managed X10. Since the X10 compiler translates managed X10 code to Java and then compiles the generated Java code to byte code, we used Java for components such as Graph DB Interface Layer, MAG Generator, etc. We used pure X10 code for constructing the distributed graph data structure. This way we were able to use X10 language features only in the components that they are needed. However, the entire XGDBench client was compiled using X10 compiler (x10c), and the benchmarking sessions were run using the X10 interpreter (x10). XGDBench client accepts a collection of input parameters that are used during the benchmarking process. Each of these parameters is described in the below subsections.

XGDBench has two phases of execution called *loading phase* and *transaction phase*. The loading phase generates an attribute graph by using the MAG algorithm

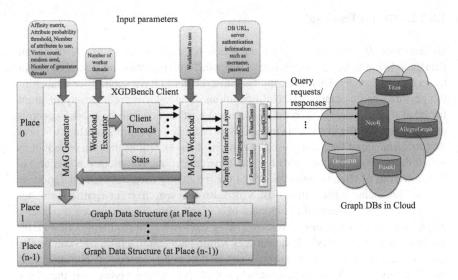

Fig. 7.13 Architecture of XGDBench client

Table 7.3 Core workloads of XGDBench

A: Update heavy
Workload A is a mix of 50/50 read/update workload. Read operations query a vertex V and read all the attributes of V. Update operation changes the last login time attribute of the vertices. Attributes related to vertex affinity are not changed
B: Read mostly
A mix of 95/5 read/update workload. Read/update operations are similar to A
C: Read only
Consists of 100% read operations. The read operations are similar to A
D: Read latest
This workload inserts new vertices to the graph. The inserts are made in such a way that the power-law relations of the original graph are preserved
E: Short range scan
This workload reads all the neighbor vertices and their attributes of a vertex A. This represents the scenario of loading the friendliest of person A on to an application
F: Traverse heavy
Consists of 45/55 mix of traverse/read operations
G: Traverse only
Consists of 100% traverse operations

shown in Algorithm 1. The transaction phase of XGDBench calls a method in *CoreWorkload* called *doTransaction()*, which invokes the basic operations such as database read, update, insert, scan, and traverse. We have implemented the workloads that satisfy the requirements stated in Sect. 7.6.2 on XGDBench, and these workloads are listed in Table 7.3.

We use throughput (operations per second), latency (milliseconds), and runtime (milliseconds) as the performance metrics in XGDBench. Furthermore, XGDBench can be configured to output a histogram of latencies for each operation.

7.6.3.1   Graph Generator

XGDBench client consists of a graph data generator (MAG Generator in Fig. 7.13) for generating the data to be loaded to the database. The workload generator is implemented using Multiplicative Attribute Graphs (MAG) model [59] as described in the previous section. As can be observed in the line 1 of Algorithm 1, the graph generator accepts an attribute matrix that is initialized with random attribute values (either 0 or 1). To ensure the repeatability of the benchmarking experiments, the attribute matrix needs to be initialized with the same attribute values across different benchmarking experiments that contain the same set of input parameters. To ensure this property, we used a single random number generator object that is initialized with some initial random seed that can be specified on the command line. We observed during our experiments that the graph generator generates the same graph across different benchmarking sessions.

7.6.3.2   Graph Data Structure

We use the DistArray of X10 to implement the distributed graph data structure of XGDBench client. This data structure is useful for storing very large graphs that cannot be stored on a single node's memory. By default, the vertex and edge information are stored in Place 0 (Place 0 runs on the node that invoked the XGDBench client.), and when the graph grows exceeding the prespecified vertex count per place, the excess vertices are transferred to the next place. We configured XGDBench's graph structure to handle up to 2^{25} (33 million) vertices per place during the experiments.

7.6.3.3   Workload Executor

The workload executor initializes multiple client threads which invoke operation sequences according to the workloads it handles. A sequential series of operations are executed by each client thread. Graph database interface layer translates these simple requests from client threads into calls against the graph database. Unlike its predecessor (YCSB), XGDBench faces a problem when implementing the multithreaded workload execution. This is because each thread needs to access the same generator object to get its next vertex/edge information. However, in YCSB there was no such requirement for querying a single object for information because the operations invoked did not have relationships like edges in graphs. Currently we synchronize only the code that obtains the next vertex/edge information from the generator which solves this problem.

7.6.3.4   Graph DB Workload

Graph DB Workload (MAG Workload in Fig. 7.13) is a component that represents a workload that can be invoked on the Graph DB Interface Layer. It wraps up the workload's properties that are specified in the property files as well as command line arguments. Furthermore, it acts as the bridge between the client threads and the graph generator. The Graph DB Workload component also forwards each operation invoked by the client threads to the Graph DB Interface Layer.

7.6.3.5   Graph DB Interface Layer

Graph DB Interface Layer consists of interfaces for different graph databases. Most of the current graph database servers have their own optimized query interfaces. For example, RexPro [7] is a binary protocol that can be utilized to send Gremlin scripts to remote Rexster instances. However, we decided to use common protocols such as HTTP/REST for implementing the Graph DB Layer because it enables us to do more fair comparison of different systems. Furthermore, there were limitations of the HTTP/REST interfaces of certain graph database servers that made us use some alternatives in combination with HTTP/REST interfaces to implement the required functions. For example, the Rexster server 2.1.0 used for Titan graph database server threw an error when we try to POST edges through HTTP/REST interface which made us use the Rexster's Gremlin interface to conduct edge insertion.

In current XGDBench implementation, our focus is on benchmarking graph database servers. The reason for this is that XGDBench is a benchmarking framework rather than a benchmark specification. If XGDBench was a benchmark specification, the specified benchmark operations would have to be implemented in the target graph database using its query language which could be either an embedded graph database or a stand-alone graph database server. Such an approach can be categorized as a white box approach because the developer can implement the benchmark specification in the way he/she wants. However, in XGDBench we treat the graph database server completely as a black box which makes the benchmarking process and the workloads executed on the graph databases work more similar to a graph-based application communicating with a stand-alone graph database server. Nevertheless, if a user wants to benchmark an embedded graph database with XGDBench, that is completely doable with the current implementation. In such a scenario the graph database client will create an embedded graph database server instance within the same JVM instance (note that managed X10 is interpreted by the system's JVM). But the benchmarking result will be interfered with by the benchmarking software itself. This is another reason for why we do not use XGDBench for benchmarking embedded graph databases.

7.6.3.6   Implementation of Traversal Operation

We implemented the traversal operation of the XGDBench by implementing BFS traversal for finding friends of friends scenario for each graph database client. The BFS traversal operation is conducted up to only two hops from a randomly chosen starting point. This is because we believe that many of the social network users are interested of finding their friends' information as well as the user's friends of friends information. It is rare that users go beyond this two-hop traversal. Here "two-hop traversal" means visiting vertices' neighbors and neighbors of neighbors by traversing the graph. Social networking happens among peers, not among strangers [86].

7.6.3.7   Implementation of Insert and Update Operations

The update operations on the graph data preserves the power-law distribution that is present in the original graph created by MAG because the update operations are conducted only on attributes that are not related to calculation of probability of an edge. Furthermore, we make sure the insert operations of the vertices done during the workload executions preserve the power-law structure. While it is rare to find graph database applications that execute 100% traverse operations, we created the workload G as a complete traverse only workload because traverse operation is one of the inherent key features of a graph database server, and it is important to compare graph traverse operation performance of graph databases.

7.6.4   Evaluation of XGDBench in HPC Cluster

7.6.4.1   Performance Evaluation of Titan

In the next half of the evaluations, we configured Titan (through Rexster 2.1.0) on Tsubame. The arrangement of the experiment node cluster is shown in Fig. 7.14.

We executed data loading and transaction workloads on the Titan Rexster server for different vertex counts. We used 24 threads for XGDBench during all the experiments because a single node on Tsubame 2.0 contains 24 hardware threads. Before each experiment round we truncated the Titan and Cassandra to make sure each experiment is started with clean graph database server. We used 100 as the initial random seed value for XGDBench. The results of the data loading phase are shown in Fig. 7.15.

The results of executing transaction phase are shown in Fig. 7.15. Note that the experiment results shown in Figs. 7.15 and 7.16 are single experiment runs.

Fig. 7.14 How XGDBench, Titan Rexster server, and Cassandra are deployed in the experiment node cluster on Tsubame

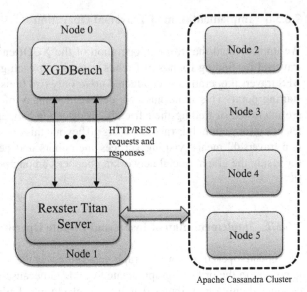

7.6.4.2   Evaluation of Graph Generation Time

We evaluated the time taken for generating large graphs with XGDBench's graph generator. The purpose of this evaluation was to identify to what extent the generator can generate large graphs. The results are shown in Fig. 7.17. We observed that XGDBench's generator is able to generate a graph with 250 thousand vertices and 622 million edges in about 315 s using a JVM heap size of 32 GB on a single node of Tsubame. While such large-scale graphs can be generated with XGDBench, benchmarking graph database servers with such gigantic graphs cannot be achieved easily because most of the current graph database servers are not capable of handling such large graphs efficiently.

7.7   Conclusion

This chapter presented our experience of design and implementation of graph data processing systems in X10. We first described about ScaleGraph graph processing library and then moved to discuss about Acacia distributed graph database server. Finally, we discussed about design and implementation of XGDBench which is a graph benchmarking framework. An important characteristic of these graph processing frameworks is that while they are completely developed in X10 from the ground-up, X10's native code invocation has helped them to leverage their underlying language back end.

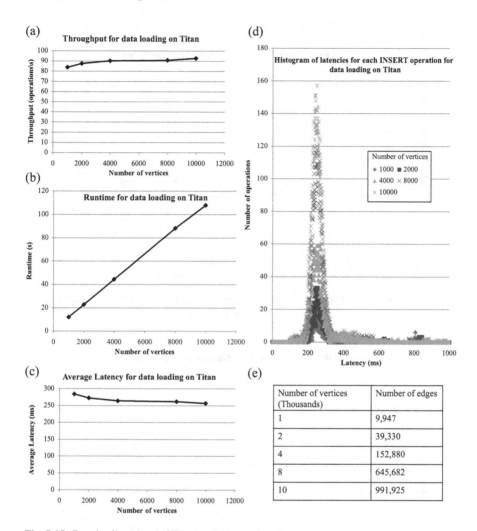

Fig. 7.15 Data loading phase of Titan on Tsubame Cloud

Through extensive scalability experiments, we have shown that X10-based graph processing applications indicate limited scalability in cluster environments. In the future we plan to extend our knowledge on the scaling bottlenecks of X10 applications further in large-scale clusters. Furthermore, we are working on extending these graph data processing frameworks to novel areas such as time-evolving graphs.

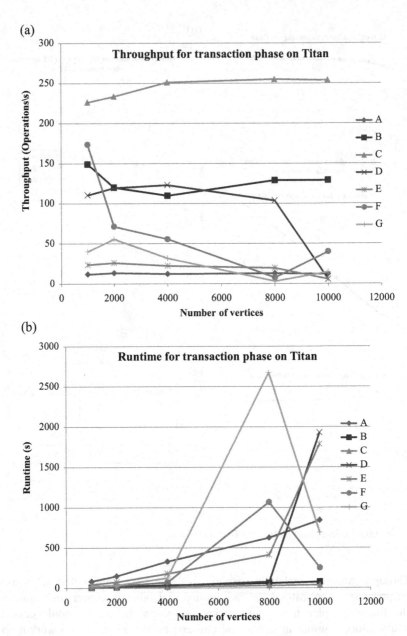

Fig. 7.16 Throughput and runtime for transaction phase of Titan on Tsubame Cloud

(a)

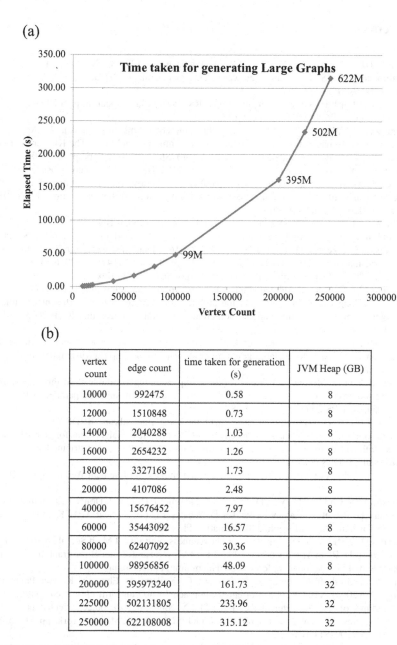

(b)

vertex count	edge count	time taken for generation (s)	JVM Heap (GB)
10000	992475	0.58	8
12000	1510848	0.73	8
14000	2040288	1.03	8
16000	2654232	1.26	8
18000	3327168	1.73	8
20000	4107086	2.48	8
40000	15676452	7.97	8
60000	35443092	16.57	8
80000	62407092	30.36	8
100000	98956856	48.09	8
200000	395973240	161.73	32
225000	502131805	233.96	32
250000	622108008	315.12	32

Fig. 7.17 Evaluation of graph generation time on XGDBench graph generator on Tsubame Cloud. The numbers on the curve in (**a**) indicate the number of edges generated in millions (M)

References

1. Abadi DJ, Marcus A, Madden SR, Hollenbach K (2009) Sw-store: a vertically partitioned DBMS for semantic web data management. VLDB J 18(2):385–406. doi:10.1007/s00778-008-0125-y
2. Agarwal S, Barik R, Sarkar V, Shyamasundar RK (2007) May-happen-in-parallel analysis of x10 programs, PPoPP '07, San Jose, pp 183–193
3. Aggarwal CC, Wang H (2010) A survey of clustering algorithms for graph data. In: Aggarwal CC, Wang H, Elmagarmid AK (eds) Managing and mining graph data. The Kluwer international series on advances in database systems, vol 40. Springer, New York, pp 275–301
4. An P, Jula A, Rus S, Saunders S, Smith T, Tanase G, Thomas N, Amato N, Rauchwerger L (2003) STAPL: an adaptive, generic parallel c++ library. In: Proceedings of the 14th international conference on Languages and compilers for parallel computing, LCPC'01. Springer, Berlin/Heidelberg, pp 193–208
5. Anthonisse J (1971) The rush in a directed graph. Technical report BN 9/71
6. Arnold M, Grove D, Herta B, Hind M, Hirzel M, Iyengar A, Mandel L, Saraswat VA, Shinnar A, Siméon J, Takeuchi M, Tardieu O, Zhang W (2016) Meta: middleware for events, transactions, and analytics. IBM J Res Dev 60(2–3):15:1–15:10. doi:10.1147/JRD.2016.2527419
7. Aurelius (2013) Rexpro. https://github.com/tinkerpop/rexster/wiki/RexPro
8. Aurelius (2015) Titan: distributed graph database. http://thinkaurelius.github.io/titan/
9. Bader D, Cong G, Feo J (2005) On the architectural requirements for efficient execution of graph algorithms. In: International conference on parallel processing, ICPP 2005, Oslo, pp 547–556
10. Bader DA, Feo J, Gilbert J, Kepner J, Koester D, Loh E, Madduri K, Mann B, Meuse T, Robinson E (2009) HPC scalable graph analysis benchmark. http://www.graphanalysis.org/benchmark/
11. Barrett B, Berry J, Murphy R, Wheeler K (2009) Implementing a portable multi-threaded graph library: the MTGL on Qthreads. In: IEEE international symposium on parallel distributed processing, IPDPS 2009, Rome, pp 1 –8
12. Batenkov D (2011) Boosting productivity with the boost graph library. XRDS 17:31–32
13. Berry J, Hendrickson B, Kahan S, Konecny P (2007) Software and algorithms for graph queries on multithreaded architectures. In: IEEE international parallel and distributed processing symposium, IPDPS 2007, Long Beach, pp 1–14
14. Bizer C, Schultz A (2009) The Berlin SPARQL Benchmark. Int J Semant Web Inf Syst 5(2):1–24
15. Blackford LS, Choi J, Cleary A, D'Azevedo E, Demmel J, Dhillon I, Dongarra J, Hammarling S, Henry G, Petitet A, Stanley K, Walker D, Whaley RC (1997) ScaLAPACK Users' guide. Society for Industrial and Applied Mathematics, Philadelphia
16. Brandes U (2001) A Faster algorithm for betweenness centrality. J Math Sociol 25:163–177
17. Chakrabarti D, Zhan Y, Faloutsos C (2004) R-MAT: a recursive model for graph mining. In: Fourth SIAM international conference on data mining, Philadelphia
18. Charles P, Grothoff C, Saraswat V, Donawa C, Kielstra A, Ebcioglu K, von Praun C, Sarkar V (2005) X10: an object-oriented approach to non-uniform cluster computing. In: Proceedings of the 20th annual ACM SIGPLAN conference on object-oriented programming, systems, languages, and applications, OOPSLA '05. ACM, New York, pp 519–538. doi:10.1145/1094811.1094852
19. Ciglan M, Averbuch A, Hluchy L (2012) Benchmarking traversal operations over graph databases. In: 2012 IEEE 28th international conference on data engineering workshops (ICDEW), Arlington, pp 186–189
20. Cong G, Almasi G, Saraswat V (2009) Fast PGAS connected components algorithms, PGAS '09. ACM, New York, pp 13:1–13:6
21. Cong G, Almasi G, Saraswat V (2010) Fast PGAS implementation of distributed graph algorithms, SC '10. IEEE Computer Society, Washington, DC, pp 1–11

22. Cooper BF, Silberstein A, Tam E, Ramakrishnan R, Sears R (2010) Benchmarking cloud serving systems with YCSB. In: Proceedings of the 1st ACM symposium on cloud computing, SoCC '10. ACM, New York, pp 143–154. doi:http://doi.acm.org/10.1145/1807128.1807152

23. Csardi G, Nepusz T (2006) The igraph software package for complex network research. Inter J Complex Syst 1695. http://igraph.sf.net

24. Cunningham D, Grove D, Herta B, Iyengar A, Kawachiya K, Murata H, Saraswat V, Takeuchi M, Tardieu O (2014) Resilient x10: efficient failure-aware programming. In: Proceedings of the 19th ACM SIGPLAN symposium on principles and practice of parallel programming, PPoPP '14. ACM, New York, pp 67–80. doi:10.1145/2555243.2555248

25. Dayarathna M, Suzumura T (2012) Xgdbench: a benchmarking platform for graph stores in exascale clouds. In: 2012 IEEE 4th international conference on cloud computing technology and science (CloudCom), pp 363–370. doi:10.1109/CloudCom.2012.6427516

26. Dayarathna M, Suzumura T (2014) Graph database benchmarking on cloud environments with XGDBench. Autom softw Eng 21(4):509–533. doi:10.1007/s10515-013-0138-7

27. Dayarathna M, Suzumura T (2014) Towards emulation of large scale complex network workloads on graph databases with XGDBench. In: 2014 IEEE international congress on big data, pp 748–755. doi:10.1109/BigData.Congress.2014.140

28. Dayarathna M, Suzumura T (2014) Towards scalable distributed graph database engine for hybrid clouds. In: 2015 5th international workshop on data-intensive computing in the clouds (DataCloud), pp 1–8. doi:10.1109/DataCloud.2014.9

29. Dayarathna M, Houngkaew C, Ogata H, Suzumura T (2012) Scalable performance of scalegraph for large scale graph analysis. In: 2012 19th international conference on high performance computing (HiPC), pp 1–9. doi:10.1109/HiPC.2012.6507498

30. Dayarathna M, Houngkaew C, Suzumura T (2012) Introducing scalegraph: an x10 library for billion scale graph analytics. In: Proceedings of the 2012 ACM SIGPLAN X10 workshop, X10 '12. ACM, New York, pp 6:1–6:9. doi:10.1145/2246056.2246062, http://doi.acm.org/10.1145/2246056.2246062

31. Dayarathna M, Herath I, Dewmini Y, Mettananda G, Nandasiri S, Jayasena S, Suzumura T (2016) Introducing acacia-RDF: an x10-based scalable distributed RDF graph database engine. In: 2016 IEEE international parallel and distributed processing symposium workshops (IPDPSW), pp 1024–1032. doi:10.1109/IPDPSW.2016.31

32. Dongarra J et al (2011) The international exascale software project roadmap. Int J high Perform Comput Appl 25(1):3–60

33. Ediger D, Jiang K, Riedy J, Bader DA, Corley C (2010) Massive social network analysis: mining twitter for social good. In: Proceedings of the 2010 39th international conference on parallel processing, ICPP '10. IEEE Computer Society, Washington, DC, pp 583–593

34. Fortunato S (2009) Community detection in graphs. CoRR abs/0906.0612

35. Freeman LC (1977) A Set of Measures of centrality based on betweenness. Sociometry 40(1):35–41

36. SPARQL G (2016) The SPARQL (pron: sparkle) query language antlr4 grammar. https://code.google.com/p/sparkle-g/

37. Garcia R, Jarvi J, Lumsdaine A, Siek JG, Willcock J (2003) A comparative study of language support for generic programming, OOPSLA'03. ACM, New York, pp 115–134

38. Gregor D, Lumsdaine A (2005) Lifting sequential graph algorithms for distributed-memory parallel computation. SIGPLAN Not 40:423–437

39. Grove D, Tardieu O, Cunningham D, Herta B, Peshansky I, Saraswat V (2011) A performance model for x10 applications: What's going on under the hood?

40. Guo Y, Pan Z, Heflin J (2005) Lubm: a benchmark for owl knowledge base systems. Web Semant 3(2–3):158–182. doi:10.1016/j.websem.2005.06.005

41. Gurajada S, Seufert S, Miliaraki I, Theobald M (2014) Triad: a distributed shared-nothing RDF engine based on asynchronous message passing. In: Proceedings of the 2014 ACM SIGMOD international conference on management of data, SIGMOD '14. ACM, New York, pp 289–300. doi:10.1145/2588555.2610511

42. Hammoud M, Rabbou DA, Nouri R, Beheshti SMR, Sakr S (2015) Dream: distributed RDF engine with adaptive query planner and minimal communication. Proc VLDB Endow 8(6):654–665. doi:10.14778/2735703.2735705
43. Hielscher F, Gottschling P (2012) Pargraph. http://pargraph.sourceforge.net/
44. Ho LY, Wu JJ, Liu P (2012) Distributed graph database for large-scale social computing. In: 2012 IEEE 5th international conference on cloud computing (CLOUD), Piscataway, pp 455–462
45. Huppler K (2009) The art of building a good benchmark. In: Nambiar R, Poess M (ed) Performance evaluation and benchmarking. Springer, Berlin/Heidelberg, pp 18–30
46. IBM (2014) X10: performance and productivity at scale. http://x10-lang.org/
47. Karypis G, Kumar V (1998) A fast and high quality multilevel scheme for partitioning irregular graphs. SIAM J Sci Comput 20(1):359–392
48. Kemal Ebcioglu VS Vijay Saraswat (2004) X10: Programming for hierarchical parallelism and non-uniform data access. In: 3rd international workshop on language runtimes, impact of next generation processor architectures on virtual machine technologies
49. Labouseur AG, Birnbaum J, Olsen J PaulW, Spillane S, Vijayan J, Hwang JH, Han WS (2014) The g* graph database: efficiently managing large distributed dynamic graphs. Distrib Parallel Databases 1–36. doi:10.1007/s10619-014-7140-3
50. Law J (2003) Review of "the boost graph library: user guide and reference manual by jeremy g. siek, lie-quan lee, and andrew lumsdaine." addison-wesley 2002. ACM SIGSOFT Softw Eng Notes 28(2):35–36
51. Lee LQ, Siek JG, Lumsdaine A (1999) The generic graph component library. SIGPLAN Not 34:399–414
52. Leskovec J (2012) Snap: Stanford network analysis project. http://snap.stanford.edu/
53. Lugowski A, Alber D, Buluç A, Gilbert J, Reinhardt S, Teng Y, Waranis A (2012, accepted) A flexible open-source toolbox for scalable complex graph analysis. In: SIAM Conference on Data Mining (SDM), Philadelphia
54. Ma L, Yang Y, Qiu Z, Xie G, Pan Y, Liu S (2006) Towards a complete owl ontology benchmark. In: Sure Y, Domingue J (eds) The semantic web: research and applications. Lecture notes in computer science, vol 4011. Springer, Berlin/Heidelberg, pp 125–139
55. Madduri K, Hendrickson B, Berry J, Bader D, Crobak J (2008) Multithreaded algorithms for processing massive graphs
56. Malewicz G, Austern MH, Bik AJ, Dehnert JC, Horn I, Leiser N, Czajkowski G (2010) Pregel: a system for large-scale graph processing. In: Proceedings of the 2010 international conference on management of data, SIGMOD '10. ACM, New York, pp 135–146
57. Marsland S (2009) Machine learning: an algorithmic perspective. Chapman & Hall/CRC, Boca Raton
58. Morsey M, Lehmann J, Auer S, Ngomo ACN (2011) Dbpedia sparql benchmark – performance assessment with real queries on real data. In: International semantic web conference (1)'11, pp 454–469
59. Myunghwan K, Leskovec J (2012) Multiplicative attribute graph model of real-world networks. Internet Math 8(1-2):113–160
60. Newmann M (2010) Networks: an introduction. Oxford University Press, Oxford/New York
61. Neumann T, Weikum G (2010) The RDF-3x engine for scalable management of RDF data. The VLDB J 19(1):91–113. doi:10.1007/s00778-009-0165-y
62. Newmann M, Barabasi AL, Watts DJ (2006) The structure and dynamics of networks. Princeton University Press, Princeton
63. NMON (2016) NMON performance: a free tool to analyze aix and linux performance. http://www.ibm.com/developerworks/aix/library/au-analyze_aix/
64. Ogata H, Dayarathna M, Suzumura T (2012) Towards highly scalable x10 based spectral clustering. In: 2012 19th international conference on high performance computing, pp 1–5. doi:10.1109/HiPC.2012.6507522

65. O'Madadhain J, Fisher D, White S, Boey Y (2003) The JUNG (Java Universal Network/Graph) Framework. Technical report, UCI-ICS
66. Papailiou N, Tsoumakos D, Karras P, Koziris N (2015) Graph-aware, workload-adaptive sparql query caching. In: Proceedings of the 2015 ACM SIGMOD international conference on management of data, SIGMOD 2015. ACM, New York, pp 1777–1792. doi:10.1145/2723372.2723714
67. Pingali K, Nguyen D, Kulkarni M, Burtscher M, Hassaan MA, Kaleem R, Lee TH, Lenharth A, Manevich R, Méndez-Lojo M, Prountzos D, Sui X (2011) The tao of parallelism in algorithms. In: Proceedings of the 32nd ACM SIGPLAN conference on programming language design and implementation, PLDI '11. ACM, New York, pp 12–25
68. Project AX (2012) Xerces-c++ xml parser. http://xerces.apache.org/xerces-c/
69. Rohloff K, Dean M, Emmons I, Ryder D, Sumner J (2007) An evaluation of triple-store technologies for large data stores. In: On the move to meaningful Internet systems 2007: OTM 2007 workshops. Lecture notes in computer science, vol 4806. Springer, Berlin/Heidelberg, pp 1105–1114
70. Sarwat M, Elnikety S, He Y, Kliot G (2012) Horton: online query execution engine for large distributed graphs. In: ICDE, pp 1289–1292
71. Schaeffer SE (2007) Graph clustering. Comput Sci Rev 1(1):27 – 64
72. Schmidt M, Hornung T, Lausen G, Pinkel C (2008) Sp2bench: a SPARQL performance benchmark. CoRR abs/0806.4627
73. Skiena SS (2008) The algorithm design manual. 2nd edn. Springer, London
74. Sourceforge (2012) Jung – java universal network/graph framework. http://jung.sourceforge.net/index.html
75. Tardieu O, Herta B, Cunningham D, Grove D, Kambadur P, Saraswat V, Shinnar A, Takeuchi M, Vaziri M (2014) X10 and apgas at petascale. In: Proceedings of the 19th ACM SIGPLAN symposium on principles and practice of parallel programming, PPoPP '14. ACM, New York, pp 53–66. doi:10.1145/2555243.2555245
76. Thakker D, Osman T, Gohil S, Lakin P (2010) A pragmatic approach to semantic repositories benchmarking. In: Aroyo L, Antoniou G, Hyvönen E, ten Teije A, Stuckenschmidt H, Cabral L, Tudorache T (eds) The semantic web: research and applications. Lecture notes in computer science, vol 6088. Springer, Berlin/Heidelberg, pp 379–393
77. Versaci F, Pingali K (2012) Processor allocation for optimistic parallelization of irregular programs. In: Proceedings of the 12th international conference on computational science and its applications – volume part I, ICCSA'12. Springer, Berlin/Heidelberg, pp 1–14
78. Vicknair C, Macias M, Zhao Z, Nan X, Chen Y, Wilkins D (2010) A comparison of a graph database and a relational database: a data provenance perspective. In: Proceedings of the 48th annual southeast regional conference, ACM SE '10. ACM, New York, pp 42:1–42:6
79. W3C (2015) RDF – semantic web standards. http://www.w3.org/RDF/
80. WANG J (2009) Sequential patterns. In: LIU L, öZSU M (eds) Encyclopedia of database systems. Springer, New York, pp 2621–2625
81. Wood D, Zaidman M, Ruth L, Hausenblas M (2014) Linked Data. Manning, Shelter Island
82. Wu B, Zhou Y, Yuan P, Jin H, Liu L (2014) Semstore: a semantic-preserving distributed RDF triple store. In: Proceedings of the 23rd ACM international conference on information and knowledge management, CIKM '14. ACM, New York, pp 509–518. doi:10.1145/2661829.2661876
83. Xia Y, Tanase I, Nai L, Tan W, Liu Y, Crawford J, Lin CY (2014) Graph analytics and storage. In: IEEE international conference on big data (Big Data), pp 942–951. doi:10.1109/BigData.2014.7004326
84. Yuan P, Liu P, Wu B, Jin H, Zhang W, Liu L (2013) Triplebit: a fast and compact system for large scale RDF data. Proc VLDB Endow 6(7):517–528. doi:10.14778/2536349.2536352
85. Zeng K, Yang J, Wang H, Shao B, Wang Z (2013) A distributed graph engine for web scale RDF data. In: Proceedings of the 39th international conference on Very Large Data Bases, VLDB Endowment, PVLDB'13, pp 265–276. http://dl.acm.org/citation.cfm?id=2488329.2488333

86. Zhao Z, Liu J, Crespi N (2011) The design of activity-oriented social networking: Dig-event. In: Proceedings of the 13th international conference on information integration and web-based applications and services, IIWAS '11. ACM, New York, pp 420–425
87. Zou L, Mo J, Chen L, Özsu MT, Zhao D (2011) gStore: answering SPARQL queries via subgraph matching. Proc VLDB Endow 4(8):482–493. doi:10.14778/2002974.2002976

Chapter 8
Implementing MapReduce Applications in Dynamic Cloud Environments

Fabrizio Marozzo, Domenico Talia, and Paolo Trunfio

8.1 Introduction

Clouds are used as effective computing platforms to face the challenge of extracting knowledge from big data repositories, as well as to provide efficient data analysis environments to both researchers and companies [1]. A key point for the effective implementation of data analysis environments on Cloud platforms is the availability of programming models that support a wide range of applications and system scenarios [2]. One of the most popular programming models adopted for the implementation of data-intensive Cloud applications is MapReduce [3].

Since its introduction by Google, MapReduce has proven to be applicable to many domains, including machine learning and data mining, log file analysis, financial analysis, scientific simulation, image retrieval and processing, blog crawling, machine translation, language modelling, and bioinformatics. It is widely recognized as one of the most important programming models for Cloud environments, being supported by leading providers such as Amazon, with its Elastic MapReduce service,[1] and Google itself, which released a MapReduce API for its App Engine.[2]

MapReduce defines a framework for processing large data sets in a highly parallel way by exploiting computing facilities available in a large cluster or through a Cloud system. Users specify the computation in terms of a map function that processes a key/value pair to generate a list of intermediate key/value pairs and a reduce function that merges all intermediate values associated with the same inter-

---

[1]http://aws.amazon.com/emr/

[2]https://cloud.google.com/appengine/docs/java/dataprocessing/

F. Marozzo (✉) • D. Talia • P. Trunfio
DIMES, University of Calabria, Rende, Italy
e-mail: fmarozzo@dimes.unical.it; talia@dimes.unical.it; trunfio@dimes.unical.it

© Springer International Publishing AG 2017

N. Antonopoulos, L. Gillam (eds.), *Cloud Computing*, Computer Communications and Networks, DOI 10.1007/978-3-319-54645-2_8

mediate key. Standard MapReduce implementations (e.g., Google's MapReduce [4] and Apache Hadoop [5]) are based on a master-slave model. A job is submitted by a user node to a master node that selects idle workers and assigns each one a map or a reduce task. When all map and reduce tasks have been completed, the master node returns the result to the user node. The failure of a worker is managed by re-executing its task on another worker, while standard MapReduce implementations do not handle master failures as designers consider failures unlikely in large clusters or in reliable Cloud environments.

On the contrary, node failures – including master failures – can occur in large clusters and are likely to happen in dynamic Cloud environments like a Cloud of clouds, which can be formed by a large number of computing nodes that join and leave the network at very high rates. Therefore, providing effective mechanisms to manage master failures is fundamental to exploit the MapReduce model in the implementation of data-intensive applications in large dynamic Cloud environments where standard MapReduce implementations could be unreliable.

P2P-MapReduce [6] exploits a peer-to-peer model to manage node churn, master failures, and job recovery in a decentralized but effective way, so as to provide a more reliable MapReduce middleware that can be effectively exploited in dynamic Cloud infrastructures. This chapter describes the P2P-MapReduce architecture, mechanisms, and implementation and provides an evaluation of its performance. The performance results confirm that P2P-MapReduce ensures a higher level of fault tolerance compared to a centralized implementation of MapReduce.

The remainder of the chapter is organized as follows. Section 8.2 provides a background on MapReduce. Section 8.3 describes the P2P-MapReduce architecture. Section 8.4 discusses the fault tolerance mechanisms used in P2P-MapReduce. Section 8.5 describes how the system has been implemented. Section 8.6 presents an evaluation of its performance. Finally, Sect. 8.7 concludes the chapter.

8.2   MapReduce Background

This section describes the operations performed by a generic MapReduce application to transform input data into output data according to the standard master-slave model and discusses some popular MapReduce frameworks.

MapReduce Users define a *map* and a *reduce* function [3]. The *map* function processes a (key, value) pair and returns a list of intermediate (key, value) pairs:

map (k1,v1) → list(k2,v2).

The *reduce* function merges all intermediate values having the same intermediate key:

reduce (k2, list(v2)) → list(v2).

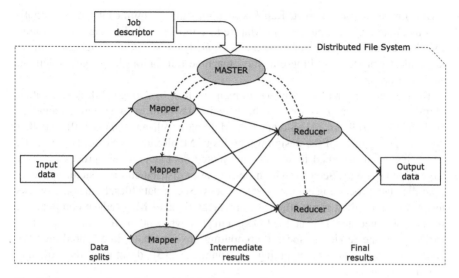

Fig. 8.1 Execution phases in a generic MapReduce application

The whole transformation process can be described through the following steps
(see Fig. 8.1):

1. A master process receives a job descriptor that specifies the MapReduce job to
   be executed. The job descriptor contains, among other information, the location
   of the input data, which may be accessed using a distributed file system or an
   HTTP/FTP server.
2. According to the job descriptor, the master starts a number of mapper and reducer
   processes on different machines. At the same time, it starts a process that reads
   the input data from its location, partitions that data into a set of splits, and
   distributes those splits to the various mappers.
3. After receiving its data partition, each mapper process executes the *map* function
   (provided as part of the job descriptor) to generate a list of intermediate key/value
   pairs. Those pairs are then grouped on the basis of their keys.
4. All pairs with the same keys are assigned to the same reducer process. Hence,
   each reducer process executes the *reduce* function (defined by the job descriptor)
   which merges all the values associated to the same key to generate a possibly
   smaller set of values.
5. The results generated by each reducer process are then collected and delivered
   to a location specified by the job descriptor, so as to form the final output
   data.

Several applications of MapReduce have been demonstrated, including performing a distributed grep, counting URL access frequency, building a reverse
Web-link graph, building a term-vector per host, building inverted indexes, and

performing a distributed sort. Ref. [5] mentions many significant types of applications implemented exploiting the MapReduce model, including machine learning and data mining, log file analysis, financial analysis, scientific simulation, image retrieval and processing, blog crawling, machine translation, language modelling, and bioinformatics.

Besides the original MapReduce implementation by Google [4], several other MapReduce implementations have been realized within other systems, including Hadoop [5], GridGain [7], Skynet [8], MapSharp [9], and Disco [10]. Another system sharing most of the design principles of MapReduce is Sector/Sphere [11], which has been designed to support distributed data storage and processing over large Cloud systems. Sector is a high-performance distributed file system; Sphere is a parallel data processing engine used to process Sector data files. Some other works focused on providing more efficient implementations of MapReduce components, such as the scheduler [12] and the I/O system [13], while others focused on adapting the MapReduce model to specific computing environments, like shared-memory systems [14], volunteer computing environments [15], desktop grids [16], and mobile environments [17].

Even though P2P-MapReduce [18] shares some basic ideas with some of the systems discussed above (in particular, [15] and [17]), it also differs from all of them for its use of a peer-to-peer approach both for job and system management. Indeed, the peer-to-peer mechanisms implemented by P2P-MapReduce allow nodes to dynamically join and leave the network, change state over time, and manage nodes and job failures in a way that is completely transparent both to users and applications.

8.3   P2P-MapReduce Architecture

The P2P-MapReduce architecture includes three types of nodes, as shown in Fig. 8.2: *user*, *master*, and *slave*. Computing nodes are dynamically assigned the master or the slave role; thus the sets of master and slave nodes change their composition over time, as discussed later. User nodes submit their MapReduce *jobs*, composed by multiple map/reduce *tasks*, through one of the available masters. The choice of the master to which to submit the job may be done on the basis of the current workload of the available masters, i.e., the user may choose the master that is managing the lowest number of jobs.

Master nodes are at the core of the system. They perform three types of operations: management, recovery, and coordination. Management operations are those performed by masters that are acting as the *primary master* for one or more jobs. Recovery operations are executed by masters that are acting as *backup master* for one or more jobs. Coordination operations are performed by the master that is acting as the network *coordinator*. The coordinator has the power of changing slaves into masters, and vice versa, so as to keep the desired master/slave ratio.

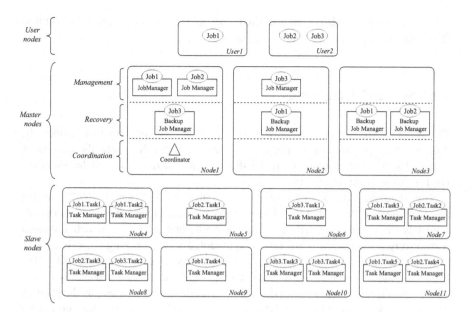

Fig. 8.2 Architecture of P2P-MapReduce

Each slave executes the tasks that are assigned to it by one or more primary masters. Task assignment may follow various policies, based on current workload, highest reliability, and so on. In our implementation, tasks are assigned to the slaves with the lowest workload, i.e., with the lowest number of assigned tasks. Jobs and tasks are managed by processes called *Job Managers* and *Task Managers*, respectively. Each primary master runs one Job Manager thread per managed job, while each slave runs one Task Manager thread per managed task. Moreover, masters use a *Backup Job Manager* for each job they are responsible for as backup masters.

Figure 8.2 shows an example scenario in which three jobs have been submitted: one job by *User1* (*Job1*) and two jobs by *User2* (*Job2* and *Job3*). Focusing on *Job1*, *Node1* is the primary master, and two backup masters are used (*Node2* and *Node3*). *Job1* is composed of five tasks: two of them are assigned to *Node4* and one each to *Node7*, *Node9*, and *Node11*.

If the primary master *Node1* fails before the completion of *Job1*, the following recovery procedure takes place:

- Backup masters *Node2* and *Node3* detect the failure of *Node1* and start a distributed procedure to elect the new primary master among them.
- Assuming that *Node3* is elected as the new primary master, *Node2* continues to play the backup function, and to keep the desired number of backup masters active (two, in this example), another backup node is chosen by *Node3*. Then, *Node3* binds to the connections that were previously associated to *Node1* and proceeds to manage the job using its local replica of the job state.

As soon as the job is completed, the (new) primary master notifies the result to the user node that submitted the managed job.

8.4 System Mechanisms

The behavior of a generic node is modeled as a state diagram that defines the different states a node can assume and all the events that determine the transitions from a state to another state. Figure 8.3 shows such state diagram modeled using the UML state diagram formalism.

The state diagram includes two macro-states, SLAVE and MASTER, which describe the two roles that can be assumed by each node. The SLAVE macro-state has three states, IDLE, CHECK_MASTER, and ACTIVE, which represent respectively a slave waiting for task assignment, a slave checking the existence of at least one master in the network, and a slave executing one or more tasks. The MASTER macro-state is modeled with three parallel macro-states, which represent the different roles a master can perform concurrently: possibly acting as the primary master for one or more jobs (MANAGEMENT), possibly acting as a backup master for one or more jobs (RECOVERY), and coordinating the network for maintenance purposes (COORDINATION).

The MANAGEMENT macro-state contains two states: NOT_PRIMARY, which represents a master node currently not acting as the primary master for any job,

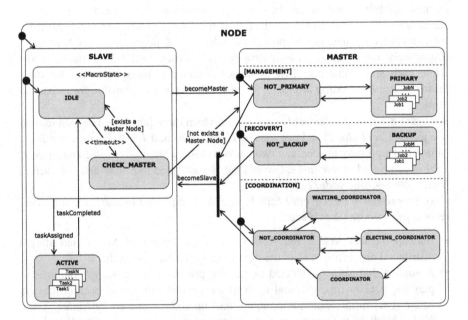

Fig. 8.3 Behavior of a generic node described by a UML state diagram

and PRIMARY, which, in contrast, represents a master node currently managing at least one job as the primary master. Similarly, the RECOVERY macro-state includes two states: NOT_BACKUP (the node is not managing any job as backup master) and BACKUP (at least one job is currently being backed up on this node). Finally, the COORDINATION macro-state includes four states: NOT_COORDINATOR (the node is not acting as the coordinator), COORDINATOR (the node is acting as the coordinator), WAITING_COORDINATOR, and ELECTING_COORDINATOR for nodes currently participating to the election of the new coordinator, as specified later.

The combination of the concurrent states [NOT_PRIMARY, NOT_BACKUP, NOT_COORDINATOR] represents the abstract state MASTER.IDLE. The transition from master to slave role is allowed only to masters in the MASTER.IDLE state. Similarly, the transition from slave to master role is allowed to slaves that are not in ACTIVE state.

8.5 Implementation

We implemented a prototype of the P2P-MapReduce framework using the JXTA framework [19]. JXTA provides a set of XML-based protocols that allow computers and other devices to communicate and collaborate in a peer-to-peer fashion. In JXTA there are two main types of peers: *rendezvous* and *edge*. The rendezvous peers act as routers in a network, forwarding the discovery requests submitted by edge peers to locate the resources of interest. Peers sharing a common set of interests are organized into a *peer group*. To send messages to each other, JXTA peers use asynchronous communication mechanisms called *pipes*. Pipes can be either point to point or multicast, so as to support a wide range of communication schemes. All resources (peers, services, etc.) are described by *advertisements* that are published within the peer group for resource discovery purposes.

All master and slave nodes in the P2P-MapReduce system belong to a single JXTA peer group called *MapReduceGroup*. Most of these nodes are edge peers, but some of them also act as rendezvous peers, in a way that is transparent to the users. Each node exposes its features by publishing an advertisement containing basic information that are useful during the discovery process, such as its role and workload. Each advertisement includes an expiration time; a node must renew its advertisement before expiration; nodes associated with expired advertisements are considered as no longer present in the network.

Each node publishes its advertisement in a local cache and sends some keys identifying that advertisement to a rendezvous peer. The rendezvous peer uses those keys to index the advertisement in a distributed hash table called Shared Resource Distributed Index (SRDI) that is managed by all the rendezvous peers of *MapReduceGroup*. Queries for a given type of resource (e.g., master nodes) are submitted to the JXTA Discovery Service that uses SRDI to locate all the resources of that type without flooding the entire network.

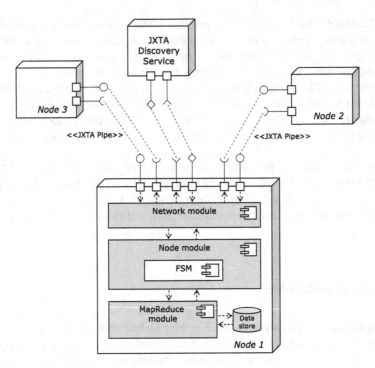

Fig. 8.4 Software modules inside each node and interactions among nodes

Pipes are the fundamental communication mechanisms of the P2P-MapReduce system, since they allow the asynchronous delivery of event messages among nodes. Different types of pipes are employed within the system: bidirectional pipes are used between users and primary masters to submit jobs and return results, as well as between primary masters and their slaves to submit tasks and receive result notifications, while multicast pipes are used by primary masters to send job updates to their backups.

Figure 8.4 uses the UML Deployment/Component Diagram formalism to describe the software modules inside each node and how those modules interact with each other in a P2P-MapReduce network.

Each node includes three software modules/layers: *Network*, *Node*, and *MapReduce*:

- The Network module is in charge of the interactions with the other nodes by using the pipe communication mechanisms provided by the JXTA framework. When a connection timeout is detected on a pipe associated with a remote node, this module propagates the appropriate failure event to the Node module. Additionally, this module allows the node to interact with the JXTA Discovery Service for publishing its features and for querying the system (e.g., when looking for idle slave nodes).

- The Node module controls the life cycle of the node in its various aspects, including network maintenance, job management, and so on. Its core is represented by the FSM component which implements the logic of the finite state machine described in Fig. 8.3, steering the behavior of the node in response to inner events or messages coming from other nodes (i.e., job assignments, job updates, and so on).
- The MapReduce module manages the local execution of jobs (when the node is acting as a master) or tasks (when the node is acting as a slave). Currently this module is built around the local execution engine of the Hadoop system [5].

8.6 Evaluation

The evaluation has been carried out by using a custom-made discrete-event simulator that reproduces the behavior of the P2P-MapReduce prototype described in the previous section, as well as the behavior of a centralized MapReduce system that performs the standard operations described in Sect. 8.2.

The simulator models joins and leaves of nodes and job submissions as Poisson processes; therefore, the inter-arrival times of all the join, leave, and submission events are independent and obey an exponential distribution with a given rate. Table 8.1 shows the input parameters used during the simulation.

As shown in the table, we simulated MapReduce systems having a size of 10,000 nodes, including both slaves and masters. In the centralized implementation, there is one master only and there are not backup nodes. In the P2P implementation, there are 1% masters (out of N), and each job is managed by one master which dynamically replicates the job state on one backup master.

To simulate node churn, a joining rate JR and a leaving rate LR have been defined. On average, every minute JR nodes join the network, while LR nodes abruptly leave the network so as to simulate an event of failure (or a graceless disconnection).

Table 8.1 Simulation parameters

Symbol	Description	Values
N	Initial number of nodes in the network	10,000
NM	Number of masters (% on N)	1 (P2P only)
NB	Number of backup masters per job	1 (P2P only)
LR	Leaving rate: avg. number of nodes that leave the network every minute (% on N)	0.025, 0.05, 0.1, 0.2, 0.4
JR	Joining rate: avg. number of nodes that join the network every minute (% on N)	equal to LR
SR	Submission rate: avg. number of jobs submitted every minute (% on N)	0.01
CT	Avg. computing time of a job (hours)	150
NT	Avg. number of tasks of a job	300

In our simulation $JR = LR$ to keep the total number of nodes approximatively constant during the whole simulation. In particular, we used five values for JR and LR: 0.025, 0.05, 0.1, 0.2, and 0.4, so as to evaluate the system under different churn rates. Note that such values are expressed as a percentage of N. For example, if $N = 10,000$ and $LR = 0.05$, there are on average 5 nodes leaving the network every minute.

Every minute, SR jobs are submitted on average to the system by user entities. The value of such submission rate is 0.01, expressed, as for JR and LR, as a percentage of N. Each job submitted to the system is characterized by two parameters, total computing time CT and number of tasks NT, whose average values are reported in the table.

For a given submitted job, the system calculates the amount of time that each slave needs to complete the task assigned to it as the ratio between the total computing time and the number of tasks required by that job. Tasks are assigned to the slaves with the lowest workload, i.e., with the lowest number of assigned tasks. Each slave keeps the assigned tasks in a priority queue. After the completion of the current task, the slave selects for execution the task that has failed the highest number of times among those present in the queue.

At the end of the simulation, we collected two main performance indicators:

- The *percentage of failed jobs*, which is the number of jobs failed expressed as a percentage of the total number of jobs submitted.
- The *percentage of lost computing time*, which is the amount of time spent executing tasks that were part of failed jobs, expressed as a percentage of the total computing time.

For the purpose of our evaluation, a "failed" job is a job that does not complete its execution, i.e., does not return a result to the submitting user entity. The failure of a job is always caused by a not-managed failure of the master responsible for that job. The failure of a slave, on the contrary, never causes a failure of the whole job because its task is reassigned to another slave.

Figure 8.5 compares the P2P and centralized implementations in terms of percentage of failed jobs.

As expected, with the centralized MapReduce implementation, the percentage of failed jobs significantly increases with the leaving rate, passing from 2.5% when $LR = 0.025$ to 38.0% when $LR = 0.4$. In contrast to the centralized implementation, the P2P-MapReduce framework is limitedly affected by job failures. In particular, the percentage of failed jobs is 0% for $LR \leq 0.2$, while it is 0.2% for $LR = 0.4$ even if only one backup master per job is used.

Figure 8.6 reports the percentage of lost computing time in centralized and P2P implementations related to the same experiments of Fig. 8.5, for different leaving rates. The figure also shows the amount of lost computing time, expressed in hours, in correspondence of each graph point for the centralized and P2P cases.

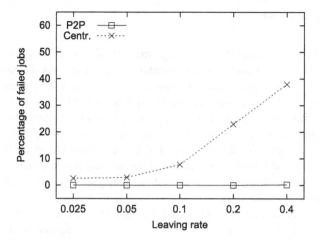

Fig. 8.5 Percentage of failed jobs

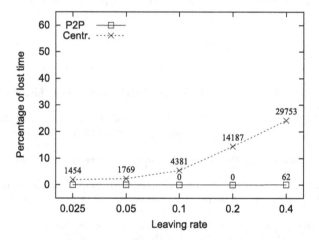

Fig. 8.6 Percentage of lost time. The numbers in correspondence of each graph point represent the amount of lost computing time expressed in hours

The lost computing time follows a similar trend as the percentage of failed jobs. For example, the percentage of lost computing time for the centralized system passes from 1.9% when $LR = 0.025$ to 24.2% when $LR = 0.4$, while the percentage of time lost by the P2P system is under 0.1% in the same configurations. The difference between centralized and P2P is even clearer if we look at the absolute amount of computing time lost in the various scenarios. In the worst case ($LR=0.4$), the centralized system loses 29753 h of computation, while the amount of lost computing time with the P2P-MapReduce system is only 62 h. An additional series of simulation results can be found in [6].

8.7   Conclusions

Providing effective mechanisms to manage master failures, job recovery, and intermittent participation of nodes is fundamental to exploit the MapReduce model in the implementation of data-intensive applications in dynamic Cloud environments where current MapReduce implementations may be unreliable.

The P2P-MapReduce model described in this chapter exploits a P2P model to perform job state replication, manage master failures, and allow intermittent participation of nodes in a decentralized but effective way. Using a P2P approach, we extended the MapReduce architectural model making it suitable for highly dynamic environments where failure must be managed to avoid a critical loss of computing resources and time.

The performance analysis conducted through simulation confirms that P2P-MapReduce ensures a higher level of fault tolerance compared to a centralized implementation of MapReduce. A prototype of the system is available at the following url: http://gridlab.dimes.unical.it/projects/p2p-mapreduce/.

References

1. Talia D, Trunfio P, Marozzo F (2015) Data analysis in the cloud. Elsevier, Amsterdam, Netherlands
2. Marozzo F, Talia D, Trunfio P (2013) Using clouds for scalable knowledge discovery applications. Lecture notes in computer science, vol 7640 LNCS. Springer, Berlin/New York, pp 220–227
3. Dean J, Ghemawat S (2008) MapReduce: simplified data processing on large clusters. Commun ACM 51(1):107–113
4. Dean J, Ghemawat S (2004) MapReduce: simplified data processing on large clusters. 6th USENIX symposium on operating systems design and implementation (OSDI'04), San Francisco
5. Hadoop (2016) http://hadoop.apache.org. (Site visited September 2016)
6. Marozzo F, Talia D, Trunfio P (2012) P2P-MapReduce: parallel data processing in dynamic Cloud environments. J Comput Syst Sci 78(5):1382–1402, Elsevier Science
7. Gridgain (2016) http://www.gridgain.com. (Site visited September 2016)
8. Skynet (2016) http://skynet.rubyforge.org. (Site visited September 2016)
9. MapSharp (2016) http://mapsharp.codeplex.com. (Site visited September 2016)
10. Disco (2016) http://discoproject.org. (Site visited September 2016)
11. Gu Y, Grossman R (2009) Sector and sphere: the design and implementation of a high performance data cloud. Philos Trans Ser A Math Phys Eng Sci 367(1897):2429–2445
12. Zaharia M, Konwinski A, Joseph AD, Katz RH, Stoica I (2008) Improving MapReduce performance in heterogeneous environments. 8th USENIX symposium on operating systems design and implementation (OSDI'08), San Diego
13. Condie T, Conway N, Alvaro P, Hellerstein JM, Elmeleegy K, Sears R (2010) MapReduce online. 7th USENIX symposium on networked systems design and implementation (NSDI'10), San Jose
14. Ranger C, Raghuraman R, Penmetsa A, Bradski G, Kozyrakis C (2007) Evaluating MapReduce for multi-core and multiprocessor systems. Proceedings of the 13th international symposium on high-performance computer architecture (HPCA'07), Phoenix

15. Lin H, Ma X, Archuleta J, Feng W-c, Gardner M, Zhang Z (2010) MOON: MapReduce on opportunistic eNvironments. Proceedings of the 19th international symposium on high performance distributed computing (HPDC'10), Chicago
16. Tang B, Moca M, Chevalier S, He H, Fedak G (2010) Towards MapReduce for desktop grid computing. Proceedings of the 5th international conference on P2P, parallel, grid, cloud and internet computing (3PGCIC'10), Fukuoka
17. Dou A, Kalogeraki V, Gunopulos D, Mielikainen T, Tuulos VH (2010) Misco: a MapReduce framework for mobile systems. Proceedings of the 3rd international conference on pervasive technologies related to assistive environments (PETRA'10), New York
18. Marozzo F, Talia D, Trunfio P (2011) A framework for managing MapReduce applications in dynamic distributed environments. Proceedings of the 19th Euromicro international conference on parallel, distributed and network-based computing (PDP 2011), Ayia Napa, pp. 149–158
19. Gong L (2001) JXTA: a network programming environment. IEEE Internet Comput 5(3): 88–95

Part IV
Multi-clouds

Chapter 9
Facilitating Cloud Federation Management via Data Interoperability

Vincent C. Emeakaroha, Phillip Healy, and John P. Morrison

9.1 Introduction

Cloud computing facilitates on-demand and scalable resource provisioning as services in a pay-as-you-go manner [2]. Cloud promises to make resources available at all times from every location. The interest of companies in deploying their business systems on the cloud to achieve an economy of scale is increasing. Currently, there is a plethora of cloud providers with individual infrastructures, APIs and application description formats. This heterogeneity has resulted in issues such as vendor lock-in that reduce consumer flexibility in terms of negotiating power, reaction to price increases and freedom to change provider [16]. Any attempt by the consumer to take advantage of multiple cloud deployments faces the problems of cross-cloud migration of resources and heterogenous data processing. The consumer has to manage a variety of resources in different representations and data formats [4]. A means of addressing this problem is the use of a generic data interchange format, which is capable of structuring and serialising data in a platform-neutral fashion.

Moreover, the volume of computing resources demanded by current data-intensive applications is rapidly increasing, thereby placing high requirements for cloud resources [19]. A single cloud provider's resources might not be enough to meet such high resource demand. Therefore, cloud providers have to rethink their business strategy and seek to increase dynamism in resource provisioning. Cloud federation offers suitable platform to address this deployment issue. A cooperative of cloud providers will enable the provisioning of applications using multiple cloud platforms. However, the management of such federated application deployment is

V.C. Emeakaroha (✉) • P. Healy • J.P. Morrison
Irish Centre for Cloud Computing and Commerce, University College Cork, Cork, Ireland
e-mail: vc.emeakaroha@cs.ucc.ie; p.healy@cs.ucc.ie; j.morrison@cs.ucc.ie

© Springer International Publishing AG 2017
N. Antonopoulos, L. Gillam (eds.), *Cloud Computing*, Computer Communications and Networks, DOI 10.1007/978-3-319-54645-2_9

challenging due to the heterogeneity of cloud platforms and data formats. Previous approaches to interoperability for federated cloud management focus mainly on the infrastructure levels, and little attention is being given to the application levels and data [3, 24].

Besides, the heterogenous nature of clouds makes inter-cloud monitoring to facilitate interoperable cloud management challenging. Existing cloud monitoring tools are mainly designed for specific platforms and have limited support for interoperability. We argue that this issue can be addressed by implementing a robust message bus system to facilitate inter-cloud management via monitoring and generic data formatting.

In this chapter, we present an architecture to facilitate federated cloud deployments management through data interoperability across clouds. The approach is based on the integration of monitoring techniques with a holistic message bus system. We propose a monitoring framework that gathers data from multiple cloud deployments. Based on this data, knowledge is drawn for managing the service provisioning and making informed decisions. The message bus system provides a holistic communication mechanism that is capable of supporting messaging at different levels of abstraction within and between clouds. It realises interoperable communication by integrating generic data interchange formats. The key contributions of this chapter include (i) presentation of a novel service monitoring framework to support the management of cloud resources and service provisioning, (ii) an interoperable communication mechanism for efficient transfer of data between clouds, (iii) analysis of different data interchange formats to identify their strengths and usage in clouds, (iv) presentation of an architecture for federated cloud deployment management and (v) presentation of a use case scenario for demonstration and evaluation of our approach.

The rest of the chapter is organised as follows: Sect. 9.2 presents a detailed description of the problem including the open challenges. It also discusses the previous research efforts in this area. In Sect. 9.3, we present our novel cloud monitoring framework. Section 9.4 discusses some data interchange formats for structuring and formatting the monitoring data in a platform-neutral manner, while Sect. 9.5 presents the holistic message bus to achieve interoperable communications. Section 9.6 presents the integration of monitoring, data interchange format and message bus to achieve an architecture for federated cloud deployment management. In Sect. 9.7, we present some performance evaluations based on a use case scenario. Section 9.8 concludes the work and highlights some future directions.

9.2 Challenges and Related Work

This section describes the challenges in this area and analyses the previous related work.

9.2.1   Challenges to Cloud Federation Deployment

Efficient provisioning of cloud services often demands finding a balance between issues. Cloud providers strive to maximise resource utilisation and minimise other factors like energy consumption while at the same time trying to maintain high quality of service. Finding this balance is difficult, especially for small and midsize enterprises that might have infrastructure constraints, scaling issues and a low budget.

Cloud federation offers providers the ability to share resources among themselves to achieve economic advantages. It allows providers to outsource services when demand exceeds their capacity and to rent out their own resources when others need them. This is driven by market growth and new forms of computational demand. The emergence of data-intensive applications and the amount of computing resources they demand are, in some cases, overwhelming for single small cloud providers.

There are, however, many open challenges to cloud federation such as how could application deployment across clouds be managed? How could data interoperability and communication be achieved? Or how can resource utilisation be monitored? In the past, cloud federation has been mainly considered in the context of outsourcing and renting infrastructure resources such as virtual machines [30]. Efforts have been made to achieve interoperability for federated cloud management at this infrastructure level [3, 8, 24]. However, little attention has been paid to the possibilities of deploying a single application using multiple cloud resources in a federation. This is a growing trend driven by cost, consumer satisfaction and resource requirements [32]. Consumers are seeking to use a composite of low-cost computing resources from different clouds to execute their application. Such deployments reduce cost for consumers because only cheap resources from multiple providers are used. The management of such federated application deployment is complex and challenging, especially due to the lack of data interoperability and interoperable communication systems.

Recently, there have been attempts to standardise various aspects of cloud Computing, such as Open Cloud Computing Interface (OCCI) [7]. Efforts have also been made to provide open implementations of cloud services, such as OpenStack [22]. Despite these efforts, cloud Computing to date has been largely characterised by competition between closed proprietary platforms.

As a result of these proprietary, vendor-specific cloud platforms and the need to provision data-intensive applications, the issues of interoperability and communication between individual cloud platforms have come to light. These issues arise from software and API incompatibilities when multiple cloud providers attempt to cooperate to achieve economy of scale among other advantages. This cooperation requires communication and transfer of data between clouds. An ideal communication system for the entire cloud stack is shown in Fig. 9.1.

A standard mechanism for performing communications such as these does not exist. A number of proprietary messaging services are available, such as Amazon's

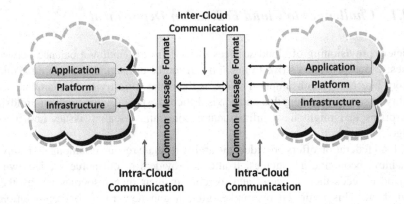

Fig. 9.1 Interoperable cloud data communication

Simple Notification, Oracle Messaging and cloudPrime. However, these services use a variety of underlying messaging technologies and incompatible message formats.

Furthermore, different monitoring tools can be used to gather detailed information at the infrastructure, platform and application levels in clouds to support the management of resources and service provisioning. However, due to heterogeneity, these monitoring tools tend to gather data in proprietary formats that are incompatible with other platforms.

Integration of a generic data interchange format for structuring data relating to cloud deployments is necessary to solve many of the issues identified above. Such a format would facilitate cloud data interoperability and thereby support the efficient management of federated cloud deployments.

9.2.2 Related Work

Currently, there is some interesting research being conducted in the area of cloud federation and interoperability. In this section, we analyse the work related to our approach.

In the area of inter-cloud federation, Demchenko et al. [6] propose an inter-cloud federation framework, which attempts to address the interoperability and integration issues in provisioning on-demand multi-provider heterogenous cloud infrastructure services. The paper describes two types of federations – consumer-side and provider-side federations. The former includes federation between cloud-based services and enterprise infrastructures, while provider-side federation is created by a group of cloud providers to outsource resources when provisioning services to consumers. They focus on the federated access control model and do not consider monitoring of deployed services nor data interoperability.

Since cloud federation started gaining attention from industry, there are many solutions coming up. Kertesz [15] characterises approaches to cloud federation that are based on their formation and interoperability issues. The paper classifies recent solutions arising from both research projects and individual research groups and shows how they attempt to conceal the diversity of multiple clouds in order to form a unified federation on top of them. The author gave some guidelines on important issues aimed at addressing interoperability, such as service monitoring, data protection and privacy, data management and energy efficiency. However, issues such as platform-neutral data formatting were not considered.

As an effort to address management issues in cloud federation, Zahariadis et al. [33] propose a management solution for cloud federation that automates service provisioning to the best possible extent. It aims to relieve developers from time-consuming configuration and provide real-time information about the whole life cycle of the provisioned service. They address this issue by introducing solutions to realise seamless deployment of services across cloud federations and the ability for services to span across different infrastructures of the federations. Furthermore, they provide monitoring of resources and data aggregation with a common structure. The paper, however, did not elaborate on the type of data interchange format used to achieve the common structure.

Mashayekhy et al. [19] present a cloud federation formation game that considers the cooperation of cloud providers in offering cloud IaaS services. On this basis, the paper designs a cloud federation formation mechanism that empowers cloud providers to dynamically form a cloud federation to achieve economic advantages. The mechanism determines the individual profits of each participating cloud provider in the federation. It ensures that the cloud provider covers its incurred cost and obtains profits based on its market power. The focus is on maximising profits, and they do not consider monitoring of the deployed services.

Nguyen et al. [21] address interoperability from the perspective of developing interoperable cloud services that can be simultaneously deployed on multiple IaaS clouds. Their approach uses a high-level abstraction layer to provide a unified interface to developers for managing the entire service life cycle. However, they do not address a means of realising data interoperability. Sotiriadis et al. [23] propose a decentralised meta-broker concept for inter-cloud resource management. In their concept, a broker is responsible for exchanging and monitoring a consumer resource request. On top of these brokers, they place meta-brokers to enable inter-cloud operation. Their approach does not consider platform-neutral messaging.

Tovarnak et al. [25] discuss requirements for the producer of monitoring information to address issues of representation, processing and distribution. To this end, they propose the use of an extensible data format to structure monitoring information to be usable by multiple consumers and thereby achieve interoperability. Their approach is event based and not general purpose. Williams et al. [30] present *Xen-Blanket*, a thin deployable virtualisation layer that can homogenise diverse cloud infrastructures. But their concept considers only the deployment of VM instances across clouds.

Wang et al. [29] discuss efficiency analysis of data interchange formats for Ajax applications. Their goals are to reduce data redundancy, improve processing time and increase the performance of Ajax applications. Their approach, however, does not consider the application of data interchange formats in clouds.

To the best of our knowledge, none of the existing work considers the integration of monitoring with a platform-neutral message bus system that uses a generic data interchange format to realise interoperability and thereby support federated cloud application deployment management.

9.3   Cloud Service Monitoring

This section presents our service monitor framework. It is designed for monitoring cloud resources and deployed application behaviour to enable efficient supervision of resource utilisation and application provisioning. We discuss its architectural design and implementation choices.

9.3.1   Architecture Design

The service monitor framework is a composed monitoring platform consisting of independent configurable monitoring tools that are managed in a decentralised manner. It is a holistic framework capable of monitoring both at the infrastructure and application levels in clouds. Since many of the cloud services today are application based, only a resource monitoring tool like [10] would be incapable of monitoring such deployments. Therefore, application level monitoring is necessary. Figure 9.2 presents the service monitor framework architecture.

As shown in Fig. 9.2, the service monitor framework consists of different components that work together to achieve its objectives. The monitor configuration/visualisation interface is the front end for configuring the monitoring tools. It allows the parameterisation of the individual monitoring tools, for example, to specify different monitoring intervals, and the selection of particular monitoring tools for specific purposes. In addition, it provides a visualisation interface for graphing the monitoring data for easy human observation of trends.

The input processing API gathers the configurations made on the front-end interface and parses them into the proper format for the service monitor core engine to understand. It is the responsibility of the service monitor core to instantiate the necessary monitoring tools with the proper configuration parameters and to co-ordinate their execution. The monitoring tools monitor the cloud resources or deployed applications to provide their current status data at run time. They are executed in parallel, and each pushes its monitoring data to the management portal for processing and decision-making.

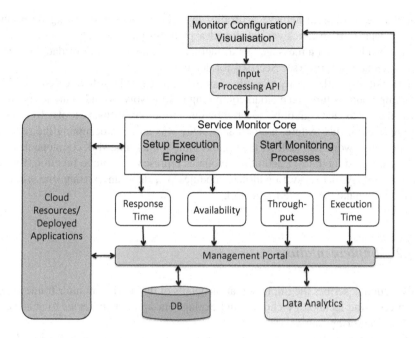

Fig. 9.2 Service monitor framework architecture

The management portal interacts with the cloud resources and deployed applications to manage them. It includes databases for storing monitoring data for historical reasons and analytic engines for analysing the monitoring data to draw control information. Based on user settings, the management portal can interact with the visualisation interface to display aggregated historical monitoring data.

The service monitor framework is designed with quality in mind. We strive to make it nonintrusive, scalable, interoperable and extensible. These qualities have been described as important features of an efficient monitoring tool in a monitoring survey paper [11]. Intrusive software is one that consumes significant resources on the monitored system, which may degrade the system performance. Therefore, to achieve nonintrusiveness in our monitoring framework, we host the monitoring software on separate nodes to the ones used to run the cloud services. However, we deploy a small agent on the computing nodes hosting the cloud services to collect the monitoring information and send them back to the monitoring nodes. This separation of responsibility also increases the scalability of the monitoring framework since it facilitates the creation of clusters of monitoring agents with decentralised control nodes.

For a monitoring tool to be usable in heterogeneous cloud platforms, interoperability is required. In the service monitor framework, we used standardised data interchange formats to achieve neutrality in serialising and formatting the monitoring data. Furthermore, we developed a platform-independent communication mechanism based on a message bus to facilitate seamless transfer of data between diverse cloud platforms (see Sect. 9.4 for details).

Extensibility is the ability to easily customise and extend a software system. This is an important feature since cloud computing is still evolving and many users have particular needs that cannot be covered by out-of-the-box software tools. To ensure the presence of this feature, a modular strategy was taken in designing the service monitor framework. This allows the organisation of the framework components into loosely coupled modules. Each of the modules represents a unique function. Based on this strategy, it is easy to add new modules or extend an existing one without having to remake the whole framework.

9.3.2   Implementation

This section describes the implementation details of the service monitor framework. We present the technology choices and explain our applied strategies to achieve a quality monitoring framework.

The monitor configuration and visualisation interface is developed using Ruby on Rails. This technology enabled a quick development and makes the interface compatible with other components. One of the attractive features of Ruby on Rails is its support for plug and play in terms of integrating new components. We exploited this feature to make the interface easily extendible with new functionalities. Ruby on Rails provides many APIs, and based on this, we used the JSON API to aggregate the inputted configuration data before transferring them to the next component to achieve efficiency.

The input processing API component is implemented as a RESTful service in Java. Since Ruby on Rails supports RESTful design, it integrates seamlessly with this component in passing down the user input data. The input processing API extracts these data and makes them available to the service monitor core component.

The service monitor core component is fully implemented in Java. It sets up and manages the execution of the user selected and configured monitoring tools. We use multithreading in this component to achieve parallel execution of the monitoring tools. The monitoring tools are developed as individual applications so that when a user wants to run particular monitoring activities, the service monitor sets up the appropriate tool based on the provided configuration parameters and arranges for a thread to execute the application.

In general, the interaction of monitoring tools with cloud resources or deployed applications is based on the type of monitoring objective the tools aim to fulfil. For example, a resource monitoring tool designed to gather low-level resource utilisation information may act as an agent that resides on the targeted cloud resource and parses different files on that system to extract data such as CPU, memory and storage utilisation. However, we implement an application-level monitoring tool to interact with the target application and must not reside on the same machine. In our approach, we use a *ping* mechanism to periodically query the status of the service. For HTTP queries, Java.Net APIs were used.

To persist the monitoring data, a MySQL database cluster was designed for the monitoring tools to achieve scalability. Each instantiated monitoring tool is automatically assigned to a database for storing its monitoring data. Hibernate is used to realise the interaction between the Java classes and the database. With Hibernate, it is easy to exchange database technologies. Thus, we are not bound to MySQL alone but could easily exchange it with other databases.

The service monitor framework enables adequate monitoring of the cloud resources and deployed application to facilitate timely and informed decision-making. This allows the management portal to outsource or rent resources and to schedule for an application migration in order to ensure high quality of service. In the next section, we discuss the data interchange formats for structuring and serialising the monitoring data.

9.4 Data Interchange Formats

As a step towards addressing the challenges of interoperability and cloud federation, we investigate data interchange formats, which provides means of structuring and serialising data for platform-neutral transmissions. In this section, we present detailed descriptions of the selected data interchange formats. The selection of these formats is based on their prominence in the existing literature.

9.4.1 eXtensible Markup Language

eXtensible Markup Language (XML) is a widely used data interchange format for structuring application data, including web services [5, 18, 31]. XML is designed to provide simplicity, generality and usability of data over the Internet [1]. Data representation in XML is text based and position independent, which makes it suitable for usage in different platforms and heterogeneous Internet environments.

An XML document is composed of units called *elements*. An element usually consists of a *start tag* and an *end tag*, and there is exactly one *"root" element* in a document. An element may contain other elements in a nested structure, i.e., if an element contains another element, it should contain both the *start tag* and *end tag* of that contained element.

One of the strengths of XML is that it is easy to read and write by both human and machine. On the down side, XML does not match with the data model of most programming languages, and it requires that the structure of data be translated into document structure, which can make the mapping complicated. Furthermore, the size of XML encoded data is larger than other representation formats due to the inclusion of many redundant tags. This verbose nature of XML can make it unsuitable for some applications, especially those operating on resource-constrained devices such as embedded systems.

9.4.2   JavaScript Object Notation

JSON is a text-oriented lightweight human readable data interchange format [18]. It is designed for the representation of simple data structures and associative arrays. JSON is programming language independent but uses conventions such as those from languages, such as Java, C, C++ and JavaScript.

When compared to XML, JSON is typically smaller in size due to the absence of extra tags. These properties make JSON a powerful language-neutral data interchange format. JSON has been used for representing many types of data including event objects [25].

In JSON, data can be organised as objects composed of key-value pairs or arrays of objects. The data are serialised into string streams, which in some instances require further conversion into binary bytes before transmission. There is a binary extension of this interchange format known as BSON. It provides, in summary, a binary serialisation of JSON.

9.4.3   MessagePack

MessagePack is a binary data interchange format [17]. It is designed for representing simple data structures such as arrays and associative arrays as compactly and simply as possible. MessagePack includes data structures that loosely correspond to those used by JSON. Its data structures are more compact than the ones in JSON, but they have limitations on array and integer sizes.

MessagePack supports various data types, including fixed-length types (e.g. integer, boolean, floating point), variable-length types (e.g., raw bytes) and container types (e.g., arrays, maps).

When compared to BSON, MessagePack is more space efficient. For example, BSON requires zero-byte terminators at the end of all strings and inserts string indexes for list elements, while MessagePack does not have those characters. Also, MessagePack allows for more compact representation of small integers, shortlists and associative arrays. Furthermore, it provides portability across many languages. Another advantage of this data interchange format is that implementations are available for a number of programming languages including C/C++, C#, Java and Python.

9.4.4   Protocol Buffers

Protocol Buffers is a binary interchange format developed by Google [14]. It provides a language- and platform-neutral way of serialising and structuring data for usage in communication. To provide smaller and faster serialisation, it encodes data into binary form. It allows users to define their suitable data structure and provides an efficient automated mechanism for serialising the structured data. Once the user defines a data structure, a compiler is used to generate code for writing and reading the structured data to and from a variety of data streams using different programming languages.

Each Protocol Buffers data element consists of a series of name-value pairs. Each data type has one or more uniquely numbered fields, and each field has a name and a value type, where value types can be numbers, booleans, strings, raw bytes, or other Protocol Buffers data types. There is a possibility of also specifying optional fields, required fields and repeated fields.

The Protocol Buffers mechanism is compact in terms of data serialisation. One of the major challenges to its use is the requirement of an extra compilation process using a proprietary compiler. The Protocol Buffers compiler currently supports Java, C++ and Python. However, there are ongoing efforts to extend to other languages.

In the next section, we present the communication message bus system that uses these data interchange formats to achieve interoperable data communication.

9.5   Messaging Bus Communication System

To communicate data between and within entities such as clouds and applications, there is a need for an efficient messaging system. We strive to design and implement a unified message bus system usable for transferring data at the different layers and levels in clouds. This section presents the details of the message bus system.

9.5.1   Intercommunication Potential

The ability to communicate data is a fundamental requirement for the management of single and distributed systems. Cloud computing and federation involve different components and layers of interaction. To enable seamless communication, we aim to realise a mechanism with the following capabilities:

- *Inter-application communication*: To enable applications executing in a cloud or in multiple clouds to interact and exchange information.
- *Intra-layer communication*: This ability embodies the interaction among resources and their control entities in a cloud layer. For example, the exchange of application behaviour data for management purposes at the cloud application layer.

- *Cross-layer communication*: Enables the management of resources and applications at different cloud layers from a central point. The cross-layer communication supports resource allocation, load balancing of virtual machines and application deployment.
- *Inter-cloud communication*: Enables the outsourcing of resources or service executions between clouds. This facilitates cloud bursting and management of different federation deployments.
- *Notification/alerting*: Enables one-way communication to notify or alert users and administrators about the occurrence of certain events.

From provider and consumer perspectives, these messaging types cover the communication requirements for efficient management of cloud service provisioning and usage.

9.5.2 Design and Implementation

The message bus system design is aimed at achieving the aforementioned intercommunication capabilities. Figure 9.3 depicts an abstract view of the message bus system.

As shown in Fig. 9.3, the message bus consists of three components: (i) producer, (ii) messaging infrastructure and (iii) consumer. In the following, we present the details of these components.

9.5.2.1 Producer

The producer is responsible for accessing the data and encoding it into messages for sending into the message broker. In some cases, the producer could be attached directly to a data generator and in other cases it could receive the data from a source. In our implementation, the producer is integrated with the monitoring to have full access to the monitoring data. It uses the platform-neutral data interchange format (see Sect. 9.4) for structuring and serialising the monitoring data before encoding it into messages.

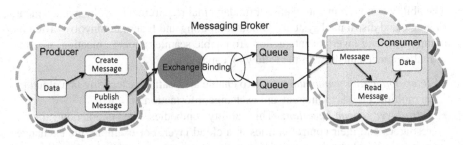

Fig. 9.3 Communication message bus overview

Using the platform-neutral data interchange format in formatting the monitoring data enables interoperable communication and understanding of these data by heterogenous cloud platforms. This is a key factor in facilitating federated cloud deployment management.

The producer has a simple interface for accessing data, and this makes it easy to integrate it into different levels in clouds, including applications, monitoring tools and management platforms.

9.5.2.2 Messaging Infrastructure

The messaging infrastructure provides the functions of a message broker. It asynchronously delivers messages from producers to consumers (synchronisation decoupling). The producer does not need to know the nature or location of a consumer. It simply sends its messages to the broker, which in turn routes them to the appropriate consumer (space decoupling). The broker therefore enables space, time and synchronisation decoupling [26]. This feature facilitates the necessarily loose relationship between a producer and a consumer, which is essential in distributed systems such as clouds and cloud federations.

In our prototype implementation, we use RabbitMQ as the messaging broker [27]. It is based on the Advanced Message Queuing Protocol (AMQP) [28]. AMQP is developed by a cooperative of industrial partners led by the financial sector with the objective of providing messaging interoperability among heterogenous platforms and message brokers. It is a binary wire-level protocol, which facilitates application-level communications.

The RabbitMQ broker consists of exchanges, bindings and queues. As shown in Fig. 9.3, the message producer sends messages into an exchange along with a routing key and not directly to a queue. The exchanges are bound to queues through binding directives. A binding directive indicates which message should be routed from an exchange to a particular queue. The message consumers set up the queues and receive messages from the queues bound to an exchange. If the routing key sent with the message matches the binding specified between the exchange and the queue, then the message is routed to the queue and received by the consumer.

We use RabbitMQ in this project because it provides well-tested open-source API implementations that are widely used in many other research projects including the Contrail project [20], which uses it in their current efforts to address interoperability at the IaaS layer [13].

9.5.2.3 Consumer

The consumer is the receiving end of the communication. It is responsible for receiving and deserialising the message body to extract the transferred data. To deserialise the data, it uses the platform-neutral data interchange format APIs to process them.

The consumer is implemented in Java, and it provides a simple interface for easy integration into different cloud levels to effect interoperable communication.

In the next section, we present the integrated architecture for federated cloud deployment management.

9.6 Cloud Federation Management

In this section, we present an architecture for federated cloud deployment management. It builds on the monitoring framework, data interchange format and messaging bus. We discuss the components, their integration and the implication of such architecture for cloud market growth.

9.6.1 Architecture Design

This architecture aims to advance cloud market growth by addressing the issues of data-intensive application deployment in clouds. The ability to compose low-cost resources from multiple clouds to provision at application level is promising. This will increase the adoption of cloud computing for heavy resource-demanding applications.

Figure 9.4 presents an abstract graphical illustration of our proposed architecture for federated cloud deployment management. The architecture is designed to achieve interoperability and interoperable communications to enhance sophisticated application deployments in clouds. Interoperability is one of the key factors that enables the cooperation of multiple cloud platforms since they are mostly proprietary and heterogenous in nature.

Our integration of monitoring and an interoperable communication message bus in this work provides many advantages, especially to support management operations. Monitoring provides in-depth information on the cloud resource utilisation status and deployed application performance. This knowledge is essential in making informed decisions about resources. The monitoring data can provide information to support on-demand resource scheduling to meet peak load, application migration to ensure quality of service or identification of unused resources that could be rented out.

As shown in Fig. 9.4, the service monitor framework is responsible for monitoring the cloud resources and deployed applications. It uses the message bus, which integrates platform-neutral data interchange formats, to transfer the monitoring data to the management interface.

The management interface is in control of the whole cloud deployment. It includes some username and password authentication mechanisms, which it shares with the monitoring component for accessing different cloud platforms. It also contains other management capabilities such as resource scheduling, application

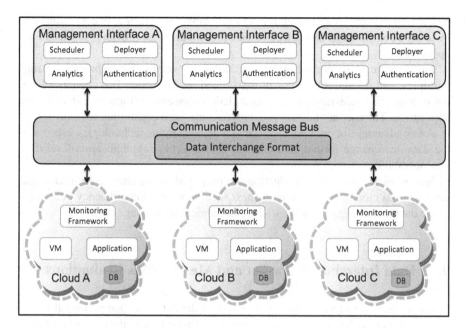

Fig. 9.4 Federated deployment management

deployment and data analytics. The monitoring data provide the source of knowledge for the management interface to determine the resource status and the performance of the deployed applications.

The architecture depicted in Fig. 9.4 presents an abstract view. The three cloud platforms shown represent an example of cloud federation. Usually, cloud federation could be formed with two or more individual cloud platforms.

In the next section, we discuss some benefits of our proposed architecture.

9.6.2 Architecture Importance for Cloud Advancement

Recent developments in genetic studies in bioinformatics [9] have shown the importance of achieving application elasticity using multiple cloud resources. Provisioning computationally intensive applications and achieving deployment flexibility are among the core concepts driving this trend. This type of service provisioning can only be facilitated by cloud federation deployments; however, its management is complex and challenging.

Our proposed architecture targets the management of federated application deployments in clouds. It has the potential to shape the future of managing on-the-fly federated application deployment. It aims to support the growing cloud market in this area by allowing varying service provisioning constellations. This offers many business opportunities and incentives to customers, for instance, in cost reduction, by using a composite of low-priced resources from different providers to execute an application.

Furthermore, it supports dynamic and automatic application deployment using multiple cloud resources based on user-specified requirements. This strategy allows a user to specify constraints such as completion time and performance goals for an application. The user application is deployed once these constraints are met.

A key advantage of our approach is that it uses emerging technologies, especially the data interchange format and message bus, in achieving application-level data interoperability.

We are in the process of evaluating the proposed architecture using real-world heterogenous clouds. However, in the next section, we present efficiency evaluation of the data interchange format with the communication message bus.

9.7   Data Interchange Format and Message Bus Evaluations

In this section, we present some evaluations of the data interchange format in the context of a cloud federation use case scenario. This serves as the first step towards evaluating our whole architecture. The goals of the evaluations are to surface their performance characteristics. We first show the data structuring capabilities and later compare the size, processing time and the amount of bandwidth consumed by each of the data interchange formats for transmission.

9.7.1   Evaluation Environment Setup

To setup the experimental environment, an OpenStack cloud platform installation running Ubuntu Linux is used. The basic hardware and virtual machine configurations of our OpenStack platform are shown in Table 9.1. We use the KVM hypervisor for hosting the virtual machines.

The physical machine resources offer the flexibility of firing up multiple virtual machines on demand for hosting different cloud services. The use of the OpenStack

Table 9.1 Cloud environment hardware

Machine type = physical machine				
OS	CPU	Cores	Memory	Storage
OpenStack	Intel Xeon 2.4 GHz	8	12 GB	1 TB
Machine type = virtual machine				
OS	CPU	Cores	Memory	Storage
Linux/Ubuntu	Intel Xeon 2.4 GHz	1	2048 MB	50 GB

platform as the evaluation environment provides the needed assurance that our approach could be used in many other cloud platforms. In the next section, we discuss the use case scenario.

9.7.2   Use Case Description

As a basis for the evaluation, we present a use case scenario of federated cloud deployments.

The use case demonstrates application execution outsourcing and the monitoring of application- and low-level resource metric data. These two data sets represent the widely communicated data types in clouds. The reason for using them is to be able to investigate the behaviour of the data interchange formats in serialising small and bigger data sets as represented by the application and resource-monitored data, respectively.

Figure 9.5 depicts the use case scenario. It shows the cooperation of three cloud providers in a federation to facilitate application deployment. In this case, cloud B is out of resources and seamlessly outsources the execution of *App B2* to cloud C. However, cloud B is responsible for managing the execution of *App B2* on cloud C's resources. So cloud B needs access to the resource status and application performance on cloud C.

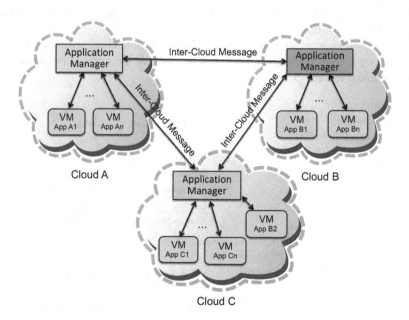

Fig. 9.5 Cloud federated use case

To derive these data, we employ our described monitoring framework to monitor and report on resource usage and application behaviour. The deployed *App B2* is a web application, and we monitor and gather seven metrics describing its performance. The resource status is determined by monitoring 53 physical/virtual machine resource metrics, such as CPUIdle, FreeDisk, Memory, etc. Since cloud can host hundreds or even thousands of virtual machines, the transmission of these monitoring data should be efficiently done to maintain performance.

We use the application monitoring data as shown in Table 9.2 to demonstrate the data structuring since they are short and simple.

In the next section, we present the data structuring capabilities.

9.7.3 Data Structuring

The data interchange formats can be categorised into two groups: (i) self-describing data interchange formats and (ii) binary (schema-based) data interchange formats. Table 9.3 present the classification of our described data interchange formats into these groups.

The two format groups have their advantages and drawbacks. The self-describing data interchange format group has the strength of being human readable and easy to understand. But, from the transmission perspective, they contain redundant components, which affect their sizes. The binary data interchange format group is not human readable. But they seem to be more efficient for transmission (see Sect. 9.7.4 for details).

In the following, we use the self-describing data interchange formats and the schema of the binary interchange formats to structure the application monitoring data presented in Table 9.2.

Table 9.2 Sample application monitoring data

Application metrics	Values
App name	Web application
App ID	178349064
Response time	5.24312 ms
Throughput	20 trans/s
Latency	3.2345 ms
Availability	99.999%
Execution time	10.5 weeks

Table 9.3 Data interchange format classification

Self-describing	Binary
XML	MessagePack
JSON	Protocol buffer

9.7.3.1   XML

Listing 9.1 presents the structuring of the monitoring data using XML.

Listing 9.1 XML Data structuring format

```
1  <webapp>
2    <appname>Web Application </appname>
3    <appid >178349064</appid >
4    <responsetime >5.24312</responsetime >
5    <throughput >20</throughput >
6    <latency >3.2345</latency >
7    <executiontime >10.5</executiontime >
8    <availability >99.999</availability >
9  </webapp>
```

As shown in Listing 9.1, XML data structuring is human readable and easy to understand. This is one of the major advantages of using XML for encoding data.

9.7.3.2   JSON

Listing 9.2 shows the structuring of the monitoring data using JSON.

Listing 9.2 JSON data structuring format

```
1  {"webapp":
2      {
3      "responsetime":5.24312,
4      "latency":3.2345,
5      "appname":"Web Application",
6      "appid":178349064,
7      "executiontime":10.5,
8      "throughput":20,
9      "availability":99.999
10     }
11 }
```

The JSON structuring is human readable but uses fewer characters to describe the data. It is, however, highly compatible with XML.

9.7.3.3   MessagePack

This is a binary data interchange format. It does not offer a human readable data structuring form, but it provides a schema for describing the data element types. The schema can be implemented in different programming languages including Java, C, C++, Ruby, Python, PHP and Erlang. In our approach, we use Java. Listing 9.3 presents the schema definition for the monitoring data.

Listing 9.3 MessagePack schema definition

```
1  @Message
2  public class WebApp {
3
4      public String appName;
5      public long appId;
6      public double responseTime;
7      public int throughput;
8      public double latency;
9      public double executionTime;
10     public double availability;
11 }
```

The "@Message" annotation indicates a MessagePack schema definition. MessagePack uses the defined schema in Listing 9.3 for serialising and deserialising data.

9.7.3.4   Protocol Buffers

This is a binary data interchange format. It uses a schema definition to describe the data, and the schema must be saved in a ".proto" file. There is a special compiler to read the schema and generate accessor classes for accessing and manipulating the data. Once the accessor classes are generated, subsequent manual editing is strongly discouraged. Protocol Buffers currently supports some programming languages including C++, Java and Python. Listing 9.4 shows the protocol buffer schema definition for the application monitoring data.

Listing 9.4 Protocol buffer schema definition

```
1  option java_package = "use.case.proto.core";
2  option java_outer_classname = "WebAppProtos";
3
4  message WebApp {
5      required string appName = 1;
6      required int32 appId = 2;
7      required double responseTime = 3;
8      required double latency = 4;
9      required int32 throughput = 5;
10     required double executionTime = 6;
11     required double availability = 7;
12 }
```

The "= 1", "= 2", etc. markers on each field identify a unique "tag" used in the binary encoding. Tags 1 to 15 require one less byte to encode as compared to higher tag numbers. This provides a means of optimisation in the encoding process [12].

This section has shown the data structuring abilities of the data interchange formats. Efforts were made to demonstrate their strength and shortcomings in terms of human readability and ease of use. In the next section, we consider and compare their serialisation compactness.

9.7.4 Serialisation Compactness

This section evaluates the serialisation compactness of the analysed data interchange formats. We compare the size, the processing time for the serialisation and the amount of used transmission bandwidth for each format to determine their performance.

The data serialisation is integrated in our implemented message bus system. When deployed, the data are serialised at the producer before being passed to the messaging infrastructure, which transmits them. The consumer receives and deserialises the data. To determine the processing time, we log the total time for structuring and serialising the data in the producer. The size of the serialised data is captured by writing them into files before sending them into the message bus. The message bus has 1 Gbit/s transmission bandwidth. Thus, we calculate the percentage of the bandwidth utilisation (BU) in transmitting the data by considering the serialised data size, the transmission bandwidth and the network overhead as expressed in equation 9.1.

$$BU = \frac{(DS + \text{Network Overhead}) * 8 * 100}{\text{Transmission Bandwidth}} \tag{9.1}$$

where DS represents serialised data size and network overhead includes the Ethernet, IP and TCP headers. Note, if the sum of the data size and network overhead is greater than 1480 bytes, the network overhead is multiplied by 2 to accommodate the packet fragmentation.

Figure 9.6 presents the achieved results of serialising the monitoring web application data including the processing time and the amount of bandwidth used for transmitting the data through the message bus.

As shown in Fig. 9.6a, the binary data interchange format group performs better than the self-describing ones in terms of serialised data sizes. The XML data interchange format outputs the largest data size, which is about 236 bytes, and hence, it has the weakest compactness. This may be attributed to the extra tags it uses in structuring/encoding data as shown in Listing 9.1. MessagePack presents the best result, which is slightly better than Protocol Buffer.

Figure 9.6b presents the processing time, that is, the time it takes for structuring and serialising the application data for each of the data interchange formats. Surprisingly, MessagePack produced the worst result among all. It took about 193 ms to process. This is interesting to note because it clearly shows where the strengths and weaknesses of this data interchange format lies. Protocol Buffers presents the best result, followed by JSON.

In Fig. 9.6c, the achieved results in terms of the amount of bandwidth consumed by each of the data interchange formats for transferring the serialised data are shown. In this aspect JSON consumed the highest amount of bandwidth in transferring the data. MessagePack produced the best results, followed by Protocol Buffer.

Figure 9.7 presents the achieved results for the second data set. It shows the sizes of the serialised resource data including the processing time and the amount of

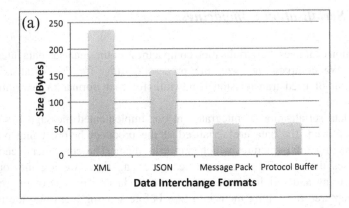

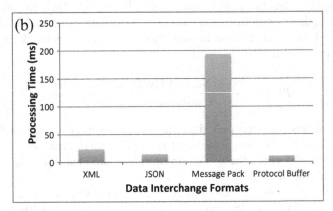

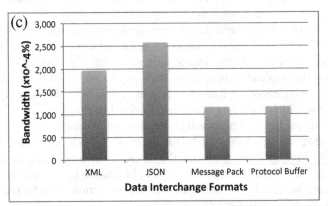

Fig. 9.6 Application metric data results. (**a**) Size (bytes). (**b**) Processing time (ms). (**c**) Bandwidth utilisation (%)

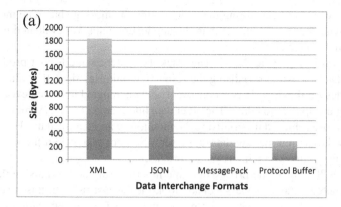

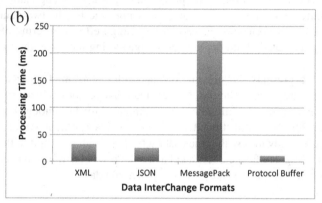

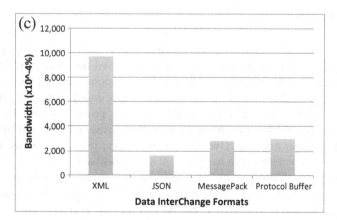

Fig. 9.7 Resource metric data results. (**a**) Size (bytes). (**b**) Processing time (ms). (**c**) Bandwidth utilisation (%)

bandwidth used for transmitting the data through the message bus. The monitoring resource data is a larger data set than the application data. We evaluated it in order to compare the results.

As shown in Fig. 9.7a, the MessagePack data interchange format produced the smallest data size while serialising the resource monitoring data. It produced a size of 264 bytes for the data. This is consistent when compared to its achieved result in serialising the application data. The other data interchange formats achieved similar results to those achieved in serialising the monitoring application data. These results show that the amount of raw data to be serialised correlates with the serialisation performance of these data interchange formats.

Figure 9.7b depicts the processing time in structuring and serialising the monitoring resource data. The MessagePack took the longest time. In this case, it took about 223 ms. This is similar to its processing time for the application data. The Protocol Buffer maintained a constant processing time for the two data sets. This is an interesting performance that could have huge effects in terms of efficiency in managing federated cloud deployments, considering the large amount of data it generates.

Figure 9.7c presents the amount of bandwidth consumed in transferring the serialised resource data. The JSON data interchange format performed best in this case. This is a very different result compared to the amount of bandwidth it consumed for the application data. Based on this result, it seems that JSON consumes less bandwidth with larger data sets. This is an assumption that we think should be investigated further. MessagePack and Protocol Buffers consumed similar amounts of resources as was the case for application data.

9.7.4.1 Short Summary

The binary data interchange format group produces very compact output while serialising data. This translates into smaller serialised data sizes. In this group, MessagePack has slightly better performance when compared to Protocol Buffers in serialising both data sets. However, in terms of processing time, Protocol Buffers is the clear winner. It even has an average constant processing time for both the smaller and bigger data sets. This is an interesting result, which could be explored further using larger data sets. Overall, there is no clear preference between the two binary formats since they both have strengths and drawbacks.

Generally, the MessagePack data interchange format seems to be the most compact in serialising both monitoring data sets. However, it incurs the highest processing overhead, which is a drawback. Protocol Buffers performs well all round with low processing time, and it produces relatively compact sizes. Its main drawback is the special compiler for generating code from the schema, which adds extra complexity to its initial setup.

In terms of bandwidth utilisation, the percentage of the message bus bandwidth used for transmitting single instances of these serialised data as shown in

Figs. 9.6c and 9.7c is small, but considering the large-scale nature of federated cloud environments, i.e., the number of virtual machines and applications to be monitored, the bandwidth utilisation can increase tremendously. This surfaces the importance of using efficient data interchange formats in order to achieve scalability and to maintain high performance, especially in managing federated application deployment.

9.8 Conclusion and Future Work

In this chapter, we proposed an architecture to facilitate the management of federated cloud deployments. The architecture aims to address the issues of data interoperability in clouds by integrating platform-neutral data interchange formats with a messaging bus and monitoring framework. Our goal is not only to achieve platform-neutral inter-cloud communication but also to extend the capability of cloud management to enable seamless federated application deployment.

The proposed monitoring framework provides the ability to measure in real-time the resource consumption of services/applications executing on cloud resources. It generates the required data to facilitate efficient management of cloud deployments.

Interoperable data transfer in our approach is enabled by a message bus system. This message bus represents a complete solution for communication in clouds. It provides intra- and inter-cloud communication, which includes interactions among applications and across cloud layers. It uses platform-neutral data interchange formats to structure and serialise the monitoring data to achieve efficiency and interoperability. The integration of monitoring with this message bus system has the potential of facilitating interoperable federated cloud management.

We presented the initial evaluation of the proposed architecture based on a cloud federation use case scenario. The focus of the evaluations was on the data interchange formats. As can be observed from the achieved results, the binary data interchange format group outperforms the self-describing data interchange format group in terms of compactness and the size of serialised data. However, this does not necessarily imply that the binary formats are superior to the self-describing formats in all aspects. These data interchange formats provided us with the ability to achieve interoperability and to support the management of federated cloud application deployments.

In the future, we aim to achieve a full evaluation of the proposed architecture using real-world heterogenous cloud platforms. This would contribute to our vision of barrier-free data-intensive application deployments using multiple clouds.

Acknowledgements The research work described in this paper was supported by the Irish Centre for cloud Computing and Commerce, an Irish National Technology Centre funded by Enterprise Ireland and the Irish Industrial Development Authority.

References

1. Bray T, Paoli J, Sperberg-McQueen CM, Maler E, Yergeau F (1997) Extensible markup language (XML). World Wide Web J 2(4):27–66
2. Buyya R, Yeo CS, Venugopal S, Broberg J, Brandic I (2009) Cloud computing and emerging IT platforms: vision, hype, and reality for delivering computing as the 5th utility. Futur Gener Comput Syst 25(6):599–616
3. Celesti A, Tusa F, Villari M, Puliafito A (2010) How to enhance cloud architectures to enable cross-federation. In: 2010 IEEE 3rd international conference on cloud computing (CLOUD), pp 337–345. doi:10.1109/CLOUD.2010.46
4. Chen G, Jagadish H, Jiang D, Maier D, Ooi BC, Tan KL, Tan WC (2014) Federation in cloud data management: challenges and opportunities. IEEE Trans Knowl Data Eng 26(7):1670–1678. doi:10.1109/TKDE.2014.2326659
5. Crockford D (2006) JSON: the fat-free alternative to XML. http://www.json.org/xml.html Accessed on 28 May 2015
6. Demchenko Y, Ngo C, De Laat C, Lee C (2014) Federated access control in heterogeneous intercloud environment: basic models and architecture patterns. In: 2014 IEEE international conference on cloud engineering (IC2E), pp 439–445. doi:10.1109/IC2E.2014.84
7. Edmonds A, Metsch T, Pappspyrou A, Richardson A (2012) Towards an open cloud standard. IEEE Internet Comput 16(4):15–25
8. Emeakaroha V, Healy P, Fatema K, Morrison J (2014) Cloud interoperability via message bus and monitoring integration. In: an Mey D, Alexander M, Bientinesi P, Cannataro M, Clauss C, Costan A, Kecskemeti G, Morin C, Ricci L, Sahuquillo J, Schulz M, Scarano V, Scott S, Weidendorfer J (eds) Euro-Par 2013: parallel processing workshops. Lecture notes in computer science, vol 8374. Springer, Berlin/Heidelberg, pp 65–74. doi:10.1007/978-3-642-54420-0_7
9. Emeakaroha V, Maurer M, Stern P, Labaj PP, Brandic I, Kreil D (2013) Managing and optimizing bioinformatics workflows for data analysis in clouds. J Grid Comput 11(3):407–428. doi:10.1007/s10723-013-9260-9
10. Emeakaroha VC, Brandic I, Maurer M, Dustdar S (2010) Low level metrics to high level SLAs – lom2his framework: bridging the gap between monitored metrics and SLA parameters in cloud environments. In: 2010 international conference on high performance computing and simulation (HPCS), pp 48–54
11. Fatema K, Emeakaroha VC, Healy PD, Morrison JP, Lynn T (2014) A survey of cloud monitoring tools: taxonomy, capabilities and objectives. J Parallel Distrib Comput 74:2918–2933
12. Google Inc. (2008) Protocol buffers. https://code.google.com/p/protobuf/. Accessed on 29 May 2015
13. Harsh P, Dudouet F, Cascella R, Jegou Y, Morin C (2012) Using open standards for interoperability issues, solutions, and challenges facing cloud computing. In: 2012 workshop on systems virtualization management (SVM) in conjunction with 8th international conference on Network and service management (CNSM), pp 435–440
14. Kaur G, Fuad M (2010) An evaluation of protocol buffer. In: Proceedings of the IEEE SoutheastCon 2010 (SoutheastCon), pp 459–462. doi:10.1109/SECON.2010.5453828
15. Kertesz A (2014) Characterizing cloud federation approaches. In: Mahmood Z (ed) Cloud computing, computer communications and networks. Springer International Publishing, pp 277–296. doi:10.1007/978-3-319-10530-7_12
16. Lewis G (2013) Role of standards in cloud-computing interoperability. In: 2013 46th Hawaii international conference on system sciences (HICSS), pp 1652–1661
17. Maeda K (2012) Comparative survey of object serialization techniques and the programming support. J Commun Comput 9:920–928

18. Maeda K (2012) Performance evaluation of object serialization libraries in XML, JSON and binary formats. In: 2012 second international conference on digital information and communication technology and it's applications (DICTAP), pp 177–182. doi:10.1109/DICTAP.2012.6215346

19. Mashayekhy L, Nejad M, Grosu D (2015) Cloud federations in the sky: formation game and mechanism. IEEE Trans Cloud Comput 3(1):14–27. doi:10.1109/TCC.2014.2338323

20. Morin C (2011) Open computing infrastructure for elastic service: Contrail approach. In: Proceeding of the 5th international workshop on virtualisation technologies in distributed computing, pp 1–2

21. Nguyen BM, Tran V, Hluchy L (2013) A novel approach for developing interoperable services in cloud environment. In: 2013 international conference on information networking (ICOIN), pp 232–237

22. Pepple K (2011) Deploying OpenStack. Ó Reilly, Sebastopol

23. Sotiriadis S, Bessis N, Antonpoulos N (2012) Decentralized meta-brokers for inter-cloud: modeling brokering coordinators for interoperable resource management. In: 2012 9th international conference on fuzzy systems and knowledge discovery (FSKD), pp 2462–2468

24. Toosi A, Calheiros R, Thulasiram R, Buyya R (2011) Resource provisioning policies to increase IaaS provider's profit in a federated cloud environment. In: 2011 IEEE 13th international conference on high performance computing and communications (HPCC), pp 279–287. doi:10.1109/HPCC.2011.44

25. Tovarnak D, Pitner T (2012) Towards multi-tenant and interoperable monitoring of virtual machines in cloud. In: 2012 14th international symposium on symbolic and numeric algorithms for scientific computing (SYNASC), pp 436–442

26. Tran NL, Skhiri S, Zimanyi E (2011) EQS: an elastic and scalable message queue for the cloud. In: 2011 IEEE third international conference on cloud computing technology and science (CloudCom), pp 391–398. doi:10.1109/CloudCom.2011.59

27. Videla A, Williams JJ (2012) RabbitMQ in action: distributed messaging for everyone. Manning Publications Company, Shelter Island

28. Vinoski S (2006) Advanced message queuing protocol. IEEE Internet Comput 10(6):87–89

29. Wang P, Wu X, Yang H (2011) Analysis of the efficiency of data transmission format based on Ajax applications. In: 2011 international conference on information technology, computer engineering and management sciences (ICM), vol 4, pp 265–268. doi:10.1109/ICM.2011.199

30. Williams D, Jamjoom H, Weatherspoon H (2012) The Xen-Blanket: virtualize once, run everywhere. In: Proceedings of the 7th ACM European conference on Computer Systems, EuroSys'12, pp 113–126. doi:10.1145/2168836.2168849

31. Yahui Y (2012) Impact data-exchange based on XML. In: 2012 7th international conference on computer science & education (ICCSE). IEEE, pp 1147–1149

32. Yang X, Nasser B, Surridge M, Middleton S (2012) A business-oriented cloud federation model for real-time applications. Futur Gener Comput Syst 28(8):1158–1167. doi:http://dx.doi.org/10.1016/j.future.2012.02.005. http://www.sciencedirect.com/science/article/pii/S0167739X12000386. Including Special sections SS: Trusting Software Behavior and SS: Economics of Computing Services

33. Zahariadis T, Papadakis A, Alvarez F, Gonzalez J, Lopez F, Facca F, Al-Hazmi Y (2014) Fiware lab: managing resources and services in a cloud federation supporting future internet applications. In: 2014 IEEE/ACM 7th international conference on utility and cloud computing (UCC), pp 792–799. doi:10.1109/UCC.2014.129

Chapter 10
Applying Self-* Principles in Heterogeneous Cloud Environments

Ioan Drăgan, Teodor-Florin Fortiş, Gabriel Iuhasz, Marian Neagul, and Dana Petcu

10.1 Introduction

The taxonomy of cloud computing, which was presented in [45], was constructed on criteria that were focused on five features: cloud architecture, virtualization management, service, fault tolerance, and security.

In general, when we are speaking about cloud architectures, we are referring to a layered architecture that permits development of applications running on an on-demand internet access service. Each of these services have to be accessible from anywhere given that there is internet connectivity.

Virtualization management is the component that takes care of abstracting the coupling between hardware components and the operating system. When it comes to virtualization, nowadays, there exists a large palette of techniques and implementations. Services can be classified in several categories, such as *software as a service* (SaaS), *platform as a service* (PaaS) etc., each of them having specific properties and offering to the users various resources that are to be consumed over the internet.

I. Drăgan (✉)
Institute e-Austria, Timişoara, Romania

"Victor Babeş" University of Medicine and Pharmacy, Timişoara, Romania
e-mail: idragan@ieat.ro

T.-F. Fortiş • G. Iuhasz • M. Neagul • D. Petcu
Institute e-Austria, Timişoara, Romania

West University of Timişoara, Timişoara, Romania
e-mail: fortis@info.uvt.ro; iuhasz.gabriel@info.uvt.ro

© Springer International Publishing AG 2017
N. Antonopoulos, L. Gillam (eds.), *Cloud Computing*, Computer Communications and Networks, DOI 10.1007/978-3-319-54645-2_10

Fault tolerance is one of the key components of any cloud architecture, and it has to deal with the cases when various building blocks fail. When speaking about fault tolerance, one refers to the case when the service running stops suddenly and another service is ready to take its place and continue the job from where the other service failed.

Another crucial component in cloud computing is security, its focus being on data, infrastructure, and virtualization of resources. The issues that arise from an unsecure environment can be catastrophic to companies where data is not only an asset but might also contain information about various clients.

Given that in recent years cloud computing gained momentum as more companies understood the concepts that govern the cloud environment, various parallel computing applications considered a migration toward the new concept. In this migration process, some of the applications partially sacrificed their performance in favor of scalability or instant availability of resources.

On the other hand, as supercomputing centers have slow procedures for admission (based on proposals and evaluations) and long waiting queues (that are serving resource-greedy batch parallel applications already tuned to match the particular architecture of the supercomputer), the new initiatives from the cloud community have started to spawn offering HPC as a service (HPCaaS) or developments that enable high-performance computing (HPC) applications. Taking this approach over the traditional HPC seems to be an appealing alternative for just-in-time parallel applications, real-time or interactive parallel applications, or even to support special environmental settings that are hard to be under user control in a supercomputing center.

Nowadays we are witnessing multiple changes in how the data- and compute-intensive services are offered due to the influences of cloud computing, autonomic computing, or the increase of the heterogeneity in terms of computing resources. As a particular case, the self-* principles may offer an interesting alternative in migrating some compute-intensive applications to tailored cloud environments.

At the moment, bare metal cloud is also gaining momentum. Although the trend is to move as many applications to cloud environments, there are multiple warnings coming from the scientific literature about the significant loss of performance relative to the case of a supercomputing usage. This is due to the fact that parallel computing applications are rather expected to run in a cloud environment in the same manner as they are running on computing centers or even supercomputers (especially for production phases of an application).

In this context, when we are speaking about application providers, they are expecting that the cloud infrastructure service behaves like a grid service rather than a supercomputer. The main difference is that individual users have more control on the software stack that is supporting the application execution. However, this is a small difference, as the grid environments currently allow to simulate cloud environments on top of grid services. While such a simulation approach is useful for the users who do not have access to supercomputers or grid environments (as they are mainly targeting academic users), an HPCaaS approach has the potential to benefit more from the automation processes associated with the cloud services.

Our chapter is intended to offer an overview of individual characteristics presented in the context of cloud computing, focusing mostly on aspects coming from the self-organization and self-management of clouds. In order to achieve this goal, we start by presenting some of the building blocks presented in literature for being able to construct such systems. That is, we first present the concepts and properties from the area of autonomic computing (see Sect. 10.2). Based on these concepts and features, we also offer a short overview of several European projects that try to tackle various problems that arise from the concepts. Next we focus our attention on principles of cloud computing (see Sect. 10.3), present the basics, and introduce the concepts that are required in order to further develop and understand the principles that are presented in various research papers as being part of the so called self-* clouds (see Sect. 10.4). We conclude this chapter with an overview of both European initiatives and with actual production-ready software that is designed in order to cover the various characteristics of such cloud systems (see Sect. 10.5).

10.2   Autonomic Computing

10.2.1   Properties of Autonomic Computing

In the visionary document on autonomic computing, Paul Horn (IBM) stated that "autonomic systems must anticipate needs and allow users to concentrate on what they want to accomplish rather than figuring how to rig the computing systems to get them there" [21]. While self-management, self-evolving, self-configuration, and others were not new, the merit of the document was to gather such characteristics and define their role in the description of much complex systems. Some of the core concepts of autonomic computing were exploited in the project eLiza. The project was designed in order to close the gap between autonomic and grid computing, given that "grids will connect heterogeneous resources anywhere in the world. It will be impossible to manually manage the complexity of such vast, interconnected systems," as a press release from 2002 specified [23].

In a simplified view, autonomic computing is often viewed as a manifestation of the automation of resource management, usually exposed in various distributed systems [26]. Indeed, according to Kephart and Chess, self-management is "the essence of autonomic computing," with self-configuration, self-optimization, self-healing, and self-protection frequently considered aspects of self-management. However, there cannot be set any limitation in relation with the other essential characteristics an autonomic computing system may have, such as self-awareness, self-regulation, self-description, or self-creation [21, 22, 39, 44].

Despite the complexity of the interdisciplinary approaches needed in order to achieve the full set of characteristics, according to [46] a minimal set of properties can be identified for any autonomic system:

1. *Automatic* – self-control of systems' internals, coupled with the self-containment ability
2. *Adaptive* – the "capability to change its operation"
3. *Aware* – awareness on its operational context and internal states, which allows a system to control its adaptive property

In fact, Schmid et al. clearly differentiate autonomic computing, as it was defined in [21], from autonomic systems, and offer a definition for the latter: "an *autonomic system* is a system that operates and serves its purpose by managing its own self without external intervention even in case of environmental changes" [46].

By its essential characteristics, cloud computing already offers an environment which exposes some of the properties of autonomic computing and autonomic systems, like the *on demand self service* or *rapid elasticity* characteristics. However, important steps are required to enable an autonomic behavior in the context of cloud computing: for example, at software-as-a-service (SaaS) level, the autonomic properties may be put in action by the means of fully automated cloud service lifecycle [19] or by employing new approaches in service brokering [12].

In order to enable automatic scalability, which is involved by the *rapid elasticity* cloud characteristic, it is supposed to support unpredictable number of demands and automatic adaptation which is required to avoid the failures of hardware resources; some techniques that are specific to autonomic systems must be also applied in the cloud context. One may consider that the *main characteristics of an autonomic cloud* are as follows, as argued in [43]:

1. *Resources variability*, which involves services for which the number of instances varies by adapting to unpredictable changes
2. *Contextual behavior*, through methods of self-management, self-tuning, self-configuration, self-diagnosis, and self-healing
3. *Easy deployment, management and robustness*, by using techniques for the design, build, deployment, and management of resources with minimal human involvement and presenting itself as a robust and fault tolerant system

One may notice that the set of properties from [43] are built in close relation with the minimal set of properties describing an autonomic system [46], with some additional requirements of robustness and fault tolerance.

10.2.2   The Autonomic Loop

In its series of autonomic computing white papers, IBM was developing the architectural blueprint for autonomic computing [3]. The autonomic manager was described as one of the core components that "manages other software or hardware

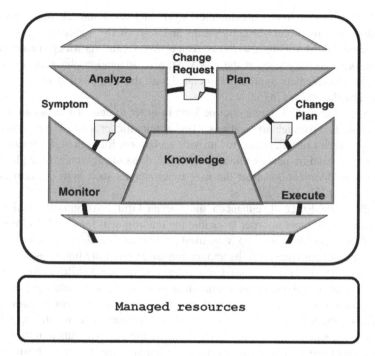

Fig. 10.1 The IBM MAPE-K autonomic loop (Source: [3])

components using a control loop, as depicted in Fig. 10.1. The control loop of the autonomic manager includes monitor, analyze, plan and execute functions." The internal structure of the autonomic manager included five core components, **M**onitor, **A**nalyze, **P**lan, **E**xecute and **K**nowledge, which inspired the acronym often used in literature: the **MAPE-K** loop. The four functions of the autonomic manager are as follows [3]:

Monitor: a function of the autonomic manager, responsible for collecting, aggregating, filtering, and reporting of various details coming from managed resources

Analyze: the function used to analyze collected data to get an understanding of current state of the system

Plan: the function of the autonomic manager needed to trigger the necessary actions to achieve certain goals and objectives

Execute: the function used to change the behavior of the managed resources.

These functions are using, analyzing, modifying, or acting based on a set of shared data, the shared knowledge, for which different types were identified: solution topology knowledge; policy knowledge; problem determination knowledge.

There exist several approaches based on the MAPE-K autonomic loop which were applied in cloud computing. In [36], the authors proposed an extension of the autonomic loop, by introducing an additional phase, the *Adaptation*, which was viewed as "a balance to the virtualization layer" and contained "all steps necessary to be done before successful deployment and start of the application.'. The new model, named A-MAPE-K, also received an update for the knowledge management phase in order to fully support the newly defined, adaptation phase. A rule-based knowledge management approach associated with this autonomic loop was further extended by the authors in [35].

Leite et al. exploited the autonomic loop in order to deliver a cloud autonomic architecture for parallel applications. The autonomic properties were used for achieving a series of objectives: to "provide a platform for high performance computing in the cloud for users without cloud skills; dynamically scale the applications without user intervention; meet the user requirements such high performance at reduced cost" [31].

In [29], Koehler et al. enhanced the Vienna Grid Environment (VGE) with some adaptive abilities in order to enable the environment for cloud deployments. The MAPE-K autonomic loop was used to enable "on demand selection and configuration of resources and the application based on utility functions."

The authors of [19] discussed the relevance of the MAPE-K functions in the context of cloud governance and management. In their analysis, the Execute function was set in relation with resource provisioning, configuration, and deployment; the Monitoring function was related with resource monitoring actions, SLA management with the Plan function, while the Analyze function was linked with the capability of application reconfiguration and thus being established links between the MAPE-K autonomic loop functions and ISO/IEC 38500, as depicted in Fig. 10.2.

10.2.3   European Initiatives for Autonomic Clouds

The set of properties for autonomic computing, autonomic systems, and the MAPE-K autonomic loop received extensive attention from a series of research projects. Such recent approaches, dealing with autonomic aspects of cloud, include several European initiatives like PANACEA,[1] HARNESS,[2] MIKELANGELO,[3] CloudLightning,[4] and SUPERCLOUD[5] are several European ongoing initiatives dealing with autonomic clouds, respectively, Autonomic HPC Clouds.

PANACEA is a FP7 project, which builds innovative solutions for a proactive autonomic management of cloud resources, based on a set of advanced machine learning techniques and virtualization, by using an "ML-based framework for

---

[1] http://projects.laas.fr/panacea-cloud/

[2] http://www.harness-project.eu/

[3] https://www.mikelangelo-project.eu/

[4] http://cloudlightning.eu/

[5] http://supercloud-project.eu

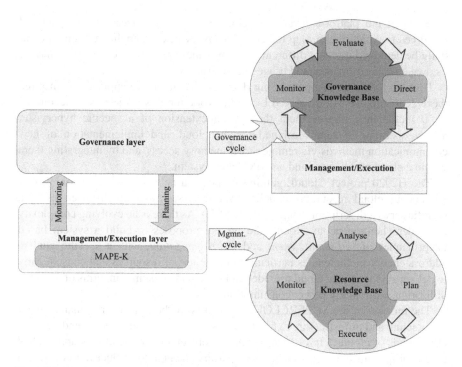

Fig. 10.2 The MAPE-K and ISO 38500 models (Source: [19])

Proactive Client-server Application Management (PCAM)" [15]. It supports a series of properties of the autonomic cloud, including (a) *self-healing* against anomalies by recovering from multiple node and link failures and using proactive rejuvenation of applications and servers for preventing crashes and increasing the availability, predicting the threshold violation of response time of servers; (b) *self-configuration* by efficiently mapping user's requirements onto distributed clouds and configuring on-the-fly in the presence of anomalies, self-optimizing using proactive migration of virtual machines from one cloud resource to another, maintaining the quality of service of end-to-end flows; (c) *self-protection* using proactive reconfiguration of overlay networks to protect against security attacks.

The FP7 HARNESS project offers an approach to the integration of heterogeneous hardware and network technologies into data center platforms, to increase performance, reduce energy consumption, and lower cost profiles for cloud applications. It develops an enhanced PaaS software stack that brings new degrees of freedom to cloud resource allocation and optimization, providing mechanisms to "automate the choice of resources that should be assigned to arbitrary non-interactive applications that get executed repeatedly" [25]. Technologies such as FPGAs, GPGPUs, programmable network routers, and solid-state disks promise increased performance, reduced energy consumption, and lower cost profiles. Specialized technologies are virtualized into resources that can be managed and accessed at the platform level. The cloud platform has access to a variety of resources to which it can map the components. A flexible application may potentially be deployed in many different ways over these resources, each option having its own cost, performance, and usage characteristics.

High-performance computing, big data, and I/O intensive applications inspired the H2020 project MIKELANGELO. The work for this project is concentrated on I/O efficiency improvement through an extension of a specific hypervisor, a new operating system[6] designed for the cloud, and implementation of new communication methods via remote direct memory access, and by integrating them within a cloud middleware and an HPC batch system.

The H2020 project CloudLightning proposes a new way of provisioning heterogeneous cloud resources to deliver services, specified by the user, using a specific service description language (CL-SDL). As there is an evolving complexity of modern heterogeneous clouds, the project proposes to build a system based on principles of *self-management* and *self-organization*, with a specific goal to address energy inefficiencies particularly in the use of resources and consequently to deliver savings to the cloud provider and the cloud consumer in terms of resource utilization, particularly power consumption [33].

The mission of the SUPERCLOUD project is to "build a security management architecture and infrastructure to fulfill the vision of user-centric secure and dependable clouds of clouds." In order to reach this objective, the paradigms approached by this project must be self-managed, with a specific goal to "reduce administration complexity through security automation" [30]. With such an approach, it is expected to tackle both the new security risks, identified in the context of multi-cloud applications, as well as the traditional ones, as previously identified in the literature. All these risks are set in the context of security, privacy, and trust, as mentioned in [52].

10.3 Cloud Architectures

Together with the large scale adoption of cloud computing, a series of reference architectures addressing various of its aspects were identified and defined. Being based on the five essential characteristics of cloud computing, with an emphasis on the *on-demand self-service*, *resource pooling* and *rapid elasticity* and being inspired by the developments in grid computing, these architectures clearly identified components that may offer the foundation for autonomic approaches for cloud computing.

---

[6]http://osv.io/

10.3.1   Service Automation

Automation, in the context of cloud computing, represents one of the challenges for improved inter-cloud workload deployments. The "NIST Cloud Computing Standards Roadmap" document mentioned it as "a future direction of workloads data and metadata standardization is to help improve the automation of inter-cloud system workload deployment," while it enables reduced costs in various distributed architectures (including cloud system, grids, and others) [40].

One of the first architectures dedicated to cloud management was defined by DMTF [17] in a series of two white papers from the Open Cloud Standards Incubator (OCSI). While the work in the first one intends to offer a unified framework for cloud interoperable management [17], the second of the DMTF documents shows, in the context of the *provision resources* or *deploy service template* scenarios, that "the Service Manager, Provisioning Manager, and Metering Manager, are functions that are most likely automated" [18].

In the IBM CCRA document [24], the *service automation management* is one of the core components for supporting the Operational Support Services (OSS) aspects of a cloud deployment. IBM's CCRA, amongst others, "combines powerful automation and services management (low touch) with rich business management functions for fully integrated, top-to-bottom management of cloud infrastructure and cloud services," and achieving the "low-cost automation required to successfully scale to economically successful cloud solutions" was identified as raising highly relevant challenges related with the cloud management platform.

In Microsoft's Cloud Services Foundation Reference Model (CSFRM) series of articles [16],[7] a specific component for coordination of automated processes "across multiple Management and Support and Infrastructure components" was identified, which was considered a key enabler for controlling service costs, while in a white paper from the Cloud Council, service automation was considered one of the security controls used for the development of a set of security use case scenarios [11].

10.3.2   Autonomic SLA Management

There were recent intense efforts in defining and implementing service level agreement (SLA) approaches for cloud resource provisioning. Service level agreements (SLA), quality of service (QoS) as well as "autonomic management system and PaaS framework" were identified at the core of several open challenges and architectural components for autonomic cloud computing, in [8]. The overall approach was described by Kertesz et al., where SLA-based cloud middleware was seen in

---

[7]https://aka.ms/csfrm,https://aka.ms/Q6voj9

the core of the implementation of the autonomic principles, and the autonomic loop is based on SLA violations while service level objectives (SLOs) offer the basis for autonomic reactions [28].

The importance of SLA-based management was also revealed in [9], where *autonomic resource management* was mentioned as one of the important research challenges in the field. In the case of SLA-based autonomic resource management, the steps from the MAPE-K autonomic loop are highly relevant, as continuous monitoring of service request and appropriate answers to requests are necessary for implementing self-management for the reservation process, self-configuration of components, adaptability to new service requirements, and others. However, for the MAPE-K loop to come into action, yet other research challenges were mentioned, such as *Service Benchmarking and Measurement* or *SLA-oriented Resource Allocation Through Virtualization*.

A slightly different approach was considered by Almeida et al. in [2], where the authors are trying to approach two different types of problems, from a provider point of view:

- The SLA management problem: minimizing resource management costs, while maximizing SLA-based revenues
- The long-term capacity planning problem: maximizing SLA-based long-term revenues, while minimizing the total cost of ownership (TCO) of resources, as a reaction to the size of a service center.

Even if their approach was not set in the context of cloud computing, the associated performance model offers results which are highly relevant for various distributed environments.

Other SLA-oriented approaches were considered in recent years, covering particular autonomic features. An autonomic approach based on SLA templates was considered in [6]. In this approach, the targeted autonomic behavior was rather for the cloud markets by using a two-step autonomic SLA mapping mechanism. A different mechanism was investigated [35], where "an autonomic SLA enactment and resource management tool for Cloud Computing infrastructures on the level of VMs" was presented, where "no a-priori learning was necessary and adaptation happens on the fly during execution."

10.3.3 Cloud Brokerage and Cloud Service Lifecycle

An autonomic computing framework is naturally implemented using multi-agent systems (with micro-services as an alternative), like in [4, 49, 50]. Alternative artificial intelligence techniques, like genetic algorithms, neural networks, or multi-objective and combinational optimization heuristics, can also be successfully applied, especially in the context of the solutions supporting cloud brokerage and cloud service lifecycle [38, 49, 53].

The relevance of the cloud broker was revealed in a Gartner report[8] from the early ages of cloud computing, as the necessary link between service consumers and service providers, designed to address three major uses: service intermediation, service aggregation, and service arbitrage. Closely related with the information from previously mentioned Gartner report, the cloud broker was later defined in a NIST document as "as an entity that manages the use, performance, and delivery of cloud services, and negotiates relationships between Cloud Providers and Cloud Consumers" [32].

The CompatibleOne project defined an "open source broker, which provides interoperable middleware for the description and federation of heterogeneous Clouds and resources provisioned by different Cloud providers" [53]. This cloud broker is at the core of the Advanced Capabilities for CORDS model (ACCORDS) cloud brokerage platform, which is built on top of the CompatibleOne Resource Description System (CORDS) model. One may notice that the architecture of this platform follows the MAPE-K principles, which are visible through its four functional steps:

1. Handling user's requirements, and creation of the CORDS manifest (the *Knowledge*) – enabling the *Monitoring* step, by specific CompatibleOne components
2. Validation of CORDS manifests and build of the provisioning plan – the *Analyze* step
3. Execution of the provisioning plan (enabled by the ACCORDS broker) – the *Plan* step
4. Cloud service delivery – the *Execution* step

In the context of the mOSAIC project,[9] a cloud agency was defined to carry out specific cloud resource brokering activities and to assist the mOSAIC PaaS during its self-deployment activities. The mOSAIC PaaS was designed as a self-deployable platform, capable to run on top of various IaaS deployments. The mOSAIC cloud agency [4, 49], which is built as a "mobile agent"-based solution, offers support for cloud resource management, by means of SLA negotiation and management. The SLA negotiation capabilities also include dynamic renegotiation of SLAs, in order to adapt itself to the time varying consumer requirements. The autonomic characteristics are exposed by different agent classes, including:

1. The *client agent* class, which dynamically creates and updates the SLAs based on users' requirements – the *plan* step
2. The *mediator agent* class, which coordinates various provider agents to assist in selecting the best provider – exposing activities from the *analyze* and *execute* steps
3. The *negotiation agent* class, which will support specific SLA-based activities in order to optimize contracts – exposing activities from the *analyze* step

---

[8]http://www.gartner.com/newsroom/id/1064712

[9]http://www.mosaic-cloud.eu/

4. The *monitor agent* class, which will collect available information necessary to assess application performance and current values of various QoS parameters, this agent class will be supported by the *benchmarker* agent type – the *monitoring step*

5. A *semantic engine*, built on top of the mOSAIC ontology [37], is used by various agents for semantic validation, translation and unification of messages coming from different sources, in order to assist in the construction of complete SLA specifications – the *knowledge* component.

An interesting approach was offered by the Cloud@Home approach, which "aims at implementing a brokering-based Cloud Provider starting from resources shared by different providers, addressing QoS and SLA related issues, as well as resource management, federation and brokering problems" [12, 13] and defines an autonomic service engine framework (CHASE – Cloud@Home Autonomic Service Engine). Another SLA-based approach for an "SLA-based Service Virtualization and on-demand resource provision" is described by Kertesz et al., which is built on top of the principles of autonomic computing, in order to deliver different functionalities including meta-negotiation, brokering, and automatic service deployment and previously identified in [5]. The SSV architecture from [27] identifies three mandatory components for the realization of the autonomic architecture: agreement negotiation, service brokering, and service deployment and virtualization, and clear mappings to the MAPE-K model were offered.

10.4   Self-*

As presented in Sect. 10.3, there are a series of reference architectures that address the problem of self-*. Most approaches described in literature are based on the concept of *matchmaking* that basically tries to satisfy all the requirements from a request based on the resources that are available. Before we can dive deeper in the concepts and principles of matchmaking, we first have to define the driving characteristics that allow us to identify and quantify the needed resources. Table 10.1 gives a short overview of the core properties that are used in order to define the self-* principles.

Lots of attention coming from various research communities was directed toward the study of the self-* properties in order to better adapt and integrate the concepts in the field of study. As presented in Sect. 10.2, some of the recent European initiatives invested lots of effort in research and are still focusing on adoption and improvement of the principles from self-* to new cloud architectures. The rest of this section tries to give a short overview of the directions identified in various research literature.

There are a couple of major directions identified by the authors in [47]. As presented, *the process of matchmaking* refers to the mechanism that allows prediction of future steps that have to be taken in order to fulfill future and current requests based on the historical information collected. In contrast to this approach,

Table 10.1 A summary of the core self-* properties

Self-* property name	Description
Self-stabilization	refers to a system that is capable of recovering to a configuration that meets all the safety properties when starting from a random initial state
Self-healing	a system is said to be self-healing if by the occurrence of an external event that destabilizes the system that state causes at most a temporary violation of the systems safety properties
Self-organizing	refers to a system with a number of processes that run simultaneously that is capable of maintaining, improving or restoration of one or more safety properties after a set of external actions have happened to the system
Self-organizing	refers to the capability of a system to optimize some objective function, that is starting from an arbitrary initial configuration it has the capability of improving its configuration in such a way that the objective function is optimized
Self-configuration	refers to the capacity of a system to organize itself, such as changing network topology or various settings of software and hardware components
Self-scaling	refers to the capability of a system to behave as expected under various configurations on the system size

basic cloud computing model does not provide any means of *prediction*. In their paper, the authors use annotated monitoring data for prediction and matchmaking process. The process of matchmaking is a crucial component when it comes to self-healing clouds. That is, in the process of on-the-fly vendor replacement for various reasons, it is crucial to have good prediction mechanisms that enable efficient solution generation. Nowadays, it is common to have services that run on multiple clouds (offered by various vendors) hence on-the-fly replacement for infrastructure parts becomes essential.

The process of matchmaking is nothing else than another component that stands between the cloud service request and the cloud service description (composition of clouds that enables run of the application). Matchmaking component is in charge of generating a large set of cloud offers for the cloud service request based on the cloud descriptions. As next step it filters out the offers that are not efficient from various points of view; here efficiency is defined by the user. Some of the classical efficiency measurements refer to cost efficiency, RAM, and CPU usage, or even storage cost can be involved in defining the cost function. Based on these cost functions, the generated offers are ranked, and a small set of offers are presented back to the cloud consumer in order to select and deploy its services.

Marinescu et al. in [34] argues that *the self-organizing and self-managing principles* for autonomic clouds are not only desirable but rather necessary for the future of cloud computing.

One classification of self-manageable cloud can be made as follows, first we have novel solutions for the cloud computing approach as presented in [7]. Second we have the solutions based on service level agreement (SLA) and negotiation, inspired from the related area of grid computing. Lastly we have a category that is inspired from principles of automatic computing adapted to meet the needs of cloud computing.

The work presented in [1] proposes an extension to the service abstraction in the context of Open Grid Service Architecture (OGSA) for quality of service (QoS) properties. This extension is intended for providing means for various requests to search in computational grids for services based on QoS criteria. The framework is intended to operate at the application layer and provide support for service discovery based on properties describing QoS. The interaction between various modules is done by either reservation of resources or by allocating resources based on a predefined budget.

Another direction coming from the Grid computing community is focused on service level agreement (SLA) brokering [41]. In a broad sense, the SLA is nothing else than a bilateral agreement between the service provider and the service consumer. This approach is based on a multi-agent system that is in charge of scheduling the various resources in order to meet the SLA. As for the negotiation protocol, a variation of the Contract Net Protocol is used. Contract Net Protocol [48] is a communication protocol that allows efficient cooperation between agents. With regard to SLAs, there exist a big variety of languages that allow end-users to specify SLAs, and there are a couple of directives that aim at standardizing how these documents should look e.g., the web service level agreement (WSLA).[10]

From the perspective of scientific computing and doing science using the cloud as back-end, there are some results summarized in [14]. In their paper, Deelman et al. focus only on one dimension by examining the trade-offs of various execution modes and provisioning plans for cloud resources. They show that in a setting where the application is data intensive with small computational granularity, the cost of computation power represents a big proportion of the overall costs for the application in test. As a case study, they used the Montage application and the Amazon EC2 fee structure.

In [5], the first steps toward a self-manageable cloud services are presented. The work is focused on presentation of core components that allow a system to keep its state stable by having services manage themselves. Alongside, a taxonomy for resource submission is developed in order to match the requirements of self-manageable cloud services. Evaluation was carried out on a system that is based on service mediation and negotiation bootstrapping.

10.5   Applications of Self-* Principles in Cloud Computing

The principles and methodologies detailed in the previous sections are being implemented in particular by cloud computing environments. The dynamic nature of cloud environments enables developers to easily use intelligent self-* style

---

[10]http://www.research.ibm.com/WSLASpecV1-20030128.pdf

methodologies and principles. One of the first principles to be tackled is that of self-optimization, also known as distributed orchestration.

Traditional orchestration usually follows a client-server type architecture pattern. This model assumes that there is a central component which handles service composition. Choreography uses interaction rules between services to achieve the same goal in a distributed manner. Distributed orchestration is situated at the intersection of these two approaches, borrowing concepts from both approaches. That is, it uses a central component of service composition, but the component is elected from a pool of peers instead of being fixed before runtime.

Dynamic resource configuration is a key issue in orchestrating dynamic massively scalable applications. This is necessary as newly provisioned resources have to be configured in order to integrate them into the already running application. This configuration is not done in a stateless manner; most often, it is based on the current state of the running application. In order to effectively orchestrate and then configure such an application, a scalable near real-time monitoring solution needs to be considered in the application design. This can take the form of a strongly coupled monitoring component present in the application architecture. Another way would be by providing mechanisms that allow application metrics (performance, quality, or any other type of metrics) to be easily consumed by external monitoring solutions. The resulting metrics can be used in the creation of both anomaly detection (both in behavior or in resource usage) and predictive workload models [10, 42].

In order to satisfy various quality of service, optimal resource selection and allocation are needed. This is still an open research topic, and a wide range of solutions have been proposed ranging from computational optimization [20] to evolutionary optimization [51]. In the FP7 FUSION project,[11] an orchestration framework was developed. The framework was designed for deployment of resources close to the user. It uses monitoring metrics related to current capability of a particular instance in order to decide if scaling or even stopping an instance is necessary.

Serf[12] is a decentralized solution for service discovery and orchestration that is designed to be lightweight, highly available, and fault tolerant. It uses a lightweight gossip protocol for communication among nodes. In order for a newly created service to join a cluster, it must know at least one member of the said cluster. Communication (in this case done UDP) is done using a fixed fanout and time interval. Its reliance on the gossip protocol means in the case of a large number of joined services, the convergence rate can become quite significant (eventual consistency). This limitation also extends to services which have a small startup time (i.e., unikernels) and a low life expectancy. In essence the service can start, fulfill its designated task, and be decommissioned before convergence can take place.

Consul[13] is built on top of Serf and leverages the membership and failure detection features built upon them in order to add service discovery. Consul focuses

---

[11] http://www.fusion-project.eu/

[12] https://www.serf.io/

[13] https://www.consul.io/

more on service level abstraction in contrast to Serf, which relies on node level abstractions. It is also important to note that while Serf sacrifices consistency for availability, Consul is the other way around; it cannot operate if the central servers cannot form a quorum. At high level, Consul is made up of Consul agents (each member of a Consul cluster must run an agent instance) that can run in server or client modes and can run HTTP or DNS. They are also responsible for running checks and keeping services in sync. In client mode, agents are basically stateless and are only responsible to forward remote procedure calls to a server. Server agents participate in the Raft quorum and are responsible to maintain the cluster state. Consensus in Consul means the election of leaders as well as the ordering of transactions. Transactions are applied to finite-state machines, and consensus requires the consistency between replicated state machines.

Akka[14] is an open source toolkit and runtime designed for the construction of concurrent and distributed applications running on the JVM. It uses an actor-based concurrency model which is message based and asynchronous. Each actor communicates directly or using routing facilities. This allows for easy scaling both horizontally and vertically. Actors are arranged hierarchically making dealing with program failure easier to handle. It has been used to create a wide array of self optimizing applications.

Configuration management systems are a key feature when designing cloud applications using self-* principles. They are used to automatically provision and configure new VMs. There are currently a wide array of such solutions likes Chef,[15] Puppet,[16] and Salt.[17] Chef in particular is one of the most notable solutions in the Infrastructure as a Code paradigm. Users write recipes that describe how the newly provisioned application VMs should be configured. The Chef server and clients use these descriptions as a basis for management. It can be argued that these configuration management systems, in many ways, adhere to a multi-agent paradigm in that there are a number of software entities that have a clear goal (in the case of Chef given by the recipes) which they have to achieve. The most important difference of this type of system and an agent based one is that in the case of configuration management each component (be it the server or the clients) has a narrow degree of autonomy to create a plan in order to achieve a given goal. The plan being defined in large part by the user. However, there are ways to generate these plans dynamically using the configuration management system only as an actuator.

In order to create a self-healing application in a cloud environment, they have to be in a place where some mechanisms allow this to happen. First a cloud environment will have to have the ability to scale some, if not necessarily all, of its components with the aid of load balancing and a mechanism to create and enforce scaling policies. For example, in the case of AWS, this can be done

---

[14]http://akka.io/

[15]https://www.chef.io/

[16]https://puppet.com/

[17]https://saltstack.com/

using EC2 autoscaling groups and elastic load balancing. Secondly, there has to be a way of monitoring the application which allows the orchestration to react based on the detected events (failures, high load, etc.). Automatic failover of unresponsive components is also key in creating a self-healing application. Once a failed component is detected, all traffic meant for that component has to be redirected to a replica. Self-healing networks need to recognize failures in a network and deal with them automatically. For example, a web server can be considered to be stateless. If one server fails, traffic to that server should be rerouted to other web servers automatically. Once the server is back online, a series of tests should be run on the server to see if it is configured correctly. Once all tests have been done, traffic can be safely rerouted to it. The abovementioned scenario can be easily implemented by taking advantage of autoscaling groups in AWS.

Druva[18] is a cloud-based storage solution which deploys its own file system called Druva cloud file system. It has source-side data de-duplication, continuous data protection, compressed and encrypted data storage, and policy-based data retention. It has many key concepts which are important in a cloud-based storage system such as durability (it uses AWS S3 and DynamoDB for file system meta-data storage). It also features self-healing capability by using inSync that continues to serve both backup and restore requests despite possible inconsistencies. It accomplishes this by periodically simulating a restore procedure. If a restore procedure fails, it executes a purge of that snapshot. An inconsistency report is generated which ensures future consistency.

10.6 Conclusion

The application of the self-* principles in heterogeneous cloud environments is a hot topic nowadays, and lots of effort is invested in the development and integration of the principles in production-ready environments. Adaption and promotion of self-* principles in the context of heterogeneous cloud environments is based on good examples from practice. An important step in this direction is the establishment of a good set of templates that can be used in order to use the self-* principles in production-ready systems.

This chapter gives an historical overview of the self-* principles and also of individual properties that make a system to be classifiable as self-* system. We also give a brief overview of the state-of-the-art literature that is guiding the field of study as well as the various research projects that have as a goal the development of various components that contribute to the composition of a self-* system. Alongside the presentation of individual characteristics of self-*, we also present interesting European initiatives aiming at improving both the theoretical and the practical part of various fields of self-* cloud environments. Last but not least this chapter also a

---

[18]http://www.druva.com/

succinct presentation of production ready tools and their characteristics offered. By combining all the ingredients presented in this chapter, we believe that the field of self-* clouds has a good starting point for further development and improvement.

Acknowledgements This work is partially funded by the European Union's Horizon 2020 Research and Innovation Programme through the CloudLightning project (http://www. cloudlightning.eu) under Grant Agreement Number 643946 and the DICE project (http://www. dice-h2020.eu/) under Grant Number 644869.

References

1. Al-Ali RJ, Rana OF, Walker DW, Jha S, Sohail S (2002) G-QOSM: grid service discovery using QOS properties. Comput Inf 21(4):363–382
2. Almeida J, Almeida V, Ardagna D, Francalanci C, Trubian M (2006) Resource management in the autonomic service-oriented architecture. In: 2006 IEEE international conference on autonomic computing
3. An architectural blueprint for autonomic computing (2005) White paper, IBM
4. Aversa R, Di Martino B, Rak M, Venticinque S (2010) Cloud agency: a mobile agent based cloud system. In: 2010 international conference on complex, intelligent and software intensive systems
5. Brandic (2009) Towards self-manageable cloud services. In: 2009 33rd annual IEEE international computer software and applications conference
6. Breskovic I, Maurer M, Emeakaroha VC, Brandic I, Dustdar S (2011) Cost-efficient utilization of public sla templates in autonomic cloud markets. In: 2011 fourth IEEE international conference on utility and cloud computing
7. Broberg J, Buyya R, Tari Z (2009) MetaCDN: harnessing 'Storage Clouds' for high performance content delivery. J Netw Comput Appl 32(5):1012–1022
8. Buyya R, Calheiros RN, Li X (2012) Autonomic cloud computing: open challenges and architectural elements. In: 2012 third international conference on emerging applications of information technology
9. Buyya R, Garg SK, Calheiros RN (2011) Sla-oriented resource provisioning for cloud computing: challenges, architecture, and solutions. In: 2011 international conference on cloud and service computing
10. Chandola V, Banerjee A, Kumar V (2009) Anomaly detection: a survey. ACM Comput Surv 41(3):15:1–15:58
11. Cloud Computing Use Cases White Paper (2010) http://www.cloud-council.org/Cloud_ Computing_Use_Cases_Whitepaper-4_0.pdf
12. Cuomo A, Rak M, Venticinque S, Villano U (2012) Enhancing an autonomic cloud architecture with mobile agents. Springer, Berlin/Heidelberg, pp 94–103
13. Cuomo A, Di Modica G, Distefano S, Puliafito A, Rak M, Tomarchio O, Venticinque S, Villano U (2012) An sla-based broker for cloud infrastructures. J Grid Comput 11(1):125
14. Deelman E, Singh G, Livny M, Berriman B, Good J (2008) The cost of doing science on the cloud: the montage example. In: 2008 SC – international conference for high performance computing, networking, storage and analysis, SC 2008
15. Di Sanzo P, Pellegrini A, Avresky DR (2015) Machine learning for achieving self-* properties and seamless execution of applications in the cloud. In: 2015 IEEE fourth symposium on network cloud computing and applications (NCCA). Institute of Electrical & Electronics Engineers (IEEE)
16. Dial J (2013) Cloud services foundation reference architecture – reference model – cloud and datacenter solutions. BLOG entry

17. DMTF (2010) Architecture for Managing Clouds A White Paper from the Open Cloud Standards Incubator. Technical report, Distributed Management Task Force
18. DMTF (2010) Use Cases and Interactions for Managing Clouds A White Paper from the Open Cloud Standards Incubator. Technical report, Distributed Management Task Force
19. Fortis T-F, Munteanu VI (2014) From cloud management to cloud governance. Continued Rise of the Cloud, pp 265–287
20. Hajjat M, Sun X, Sung YWE, Maltz D, Rao S, Sripanidkulchai K, Tawarmalani M (2010) Cloudward bound: planning for beneficial migration of enterprise applications to the cloud. SIGCOMM Comput Commun Rev 40(4):243–254
21. Horn P (2001) Autonomic computing: IBM's Perspective on the State of Information. Technical report, IBM
22. Huebscher MC, McCann JA (2008) A survey of autonomic computing-degrees, models, and applications. ACM Comput Surv 40(3):1–28
23. IBM's project eLiza closing the gap between autonomic and grid computing (2002) http://www.itweb.co.za/index.php?option=com_content&view=article&id=85862
24. IBM (2011) Getting cloud computing right. Technical report, IBM
25. Iordache A, Buyukkaya E, Pierre G (2015) Heterogeneous resource selection for arbitrary HPC applications in the cloud. In: Lecture notes in computer science, vol 9038. Springer Science + Business Media, pp 108–123
26. Kephart JO, Chess DM (2003) The vision of autonomic computing. Computer 36(1):41–50
27. Kertesz A, Kecskemeti G, Brandic I (2014) An interoperable and self-adaptive approach for sla-based service virtualization in heterogeneous cloud environments. Futur Gener Comput Syst 32:5468
28. Kertesz A, Kecskemeti G, Brandic I (2011) Autonomic sla-aware service virtualization for distributed systems. In: 2011 19th international Euromicro conference on parallel, distributed and network-based processing
29. Koehler M, Kaniovskyi Y, Benkner S (2011) An adaptive framework for the execution of data-intensive mapreduce applications in the cloud. 2011 IEEE international symposium on parallel and distributed processing workshops and Phd Forum
30. Lacoste M, Charmet F (2015) Towards user-centric management of security and dependability in clouds of clouds. E-Democracy–Citizen Rights in the World of the New Computing Paradigms, pp 198201
31. Leite AF, Raiol T, Tadonki C, Walter MEMT, Eisenbeis C, de Melo ACMA (2014) Excalibur: an autonomic cloud architecture for executing parallel applications. In: Proceedings of the fourth international workshop on cloud data and platforms – CloudDP 14
32. Liu F, Tong J, Mao J, Bohn R, Messina J, Badger L, Leaf D (2012) NIST cloud computing reference architecture: recommendations of the national institute of standards and technology (Special Publication 500–292). CreateSpace Independent Publishing Platform
33. Lynn T, Xiong H, Dong D, Momani B, Gravvanis G, Filelis-Papadopoulos C, Elster A, Khan MMZM Tzovaras D, Giannoutakis K et al. (2016) CLOUDLIGHTNING: a framework for a self-organising and self-managing heterogeneous cloud. In: Proceedings of the 6th international conference on cloud computing and services science. Scitepress, pp 333–338
34. Marinescu DC, Morrison JP, Paya A (2015) Is cloud self-organization feasible? Springer International Publishing, pp 119–127
35. Maurer M, Brandic I, Sakellariou R (2012) Self-adaptive and resource-efficient sla enactment for cloud computing infrastructures. In: 2012 IEEE Fifth International Conference on Cloud Computing
36. Maurer M, Breskovic I, Emeakaroha VC, Brandic I (2011) Revealing the MAPE loop for the autonomic management of cloud infrastructures. In: 2011 IEEE symposium on computers and communications (ISCC)
37. Moscato F, Aversa R, Di Martino B, Fortis T-F, Munteanu VI (2011) An analysis of mosaic ontology for cloud resources annotation. In: 2011 Federated Conference on Computer Science and Information Systems (FedCSIS), pp 973–980

38. Munteanu VI, Fortis T-F, Negru V (2013) An evolutionary approach for sla-based cloud resource provisioning. In: 2013 IEEE 27th international conference on advanced information networking and applications (AINA)
39. Nami MR, Bertels K (2007) A survey of autonomic computing systems. In: Third international conference on autonomic and autonomous systems, (ICAS'07). IEEE, pp 26–26
40. NIST Cloud Computing Standards Roadmap Working Group (2013) NIST Cloud Computing Standards Roadmap. Technical report, National Institute of Standards and Technology
41. Ouelhadj D, Garibaldy J, MacLaren J, Sakellariou R, Krishnakumar K (2005) A multi-agent infrastructure and a service level agreement negotiation protocol for robust scheduling in grid computing. In: Advances in grid computing, pp 651–660
42. Patcha A, Park J-M (2007) An overview of anomaly detection techniques: existing solutions and latest technological trends. Comput Netw 51(12):3448–3470
43. Petcu D (2014) Building automatic clouds with an open-source and deployable platform-as-a-service. In: Advances in parallel computing. Cloud computing and big data. IOS Press, pp 3–19
44. Poslad S (2009) Autonomous systems and artificial life. John Wiley & Sons, pp 317–341
45. Rimal BP, Choi E, Lumb I (2009) A taxonomy and survey of cloud computing systems. In: Proceedings of the 2009 fifth international joint conference on INC, IMS and IDC, NCM '09. IEEE Computer Society, Washington, DC, pp 44–51
46. Schmid S, Sifalakis M, Hutchison D (2006) Towards autonomic networks. Springer, Berlin/Heidelberg, pp 1–11
47. Serrano M, Le-Phuoc D, Zaremba M, Galis A, Bhiri S, Hauswirth M (2013) Resource optimisation in IoT cloud systems by using matchmaking and self-management principles. Springer, Berlin/Heidelberg, pp 127–140
48. Smith RG (1980) The contract net protocol: high-level communication and control in a distributed problem solver. IEEE Trans Comput C-29(12):1104–1113
49. Venticinque S, Aversa R, Di Martino B, Rak M, Petcu D (2011) A cloud agency for SLA negotiation and management. Lecture notes in computer science. Springer, Berlin/New York, pp 587–594
50. Venticinque S, Aversa R, Di Martino B, Petcu D (2011) Agent based cloud provisioning and management – design and prototypal implementation. In: Proceedings of the 1st international conference on cloud computing and services science, pp 184–191
51. Wada H, Suzuki J, Yamano Y, Oba K (2011) Evolutionary deployment optimization for service-oriented clouds. Softw Pract Exper 41(5):469–493
52. Yaich R, Idrees S, Cuppens N, Cuppens F (2015) D1.2 SUPERCLOUD self-management of security specification. Project deliverable, SUPERCLOUD Project
53. Yangui S, Marshall I-J, Laisne J-P, Tata S (2013) Compatibleone: the open source cloud broker. J Grid Comput 12(1):93109

Part V
Performance and Efficiency

Chapter 11
Optimizing the Profit and QoS of Virtual Brokers in the Cloud

Santiago Iturriaga, Sergio Nesmachnow, and Bernabé Dorronsoro

11.1 Introduction

The paradigm of cloud computing [10] has evolved extremely fast in the last years, thanks to the unique properties it offers, such as flexibility, fail over mechanisms, and the (apparently) unlimited computational power. The main features of the cloud computing model are achieved by using the hardware virtualization technology. This technology allows splitting a single physical computing resource into several separated virtual resources which can be used to perform different computing tasks or to offer different services. Regarding computing hardware, cloud computing is based on virtual machines (VMs) that can be dynamically allocated and deallocated to the physical resources (servers) according to demand and availability. The cloud provider has the possibility of applying consolidation strategies to group a number of VMs into the same physical server. Furthermore, when the available resources owned by the provider are not enough for the current demand at a given peak time, specific techniques such as *cloud bursting* [14] can be used to get additional resources from external clouds, therefore extending the computing capacity of the facility in a transparent way to the users.

Among the different provisioning models that cloud computing offers, we deal in this chapter with the optimization of IaaS-oriented cloud services, which is the most flexible model to deploy applications but also the most challenging for the user. IaaS allows the user to significantly reduce infrastructure costs (e.g., from purchasing, installation/configuration, administration, and maintenance among

S. Iturriaga (✉) • S. Nesmachnow
Universidad de la República, Montevideo, Uruguay
e-mail: siturria@fing.edu.uy; sergion@fing.edu.uy

B. Dorronsoro
Universidad de Cádiz, Cádiz, Spain
e-mail: bernabe.dorronsoro@uca.es

© Springer International Publishing AG 2017
N. Antonopoulos, L. Gillam (eds.), *Cloud Computing*, Computer Communications and Networks, DOI 10.1007/978-3-319-54645-2_11

others) providing flexibility comparable to an in-house infrastructure. Furthermore, by dealing with IaaS-oriented services, a cloud system can provide PaaS and SaaS services in a more efficient way. Since those models are built upon IaaS services, the deployment of VMs can be customized to offer better PaaS and SaaS services to its customers [18].

Since cloud computing became a successful computing model in many application domains [4], the number of cloud providers has increased notably in the last decade. Among many well-known cloud providers, we can name Amazon Elastic Compute Cloud, Google App Engine Cloud Platform, Microsoft Azure, VMware vCloud Air, and Rackspace. Many other companies offer small-scale services in the cloud, too. Each provider competes for a market share, usually applying aggressive strategies and offering many services, applications, bundles, and also different prices and rates, thus overwhelming cloud end users with many options. Up to now, no standardization exists among cloud providers; hence each one offers a set of services with its own characteristics and pricing.

The lack of standardization and the increasing number of cloud providers have made it challenging for end users to choose an adequate provider for their applications. To cope with this, a new kind of player—the *cloud broker*—has emerged as an intermediary between end users and providers [6]. The cloud broker is an agent that manages a portfolio of cloud providers and offers consulting services, advising end users which are the most suitable providers for them and the best way to deploy their applications. This is a complex task in which the cloud broker must take into account providers' characteristics such as pricing, performance, service level agreements (SLA), security, privacy, and any other feature that may affect the user application. However, the services of a cloud broker are usually expensive, increasing the budget of the end user.

Nesmachnow et al. [17] introduced a new brokering model which takes advantage of the pricing structure of the cloud providers to produce revenue without increasing the budget of the end user. In this new model, the cloud broker is called a *virtual broker*, because it owns a number of virtual resources: it rents a number of VMs from different providers for a long period of time with a significant discount in price (i.e., up to 75%). Then, it sublets these VMs on an on-demand basis to end users at cheaper prices than those of the cloud providers. We also introduced the profit optimization problem for the virtual broker and proposed batch-oriented algorithms for solving the planning problem taking into account profit and quality of service (QoS) metrics. We proved that the virtual broker is capable of generating revenue with very competitive pricing.

This chapter summarizes our previous work and extends it by improving the problem formulation using a multi-objective approach to consider both profit and QoS simultaneously. In this formulation the profit objective is the total economic profit of the virtual broker, while the QoS objective is the sum of the waiting time of all VM requests. We design six heuristic algorithms for tackling the problem and accurately compute trade-off values between both objectives. These new algorithms allow further studying the efficacy of the virtual brokering approach by comparing the obtained results applying a Pareto dominance analysis of accurate trade-off solutions.

We design two online scheduling algorithms and four offline scheduling algorithms. Online algorithms are defined as being non-batch oriented, meaning they schedule requests as soon as they arrive without creating batches and without delay. On the contrary, offline algorithms accumulate arriving requests into batches and schedule a whole batch of requests each time. To compare online and offline algorithms is relevant since creating larger batches provides the scheduling algorithms with greater context insight. But at the same time, the size of the batch affects the QoS of the system since the VM requests must be delayed briefly for creating each batch.

The main contributions of the research reported in this chapter are:

- The design of six fast optimization techniques to efficiently solve the problem of optimizing the profit of the virtual broker and the QoS provided to its customers.
- The experimental evaluation performed in a benchmark set of realistic problem instances, including data from real cloud IaaS providers. These experiments demonstrate that the proposed methods are accurate and efficient strategies to solve the problem, finding good quality schedules that account for both the virtual broker profit and QoS provided to the cloud users.
- The reported results represent the new state of the art for this problem when considering the virtual brokering approach.

The paper is structured as follows. The next section presents the current cloud brokering model and introduces the new virtual brokering model. The optimization problem addressed in this work and a review of the existing work on related brokering proposals for cloud computing are presented in Sect. 11.3. The six scheduling heuristics proposed for addressing the virtual brokering optimization problem are described in Sect. 11.4. The experimental evaluation over a set of realistic workloads and scenarios is reported in Sect. 11.5. Finally, Sect. 11.6 presents the conclusions and formulates some open lines for future work.

11.2 Brokering and Virtual Brokering in Cloud Computing Systems

This section introduces the main concepts about brokering models and services and describes our proposal for a virtual broker for IaaS services.

11.2.1 Cloud Brokering

A *cloud broker* is defined as "a cloud service partner that negotiates relationships between cloud service customers and cloud service providers," according to the International Organization for Standardization [13]. The figure of the cloud broker [11] emerged as an important actor to assist cloud users in the quest of finding the best choices of both hardware and software for implementing, deploying, and/or executing their applications.

Cloud brokers are important agents to manage the different types of cloud infrastructures. The most recognizable and popular type of cloud are *public clouds*, which follow the standard model for providing services based on virtualized environments. Public clouds provide services to multiple clients using the same shared infrastructure and a multitenancy model for applications. Public clouds are mostly used individually by users that do not have important concerns about processing time or security, but they are also useful for industries and companies to store and process nonsensitive data and other day-to-day collaborative operations. Public clouds provide the standard features of scalability, flexibility, reliability, and pay-as-you-use utility pricing for users.

Private clouds, usually also named as internal cloud or corporate cloud, are based on the same features as public clouds but based on a proprietary infrastructure and/or software. Private clouds are dedicated to a single organization, which makes use of the resources and services to handle critical processes which have strong uptime requirements, to store and handle sensitive data, or those that have large security concerns. Private clouds tend to be small, due to the ownership costs and management costs that cannot be delegated to third parties.

Finally, a *hybrid cloud* is a type of cloud that makes use of both private and public services and resources in a coordinated way. This model allows scaling the operation beyond a private infrastructure, delegating noncritical processes and data to the public cloud, while keeping sensitive data and processing in the private cloud. Processes and data can move between private and public clouds depending on (variable) situations, such as changes in cost or changes on demand. Thus, hybrid clouds provide the users the most flexible option to deploy their applications, especially for dynamic operations, for example, workload peaks. The technique that allows scaling up to get additional resources and services from a public cloud is called *cloud bursting*. The hybrid model allows getting the most from cloud resources and services, but it also requires an advanced management from both technical and economical point of views. Issues such as compatibility, connectivity, interoperability, and resource planning are critical for the correct operation of the hybrid cloud.

Cloud brokers can play different roles according to the type of cloud they work over. The broker can focus on specific actions and services for the public, private, or hybrid cloud, such as the ones described in the following subsection.

11.2.2 Broker Types

An effective broker should guide users toward the most adequate cloud solutions for their needs, creating and offering added value over basic cloud services. This way, users will be attracted to use the broker services and make the brokering model useful and profitable. The main concepts of cloud brokering apply to both the traditional broker and the virtual broker.

Two main sources of users' motivation emerge as possible targets for brokers to attract users: the QoS point of view and the economic point of view. On the one hand, brokers can focus on offering better services by improving the QoS of external services and applications in their portfolio. On the other hand, brokers can focus on improved and attractive pricing models, such as the one we exploit in this chapter. These two main aspects directly impact on the broker *reputation*, which is certainly an important feature in a market with a large number of actors offering brokering services. We will also consider this important issue in the model for our virtual broker.

Regarding brokering services, the literature recognizes two different classifications: the ones proposed by Gartner [12] and by the National Institute of Standards and Technology (NIST) of the US Department of Commerce [3]; both classify cloud services into three categories. On the one hand, the classification proposed by Gartner defines three main types of services that fulfill distinct needs (we include a brief description of each service type over the IaaS model):

- *Aggregation brokers*: These brokers provide bundles of services and platforms with different features that gather software and hardware services from multiple providers. The broker accounts for managing SLAs for the users. In the IaaS model, aggregation services are provided by brokers that offer cloud computing platforms with different features (e.g., computing power, storage, geographical location, security, and access among others) following the single system image concept, usually applied in distributed computing. A simple method for implementing aggregation is the low-level hardware-as-a-service (HaaS) paradigm that provides access to infrastructure from several cloud providers in a pay-as-you-use model for cloud users. But the broker can also offer services that implement a distributed system, including single IP address space, checkpointing, process migration, single process space, and unified view of the file system among others.
- *Integration brokers*: These brokers provide services focused on creating a unified system using capabilities from several providers. A typical example of integration broker is the one that allows implementing the concept of hybrid cloud. Specific services are offered by brokers for the integration of public and private clouds. This model is usually implemented for high level services, but integration of low-level IaaS services is also possible, for example, when a broker provides assistance for the management of cloud bursting techniques.
- *Customization brokers*: These brokers provide services that allow personalizing existing services, usually combining aggregation, integration, and other specific features oriented to add value and build new products. Customization is useful for creating new and sophisticated services, which are usually focused on specific platforms, but can be used generally too. In the IaaS model, customization can be applied to create managing services, for example, to provide support for heterogeneous platforms including different hardware and devices.

On the other hand, the definition proposed by NIST groups broker services in the following categories:

- *Intermediation brokers*: These brokers provide intermediation services as defined by NIST. An intermediation service is an improvement or enhancement over some given service. This improvement may be related to QoS activities, security, performance reporting, or some other capability.
- *Aggregation brokers*: These brokers provide aggregation services which combine and integrate multiple services into new services. These brokers must integrate data and processes and ensure security in service-to-service interaction.
- *Arbitration brokers*: Arbitration services are a more flexible form of aggregation services. In an aggregation service, all aggregated services are fixed and do not change over time. However, in an arbitration service, the broker can dynamically aggregate services according to a business-aware algorithm to achieve some advantage related to pricing, features, or some other.

According to the mentioned classifications, our virtual broker would fall into the categories of *integration brokers* and *intermediation brokers*.

11.2.3   The Virtual Broker for IaaS

Traditional brokering. As intermediary agent between cloud providers and cloud users, a traditional cloud broker, offers several services. The most common service offered by brokers is assisting users to find the best cloud options and providers to satisfy users' requirements or to deploy users' applications. The "best" option can be defined regarding many factors, including economic cost, QoS, reliability, security and privacy, and several other criteria. Other more sophisticated services can be offered by the broker (as described in the previous subsection), but in general they all work following the specific methodology for the interactions between users, broker, and providers that we describe in Fig. 11.1.

When using the services of a traditional broker T, users contact the broker asking assistance for meeting specific needs (this interaction is represented with the blue arrow in Fig. 11.1, labeled "T1"). The cloud broker searches cloud providers (within his portfolio, or looking for different options in the public cloud) to find a set of alternatives for the user (gray arrows in Fig. 11.1, labeled "T2"). This information is then offered to the user, who may deal directly with the cloud provider(s) or interact through the cloud broker (orange arrows in Fig. 11.1, labeled "T3.1" and "T3.2").

The traditional cloud brokering approach has some limitations. For instance, it limits the added value that broker offers to users when acting just as an intermediary to find services in the public cloud (orange arrow labeled "T3.1" in Fig. 11.1). However, this approach is also open to many possibilities for developing new business models. Our proposal for the virtual broker is based on concentrating the interactions in the broker and taking advantage of existing pricing schemes for IaaS services, as we describe in the next subsection.

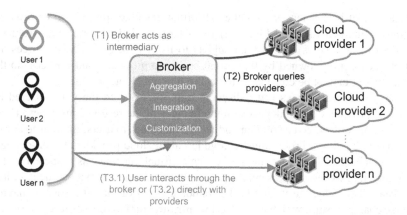

Fig. 11.1 Diagram of the interactions between users, a traditional broker, and cloud providers

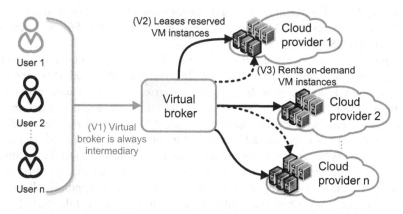

Fig. 11.2 Diagram of the interactions between users, the virtual broker [17], and cloud providers

Virtual brokering. The virtual broker presented by Nesmachnow et al. [17] and Alsina et al. [1] is based on an economic model that exploits some features of current pricing schemes of public IaaS providers. On the one hand, under the current situation, renting a specific virtual machine on a given cloud provider is usually more expensive when the request is submitted on demand than when a reserved instance is used (e.g., from 0.18 USD/h [reserved instance] to 0.41 USD/h [on-demand instance]). On the other hand, public IaaS providers, such as AWS, Azure, and Google, have significant discounts for volume usage. For example, reserved instances by Amazon allow customers to get a discount of up to 60% when compared to on-demand EC2 prices. However, to get these discounts, customers are required to reserve the virtual machines for a long period of time. This policy is applied to promote long-term provisioning of virtual machines, which accounts for better hardware amortization and thus increased revenue for cloud providers. The diagram on Fig. 11.2 presents the interactions in the virtual brokering model.

The virtual broker leases a number of virtual machines referred to as *reserved instances* (marked in green Fig. 11.2) for a large period of time (e.g., from six months to a few years) that it then sublets to its customers. These resources are not physical servers owned by the virtual broker to provide cloud services, so the virtual broker cannot be considered to be a traditional cloud provider.

The virtual broker pays a flat discount rate according to the plans offered by the cloud providers which depends on the features of the reserved instances. These resources are outsourced as on-demand virtual machines to users. In order to attract customers, the virtual broker must charge less than cloud providers for on-demand virtual machines. In our case, the broker rents virtual machines as proposed by the IaaS model; however, the presented schema can be extended to models such as SaaS and PaaS. This way, the virtual broker builds a cloud of virtual resources having diverse characteristics, which is used as the infrastructure to offer different services.

Under this pricing schema, the virtual broker could generate a profit, as a consequence of the significant price differences between reserved and on-demand virtual machines. For example, price differences for reserved and on-demand virtual machines ranges between 34%–55% in Amazon EC2 and 25%–56% in Microsoft Azure cloud IaaS services.

Reputation is crucial for a virtual broker, as it is dealing with a very dynamic market with many similar agents that provide services on the cloud. Rejecting user requests is not desirable, as the broker gains negative reputation and the user might not be willing to hire the broker services in the future. In case the virtual broker cannot accommodate a specific upcoming request before the demanded deadline, it must either use a larger available reserved instance (i.e., offering the user more resources than (s)he requested), or buy an on-demand instance to fulfill the request. In any case, the broker must charge the cost of the virtual machine originally requested by the user, coping with any additional cost. This approach allows the virtual broker to keep a positive reputation among its customers at the cost of some negative impact on its revenue.

The success of the economical model applied by the virtual broker relies on two key aspects:

1. An accurate forecasting of resources requested by users, in order to fulfill their demands. This estimation can be performed by applying a market analysis in order to study the needs and how attractive is the proposed model within a given area of application or users from a cloud community. An accurate forecasting technique is not critical for the adequate operation of the virtual broker model because the broker has the capability of renting on-demand virtual machines to guarantee that users are served. Nevertheless, the more accurate the forecasting technique is, the more accurately the virtual broker can estimate the number of reserved instances to rent. This is useful for maximizing the profit of the virtual broker because overestimating demand would increase costs, while underestimating it would decrease revenue;

2. The utilization of accurate scheduling algorithms (such as greedy heuristics or evolutionary algorithms) for managing the available reserved instances and scheduling them to customers' VM requests in order to maximize their usage, the proper location of requests to resources, and the hiring of on-demand virtual machines when needed.

Rogers and Cliff [19] proposed a brokering business model similar to the one we propose in this work but using a collaborative forecasting and dynamic pricing approach. The model by Rogers and Cliff requires each customer to forecast its own VM resource usage and rewards the most accurate forecasting customers by lowering their resource renting costs. These forecasts are used by the broker to determine the amount of reserved instances to rent. Recently, Cartlidge and Clamp [5] showed that the model proposed by Rogers and Cliff [19] is not viable with the pricing schemes from 2014, and they claim that "the window of opportunity has now closed." In this work, we present a new economic model which differs from the one by Rogers and Cliff in several aspects and opens a new window of opportunity for the virtual broker.

Our research studies the viability of the proposed economic model for the virtual broker, and we propose specific planning algorithms to be applied in order to maximize the broker profit and the QoS offered to users. Statistic approaches can be applied for forecasting the required reserved instances, for example, as proposed by De Felice and Yao [8]. Our algorithms assume that a given virtual cloud is already reserved by the virtual broker. We focus on the comparison of online and offline methods to manage the reserved instances to satisfy users' request, according to specific service levels agreed by users and the broker.

The virtual broker rents a *distributed* infrastructure, possibly including reserved instances from many IaaS providers and geographically located in different data-centers around the globe. As a consequence, it is very important to consider the geographical location of resources, applications, and users and also the possible communications between applications and users.

We focus on designing greedy heuristic scheduling algorithms to manage a set of reserved virtual resources in order to satisfy as many user requests as possible, without relying on on-demand resources. Only when the broker cannot fulfill the contracted SLA, a kind of cloud bursting approach is applied, renting on-demand virtual machines.

11.3 Virtual Machine Planning for a Virtual Cloud Broker

This section defines the virtual machine planning problem for a virtual cloud broker. First, we introduce the general problem formulation. After that, we present an extended problem formulation which considers geolocalization and various types of applications.

11.3.1 Problem Formulation

The ultimate goal of the virtual broker is to maximize its revenue. To accomplish this task, the virtual broker must efficiently manage its reserved instances to cope with as many user requests as possible. In the case it cannot fulfill all requests without violating the contracted SLA, it must rent on-demand VM instances from the public cloud to satisfy demand, despite its revenue loss.

We define the SLA to be deadline based; thus it is associated with each customer request. In its most simple formulation, the objective of our problem is to find a mapping function to schedule customers' requests into VM instances, maximizing the revenue of the virtual broker while satisfying their deadlines. In order to formulate this objective, we must introduce some definitions.

- The set of VM requested by the virtual broker's customers $VM = \{v_1, \ldots, v_n\}$. Each request v_i with a hardware demand given by its required processor speed $P(v_i)$, number of cores $nc(v_i)$, memory size $M(v_i)$, and persistent storage space $S(v_i)$. The arrival of these requests follows a stochastic homogeneous Poisson process with an arrival rate of λ.
- The customer must specify the time length $T(v_i)$ and deadline $D(v_i)$ of each request. The time length is the amount of time the customer will use the VM, while the deadline is the maximum amount of time the customer is willing to wait for the VM to be available.
- The set of reserved VM instances leased by the virtual broker $RI = \{r_1, \ldots, r_m\}$ with $m \ll n$. Each reserved VM r_j with hardware characteristics given by its processor speed $P(r_j)$, number of cores $nc(r_j)$, memory size $M(r_j)$, and persistent storage space $S(r_j)$.
- The cost function $C(r_j)$ defines the cost the virtual broker must pay for renting the reserved VM instance r_j for each time unit. Additionally, $COD(r_j)$ is the cost the virtual broker must pay for renting the same instance as an on-demand instance for each time unit.
- The pricing function $p(r_j)$ defines the price the virtual broker charges its customers for VM instance r_j, for each time unit.

We consider all time units to be expressed in an hourly basis. This is a realistic consideration since most cloud providers charge per hour for VM instances. Also, it is key to highlight that for this model to be profitable, two things must be ensured. First, $C(r_j) \ll COD(r_j)$, since this model would be unprofitable if the discount for the reserved instances owned by the virtual broker is not large enough. Second, $C(r_j) < p(r_j) < COD(r_j)$, this is key for attracting customers and generating revenue.

The objective of our problem is to find a mapping function $f : VM \to RI$ to assign VM requests to VM instances which maximizes the profit of the virtual broker as shown in Eq. 11.1.

$$O_p = \max \sum_{j=1}^{m} \sum_{i:f(v_i)=r_j} \big(p(BF(v_i)) - C(r_j)\big) \times T(v_i)$$

$$+ \sum_{h:ST(v_h)>D(v_h)} \big(p(BF(v_h)) - COD(BF(v_h))\big) \times T(v_h) \qquad (11.1)$$

where $BF(v_i)$ is a simple function that returns the cheapest VM instance that is suitable for request v_i. That is, $BF(v_i)$ considers every VM instance which meets or exceeds the hardware requirements of request v_i and selects the VM instance which has the cheapest on-demand cost. Finally, $ST(v_h)$ is the starting time of request v_h according to the scheduling function f.

As we already discussed, the virtual broker must satisfy all requests from its customers. If it is unable to satisfy the deadline of a request v_i with the reserved VM instance given by $BF(v_i)$, the virtual broker has two alternatives. If it has reserved VM instances available with larger capacity than $BF(v_i)$, it may assign one of them to request v_i. Otherwise, the virtual broker must lease an on-demand VM instance from a cloud provider to satisfy request v_i. Either way, this will generate a loss in revenue, since the virtual broker must charge $p(BF(v_i))$ for request v_i.

This problem is different from the classical VM deployment in physical servers typically addressed in cloud computing to efficiently manage the resources of the cloud provider [4, 20, 22, 23]. In contrast, we focus on mapping all VM requests into the available RIs, taking into account that the assigned RIs must provide similar or better performance than the corresponding VM request. Therefore, this is a resource allocation problem with additional constraints, making it more complex than the resource allocation problem (the resource allocation problem itself is NP-hard [21]). In our problem, the virtual broker relies on the cloud provider to meet the SLA, thus the broker just needs to ensure that all VMs are assigned to RIs with similar or larger capacity.

Since we do not consider geographic localization in this formulation, we consider it to be a location-agnostic formulation. Next we present an extended formulation which includes geographic localization.

11.3.2 Extended Problem Formulation

In the previous section, we presented a formulation that takes into account all the fundamental aspects of our problem. In this section we further extend our previous formulation in order to address a more realistic scenario. In this extended, location-aware formulation, we consider the geographic localization of customers and cloud providers, the type of application of each VM request, and the cost of the data transferred by each application through the network. On top of this, we also consider a SLA-related objective to be optimized simultaneously with the profit objective we defined previously. Let us introduce some additional elements, on top of the ones introduced on our previous formulation.

- Two types of customers' requests: computation tasks (CT) and web services (WS). A computation task is a noninteractive application which may be executed at any time just before its deadline $D(v_i)$. Because of noninteractive nature, there is flexibility on its starting time. On the contrary, a web service is an interactive task; thus it must be started right away without delay. That is, there is no flexibility on their starting time.
- A set of geographic zones $C = \{z_1, \ldots, z_l\}$. Each VM instance is located in a geographic zone z_j which depends on the geographic location of its hosting cloud provider. Each application transfers data to and from users, which in turn are also located in some geographic zone. Hence, we define a function $DTC(z_j, z_i)$ which models the data transfer cost per hour for transferring data between zone z_i and z_j. For VM request v_i, the rate of data transferred between each zone z_i is given by $DTD(v_j, z_i)$, with $\sum_{i=1}^{l} DTD(v_j, z_i) = 1 \; \forall v_j \in VM$.

The objective of the extended problem formulation is to find a mapping function $f : VM \rightarrow RI$ to assign VM requests to VM instances which maximizes the profit for the virtual broker and also minimizes the waiting time for the customer's requests. In this multi-objective formulation, the QoS is related to the waiting time of the VM requests, i.e., the time lapse since the VM request arrives up until the VM instance starts its execution. Equation 11.2a shows the profit maximization objective (O_p), while the QoS objective (O_q) is modeled in Eq. 11.2b by the minimization of the waiting time of customer's requests. In Eq. 11.2b, $AR(v_i)$ is the arrival time of the customer's VM request v_i.

$$O_p = \max \sum_{j=1}^{m} \sum_{i: f(v_i)=r_j} \left(p(BF(v_i)) - C(r_j) \right) \times T(v_i)$$

$$+ \sum_{h: ST(v_h) > D(v_h)} \left(p(BF(v_h)) - COD(BF(v_h)) \right) \times T(v_h) + \qquad (11.2a)$$

$$\sum_{i=1}^{n} \sum_{k=1}^{l} DTD(v_i, z_k) \times DTC(f(v_i), z_k) \times DT(f(v_i))$$

$$O_q = \min \sum_{i=1}^{n} ST(v_i) - AR(v_i) \qquad (11.2b)$$

11.4 The Proposed Scheduling Methods

In this section we introduce a set of efficient scheduling algorithms for solving the two formulations of the virtual machine planning problem presented in the previous section. We originally proposed these heuristics in [16] for solving a simpler formulation of the problem proposed in this work. We designed them to be efficient and effective and capable of scaling up to several hundreds of VM requests. They aim to provide a trade-off between user-related and system-related criteria. User-related criteria evaluate the algorithm from the user perspective and include metrics such as response time, waiting time, and turnaround time. Likewise, system-related criteria evaluate the algorithm from the system perspective and include metrics like VM utilization, profit, and throughput. The presented heuristics consider two different scheduling approaches: *online scheduling* and *batch scheduling*. Next we describe each scheduling approach along with each heuristic.

11.4.1 Online Scheduling Heuristics

The *online scheduling* approach consists in immediately assigning VM requests to VM instances upon each request arrival, considering the workload queue of each VM instance for load balancing. This approach is depicted in Fig. 11.3. The online approach is agile in the sense that VM requests are assigned to a VM instance without delay. However, this does not mean the VM requests are executed right away. It is most likely they will be queued at their assigned VM instances waiting for their time to start executing.

The online heuristics we designed for this chapter are:

- *Best fit resource* (BFR). This heuristic assigns each VM request to the VM which best fits the request of the customer, disregarding the deadline values. If there is no reserved VM instance which best fits and satisfies the deadline of the request, then an on-demand best fit VM instance is rented. The best fit is defined as a VM instance with the same number of cores as requested and the closest amount of

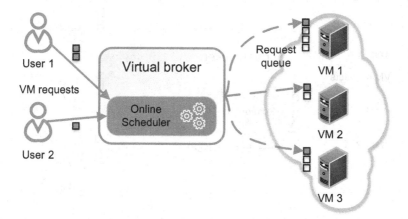

Fig. 11.3 Schema of the online scheduling model

memory to the requested value. The approach used in this heuristic intends to take advantage of assigning the requests to those VM instances that fit the most, making room for most restrictive requests to be executed in larger reserved VM instances.

- *Cheapest instance* (CI). This heuristic selects the cheapest VM instance that allows the execution of each request. This heuristic is intended to reduce the average waiting time of VM requests on the cloud system. An on-demand VM instance is rented only if there is absolutely no reserved VM instance which can satisfy the deadline of the VM request.

11.4.2 Offline Scheduling Heuristics

The *batch scheduling* approach arranges the arriving VM requests in batches. To achieve it, this approach makes use of an auxiliary batch queue where arriving requests are queued. Every T seconds, all VM requests in the batch queue are removed from it and scheduled to the VM instances considering not just the request queue of each VM instance but also all the VM requests in the request batch. Since VM requests in the same batch are scheduled together, the batch scheduling algorithm has a larger amount of information to schedule and accommodate requests than the online scheduling algorithm. This usually means the batch approach is able to compute more accurate schedules than the online approach. However, it is also less agile than the online approach because a request must wait in the batch queue until the batch is complete before it is scheduled to a VM instance. This approach is depicted in Fig. 11.4.

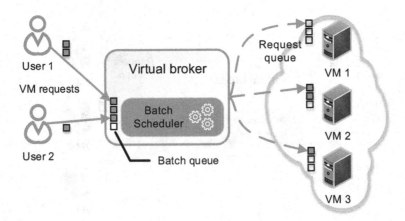

Fig. 11.4 Schema of the batch scheduling model

Next, we present a set of batch scheduling algorithms for the virtual machine planning problem.

- *Shortest request to cheapest instance* (SRCI). This heuristic sorts by duration the VM requests in the batch queue and selects the cheapest instance that allows the execution of each request. Just as CI, an on-demand VM instance is rented only if there is absolutely no reserved VM instance which can satisfy the deadline of the VM request. SRCI is similar to the well-known Shortest Job to the Fastest Resource (SJFR) heuristic for makespan optimization. As SJFR, the SRCI heuristic is intended to maximize the broker profit, as well as to minimize the response time perceived by the user of the cloud infrastructure: since shortest requests are assigned to execute first, they will finish earlier, and users with short computing time demands will find that their requests are completed very fast.
- Earliest Deadline First (EDF). This heuristic gives priority to those VM requests with the earliest deadlines (without taking into account their arrival time), and assigns each request to the suitable VM instance with the earliest availability. An on-demand VM instance is rented if the earliest available reserved VM instance cannot satisfy the deadline of the VM request. The main idea behind this heuristic is execute the more restrictive requests first, in order to avoid the penalization of buying on-demand instances due to deadline violations.
- Earliest Finishing Task (EFT). This heuristic gives priority to those VM requests that can be finished the soonest. The availability of each suitable VM instance for the request is considered to compute the finish time. The main idea behind this heuristic is to take advantage of executing the requests that can be finished the soonest to increase the availability of VM instances. As before, an on-demand VM instance is rented if no reserved VM instance can satisfy the deadline of the VM request.
- Shortest Task First (STF). It gives priority to VM requests with shorter execution times, following the idea of the STF method for makespan minimization. The heuristic searches for the shortest unattended VM request, and it assigns it to the lowest-cost VM instance that satisfies its hardware requests. Similarly, an on-demand VM instance is rented if no reserved VM instance can satisfy the deadline of the VM request.

11.5 Experimental Evaluation

In this section we present the results of the experimental analysis of the online and offline scheduling algorithms. First, we present the problem instances and the computing infrastructure for the experiments. Next, we present and discuss the results of our experimental analysis.

11.5.1 Problem Instances

We create a set of real-world problem instances based on data gathered from public reports and webpages from cloud providers [2, 15]. On top of that, we model the workload of customer's requests using real data from our high-performance computing facility [7] and from the parallel workload archive [9].

Each problem instance is defined by a workload file and a scenario file. The workload file contains the workload of customer's requests, while the scenario file describes the VM hardware characteristics, their renting prices, and the number of reserved VM instances. We consider scenarios with 10, 20, 30, and 50 reserved instances combining VMs from Amazon and Azure providers. We consider workloads of 50, 100, 200, and 400 requests, arriving according to a Poisson process, with length between 10 and 200 time units and deadlines defined according to real data from cloud logs. The combination of these scenarios and workloads samples a wide range of heterogeneous problem instances. On the one hand, the problem instance considering 50 customer's requests and 50 reserved instances models a very lightly loaded instance where reserved VMs are mostly idle. On the other hand, the problem instance considering 400 customer's requests and only 10 reserved VMs models the most heavily loaded instance.

Furthermore, for the location-aware problem, we consider five geographical zones: South America, North America, Europe, Asia, and Oceania. We define two data traffic scenarios, one for requests with low networking usage and another for high networking usage. The low data traffic scenario considers a total data traffic for all requests between 10 and 20 GB, while the high data traffic scenario considers traffic between 50 and 250 GB. Finally, we consider the application type of customer's requests to be 70% computation tasks (CT) and 30% web services (WS).

Our pricing policy considers a 20% price reduction compared to the on-demand pricing offered by cloud providers. That is, $p(b_j) = 0.8 \times COD(b_j)$. This is a very attractive pricing reduction for cloud customers.

In total, we consider 400 instances for the location-agnostic problem and 800 instances for the location-aware problem.

11.5.2 Computing Infrastructure

The proposed heuristics are implemented in C using GNU gcc. The experimental analysis is performed on a 24-Core AMD Opteron Magny-Cours Processor 6172 at 2.1 GHz, with 24 GB RAM and CentOS Linux, hosted at the Cluster FING HPC facility from Universidad de la República, Uruguay [7].

11.5.3 Experimental Results for the Location-Agnostic Problem

In this section we present and discuss the results computed by the schedulers for the location-agnostic problem. Figure 11.5 presents the profit computed by each scheduling algorithm grouped by the size of the request workload. Each workload size aggregates 100 different instances which consider different stress scenarios for the infrastructure of reserved VMs.

Figure 11.5 shows a wide range of extreme values which represent the most lightly loaded and most heavily loaded scenarios for each workload size. On the one hand, for the most lightly loaded scenarios, profit is high since reserved instances are plenty and nearly no on-demand instances are needed. On the other hand, profit

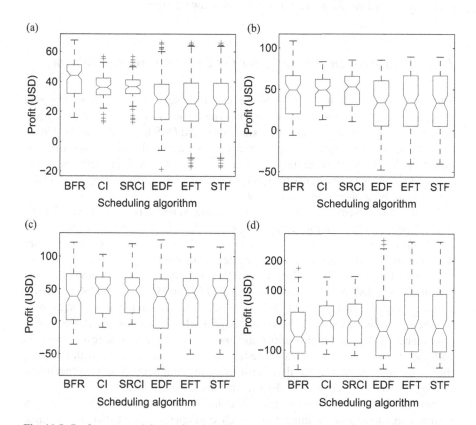

Fig. 11.5 Profit computed by each scheduling algorithm for the location-agnostic problem formulation aggregated by workload size. (**a**) Workload with 50 customer's requests. (**b**) Workload with 100 customer's requests. (**c**) Workload with 200 customer's requests. (**d**) Workload with 400 customer's requests

is very low (sometimes there is even a budget deficit) for the most heavily loaded scenarios, since reserved instances are not enough to cope with the demand and the virtual broker is forced to lease on-demand instances too frequently.

Figure 11.5a, b shows BFR, CI, and SRCI are the best performing algorithms for lightly and moderately loaded scenarios. CI and SRCI are more reliable, but BFR is able to compute the best schedules. Figure 11.5d shows no scheduler is able to reliably compute profitable schedules for the most heavily loaded scenarios. Nevertheless, CI and SRCI are the best alternatives in these scenarios, since all the others compute negative profits in median.

All considered, for the most simple location-agnostic formulation, the best performing schedulers are the online scheduler (CI) and the offline scheduler (SRCI). The offline schedulers do not seem to take any advantage of the additional scheduling insight provided by the batch queue. Next, we present and discuss the results computed for the more realistic location-aware problem.

11.5.4   Experimental Results for the Location-Aware Problem

This section presents the results of the experimental analysis of the proposed schedulers for the location-aware problem. The location-aware problem addresses two different objectives: the profit maximization and QoS maximization. Hence, in this section we start by discussing the results related to the profit maximization objective. We analyze separately the low network and the high network traffic scenario. After that, we discuss the QoS maximization in a similar way. And finally we compare both objectives simultaneously.

Figure 11.6 presents the results of the proposed schedulers when addressing the low network traffic scenario aggregated by workload size. Results show CI and SRCI are clearly the most accurate heuristics. Both are able to compute better schedules in median than any other scheduler in any scenario.

On the other hand, Fig. 11.7 shows results for the high network traffic scenarios are more contested. Along with CI and SRCI, BFR and EDF are also able to compute competitive schedules for the lightly loaded and moderately loaded scenarios. Nevertheless, for the most loaded scenario, again SRCI is the most profitable choice, with higher median and higher upper and lower whiskers. All these results position SRCI as the most reliable overall scheduler for profit optimization, with CI being the second most reliable scheduler. Considering the simplicity of online scheduling, CI may be even preferable over SRCI if we consider profit alone.

Let us compare the results of the schedulers when considering QoS. The QoS metric is related to the waiting time of all customer's request, that is, the time the customer has to wait before its request starts its execution (i.e., $WT(v_i) = ST(v_i) - AR(v_i)$). For simplicity we discuss the results computed by each scheduler by comparing the waiting time metric.

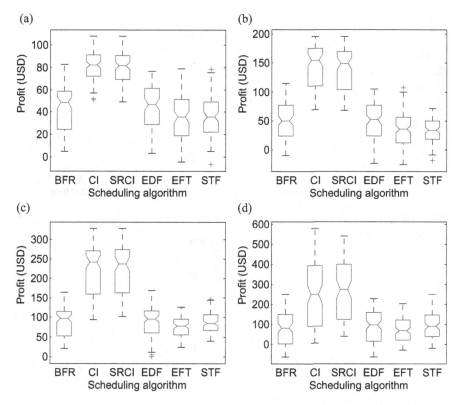

Fig. 11.6 Profit computed by each scheduling algorithm for the location-aware problem formulation for a low networking scenario aggregated by workload size. (**a**) Workload with 50 customer's requests. (**b**) Workload with 100 customer's requests. (**c**) Workload with 200 customer's requests. (**d**) Workload with 400 customer's requests

Figure 11.8 presents the waiting time computed by each scheduler aggregated by workload size. Results show SRCI computes the schedules with the lowest median waiting time and the lowest worst waiting time. SRCI reliably provides the best QoS for nearly every scenario considered, with the only exception of a few outlier schedules.

Overall, experimental analysis shows SRCI to be the best scheduling algorithm for our problem. Both SRCI and CI compute the most profitable schedules, outperforming all other schedulers especially for the low networking scenarios. However, CI is not able to keep up with SRCI when considering the QoS provided by their schedules. SRCI clearly computes the schedules with the best QoS in every scenario.

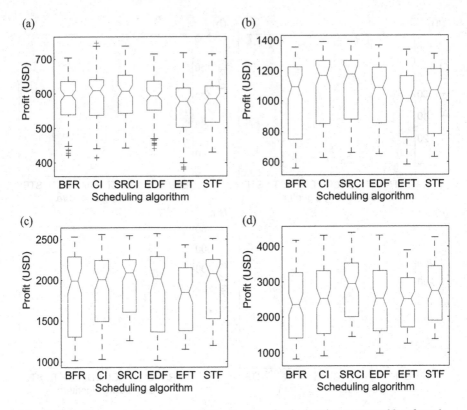

Fig. 11.7 Profit computed by each scheduling algorithm for the location-aware problem formulation for a high networking scenario aggregated by workload size. (**a**) Workload with 50 customer's requests. (**b**) Workload with 100 customer's requests. (**c**) Workload with 200 customer's requests. (**d**) Workload with 400 customer's requests

Figure 11.9 presents the average relative profit and waiting time computed by each scheduler aggregated by workload size. Results presented in Fig. 11.9 confirm previously presented results. SRCI computes the most profitable schedules while also providing the best QoS. CI computes competitive results in terms of profit, but SRCI is able to clearly outperform CI in terms of QoS by taking advantage of the batch queue.

11.6 Conclusions and Future Work

In this work we present the virtual broker model for cloud infrastructures. This brokering model extends previous models by proposing the broker to lease a set of virtual resources. By taking advantage of bulk discounts, the virtual broker is able to sublease these resources to its customers at cheaper prices than the cloud providers.

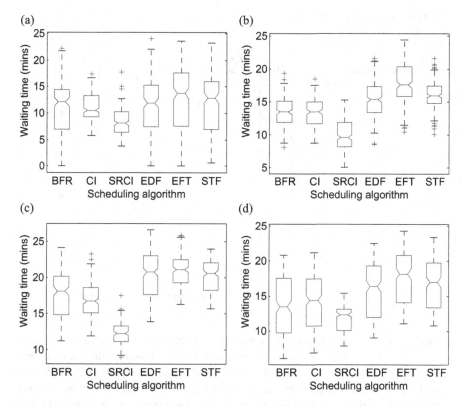

Fig. 11.8 Waiting time computed by each scheduling algorithm for the location-aware problem formulation aggregated by workload size. (**a**) Workload with 50 customer's requests. (**b**) Workload with 100 customer's requests. (**c**) Workload with 200 customer's requests. (**d**) Workload with 400 customer's requests

However, for this model to be effective, the virtual broker must schedule its leased resources effectively in order to maximize its profit. Hence, we introduce a mathematical formulation for the problem of optimizing the profit of the virtual broker, and we design six simple heuristics for solving the optimization problem. Experimental evaluation shows the virtual brokering model is profitable in most situations even when considering a simple scheduling approach.

We further study the virtual brokering model by proposing a more realistic problem formulation. We extend the previous problem formulation by considering geographical location of customers, requests of different application types, network data transmission, and QoS provided to customers. Experimental evaluation shows again the virtual broker is able to make profit in most scenarios while delivering an adequate QoS to its customers. The SRCI scheduling is the most accurate scheduler for addressing this extended problem formulation, computing schedules with high profit for the virtual broker and low waiting time for the customers.

Fig. 11.9 Average relative profit and relative waiting time computed by each scheduler for the location-aware problem aggregated by workload size

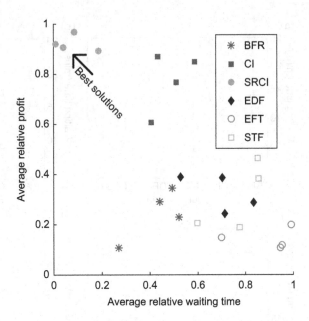

In case that the pricing model for renting VMs in the cloud changes drastically, our model and methods would still have a window of opportunity, taking into account the main differences between our model and the one proposed by Rogers and Cliff [19] and later analyzed by Cartlidge and Clamp [5]. Some minor adjustments might be needed in the price offered to users, and the overall broker profit might reduce, but the business model will still be valid.

The main lines of future work include further studying the proposed methods in overloaded situations to test the scalability of our methods. Furthermore, we propose to study more accurate methods, such as algorithms based on computational intelligence, for addressing the proposed problem. Regarding this, we propose to adapt the evolutionary technique introduced by Nesmachnow et al. [17] to address the problem proposed in this work. This evolutionary technique is relevant to our problematic since Nesmachnow et al. showed it to be more accurate than a set of eight greedy heuristics when addressing a problem similar to the one proposed in this work without considering geolocalization.

Also, it is relevant to study the application of the proposed model to other realistic applications (such as massive online gaming and audio and video streaming) and other cloud service models (such as platform as a service and function as a service). For this, our model must be further extended to incorporate a larger set of characteristics (such as the network scheme), and it must be able to describe a wider scope of applications (such as applications that do not follow the deadline QoS model). Finally, the development of precise forecasting methods is key to accurately predict the volume of VM requests. This is a must for the virtual broker to efficiently manage its reserved resources.

Acknowledgements Bernabé Dorronsoro would like to acknowledge the Spanish MINECO for the support provided under contracts TIN2014-60844-R (the SAVANT project) and RYC-2013-13355. Santiago Iturriaga and Sergio Nesmachonow acknowledge ANII and PEDECIBA (Uruguay) for supporting this research.

References

1. Alsina J, Iturriaga S, Nesmachnow S, Tchernykh A, Dorronsoro B (2016) Virtual machine planning for cloud brokering considering geolocation and data transfer. In: IEEE international conference on cloud computing technology and science, pp 352–359
2. Amazon (2016) Amazon Web Services. Online, http://aws.amazon.com/. Accessed on Nov 2016
3. Bohn RB, Messina J, Liu F, Tong J, Mao J (2011) NIST cloud computing reference architecture. In: IEEE world congress on services, Washington, DC, pp 594–596
4. Buyya R, Broberg J, Goscinski AM (2011) Cloud computing principles and paradigms. Wiley Publishing, Hoboken
5. Cartlidge J, Clamp P (2014) Correcting a financial brokerage model for cloud computing: closing the window of opportunity for commercialisation. J Cloud Comput Adv Syst Appl 3(2):1–20
6. Chhetri MB, Chichin S, Vo QB, Kowalczyk R (2013) Smart cloud broker: finding your home in the clouds. In: 28th international conference on automated software engineering, Silicon Valley, pp 698–701
7. Cluster FING (2015) High Performance Computing at Universidad de la República. Available online at http://www.fing.edu.uy/cluster. Accessed Aug 2016
8. De Felice M, Yao X (2011) Short-term load forecasting with neural network ensembles: a comparative study. IEEE Comput Intell Mag 6(3):47–56
9. Feitelson D (2016) Parallel workload archive. Available online at http://www.cs.huji.ac.il/labs/parallel/workload. Accessed Aug 2016
10. Foster I, Zhao Y, Raicu I, Lu S (2008) Cloud computing and grid computing 360-degree compared. In: Grid computing environments workshop, Austin, pp 1–10
11. Grozev N, Buyya R (2014) Inter-cloud architectures and application brokering: taxonomy and survey. Softw Pract Exp 44(3):369–390
12. Guzek M, Gniewek A, Bouvry P, Musial J, Blazewicz J (2015) Cloud brokering: current practices and upcoming challenges. IEEE Cloud Comput 2(2):40–47
13. International Standards Organization/International Electrotechnical Commission (2014) Information technology–cloud computing–overview and vocabulary. International Standard 17788:2014
14. Mattess M, Vecchiola C, Garg S, Buyya R (2011) Cloud bursting: managing peak loads by leasing public cloud services. CRC Press, Boca Raton
15. Microsoft (2016) Microsoft Azure. Online, https://azure.microsoft.com/. Accessed on Nov 2016
16. Nesmachnow S, Iturriaga S, Dorronsoro B, Talbi EG, Bouvry P (2013) List scheduling heuristics for virtual machine mapping in cloud systems. In: VI high performance computing Latin America symposium, Mendoza, pp 37–48
17. Nesmachnow S, Iturriaga S, Dorronsoro B (2015) Efficient heuristics for profit optimization of virtual cloud brokers. IEEE Comput Intell Mag 10(1):33–43
18. Rimal BP, Choi E, Lumb I (2009) A taxonomy and survey of cloud computing systems. In: Fifth international joint conference on networked computing, advanced information management and service, and digital content, multimedia technology and its applications, Seoul, pp 44–51

19. Rogers O, Cliff D (2012) A financial brokerage model for cloud computing. J Cloud Comput Adv Syst Appl 1(2):1–12
20. Schwiegelshohn U, Tchernykh A (2012) Online scheduling for cloud computing and different service levels. In: IEEE international parallel and distributed processing symposium, Anchorage, pp 1061–1068
21. Tang C, Steinder M, Spreitzer M, Pacifici G (2007) A scalable application placement controller for enterprise data centers. In: International conference on World Wide Web, Banff, pp 331–340
22. Tchernykh A, Lozano L, Schwiegelshohn U, Bouvry P, Pecero JE, Nesmachnow S (2014) Bi-objective online scheduling with quality of service for IaaS clouds. In: IEEE international conference on cloud networking, pp 307–312
23. Tchernykh A, Lozano L, Schwiegelshohn U, Bouvry P, Pecero JE, Nesmachnow S (2014) Energy-aware online scheduling: ensuring quality of service for IaaS clouds. In: Proceedings of the international conference on high performance computing & simulation, New Orleansm, pp 911–918

Chapter 12
Adaptive Resource Allocation for Load Balancing in Cloud

Somnath Mazumdar, Alberto Scionti, and Anoop S. Kumar

12.1 Introduction

Cloud computing, or simply Cloud, is a computational as well as an infrastructural model, which aims at providing enormous computational power as a utility service by federating physical resources and associated services. Since its initial adoption, several research works have been done to make Cloud a robust computing model. Its attractiveness derives from its capability of scaling and offering a reliable service through a standard web access. A growing number of users who work on large data sets (or so-called Big Data) mostly running lengthy jobs found Cloud very efficient, regarding cost and ease of manageability.

Cloud is a successful example of a heterogeneous computing platform. Heterogeneity in data centres (DCs) is present in many forms: from different implementations of the same instruction set architecture (ISA) to reconfigurable and custom devices (e.g., FPGAs). This vast architectural diversity of hardware in DCs may benefit many applications: for instance, recently FPGA-based acceleration approach has been successfully applied to speed up the search engine service *Bing Search* [56]. However, some of the challenges faced by DCs are (*i*) the appropriate dimensioning of the set of resources used to cover incoming application requests and (*ii*) the efficient distribution of the workload among the nodes of the infrastructure.

S. Mazumdar (✉)
Università di Siena, Via Roma 56, Siena, Italy
e-mail: mazumdar@dii.unisi.it

A. Scionti
Istituto Superiore Mario Boella, Via P. C. Boggio 61, Torino, Italy
e-mail: scionti@ismb.it

A.S. Kumar
BITS Pilani – K.K. Birla Goa Campus, 403726, Goa, India
e-mail: anoopk@goa.bits-pilani.ac.in

© Springer International Publishing AG 2017
N. Antonopoulos, L. Gillam (eds.), *Cloud Computing*, Computer Communications and Networks, DOI 10.1007/978-3-319-54645-2_12

Thus, an efficient allocation of the physical resources becomes a key feature to maintain a robust execution environment. Furthermore, it also helps service providers to offer a high level of quality of service (QoS) also during unexpected events or failures.

Cloud's success is due to the elasticity or dynamic scalability, which requires physical servers to be provisioned (i.e., scale up and down) as quickly as possible. The capacity of a typical DC is huge, but not "infinite". A DC has thousands of running servers arranged in multiple racks, paying 40%–50% of its total expenses as power bills [28, 37]. However, the average server utilisation remains between 10% and 50% in most of the DCs [4, 5], and, further, idle servers can consume up to 60% of their peak power [5, 26, 30]. In general, the power efficiency of servers can be increased by reducing the number of idle servers and maximising their usage. To that end, multiple services can be packed on the same physical machine efficiently. Server consolidation, which addresses this problem, is a combinatorial optimisation problem and can be reduced to a bin-packing problem [17].

Virtual machines (VMs) are the basic resource block for running jobs, and packing VMs inside a physical server represents an example of an online bin-packing problem [18]. When the number of VM types is few, then packing them inside the available servers is a "bit simpler" (e.g., some Cloud providers use a pool of single sized VMs, which makes their allocation on the physical machines trivial). However, in public DCs, for different user requirements, there exist various VM types (i.e., VMs with various configurations regarding CPU, memory, network, and storage capabilities), so in this case, efficiently packing the VMs inside the servers is complex. Virtualisation [53] is a widely used technique to increase server utilisation, and due to virtualisation, servers with different resource capacities can dynamically host different types of VMs. Hypervisors are responsible for VM management and play a fundamental role in scheduling their allocation to the physical servers, but hypervisors also consume computing resources for maintaining VMs. The arrival of user requests for acquiring resources (VMs) in a DC can be effectively modelled as a stochastic process. The dynamism in the resource allocation is because the Cloud allows acquiring and releasing resources in real-time. The stochastic nature of Cloud workload and worst-case resource usage policy (i.e., resources are usually provisioned to their peak usage) employed by most DCs lead to poor resource utilisation [64, 71]. Thus, there is a need for an efficient proactive resource allocation strategy (PRAS) which can be useful in reducing the workload imbalance and also optimising resource utilisation by predicting the future workload. In general, the resource acquisition patterns present two components: one is a stable part and burstiness characterises the other. Fortunately, the stable pattern occurs more often than burstiness, meaning that real-world traces show that application access patterns are more correlated than random patterns [61, 66]. Time series analysis can find repeating patterns in the workload traces and also can forecast future VM requests.

In this chapter, we discuss a framework for PRAS developed for the Infrastructure-as-a-Service (IaaS) service model, which not only efficiently predicts the incoming VM requests but also maps VMs onto the servers. PRAS works in two steps: (*i*) it predicts the future workload (incoming VM counts) and, (*ii*) next, it employs a resource allocation strategy based on a heuristic using the predicted value. For the first step, we picked the best predictor from the three well-known variants of the autoregressive moving-average (ARMA) model (i.e., autoregressive integrated moving-average, ARIMA; seasonal autoregressive integrated moving-average, SARIMA; and autoregressive fractionally integrated moving-average, ARFIMA) [11] and compared their forecasting accuracy. Next, we have employed particle swarm optimization (PSO) [24], to schedule the resource assignment. PSO is inspired by the interaction between swarm members, requiring no supervision or a priori knowledge. This approach can better adapt itself to changes by exploiting inherited "memory" of both the predictive model and the optimisation heuristic, which can further lead to better energy savings and improved reliability. We also present experimental results to demonstrate the feasibility of the proposed system.

The rest of the chapter is organised as follows. Section 12.2 introduces state-of-the-art related works; Sect. 12.3 gives an overview of the current evolution of the Cloud paradigm. In Sect. 12.4, we detail the Cloud hardware resources, while Sect. 12.5 elaborates the workload management challenges in Cloud. Next, in Sect. 12.6, we explain our PRAS-based framework and its results in Sect. 12.7. Finally, we conclude the presented chapter in Sect. 12.8.

12.2   Related Work

Energy efficiency in Cloud computing domain is a well-researched area, and in past years, various approaches have been proposed [41]. Most of these approaches improve the resource allocation aiming at more efficiently using computational capabilities and further reducing energy cost. Among them, the popular method-ologies are Best Fit [6], First Fit [9, 50, 70], constraint satisfaction problem (CSP) [34, 68], control theory [80], game theory [3, 73], genetic algorithms (GA) and their variants [57, 76], queuing model [44, 67], and also various forms of heuristics [15, 29, 43, 55]. It is interesting to note that greedy algorithms are also used in commercial products (e.g., the distributed resource scheduler (DRS) tool from VMware [36]).

Time series-based prediction is well known, and it also has a comprehensive set of literature. Autoregressive (AR) model is a simplified approach for modelling univariate time series. AR can be combined with the moving-average (MA), leading to the well-known ARMA model. ARMA has been already used to forecast Cloud-based services [32, 59, 65]. In [32], authors proposed a framework for characterising and forecasting the access patterns of YouTube videos. In this work, ARMA model was employed on the principal components of the data instead of the individual time series. In this work, daily video access demand was predicted using 1-week datasets. Tirado et al. [65] present a load forecasting model based on an ARMA model to improve the server utilisation and load imbalance by replicating and consolidat-ing resources based on a configurable utilisation threshold. The workload (trace collected from an online music service) is predicted by an AR model capturing trends and seasonal patterns by employing multiplicative seasonal autoregressive moving-average model. Authors in [59] develop a look-ahead resource allocation algorithm based on model predictive control. The proposed model predicts the future workload based on a limited horizon. Here, a second-order ARMA has been used for estimating the incoming workload of the system for future time periods, and resource allocation is adjusted ahead of time. Chandra et al. [13] proposed a system architecture that combines online measurements (e.g., the workload characteristics and the current state of the system) with prediction and resource allocation techniques. This framework uses the AR model to predict workload and then employ a constrained non-linear optimisation method (i.e., queuing theory) to allocate the server resources (CPU, network, and disk space) dynamically. Similarly, Chen et al. [15] propose an energy-efficient server provisioning and load dispatching method in a single framework, using an AR model and a heuristic for distributing the load among the servers.

Differently, from these works, we are focused on the variants of ARMA models and the measurement of their efficiency in forecasting future workload of the DC. Recently, Kumar et al. [42] showed that ARIMA could forecast CPU, RAM, and also network patterns with a very low forecasting error rate while outperforming SARIMA and ARFIMA model regarding forecast accuracy. In this work, the Wikipedia grid traces are used in the experiment. Earlier, Dinda et al. [20] predicted the task's running time by exploiting multiple (AR, MA, ARMA, ARIMA, and ARFIMA) linear time series models, and authors claimed that ARIMA model performs well in capturing the nonstationary behaviour (i.e., it performs better in describing mean, variance, autocorrelation of time series, which in turn change over time) of time series, while ARFIMA is more appropriate for extracting statistical self-similar or long memory patterns embedded in the data.

ARIMA has been employed for load prediction based on both CPU utilisation only [27, 48] and a combination of CPU and memory [79] for improving the dynamic capacity provisioning. Authors in [48] present a control theory-based performance management approach to execute scientific applications in a distributed environment such as that offered by a DC and that uses loop scheduling technique. Here, the ARIMA model is used for estimating the percentage of CPU capacity that is available for the execution process loop. In [27], authors proposed a proactive framework, where the ARIMA model has been used to predict the future workload regarding CPU load, while VM migration has been used extensively to optimise the overall resource allocation. In [79], the authors proposed a solution based on a model predictive control (MPC) policy for the dynamic server provisioning problem, to minimise the total energy cost and also to satisfy the task scheduling delay. In particular, authors used the ARIMA model to forecast the future usage of CPU and RAM. In a recent work [12], ARIMA has been used for forecasting the future application workload behaviour in Cloud. In this work, the forecasted value is fed into the queueing model for calculating the number of required VMs. Seasonal ARIMA (SARIMA) was mostly used in analysing and predicting the network traffic [14, 63]. However, recently, the SARIMA model has also been used for forecasting server workloads too [19]. Adzigogov et al. [2] proposed a Grid meta-scheduler which predicts CPU and memory usage by implementing different variants of the AR model (i.e., specifically AR, ARIMA, ARFIMA). In the experiments, authors claim that AR and ARFIMA performed well for forecasting the resource usage.

In DCs, automated provisioning of VMs is also proposed via dynamic scaling algorithm without using any predictive method. In [38], the authors propose a hybrid scaling technique that employs reactive rules to scale up (mainly based on CPU utilisation) and a regression-based approach for scaling down when needed. The proposed technique actively monitors the response times for requests to a multi-tier web application to collect CPU utilisation-related data and employs heuristics to identify the bottlenecks in the system. In [7], authors propose an energy-efficient threshold-based dynamic consolidation approach of VMs, with dynamic adjustment of the threshold values. It employs dynamic thresholds, which are calculated considering the running application conditions. In this work, the adaptive utilisation threshold is based on a statistical analysis of the historical data of the VMs. Chieu et al. [16] proposed dynamic scaling of Cloud web applications based on thresholds. The proposed dynamic scaling algorithm relies on the number of active sessions, and the scaling algorithm fits in the front-end load balancer. However, the selection of the threshold value remains an open issue, and improper selection of values may lead to a degradation of the algorithm performance. Lim et al. [45] designed a proportional threshold technique based on an integral controller, which can adjust the number of VMs based on the average CPU usage. Authors have applied a simple MA method to remove the noise from the time series data.

Particle swarm optimization (PSO) has been widely used in resource allocation problems [46, 75, 77, 78]. Zhan et al. [77] proposed a hybrid PSO algorithm by combining the standard PSO algorithm with the simulated annealing (SA) algorithm called as particle swarm-simulated annealing. It primarily aims at improving convergence rate and also the solution quality by adding SA into every iteration of PSO. This approach improves the average task execution time and also the resource utilisation. In [46], an improved version of PSO-based task scheduling model has been proposed, to solve the load balancing problem of VMs in Cloud. To this end, the proposed solution optimises the task execution time and the resource utilisation. In this paper, authors introduced a mutation mechanism and a self-adapting inertia weight method to the standard PSO to improve convergence speed and efficiency. Zhang et al. [78] describe a hierarchical PSO-based application scheduling algorithm for Cloud, where the primary goal is to minimise both the load imbalance and also the internetwork communication cost. Similar to the previous work, to avoid plunging into the local optimum and also to provide effective local and global search, an inertia weight has been introduced into the model. In [51], a PSO-based method to minimise both communication and execution costs of applications has been proposed. Here, authors claim that PSO outperforms the best resource selection (BRS) algorithm. Revised discrete PSO (RDPSO) [75] is proposed to schedule a set of workflow applications in Cloud. The solution of RDPSO is represented by the set of pair task service and considers both data transmission and computational costs. In this model, each particle learns from both different exemplars and also from other feasible pairs of different dimensions. Similar to [51], authors also claim that RDPSO can achieve better performance on makespan and cost optimisation compared to the standard PSO and BRS. In [82], an integer programming model is used for solving the resource allocation problem, and a self-adaptive learning PSO (SL-PSO)-based scheduling approach is also proposed. The algorithm aimed at optimising the user-level QoS, as well as the economic profit. Likewise, self-adaptive PSO (SA-PSO) has been used to implement meta-schedulers for mapping VMs onto a set of servers, by fulfilling resource requirements of a maximum number of workloads [40]. In the proposed solution, to improve the quality of the solutions, the PSO algorithm also incorporates the processor transitions to various sleep states and their corresponding wake-up latencies.

12.3   Cloud Computing Continuum

Cloud provides a way to access computing resources without hosting them on premise. The three standard service models of Cloud (Software-as-a-Service, SaaS; Platform-as-a-Service, PaaS; and Infrastructure-as-a-Service, IaaS) differ from each other for the level of abstraction and the way the user accesses computing resources. In this chapter, we focus on the IaaS service model. At IaaS level, resource allocation problem emerges as one of the main challenges to address. In recent years, there has been an evolution of the Cloud spectrum. With the fast growth of the number of small embedded devices connected to the Internet [25], Cloud providers need to support them anywhere at any time, through the extension of the Cloud paradigm. The extensive computational infrastructure support of Cloud helps to integrate Cloudlets, Fog computing, and the "Cloudification" of the Internet of things (IoT) within traditional infrastructures (see Fig. 12.1).

12.3.1   Cloudlets

In recent years, mobile computing gained a momentum due to the enormous progress in low-power embedded hardware platforms. However, limitation in the processing and storage capacity of such systems requires off-loading high computational demanding tasks to more reliable infrastructures. In this case, Cloud becomes an optimal choice. Cloud infrastructures began to reduce the latency for processing jobs and to support almost real-time services aiming at supporting mobile computing applications. The proposed solutions are termed as Cloudlets [60], often known as "Datacenter-in-a-Box": trusted, capable systems co-located with the point of presence (e.g., a wireless access point), equipped with a fixed number of servers. This approach is quite similar to the in-network services

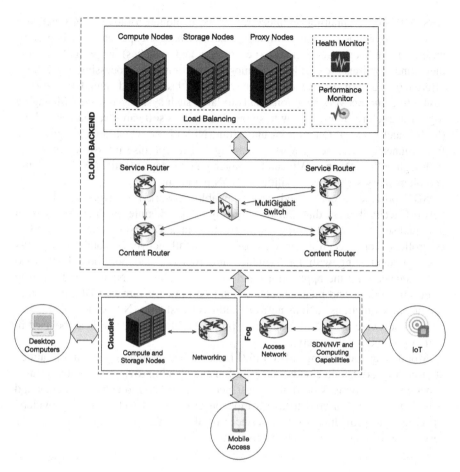

Fig. 12.1 The Cloud computing continuum: an overview of Cloud computing, Cloudlets, Fog computing, and IoT services. In *bottom*, Fog- or Cloudlet-based execution paradigm directly communicates with user via mobile devices and thus providing the better latency-based solution. While at the *top*, the traditional Cloud DCs are connected (via the complex network hardware) to the Fog and Cloudlets. Cloud DCs are still acting as a backbone to the Fog or to the Cloudlet

or middleboxes (e.g., content caches, load balancers). Using Cloudlets, mobile users can easily and quickly instantiate custom VMs on the cluster of commodity machines, without the need for accessing traditional Cloud services.

12.3.2 Fog Computing

Fog computing [10, 69] extends Cloud computing by transferring and processing jobs at the edge of the network to reduce the access latency and to improve

QoS [69]. Fog computing architecture can be exploited to adapt user's network conditions dynamically, thus optimising the user access experience. In Fog computing, the network access points (i.e., routers and switches) are virtualised, and their functionalities are melded with more general purpose processing capabilities offered in the form of specific services [74]. A less defined boundary between computing and network functions leads to label such systems as "fog". Managing fog infrastructures requires new technologies, such as software-defined networking (SDN)[1] and network function virtualization (NFV) [47], which are emerging as a front runner to increase network scalability and to optimise infrastructural costs. Although both SDN and NVF can be implemented independently, NVF is a highly complementary set of functionalities to SDN paradigm.

SDN provides a centralised, programmable network framework (of different network technologies) that can dynamically (more flexible and agile) provision a virtualised server and storage infrastructure in a DC. SDN consists of SDN controllers (for a centralised view of the overall network), southbound APIs (for communicating with the switches and routers), and northbound APIs (to communicate with the applications and the business logic). NFV provides a way to design, deploy, and manage fully virtualised infrastructure in a DC. It helps to run network functions such as network address translation (NAT) and firewall as a piece of software instead of running on proprietary hardware. NVF can be used in both wired and wireless networks.

Mobile edge computing (MEC) [52] is also a new computing paradigm, aimed at providing a dynamic content optimisation and also improving the quality of user experience. It leverages on radio access networks (RANs) to enhance latency and bandwidth mainly offered to application developers and web content providers. MEC aims at providing a set of services by the amalgamation of Cloud and IT services at the edge of the mobile network.

12.3.3 Cloud-IoT

Looking at the Internet of things (IoT) landscape [31, 35], Cloud provides a virtualised infrastructure, as well as SDN support for collecting, aggregating, and analysing data streams generated by smart sensors. Cloud-IoT applications are quite different compared to the traditional Cloud applications and services (due to a diverse set of network protocols and the integration of specialised hardware and software solutions). From this standpoint, Cloud-based IoT platforms are a conglomeration of APIs and machine-to-machine communication protocols, such as REST, WebSockets, and IoT-specific ones (e.g., message queuing telemetry

---

[1]https://www.opennetworking.org/sdn-resources/sdn-definition

transport – MQTT[2] and constrained application protocol, CoAP).[3] MQTT is the protocol built for machine-to-machine communication and IoT, while CoAP has been developed to allow low-power devices to communicate with Cloud infrastructures. The management APIs offer provisioning, managing, and troubleshooting features for the devices/machines, while the integration mediates access to traditional services through traditional Cloud infrastructures (e.g., some IoT applications are designed to interface with popular social networks).

12.4 Cloud Hardware Resources

Broadly speaking, DCs can be classified depending on the number of servers available in the DC infrastructure, which can range from few hundreds to hundreds of thousands of rack servers, but, in all cases, DCs are equipped with a large number of active servers. DCs maintain a pool of physical machines which are heterogeneous regarding core count and ISA. In recent years, heterogeneity expanded in such a way that it now comprises also low-power processors previously employed only in mobile devices, although traditional server processors still represent the majority [58]. Another source for improving efficiency and gaining performance comes from the adoption of high-density server systems, which are designed to aggregate a large set of server nodes within a standard chassis (e.g., HPE Moonshot system). With a strong preponderance of the X86 architecture, other systems based on powerful manycores are gaining interest (e.g., Kalray's MPPA-256 Processor [21] and Adapteva's Epiphany multicore [1]). Since more and more applications can benefit from execution on specialised parallel processors, heterogeneous hardware acceleration platforms (e.g., GPU and the Intel Xeon Phi) [49] also entered into the Cloud computing market. Another example of such diversity is represented by the growing adoption of field-programmable gate array (FPGA) accelerators. Several applications have been demonstrated to greatly benefit from the acceleration on specific circuits and significant parallelism offered by FPGAs [54, 56].

Two main factors that contribute to the limit of scalability in a DC are the power consumption and the components' reliability. Figure 12.2 shows the internal architecture of a processor, highlighting the numerous components that contribute to power inefficiency and reliability issues. There is also a big issue in moving the generated heat away from the processing elements. Similarly, the capability of integrating more components and functionalities inside the cores exposes the reliability issues. The more components there are in the system (e.g., cores, memory modules, accelerators, network interfaces), the higher the likelihood of failures. The adoption

---

[2]http://docs.oasis-open.org/mqtt/mqtt/v3.1.1/mqtt-v3.1.1.html
[3]http://coap.technology/

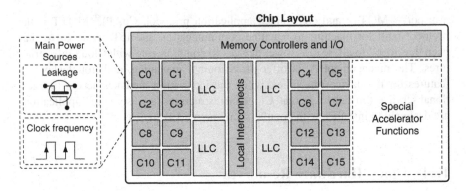

Fig. 12.2 An example of the internal organisation of a modern server processor with the main components consuming the largest part of the power budget. Sources of main energy consumption are highlighted too

of smaller transistor features makes electronic devices more sensitive to stress conditions (such as hotspots in the silicon chips, high-energy particles, ageing), and it leads to an increase of the statically dissipated power (i.e., leakage currents become dominant since transistors' isolation layers are less effective). A correct distribution of a server load represents a way to address reliability issues, using minimisation of the stress conditions acting on each server. However, sometimes hardware performance starts to degrade significantly and becomes *limping hardware or limpware* [22]. On the other hand, power consumption is dominated by the clock speeds, which in turns drives the performance of the processor. Higher clock speed allows executing a large number of instructions per unit of time, however, causing an increase in the dynamic power consumption. Dynamic voltage frequency scaling (DVFS) is a widely used technique for power reduction in servers [72, 81]. DVFS refers to the capability of the system to tune the supply of voltage and the clock frequency at the run time, depending on the workload conditions. Similarly, power-gating (PG) and clock-gating (CG) techniques aim at completely cutting off the power or the clock signal whenever the CPU is not used. Although DVFS, PG, and CG techniques provide considerable benefits regarding power saving, approaching the energy efficiency in a DC requires a more holistic strategy. Being able to schedule jobs on the processing elements correctly greatly helps to reduce the number of active servers with low load conditions.

12.5 Workload Management

Due to the dynamic nature of Cloud workloads, scheduling VMs on the fly on a given host machine is a complex task. Complexity is getting higher due to the failures of physical machines and unavailability when acquiring needed resources for allocation. Incoming requests (allocation of VMs) are stored in a queue waiting to be processed on a first-come-first-served (FCFS) basis. Workload diffusion can be used to distribute jobs among physical machines effectively. In Cloud, it can be achieved by successful VM completion and VM migration. Also, scheduling policy is getting complex when jobs have their priority or fairness which needs to be maintained. With the proper scheduling strategy, it is possible to optimise the utilisation of resources, improve the job throughput, and also reduce the total turnaround time of tasks. However, to counter the "slashdot effects", it would be desirable to put a proactive workload management framework that can adjust resource allocation based on the actual applications' needs.

12.5.1   Load Balancing Techniques

Load balancing refers to the set of techniques, both software and hardware, used to distribute the load in a system where multiple agents can serve input requests. Load balancing can be implemented at different levels of the Cloud, but IaaS layer provides more control for balancing the workload. At the infrastructure level, multiple services expose their functionalities through a virtual IP address which is mapped to a set of direct IP addresses associated with the working servers (by the load balancer agent). This assignment mechanism refers to the request for instantiating VMs on the available physical servers. Examples of well-known proprietary load balancers used by public Cloud providers are Elastic load balancer[4] and F5.[5]

Most of the hardware load balancers work directly at the network level, by routing incoming traffic to the appropriate servers based on a set of established rules (i.e., rules are used to implement filters acting on the IP addresses of the packets traversing the network). These hardware load balancers offer high performance and throughput. As the demand for Cloud services grows, software counterparts also become very much effective by supporting distributed and more flexible data plane running on commodity servers. Conversely, "pure" software load balancers suffer from low performance and sustained throughput, making them less attractive for latency-sensitive applications. Thus, most of the commercial solutions resort to a hybrid approach. The mechanism resembles the one used by modern microprocessors to manage virtual-to-physical memory address translation, and it can be easily implemented on modern network switches. Due to the dynamic nature of the Cloud workloads, load balancers must be dynamically able to migrate already assigned VMs on a different server to balance the load in the system (VM migration). To that end, fast scheduling mechanisms must be provided: heuristics can be employed as core components of any load balancing system to address this challenge. In the following, we describe a framework that takes advantage from

---

[4]https://aws.amazon.com/elasticloadbalancing/
[5]https://f5.com/glossary/load-balancer

coupling one of such fast metaheuristics (specifically PSO) with a prediction model for the incoming requests, which provides an efficient mechanism to distribute the workload in the Cloud infrastructure.

12.5.2   Existing Proactive Measures

The flexibility of Cloud to allow adding and removing computing resources at run time might suffer from resource fragmentation if improper server management is in action. DC servers face large fluctuating workloads, and to counter this situation, automatic resource scaling (up/down, auto-scaling) systems are in place. Auto-scaling techniques can be either threshold based or schedule based. In the former method, mainly two rules (each for up and down) are configured. For scaling up or down, some pre-specified thresholds are set, and whenever the utilisation level of some specific resource (e.g., the CPU utilisation or the average response time) is met, actions are taken accordingly (i.e., rules are applied). It works as a reactive system and is widely used by the public Cloud service providers. Improper choice of the thresholds can significantly degrade the performance, and oscillation can be introduced in the system [23].

Conversely, schedule-based approach extracts the pattern from the workload traces, and the scaling policy is adjusted accordingly. The efficiency of the technique solely depends on the capability of understanding the nature of the workload. To this purpose, schedule-based auto-scaling systems include proactive methods, use a prediction model to anticipate future workloads, and allocate the resources accordingly. Choosing the proper prediction model is also not trivial, and the forecasting accuracy mainly depends on the optimal predictive model for the data sets. Voting-based resource/VM allocation is also in use by a public service provider,[6] which is also quite similar to threshold-based scaling model. From academics, mostly the proposed techniques are based on resource utilisation [16], proportional threshold [33, 45], and dynamic threshold [7]. However, there are also existing works which used time series prediction models and prediction-based resource allocation strategies for auto-scaling in Cloud [39, 62], with promising results.

12.6   PRAS: Proactive Resource Allocation Strategy

Cloud is a collection of well-connected networks of servers or commodity machines. For ease of system manageability, cluster concept can be used to improve location policy. Proactive resource allocation strategy (or proactive resource allocation

---

[6]http://support.rightscale.com/12-Guides/Dashboard_Users_Guide/Manage/\Arrays/Actions/Set_up_Autoscaling_using_Voting_Tags/index.html

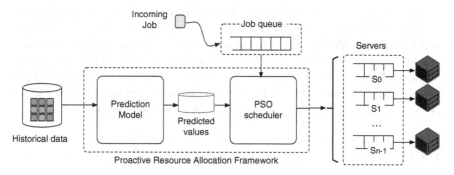

Fig. 12.3 Generic framework of proactive resource allocation strategy

framework) is based on three primary policies. Specifically, they are (*i*) information policy, (*ii*) transformation policy, and (*iii*) location policy. In information policy, historical data are used for predicting user's request by employing a time series model. Next, heuristics or algorithms are used to perform resource allocation by solving last two policies. In Fig. 12.3, we present the main architecture of our proactive resource allocation framework. It consists of two main components: the prediction model and the PSO-based scheduler. The former is in charge of forecasting the future workload on the system, while the latter is responsible for allocating resources (i.e., physical servers) for the predicted load (i.e., VMs). The prediction model is based on the seasonal variant of the ARIMA model, and it uses historical data as the input for predicting the future system load. Input requests are collected on the main queue (Job Queue – JQ), which is used by the PSO-based scheduler to select the effective set of VMs to allocate on the available physical servers. The selection process takes into account output information provided by the prediction module. Allocated VMs are assigned to physical machines by issuing requests on their input queues (s_i).

12.6.1   Prediction

In Cloud, users request VMs by specifying the type together with the required number. It has been found that "univariate" time series model is a good instrument for identifying user access patterns as it is a scalar observation recorded serially over equal time increments. "Pure load balancing" is not a very practical approach to managing the workloads in DCs. Analysing the data usage patterns, we can discover that user requests also follow some seasonality (or trend). In general, the workload estimation can be done using the standard deviation of CPU utilisation [15]. The CPU usage can be used as an estimator of energy cost, and here, we consider the linear power model similar to [15, 26]. In a linear power model, the power consumption of a server increases linearly as the CPU utilisation increases.

AR is a linear regression of the current value of the set of one or more prior values belonging to another set. When AR model is combined with moving-average (MA), it is known as ARMA model. We use three state-of-the-art variants (integrated, seasonal, and fractional) of ARMA model for out-sample prediction with a 1-h prediction horizon. We also compare each model in their forecasting accuracy and execution time. It is also interesting to note from the results that the choice of the prediction model can affect subsequent resource allocation.

12.6.1.1 ARIMA

ARIMA model is a generalisation of the ARMA class which incorporates non-stationary univariate time series. Stationary time series has its mean, variance, and autocorrelations constant in time. ARIMA includes three main components. They are the lag of the stationary series, the lag of the forecast errors, and the integrated (I) component which allows the series to be differentiated. ARIMA models hold the generalised properties of a random walk, exponential smoothing, and stationary regression models. In ARIMA terminology, p is the number of AR terms, d the number of nonseasonal differences, and q is the number of MA terms. An $ARIMA(p, d, q)$ model for a univariate time series X_t can be defined as follows:

$$\Phi(L)(1 - L)^d(X_t - \mu) = \Theta(L)\epsilon_t, \quad \epsilon_t \sim N_{iid}(0, \sigma^2) \tag{12.1}$$

In Eq. 12.1, L is the lag operator, μ is the mean, and ϵ_t is the residual term which follows an independent and identically distributed normal distribution (N_{iid}). The differencing parameter d takes integer values in the ARIMA models. Before fitting the ARIMA on the datasets, we first need to understand the order of differencing and then the numbers of AR and MA terms. The differencing value can be scaled up or down if the sum of AR coefficients and the sum of MA coefficients are close to 1.

12.6.1.2 SARIMA: Seasonal ARIMA

ARIMA can also support seasonality. A seasonal ARIMA model is also known as SARIMA (seasonal ARIMA) and can be written as:

$$SARIMA = ARIMA(p, d, q)(P, D, Q)_h \tag{12.2}$$

In Eq. 12.2, the first term (p, d, q) supports the nonseasonal part of the model where p is the AR order, d is the order of integration, and q is the MA order. The last term $(P, D, Q)_h$ supports the seasonality of the time series (h is equal to the number of periods). In SARIMA model, seasonal differencing (D) is used to remove the nonstationary component from the data sets. If there is seasonality, then D is set to one; otherwise, it is zero, and the number of regular differences (i.e., parameter d) is $d \leq 3$. The seasonal part consists of the back shifts of the seasonal data sets. We also represent the standard SARIMA model for a given time series X_t in Eq. 12.3.

$$\Phi(B^h)\phi(B)\nabla_H^D\nabla^d X_t = \alpha + \Theta(B^h)\theta(B)Z_t$$

$$\nabla_h^D X_t = (1 - B^h)^D X_t$$

$$(12.3)$$

where α is the intercept; $\phi(B)$ and $\theta(B)$ are the back-shift operators for AR and MA, respectively; B^h is the differencing back-shift operator; and D is the seasonal difference $(D = 1, 2, \ldots)$.

12.6.1.3 ARFIMA

ARFIMA indicates the presence of self-similar structures or long memory in the given series. ARFIMA is one of the best-known classes of long memory models, while ARIMA can be considered a short memory series. The main objective of ARFIMA is to measure the persistence to incorporate the long-term correlations in the time series data. ARFIMA allows the series to be fractionally integrated by generalising the ARIMA model's integer order of integration to allow the d parameter to have fractional values $(0 \leq d \leq 0.5)$. Parameter d indicates the presence of long memory or self-similar patterns in the data. Equation 12.4 represents the general form of the ARFIMA model:

$$\Phi(B)y_t = \Theta(B)(1 - B)^{-d}\epsilon_t$$

$$(12.4)$$

where $\Phi(B) = 1 - \phi_1(B) - \cdots - \phi_p(B)^p$ presents AR part, $\Theta(B) = 1 + \theta_1(B) + \cdots + \theta_q(B)^q$ represents MA operators, $\Phi(B)$ and $\Theta(B)$ have no common roots, B is the back-shift operator, and $(1 - B)^{-d}$ is the fractional differencing operator.

12.6.2 Particle Swarm Optimization-Based Scheduling

In the server consolidation problem (SCP), VM allocation is tackled by taking into account VM migrations. SCP belongs to the combinatorial optimisation class, and the problem can be further reduced to a bin-packing problem. PSO [24] is a metaheuristic developed by Kennedy and Eberhart in 1995 to optimise multimodal continuous problems. Compared with other evolutionary-based techniques, it provides higher-quality solutions, with faster convergence. Similar to other evolutionary-based heuristics, such as genetic algorithms (GAs), PSO is a population-based stochastic optimisation approach, where a group of independent solutions are used to sample the search space and discover the optimal solution. In

PSO, a group of particles are evolved over time, by moving their position into a multivariable search space. Passing from one position in a given instant of time to another position is made by taking into account the velocity of the particles. The particles' velocity and their positions are taken care by two components, which are described as two factors incorporating a form of distributed intelligence:

- *Cognitive factor* encodes the information regarding the history of the best position assumed by the particles at the time t.
- *Social factor* encodes the information relating to the history of the best position assumed by the neighbourhood of the particle at the time t.

These two factors are used to adapt the velocity of the particles in such a way it can steer the position towards the optimal solution. In PSO, there are no operators devoted to combining solutions belonging to the same population. The social factor allows to incorporate the knowledge collected by other particles. The topology of the neighbourhood influences the behaviour of the heuristic, although the entire set of particles is used as the neighbourhood (i.e., *lattice model*). The lattice model also has the advantage of keeping the number of operations used to determine the absolute best position low. Equation 12.5 shows the general rule used to update the velocity of the particle i at time t.

$$V_i^{t+1} = \omega V_i^t + \phi_1 r_1 (B_i^t - X_i^t) + \phi_2 r_2 (\hat{B}^t - X_i^t) \qquad (12.5)$$

In Eq. 12.5, ω parameter is called *inertia factor*, and it is used to determine the fraction of the current velocity (i.e., it determines how fast we want to move the particle to the next position, compared to the current velocity). Inertia is a time-variable parameter, kept high (e.g., a typical value is 0.9) at the beginning of the evolution phase to allow particles exploring the search space (exploration phase). Later, it is reduced to lower values (e.g., a typical value is 0.1) in the last part of the evolution cycle (exploitation phase). B_i^t and $\hat{B}^t$ are, respectively, the best position assumed by the particle and by the whole swarm at the time t. ϕ_1 and ϕ_2 are parameters that greatly influence the algorithm convergence and are kept constant (several works demonstrated empirically that setting $\phi_1 = \phi_2 = 2$ provides the best trade-off between probability of convergence and algorithm efficiency). Finally r_1 and r_2 are two stochastic variables with a uniform distribution $\mathcal{U}(0, 1)$. Equation 12.6 shows how the position of each particle is updated:

$$X_i^{t+1} = X_i^t + \chi V_i^{t+1} \qquad (12.6)$$

The parameter χ is called *constriction factor*. It can be used to adapt the final velocity in such a way the change to the position of the particle is small enough not to compromise the overall adaptation given by the cognitive and social factors.

In such adaptive optimisation heuristics, an initial set of solutions is randomly generated by the algorithm. In the case of PSO, solutions represent the particles' position in the search space. By using a *fitness evaluation function* (i.e., the objective function to optimise), each candidate solution is evaluated and ranked based on its fitness value. PSO received attention for developing adaptive resource allocators thanks to the quality of the solution that they provide, and their inherently parallel nature, that makes them well suited for modern massive multi-/manycore processors largely available in modern DCs.

12.6.2.1 VM Allocation

In allocating VMs on a given set of physical servers, with the aim of reducing the number of active servers, we can model the problem as follows. Given a set S of physical servers and a set V of VMs, we want to assign the maximum number of VMs denoted as $v_j \in V$ to the servers $s_i \in S$, in such a way the sum of required resources of the VMs to each server does not exceed the amount of available free resources on the servers.

Equation 12.7 allows to model this objective function (F_o) as follows:

$$F_o = \max \left\{ \sum_{i=0}^{|S|-1} \sum_{j=0}^{|V|-1} a_{ij} \cdot v_j \right\} + \min \{\sigma_S\} \tag{12.7}$$

where $|S|$ and $|V|$ denote, respectively, the cardinality of the set of servers S and of the VMs V. When asserted, boolean variables a_{ij} allow to assign the VM j to the server i. Finally, σ_S takes care of the distribution of the VMs among the active servers (i.e., a server s_i for which exists at least one of the $a_{ij} = 1$).

$$\sigma_S = \sqrt{\frac{\sum_{i=0}^{|S|-1} \sum_{j=0}^{|V|-1} (v_j \cdot a_{ij} - \overline{V})^2}{|V|-1}} \qquad \overline{V} = \frac{\sum_{i=0}^{|S|-1} \sum_{j=0}^{|V|-1} v_j \cdot a_{ij}}{|V|} \tag{12.8}$$

Equation 12.8 shows how to take into account the way the load is distributed on the servers. Minimising the standard deviation in this distribution, the function F_o tries to reduce the imbalance in the load distribution, thus contributing to reduce power consumption on the active servers. On the other hand, maximising the number of assigned VMs to a given server allows reducing the number of active servers. To correctly optimise this objective function, the following constraint must be satisfied:

$$\sum_{j=0}^{|V|-1} a_{ij} \cdot v_j \leq s_i, \quad \forall i \in \{0, \cdots, |S| - 1\} \tag{12.9}$$

Since both VMs and servers are characterised by the set of resources, they, respectively, require and offer on the maximum resources available. We express the quantities s_i and v_j as the ratio between the assigned (VM) or free (server) resources and the maximum available resources. For instance, if a certain VM requires four CPU cores and the maximum CPU cores in the system is set to ten, then the VM will be characterised by a CPU utilisation of 0.4. Similarly, a server with five CPU cores free will be characterised by a CPU offer of 0.5. Both servers and VMs are characterised by a set of three distinctive features which globally represent the full set of resources. They are CPU core fraction, the amount of main memory, and the network bandwidth required.

To find a solution for the stated problem using the PSO algorithm, we need to transform the objective function F_o (see Eq. 12.7) in such way it can be conveniently minimised. To this end, the first term of the function F_o is substituted by another term, as follows:

$$\Delta = \frac{1}{\sum_{i=0}^{|S|-1} \sum_{j=0}^{|V|-1} a_{ij} \cdot v_j} \implies F_o = \min\{\Delta + \sigma_S\} \qquad (12.10)$$

12.7 Evaluation

The proposed framework is designed to provide adaptability to the Cloud resource schedulers. The ability of such components to efficiently performing resource allocation to the requesting VMs plays a vital role in supporting Cloud QoS. A fair distribution of the workload contributes to increase the efficiency and reliability of the whole DC. Experimental results demonstrate the effectiveness of this approach, which can outperform a traditional Cloud scheduling policy such as First Fit.

12.7.1 Prediction Results

For our analysis, we have collected a trace for incoming VM requests over a period of 7 days from a private Cloud, shown in Fig. 12.4. The granularity of the incoming VM request is 6 min, and using the trace, we perform out-sample, multistep forecasting. To compare the forecasting accuracy, we consider two well-known forecasting error measures: mean absolute percentage error (MAPE) and root mean squared error (RMSE). MAPE is the sum of all prediction errors divided by the sum of actual values, while RMSE is a more rigorous error measure, and the standard error (SE) provides the details of the error distribution (see Eq. 12.11).

$$MAPE = \frac{1}{n} \sum_{t=1}^{n} \left| \frac{X_t - \widehat{X}_t}{X_t} \right|$$

$$(12.11)$$

$$RMSE = \sqrt{\frac{1}{n} \sum_{t=1}^{n} (X_t - \widehat{X}_t)^2}$$

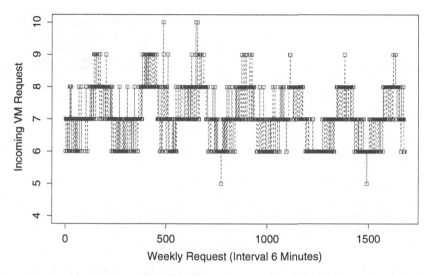

Fig. 12.4 Representation of incoming VM request for 7 days

Table 12.1 Prediction models: ARIMA input parameters are (3,1,2), SARIMA input parameters are (2,1,2)(1,1,1), and ARFIMA input parameters are (0,d,1). Standard errors are reported in parenthesis

Model	AR(1)	AR(2)	AR(3)	d	MA(1)	MA(2)	SAR(1)	SMA(1)
ARIMA	1.3475	−0.5905	−0.1456	–	−1.6867	0.8582	–	–
	(0.029)	(0.040)	(0.0276)		(0.0176)	(0.0160)		
SARIMA	1.4798	−0.7918	–	–	1.7279	0.8726	−0.1526	−1.0
	(0.0200)	(0.0192)			(0.0158)	(0.0162)	(0.0256)	(0.0087)
ARFIMA	–	–	–	0.477	−0.2842	–	–	–
				(0.0213)	(0.0246)			

We have used three widely used univariate time series models for predicting incoming VM request of a DC over a 1-h window. First, we consider the ARIMA model; next we incorporate the idea of seasonality by implementing the seasonal ARIMA (SARIMA) model. Finally, we check the possibility of fractional integration and long memory by estimating the ARFIMA model (fractional ARIMA). The optimal lag values for all the models were calculated using Akaike information criteria (AIC). The estimated values are given in Table 12.1 where standard errors are in the parenthesis.

From the standard error values, we can observe that parameters are statistically significant. The presence of seasonality in the data is verified by the values of the seasonal AR and MA coefficient. Further, the presence of long memory is confirmed as the fractional integration parameter d is statistically significant and less than 0.5. Next, we analyse the ability to predict for the three estimated models (see Fig. 12.5).

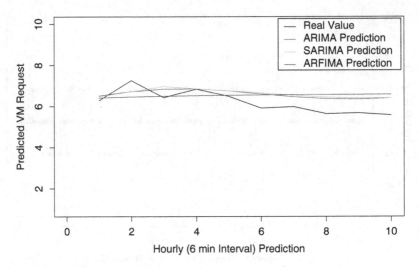

Fig. 12.5 Comparison of prediction between ARIMA, SARIMA, and ARFIMA models

Table 12.2 Forecasting error comparison and the execution time for the three analysed prediction models

Performance	ARIMA(3,1,2)	SARIMA(2,1,2)(1,1,1)	ARFIMA(0,0.48,1)
MAPE	2.092558	2.066657	2.277271
RMSE	0.02313968	0.02292463	0.02465025
Exe. time (seconds)	2.712	12.376	2.108

From the results, it is evident that SARIMA model has outperformed other models regarding forecast accuracy (it is evident from the RMSE and MAPE values). ARIMA model is found out to be the second best in prediction (see Table 12.2). The value of d is found to be 0.48 in the ARFIMA model. Hence, the presence of long memory is confirmed. However, it does not increase the forecast performance of the ARFIMA model. The superior performance of the SARIMA model indicates that there are seasonal patterns present in the analysed data. Finally, regarding computation time, ARFIMA model is found to be the fastest model, whereas SARIMA model requires the largest amount of time. This delay could be justified by the fact that the SARIMA model estimates more parameters as it incorporates seasonal patterns. Thus, in this part of the experiment, we have shown how the selection of model can affect the forecasting accuracy together with running time. The execution time should also be considered during the selection of the model. Because the real-time applicability of the model can come into question when the data sets get larger.

12.7.1.1 PSO Results

The output of the prediction model can be effectively used to drive the allocation of the DC resources, by running a metaheuristic that provides a possible resource schedule in a very short time. To show the effectiveness of the proposed method, we considered a test case where input requests are collected in an input queue. Allocation is performed analysing a window of $R \leq Q_{size}$ requests, where Q_{size} accounts for the maximum number of requests that can be presented at the input of the scheduler. Once a schedule is produced for the current window, only the VMs that effectively have been allocated are removed from the queue. The other requests are kept in the queue for the next iteration. Experimental setup used a window with a fixed size of $R = 80$ (the entire pool of predicted VMs to allocate is set to $Q_{size} = 240$), with a pool of available servers that is predicted to be of five servers. Although the number of servers in the experiments appears to be tiny, it is worth noting that the ratio between the available servers and the number of VMs to allocate is equal to 0.06, making the instance of the problem complex for any resource allocation algorithm (especially if the solution has to be generated dynamically). In experiments, it has been seen that the servers generated traffic follows localisation [8] thus running the small problem instances in parallel can be of great use. For more complex situations of the allocation problem (e.g., where a quite larger window is used, as well as the number of servers available is higher), the scheduler algorithm can leverage on its inherited parallel nature and the availability of multi-/manycore processors. By allowing groups of candidate solutions to be analysed in parallel by multiple cores on modern processors (or even better on large multithreaded systems, such as GPUs and Intel Xeon Phi coprocessor), the execution time may be kept reasonable. Furthermore, specific problem knowledge can be incorporated in the PSO heuristic to speed up its execution (i.e., reducing the number of required iterations to converge).

For comparison purpose, we have used the well-known First Fit allocation policy. In Fig. 12.6, we present the fitness value (of both PSO-based algorithm and also the First Fit) over the time related to the solutions for the problem. The simple logic employed by the First Fit algorithm allows performing initially better. However, the algorithm is not able to effectively explore the complete solution space. Conversely, the ability of PSO to intelligently sample the search space allows it to discover a solution with a lower fitness. This approach lets the PSO algorithm to quickly outperform the First Fit, leaving the algorithm to explore more the solution space. It is worth to note that presented results (see Fig. 12.6) are provided for the standard version of the PSO algorithm, without any specific problem knowledge integrated and without any parallelisation mechanism.

Regarding execution time, First Fit is faster (taking a few seconds) compared to the PSO model. The PSO-based algorithm took less than 20 s to complete the solution space exploration while running as a single-threaded instance/task.

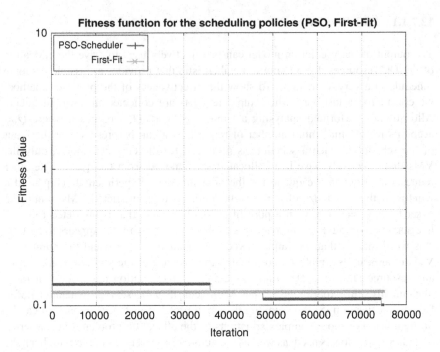

Fig. 12.6 Comparison of the fitness function over the time for the First Fit and PSO-based allocation algorithms

However, it is important to observe two specific aspects of the PSO scheduler. They are (*i*) its inherited parallel nature that can take enormous advantages from recent multi-/manycore processors and (*ii*) the capability of incorporating a memory effect. While the former aspect greatly contributes to speed up the execution, the latter aspect represents a remarkable factor. In fact, since the distribution of requests are not totally random, it leaves space for the evolutionary algorithm to exploit accumulated knowledge from previous iterations (i.e., when the scheduler moves from one window to the next one, the current best solution can be used to initialise the population of solution candidates). In this last experiment, we have shown that even a simpler form of the PSO-based solution can outperform the well-known First Fit algorithm regarding allocation efficiency. The performance can also be improved further by adding parallelism, and the complexity of the scheduling model can be increased by adding more resource-related constraints.

12.8 Conclusions and Future Work

Maintaining a power-efficient Cloud infrastructure is not easy, and the complexity of Cloud resource management is further increased by the dynamic access patterns of the users. Although many good works have been done to make the model of the problem as real as possible by adding realistic features, these proposals quickly fail when implemented as a real-time solution. In this chapter, we advocate for an adaptive resource allocation mechanism in Cloud which is still an open research problem. Here, we first give an overview of the current state of the Cloud paradigm and then discuss the underlying resources. Next, we advocate for a proactive resource allocation strategy for better resource allocation. We believe that if the first part (forecast) of the framework is efficient, then we do not need a complex allocation policy (second part). During the experiments, we have shown that (for our case) the SARIMA is more efficient to predict future VM requests compared to other state-of-the-art predictors. Passing such inputs to a metaheuristic (such as PSO), we can make an adaptive resource allocation framework for Cloud. The future direction of this work would be optimising the PSO for better convergence speed and quality of the solution. Few related approaches have been discussed in the chapter, but further tuning the control parameters (such as velocity clamping, inertia weight, constriction coefficient) could lead to better solutions. Searching space extension or hybrid PSO can also provide better performance. Apart from that, it could also be interesting to develop more robust hybrid prediction model by combining other models with the state-of a the-art models.

References

1. Adapteva Inc. (2013) Epiphany architecture reference. http://adapteva.com/docs/epiphany_arch_ref.pdf
2. Adzigogov L, Soldatos J, Polymenakos L (2005) Emperor: an ogsa grid meta-scheduler based on dynamic resource predictions. J Grid Comput 3(1–2):19–37
3. Ardagna D, Panicucci B, Passacantando M (2011) A game theoretic formulation of the service provisioning problem in cloud systems. In: Proceedings of the 20th international conference on world wide web. ACM, pp 177–186
4. Barroso LA, Clidaras J, Hölzle U (2013) The datacenter as a computer: an introduction to the design of warehouse-scale machines. Synth Lect Comput Archit 8(3):1–154
5. Barroso LA, Hölzle U (2007) The case for energy-proportional computing. Computer 40:33–37
6. Beloglazov A, Abawajy J, Buyya R (2012) Energy-aware resource allocation heuristics for efficient management of data centers for cloud computing. Futur Gener Comput Syst 28(5):755–768
7. Beloglazov A, Buyya R (2010) Adaptive threshold-based approach for energy-efficient consolidation of virtual machines in cloud data centers. In: Proceedings of the 8th international workshop on middleware for grids, clouds and e-science, vol 4. ACM,
8. Benson T, Akella A, Maltz DA (2010) Network traffic characteristics of data centers in the wild. In: Proceedings of the 10th ACM SIGCOMM conference on internet measurement. ACM, pp 267–280
9. Bobroff N, Kochut A, Beaty K (2007) Dynamic placement of virtual machines for managing SLA violations. In: 10th IFIP/IEEE international symposium on integrated network management, IM'07, pp 119–128
10. Bonomi F, Milito R, Natarajan P, Zhu J (2014) Fog computing: a platform for internet of things and analytics. In: Bessis N, Dobre C (eds) Big data and internet of things: a roadmap for smart environments. Springer, Cham, pp 169–186
11. Box GE, Jenkins GM, Reinsel GC, Ljung GM (2015) Time series analysis: forecasting and control. Wiley, Hoboken

12. Calheiros RN, Masoumi E, Ranjan R, Buyya R (2015) Workload prediction using ARIMA model and its impact on cloud applications QoS. IEEE Trans Cloud Comput 3(4):449–458
13. Chandra A, Gong W, Shenoy P (2003) Dynamic resource allocation for shared data centers using online measurements. In: International workshop on quality of service. Springer, pp 381–398
14. Chen C, Pei Q, Ning L (2009) Forecasting 802.11 traffic using seasonal ARIMA model. In: International forum on computer science-technology and applications, IFCSTA'09, vol 2, pp 347–350
15. Chen G, He W, Liu J, Nath S, Rigas L, Xiao L, Zhao F (2008) Energy-aware server provisioning and load dispatching for connection-intensive internet services. In: NSDI, vol 8, pp 337–350
16. Chieu TC, Mohindra A, Karve AA, Segal A (2009) Dynamic scaling of web applications in a virtualized cloud computing environment. In: IEEE international conference one-business engineering, ICEBE'09, pp 281–286
17. Cook SA (1971) The complexity of theorem-proving procedures. In: Proceedings of the third annual ACM symposium on theory of computing. ACM, pp 151–158
18. Csirik J, Woeginger GJ (1998) On-line packing and covering problems. Springer, Berlin/New York
19. Debusschere V, Bacha S et al (2012) Hourly server workload forecasting up to 168 hours ahead using seasonal ARIMA model. In: 2012 IEEE international conference on industrial technology
20. Dinda PA, O'Hallaron DR (1999) An evaluation of linear models for host load prediction. In: Proceedings of the eighth IEEE international symposium on high performance distributed computing, pp 87–96
21. de Dinechin BD, de Massas PG, Lager G, Léger C, Orgogozo B, Reybert J, Strudel T (2013) A distributed run-time environment for the Kalray MPPA®-256 integrated manycore processor. Procedia Comput Sci 18:1654–1663
22. Do T, Hao M, Leesatapornwongsa T, Patana-anake T, Gunawi HS (2013) Limplock: understanding the impact of limpware on scale-out cloud systems. In: Proceedings of the 4th annual symposium on cloud computing. ACM, p 14
23. Dutreilh X, Moreau A, Malenfant J, Rivierre N, Truck I (2010) From data center resource allocation to control theory and back. In: 2010 IEEE 3rd international conference on cloud computing, pp 410–417
24. Eberhart RC, Kennedy J et al (1995) A new optimizer using particle swarm theory. In: Proceedings of the sixth international symposium on micro machine and human science, vol 1, pp 39–43
25. Evans D (2011) The internet of things how the next evolution of the internet is changing everything. White paper by Cisco Internet Business Solutions Group (IBSG), pp 1–11
26. Fan X, Weber WD, Barroso LA (2007) Power provisioning for a warehouse-sized computer. In: ACM SIGARCH computer architecture news, vol 35. ACM, pp 13–23
27. Fang W, Lu Z, Wu J, Cao Z (2012) Rpps: a novel resource prediction and provisioning scheme in cloud data center. In: 2012 IEEE ninth international conference on services computing (SCC), pp 609–616
28. Filani D, He J, Gao S, Rajappa M, Kumar A, Shah P, Nagappan R (2008) Dynamic data center power management: trends, issues, and solutions. Intel Technol J 12(1):59–67
29. Ghribi C, Hadji M, Zeghlache D (2013) Energy efficient VM scheduling for cloud data centers: exact allocation and migration algorithms. In: 2013 13th IEEE/ACM international symposium on cluster, cloud and grid computing (CCGrid), pp 671–678
30. Greenberg A, Hamilton J, Maltz DA, Patel P (2008) The cost of a cloud: research problems in data center networks. ACM SIGCOMM Comput Commun Rev 39(1):68–73
31. Gubbi J, Buyya R, Marusic S, Palaniswami M (2013) Internet of things (IoT): a vision, architectural elements, and future directions. Futur Gener Comput Syst 29(7):1645–1660
32. Gürsun G, Crovella M, Matta I (2011) Describing and forecasting video access patterns. In: 2011 Proceedings IEEE INFOCOM, pp 16–20

33. Hasan MZ, Magana E, Clemm A, Tucker, L, Gudreddi SLD (2012) Integrated and autonomic cloud resource scaling. In: 2012 IEEE network operations and management symposium, pp 1327–1334

34. Hermenier F, Lorca X, Menaud JM, Muller G, Lawall J (2009) Entropy: a consolidation manager for clusters. In: Proceedings of the 2009 ACM SIGPLAN/SIGOPS international conference on virtual execution environments. ACM, pp 41–50

35. Hwang K, Dongarra J, Fox GC (2013) Distributed and cloud computing: from parallel processing to the internet of things. Morgan Kaufmann, Waltham

36. Infrastructure V (2006) Resource management with VMware DRS. VMware Whitepaper

37. Interconnect EE, Living S, Computing G (2008) Technology with the environment in mind. Intel Technol J 12(1):59–67

38. Iqbal W, Dailey MN, Carrera D, Janecek P (2011) Adaptive resource provisioning for read intensive multi-tier applications in the cloud. Futur Gener Comput Syst 27(6):871–879

39. Islam S, Keung J, Lee K, Liu A (2012) Empirical prediction models for adaptive resource provisioning in the cloud. Futur Gener Comput Syst 28(1):155–162

40. Jeyarani R, Nagaveni N, Ram RV (2012) Design and implementation of adaptive power-aware virtual machine provisioner (APA-VMP) using swarm intelligence. Futur Gener Comput Syst 28(5):811–821

41. Kaur T, Chana I (2015) Energy efficiency techniques in cloud computing: a survey and taxonomy. ACM Comput Surv (CSUR) 48(2):22

42. Kumar AS, Mazumdar S (2016) Forecasting HPC workload using ARMA models and SSA. In: Proceedings of the 15th IEEE conference on information technology (ICIT), pp 1–4

43. Li K, Tang X, Li K (2014) Energy-efficient stochastic task scheduling on heterogeneous computing systems. IEEE Trans Parallel Distrib Syst 25(11):2867–2876

44. Li L (2009) An optimistic differentiated service job scheduling system for cloud computing service users and providers. In: Third international conference on multimedia and ubiquitous engineering, MUE'09, pp 295–299

45. Lim HC, Babu S, Chase JS, Parekh SS (2009) Automated control in cloud computing: challenges and opportunities. In: Proceedings of the 1st workshop on automated control for datacenters and clouds. ACM, pp 13–18

46. Liu Z, Wang X (2012) A PSO-based algorithm for load balancing in virtual machines of cloud computing environment. In: International conference in swarm intelligence. Springer, pp 142–147

47. Martins J, Ahmed M, Raiciu C, Olteanu V, Honda M, Bifulco R, Huici F (2014) Clickos and the art of network function virtualization. In: Proceedings of the 11th USENIX conference on networked systems design and implementation. USENIX Association, pp 459–473

48. Mehrotra R, Banicescu I, Srivastava S, Abdelwahed S (2015) A power-aware autonomic approach for performance management of scientific applications in a data center environment. In: Khan SU, Zomaya AY (eds) Handbook on data centers. Springer, New York, pp 163–189

49. Mittal S, Vetter JS (2015) A survey of CPU-GPU heterogeneous computing techniques. ACM Comput Surv (CSUR) 47(4):69

50. Murtazaev A, Oh S (2011) Sercon: server consolidation algorithm using live migration of virtual machines for green computing. IETE Techn Rev 28(3):212–231

51. Pandey S, Wu L, Guru SM, Buyya R (2010) A particle swarm optimization-based heuristic for scheduling workflow applications in cloud computing environments. In: 2010 24th IEEE international conference on advanced information networking and applications, pp 400–407

52. Patel M, Naughton B, Chan C, Sprecher N, Abeta S, Neal A et al (2014) Mobile-edge computing introductory technical white paper. White Paper, Mobile-edge Computing (MEC) industry initiative

53. Pearce M, Zeadally S, Hunt R (2013) Virtualization: issues, security threats, and solutions. ACM Comput Surv (CSUR) 45(2):17

54. Pell Oliver MOTKH, Luk W (2013) High-performance computing using FPGAs, pp 747–774. Springer, New York

55. Petrucci V, Carrera EV, Loques O, Leite JC, Mosse D (2011) Optimized management of power and performance for virtualized heterogeneous server clusters. In: 2011 11th IEEE/ACM international symposium on cluster, cloud and grid computing (CCGrid), pp 23–32
56. Putnam A, Caulfield AM, Chung ES, Chiou D, Constantinides K, Demme J, Esmaeilzadeh H, Fowers J, Gopal GP, Gray J, Haselman M, Hauck S, Heil S, Hormati A, Kim JY, Lanka S, Larus J, Peterson E, Pope S, Smith A, Thong J, Xiao PY, Burger D (2016) A reconfigurable fabric for accelerating large-scale datacenter services. Commun ACM 59(11):114–122
57. Quang-Hung N, Nien PD, Nam NH, Tuong NH, Thoai N (2013) A genetic algorithm for power-aware virtual machine allocation in private cloud. In: Information and communication technology. Springer, Berlin/Heidelberg, pp 183–191
58. Reddi VJ, Lee BC, Chilimbi T, Vaid K (2011) Mobile processors for energy-efficient web search. ACM Trans Comput Syst (TOCS) (3):9
59. Roy N, Dubey A, Gokhale A (2011) Efficient autoscaling in the cloud using predictive models for workload forecasting. In: 2011 IEEE international conference on cloud computing (CLOUD), pp 500–507
60. Satyanarayanan M, Bahl P, Caceres R, Davies N (2009) The case for VM-based cloudlets in mobile computing. IEEE Pervasive Comput 8(4):14–23
61. Schroeder MR (2012) Fractals, chaos, power laws: Minutes from an infinite paradise. Courier Corporation, New York
62. Shen Z, Subbiah S, Gu X, Wilkes J (2011) Cloudscale: elastic resource scaling for multi-tenant cloud systems. In: Proceedings of the 2nd ACM symposium on cloud computing. ACM, p 5
63. Shu Y, Yu M, Liu J, Yang OW (2003) Wireless traffic modeling and prediction using seasonal ARIMA models. In: IEEE international conference on communications, ICC'03,vol 3, pp 1675–1679
64. Srikantaiah S, Kansal A, Zhao F (2008) Energy aware consolidation for cloud computing. In: Proceedings of the 2008 conference on power aware computing and systems, San Diego, vol 10
65. Tirado JM, Higuero D, Isaila F, Carretero J (2011) Predictive data grouping and placement for cloud-based elastic server infrastructures. In: Proceedings of the 2011 11th IEEE/ACM international symposium on cluster, cloud and grid computing. IEEE Computer Society, pp 285–294
66. Urdaneta G, Pierre G, Van Steen M (2009) Wikipedia workload analysis for decentralized hosting. Comput Netw 53(11):1830–1845
67. Urgaonkar B, Shenoy P, Chandra A, Goyal P, Wood T (2008) Agile dynamic provisioning of multi-tier internet applications. ACM Trans Auton Adapt Syst (TAAS) 3(1):1
68. Van HN, Tran FD, Menaud JM (2010) Performance and power management for cloud infrastructures. In: 2010 IEEE 3rd international conference on cloud computing (CLOUD), pp 329–336
69. Vaquero LM, Rodero-Merino L (2014) Finding your way in the fog: towards a comprehensive definition of Fog computing. ACM SIGCOMM Comput Commun Rev 44(5):27–32
70. Verma A, Ahuja P, Neogi A (2008) pmapper: power and migration cost aware application placement in virtualized systems. In: Middleware 2008, pp 243–264. Springer
71. Vogels W (2008) Beyond server consolidation. Queue 6(1):20–26
72. Von Laszewski G, Wang L, Younge AJ, He X (2009) Power-aware scheduling of virtual machines in dvfs-enabled clusters. In: IEEE international conference on cluster computing and workshops, CLUSTER'09, pp 1–10
73. Wei G, Vasilakos AV, Zheng Y, Xiong N (2010) A game-theoretic method of fair resource allocation for cloud computing services. J Supercomput 54(2):252–269
74. Willis DF, Dasgupta A, Banerjee S (2014) Paradrop: a multi-tenant platform for dynamically installed third party services on home gateways. In: Proceedings of the 2014 ACM SIGCOMM workshop on distributed cloud computing. ACM, pp 43–44
75. Wu Z, Ni Z, Gu L, Liu X (2010) A revised discrete particle swarm optimization for cloud workflow scheduling. In: 2010 international conference on computational intelligence and security (CIS), pp 184–188

76. Xu J, Fortes JA (2010) Multi-objective virtual machine placement in virtualized data center environments. In: Green computing and communications (GreenCom). 2010 IEEE/ACM international conference on cyber, physical and social computing (CPSCom), pp 179–188
77. Zhan S, Huo H (2012) Improved PSO-based task scheduling algorithm in cloud computing. J Inf Comput Sci 9(13):3821–3829
78. Zhang H, Li P, Zhou Z, Yu X (2012) A PSO-based hierarchical resource scheduling strategy on cloud computing. In: International conference on trustworthy computing and services. Springer, pp 325–332
79. Zhang Q, Zhani MF, Zhang S, Zhu Q, Boutaba R, Hellerstein JL (2012) Dynamic energy-aware capacity provisioning for cloud computing environments. In: Proceedings of the 9th international conference on autonomic computing. ACM, pp 145–154
80. Zhang Q, Zhu Q, Boutaba R (2011) Dynamic resource allocation for spot markets in cloud computing environments. In: 2011 fourth IEEE international conference on utility and cloud computing (UCC), pp 178–185
81. Zhuravlev S, Saez JC, Blagodurov S, Fedorova A, Prieto M (2013) Survey of energy-cognizant scheduling techniques. IEEE Trans Parallel Distrib Syst 24(7):1447–1464
82. Zuo X, Zhang G, Tan W (2014) Self-adaptive learning PSO-based deadline constrained task scheduling for hybrid IaaS cloud. IEEE Trans Autom Sci Eng 11(2):564–573

Chapter 13
Datacentre Event Analysis for Knowledge Discovery in Large-Scale Cloud Environments

John Panneerselvam, Lu Liu, and Yao Lu

13.1   Introduction

The emergence of Cloud Computing in recent years has achieved tremendous outreach in both academia and industry. Cloud providers are contractually committed to avail services and provision resources within the bounds [5] of the initial negotiated SLA (service level agreement) with the clients. SLA is paramount in determining the performance of the Cloud providers in satisfying the user requests with the measure of Quality of Service (QoS) and Quality of Expectations (QoE) of the users. A typical Cloud Computing environment is composed of massive datacentres encompassing large numbers of servers hosting the operation of the virtual machines (VMs). Jobs arriving at a datacentre for processing are usually scheduled, allocated with appropriate resources and are executed at the back-end servers. The server resources are orchestrated to execute the tasks effectively within the allocated resource levels. A scheduler in the datacentre receives, finds and allocates the jobs onto VMs encapsulated onto the physical servers for processing. Emerging multi-provider Cloud service infrastructure enables the job execution to utilise resources from different Cloud datacentres. The exchange of services within multiple Cloud datacentres are enabled by the meta-schedulers and Cloud brokers which are responsible for identifying and locating the desired services based on the

J. Panneerselvam (✉) • L. Liu
Department of Electronics, Computing and Mathematics, University of Derby, Derby, UK
e-mail: j.panneerselvam@derby.ac.uk; l.liu@derby.ac.uk

Y. Lu
School of Computer Science and Telecommunication Engineering, Jiangsu University, Jiangsu, China
e-mail: luyao478208892@163.com

© Springer International Publishing AG 2017
N. Antonopoulos, L. Gillam (eds.), *Cloud Computing*, Computer Communications and Networks, DOI 10.1007/978-3-319-54645-2_13

job requirements. Other than the compute and storage components, datacentres also comprise cooling components to maintain the reliability and longevity of the server resources such as air-conditioning, water-based cooling systems, etc. Maintaining the server resources in a 'readily-available' state is essential for achieving timely scheduling of the incoming jobs. Switching the server resources off and turning on after the job arrival in an attempt to conserve energy might delay the availability of the server resources. Server switching is usually governed by the wake-up latencies which determine the boot-up times required by servers to become available for processing.

A single job may encompass one to several tasks [13] which are scheduled accordingly onto the Cloud servers and allocated with resource levels in terms of CPU core counts, memory and disk spaces. Allocated resource levels are usually determined based on the resource requirements of the users and the computational intensity of the jobs. CPU resources are usually evaluated in terms of core counts, while the memory and disk space requirements are evaluated in terms of the memory bytes. It is commonly being argued that the initial evaluation of the resource requirements for jobs exceed far beyond the actual execution requirements. The scheduled jobs are usually executed smoothly upon allocating the required level of server resources, when there are no intrinsic and extrinsic termination causes. But the actual execution of the tasks could face various types of terminations [2] resulting in execution failures; such terminated jobs are most often resubmitted and rescheduled for processing. The current status of jobs and tasks [11] are classified as un-submitted, pending, running and dead depending on their status at the back-end server.

Understanding the nature of the incoming user requests and the server resources benefits the providers with the necessary knowledge to choose appropriate server resources for allocating jobs with optimum provisioning of resource levels. Optimum level of resource provisioning for the user requests helps the providers to accommodate more workloads onto the server resources and to reduce the energy implications of the datacentres. But the characteristics [9] of the Cloud workload are still not perfectly clear, thus modelling the behaviours of the Cloud workloads at the datacentres is challenging. The dynamic nature and the inherent diversity of the Cloud workloads demand an extensive and continuous analysis for characterising the incoming workloads, since the users of Cloud services generally coexist from different business contexts and submit workloads of diverse resource requirements, characterising diverse arrival frequency and resource consumption patterns. Furthermore, a single datacentre environment usually comprises heterogeneous servers in terms of the operating system, server capacities, utilisation levels and operating temperature, etc. Such intrinsic and extrinsic heterogeneities [10] of both the user requests and the server resources impose various levels of complexities in the datacentre management for achieving efficient execution of the user requests. With this in mind, this chapter deeply studies the characteristics of the incoming workloads and the server resource usage patterns in a large-scale datacentre execution and presents an empirical analysis of the various execution events with the motivation of exhibiting the trend and knowledge inherent among the datacentre execution events, ultimately to benefit decision making for optimum and effective datacentre management.

The remainder of this paper is organized as follows:

Section 13.2 presents an overview of the characteristics of the Cloud workloads.

Section 13.3 defines the inherent Cloud periodicity patterns and predictability of Cloud Computing.

Section 13.4 introduces the datacentre trace logs explored in this study.

Section 13.5 presents an empirical analysis conducted on the incoming job arrival trend and user behaviours in terms of job submission.

Section 13.6 covers the analysis conducted on the server farm usage pattern.

Section 13.7 presents an analysis conducted on the nature of the incoming workloads in terms of their resource intensiveness.

Section 13.8 concludes this chapter along with the future research directions.

13.2   Cloud Workload Analytics

Cloud workloads can be witnessed as jobs encompassing tasks and exhibit temporal and spatial correlations [8] as they are driven by repeatable business behaviours. Such workloads originate from users, and the active number of concurrent users in a service session is crucial in determining the required amounts of active resources in the server farm. Usually, Cloud providers employ a higher level of parallelism under increased level of concurrent users. The demand for CPU cores generally increases with increasing number of concurrent users, as the demand for CPU witnessed at 20% under 100 concurrent users and 70% fewer than 300 concurrent users in a datacentre analysis. The duration [1] of the workloads is tri-modal and classified as short, medium and long running jobs. Cloud workloads are mostly shorter in duration and are submitted at higher frequencies within shorter intervals and use the allocated resources well up to the allocated margin. Shorter duration jobs are further classified as highly parallel user requests requiring both CPU and memory resources to shorter CPU and shorter memory intensive tasks, respectively. Medium jobs usually have a fair resource utilisation profile and are more often memory intensive. Medium jobs arrive less frequently than the short jobs but more frequently than the long jobs. Though fewer in number, long running jobs consume maximum amounts of resources and are highly CPU intensive. In order to model the resource utilisation profiles of the workloads, job duration [1] has further been classified as short jobs, approaching mid, medium, receding long and long jobs accordingly. Long running jobs are further classified as encompassing user facing tasks and compute intensive tasks. The former run continuously with quicker responses and interactions with the users, and the latter generally refer to the processing of the weblogs.

In general, majority of the Cloud jobs run for less than 15 min [7], and very few jobs run for more than 300 min with the duration of latency sensitive jobs being less than 30 min on average. The incoming workloads are usually characterised with various levels of latency sensitivity [11] depending on their computational intensity, which defines the allowed timescale within which the job should be processed. Cloud datacentres usually face workloads of various latency levels, though a majority of the Cloud workloads are jobs characterising lower levels of latency sensitiveness. Task duration heavily depends on the nature of the user behaviours and their interactions. For instance, a simple search and retrieval job may run for shorter duration than those of downloading massive data or watching movies. Generally, a single job may contain tasks of both shorter and longer durations, and tasks running longer consume more of the resources than those running shorter within the same job.

Alongside job duration, the number of tasks encompassed within the incoming jobs is crucial in determining the execution profiles of the jobs. Most of the jobs in Cloud datacentres encompass small to medium number (100 on average) of tasks, and very few jobs have a single task. On the contrary, very few jobs also contain more than 2000 [7] tasks. Thus a majority of the Cloud users submit jobs with smaller number of tasks, and very few users submit jobs encompassing larger proportion of tasks. In the case of jobs submitted with a single task, the execution duration of the task is actually the execution duration of the entire job. With jobs encompassing several tasks, the execution duration of the job is the accumulation of all the tasks contained within that particular job. The smaller number of jobs with increased number of tasks and the larger number of jobs with fewer tasks have distinctive impacts on the overall datacentre behaviour. Jobs are generally attached with various constraints ([3]) such as scheduling constraints, specified server requirements, etc. An efficient Cloud infrastructure effectively manages such constraints but there are few jobs witnessed to have more than 400 constraints. Intrinsic and extrinsic dynamicity among the user-submitted workloads make them behave distinctively in the datacentre resources in terms of their resource usages, energy consumption and execution duration, etc., adding to the complexities in datacentre management.

13.3 Cloud Predictability

Interestingly, both the Cloud workloads and the server resources exhibit similar behaviours at various levels of the Cloud process infrastructure. Workload patterns generally follow a periodical behaviour despite their heterogeneity and are found to be more uniform when compared to the user diversity. Repeating patterns [8] in the behaviours of the virtual machines (VMs) in the Cloud datacentre could be attributed to their processing approach and related characteristics such as thresholds and image similarities. VM threshold pattern can be used to categorise the VMs according to their resource utilisation profiles, which helps scheduling and allocating jobs onto the servers effectively. Image similarity pattern studies the similarities among the VMs which help storing identical images together thereby benefits reducing the storage space of the VMs. Relationship pattern determines the degree of association between any two parameters and helps to identify the correlation among the workloads, which helps grouping similar workloads together for efficient processing. Variability pattern studies the covariance among both the workload and the VM groups. Periodicity pattern identifies the recurring behaviours among the incoming workloads, which are usually evident among the arrival frequency, resource requirements, etc. The accuracy of such pattern identification can be enhanced by extracting the statistical properties of the workloads and the machine parameters which remain consistent over a significant amount of time.

In general, Cloud datacentres encounter repeated submissions of jobs in a timely fashion which characterises their periodicity. For instance, generating weather reports and road traffic information is a typical example of a timely recurring job submission. Jobs are assigned with a random string of user ID, and jobs submitted by a single user are usually allocated with the same user ID. But a single user may have various user profiles with different user IDs, which would lead to the generation of various user driven profiles for a single user. It is much harder to match the ownerships of the jobs submitted by a single user in spite of being submitted under different user IDs. But jobs characterising similar behavioural patterns closely correlated with the user profiles of similar characteristics can be treated in a common way for predictive analytics. Another challenge imposed by the workload behaviour is the job submissions from brand new users. Newly arriving jobs may or may not have a pre-existing user or job profiles to which they can fit into. If they don't fit into an existing profile, then new job behavioural profiles should be created for every new user. Cloud workloads may also contain anomalies [14] and jobs submissions from malicious users. Such anomalies generally show an abnormal pattern of the behavioural profiles. Some of the runtime factors such as user access patterns, user concurrency and resource usages often result in contextual anomalies which are unavoidable in Cloud environments. It is possible that these anomalies could also be considered as newly arriving jobs submitted by brand new users, and conversely genuine workloads might also be classified as anomalies. The possibility of classifying anomalies into new patterns further increase from the oscillatory behaviours of the workloads and the measure of uncertainty of noise among the workloads. In general, genuine workloads may characterise dense neighbourhoods, whereas anomalies fall far from such dense neighbourhoods. But, anomalies may cause false nearest neighbourhoods, which causes the anomalies to fall closer to the dense clusters of genuine workloads.

Usually, Cloud providers tend to expose ample coarse grain parallelism in order to harness larger clusters of machines, where the clusters are connected by a high bandwidth cluster network for the purpose of processing the user requests. Every machine cluster has a cluster management system which is responsible for scheduling and allocating tasks to individual VMs within that particular cluster.

Though each machine within a given cluster may have its own capacity characterised by the CPU and memory capacity, etc., the characteristics of all the machines within the same cluster would be fairly homogeneous. Thus, the VM clusters facilitate the prediction of workload variations over the entire cluster, which assist predicting the workload patterns on individual VMs. A stronger workload correlation is obvious among the VMs running applications in a collaborative fashion. Such a spatial correlation among groups of VMs helps to filter the noise at the individual VM levels for accurate predictive analytics. Physical machine clusters are generally formed based on the server architecture, operating platform, CPU capacity and Memory capacity, whereas VMs are clustered based on their image similarity, threshold levels, allocated CPU and memory. In the presence of a cache at the hypervisor level, multiple VMs tend to share common chunks of VM images composed of same OS and execute similar workloads. But duplicated chunks can also exist among the VM images. Process clusters are naturally formed in the Cloud infrastructure, where tasks belonging to the same job may be executed in the same or different compute clusters located in the same or different physical server.

Quantifying machine events in clusters helps achieving appropriate allocation of VMs for the incoming jobs, load balanced resource allocation, reducing the machine failures and further identifying the causes of machine failures. Machine usage patterns generally exhibit temporal locality which can be extracted from their CPU usage profiles. The frequency at which the machine events are triggered and machine usage patterns helps server farm maintenance for managing resource availability.

Most of these metric parameters exhibit temporal and/or spatial variations and correlations, which could be both significant positives (maximum correlations) and significant negatives (minimum correlations). Significant positive represents the persistence of a system metric to remain almost the same for a consistent time period. The degree of these positives and negatives should be carefully attributed for behaviour modelling, since clusters of significant positives lead to effective prediction analysis whereas clusters of significant negatives not only affects the prediction accuracy but further causes SLA violations and QoS degradations. These correlation metrics exhibit dynamic shifts with time as the workloads fluctuate over time [6] due to the time-of-the-day, day-of-the-week, week-of-the-month and month-of-the-year effects. Thus it is essential to study and model the association of both the incoming workload patterns and machine usage patterns with the time driven periodical effects.

13.4 Datacentre Trace Sample

This work conducts empirical analysis based on the Cloud trace logs [4] released by Google, featuring more than 650,000 jobs over 28 days of datacentre execution. The statistical observations of the trace logs [11] are presented in Table. 13.1. The trace log data has been sampled on a daily basis with a single day spanning across 24 h

Table 13.1 Trace log
statistics

Number of days	28
Total number of job submissions	650,892
Total number of task submissions	46,093,201
Number of operating servers	12,500
Average number of users per day	190

starting from 12:00 am for a given day. In order to accurately model the time-of-the-day and day-of-the-week effects, the trace log data has been sampled in such a way that the trace time starts exactly at 12:00 am on a Sunday. This datacentre trace data have been deeply explored in order to the extract the inherent trend among the submission and execution events to benefit effective decision making in Cloud datacentre management.

13.5 Submission Event Analysis

Figure 13.1 presents the statistical observation of the total number of job and task submissions on a daily basis. From Fig. 13.1, it can be clearly observed that a weekly trend is evident among the incoming number of job submissions as the arrival shows an increasing/declining trend over the weekdays and weekends, respectively. On a coarse grain analysis, this arrival trend can be postulated to the operating business days. But the weekly arrival trend is hardly evident among the incoming number of task submissions. An abrupt spike is evident in the number of jobs arrived on Day 18, but it encompasses a lower number of tasks. Day 10 characterises a fewer number of jobs but encompasses an increased number of tasks. Thus the arriving trend of jobs and tasks are loosely correlated within the same day, since days with increased number of jobs encompass fewer tasks and vice versa. From this observation, it is clear that tasks and jobs are independent to each other; tasks contained within similar jobs may vary abruptly. An abrupt spike is evident among the number of jobs arrived on Day 18 because a single user suddenly submitted around 81% of the total jobs. Such a sudden arrival of the jobs is a rare event, resulting from a rare user submitting once-in-a-life-time workloads.

For deeper exploration on the job trend, Day 3 Wednesday has been randomly chosen to analyse the job arrival pattern during different time of the day for the purpose of characterising the periodical effects on job submission. Since jobs are driven by the users, it is worthy to observe the usage patterns of Cloud users during different times of day. With this in mind, Day 3 has been sampled into six different segments for deriving insights during receding midnight (12 am – 4 am), early morning (4 am – 8 am), morning (8 am – 12 pm), noon (12 pm – 4 pm), evening (4 pm – 8 pm) and approaching midnight (8 pm – 12 am), respectively, in order to observe the job arriving trend during off-peak and peak time business hours of datacentre execution.

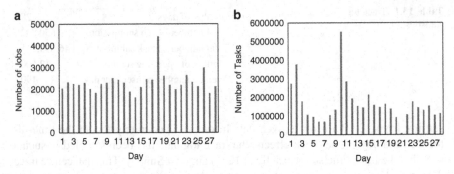

Fig. 13.1 Submission event statistics: (**a**) jobs, (**b**) tasks

It is obvious in a datacentre that a single job may characterise one to several submissions within a single day. Similarly, users submitting jobs might submit one to several jobs within a single day and might submit a single job several times. Jobs submitted more than once within a single day might generate a recurring pattern of resubmissions, and in addition, jobs facing terminations are most often resubmitted within a short succession. Figure 13.2a presents the statistical observations of the number of jobs submitted during different times of the day in Day 3. Figure 13.2b presents the data distribution of the job submission trend for the number of times a job is submitted, fitted with the closest theoretical distribution for the entire day. It can be observed that the job arrival trend is fluctuating during different hours of the day; the number of jobs arrived are increasing during the day time and declining towards the night time, exhibiting a diurnal trend of job arrival. Further, from the distribution analysis, it is clear that the curve is significantly positively skewed and predominantly fits gamma and 3 parameter Weibull distributions, insisting that Cloud datacentres face a majority of the jobs submitted for a few times, and a minority of the submitted jobs involve several resubmissions, respectively. Figure 13.3a presents the statistical observations of the active number of users during different times of the day during Day 3. Further Fig. 13.3b presents the data distribution for the number of times a job is submitted triggered by the users for the entire day. Similar to the job submission trend, the number of active users submitting jobs is high during the day time, again exhibiting a diurnal trend of active users. On a coarse grain analysis, a close correlation is evident among the number of active users and the number of jobs arrived at the datacentre. Further, the distribution curve of the job submission trend from different users predominantly fit Lognormal and three parameter Weibull distributions and are positively skewed, suggesting that Cloud datacentre comprise a majority of users submitting a fewer number of jobs and a very few users characterise majority of the jobs submissions, respectively. The data distribution statistics for both the job and user trend is illustrated in Table 13.2.

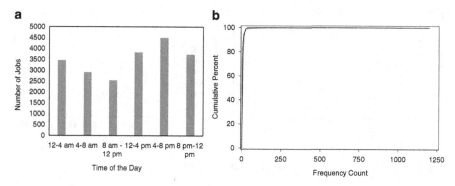

Fig. 13.2 Job statistics: (**a**) submissions, (**b**) distribution

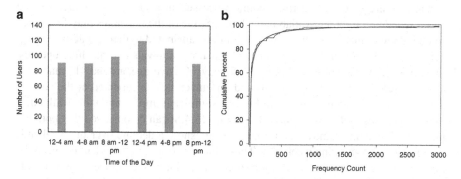

Fig. 13.3 User statistics: (**a**) active users, (**b**) distribution

Table 13.2 Data distribution trend for job submission

Trend	Distribution	Parameters	Skewness
Jobs	Gamma	$\alpha = 0.6465\ \sigma = 6.1738$	26.6112706
	3P Weibull	$\theta = 0.999\ c = 0.2407\ \sigma = 0.0653$	
Users	Lognormal	$\sigma = 1.946\ \varsigma = 2.6876$	6.11923945
	3P Weibull	$\theta = 0.999\ c = 0.3633\ \sigma = 26.36$	

13.6   Machine Usage Analysis

13.6.1   Machine Events

It is natural in a Cloud processing environment that individual machines may become unavailable due to hardware failures and sever downtimes for upgrades. Such machines are taken offline to apply the necessary repairs before bringing

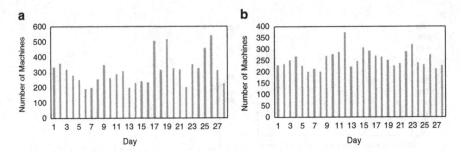

Fig. 13.4 Machine event statistics: (**a**) removals, (**b**) updates

them online in order to confront the unexpected failures. Most of these machine downtimes are shorter, and tasks being processed in such machines are stopped and rescheduled to other available machines. Some of the machines may face more frequent downtimes than others, which could be attributed to their capacity, ageing, etc. Figure 13.4 illustrates the number of machine removals and machine updates, respectively, over the observed period of 28 days. On average, around 311 machines are removed due to failures, and around 255 machines are updated at the studied datacentre traces. Such events would have a significant impact upon the availability of the machines in the server farm. From Fig. 13.4, it can be observed that both the number of machine removal and update events show a decline over the weekends compared to those during weekdays. Thus a close correlation is evident between the machine events and the number of job submissions; increased number of job arrivals naturally demands more availability of the machines in the server farm.

13.6.2 Machine Usage Frequency Analysis

Server resources in a Cloud datacentre can be viewed as common and uncommon servers. Common servers are those resources used quite often and characterised by low utilisation profiles, whereas uncommon servers show higher utilisation rates and are used occasionally. Servers in the datacentres are usually assigned with a permanent machine ID; jobs arriving at the datacentres are allocated from the temporarily deployed VMs onto these permanent machines. Schedulers in the datacentre receive the jobs and find the appropriate physical machines to allocate the tasks for processing. This process of selecting machines is usually governed by various factors such as the machine availability status, current server load, utilisation levels, nature and intensities of the jobs, etc. This section analyses the machine usage patterns based on the actual scheduling of the tasks. For this analysis, Day 3, Wednesday, has been randomly chosen for delving into the machine events in order to exhibit the machine usage patterns. A total of 12,503 servers have

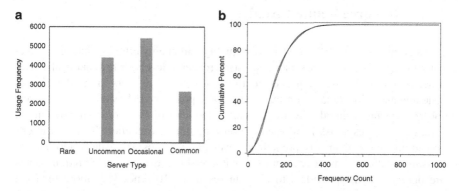

Fig. 13.5 Machine usage frequency: (**a**) quantification, (**b**) data distribution

Table 13.3 Data distribution parameters for machine usage

Distribution	Parameters	Skewness
Weibull	$c = 1{,}7518\ \sigma = 157.18$	0.85857994
3P gamma	$\theta = 26.88\ \alpha = 4.109\ \sigma = 40.69$	0.85857994

been utilised for scheduling the incoming tasks during Day 3 across a period of 24 h. Interestingly, an extreme dynamism is evident in the usage patterns of these 12,503 servers, since the usage frequency of the machines in the server farm ranges from once to a few hundred times. A total of 31 machines has been utilised only once for the whole day; such machines are generally the uncommon servers used occasionally. On the contrary some of the other machines have been consistently utilised for job scheduling throughout the entire day. In order to exhibit the usage patterns of the server, the machines are classified based on their usage frequency as rare (used once), uncommon (used for less than 100 times), occasional (used between 100 and 200 times) and common servers (used for more than 200 times). Figure 13.5a presents the usage frequency patterns for the 12,503 machines in the server farm during a period of 24 h in Day 3. It can be observed that nearly half of the servers are occasional servers, accounting for 43.2%, followed by uncommon servers, accounting for 35.21%, and common servers used for 21.27% and rare servers accounting only for 0.248% of the total machine usages. Figure 13.5b illustrates the distribution of the machine usage frequency pattern in terms of the cumulative distribution function (cdf) fitted with the closest theoretical distribution. The machine usage frequency distribution predominantly fits Weibull and 3-parameter gamma distribution for Day 3. Table 13.3 presents the statistics for the data distribution analysis for machine usage pattern over 24 hours in Day 3. It can be observed that the distribution is positively skewed at 0.8585, insisting that fewer proportions of the server farms characterise maximum utilisation within a single day; 21.27% of the total servers have been consistently utilised for majority of the incoming jobs or processing within a single day.

13.7   Resource Request Analysis

It is a common belief that good service quality and energy efficient datacentre execution cannot coexist, since user requesting resource levels shift dynamically over time. Based on the user requested requirements, the schedulers in the datacentres schedule and allocate tasks on the servers with predefined allowed resource levels for task execution. In other words, this allocated level of resources is the maximum level of resources a task is allowed to consume during execution. Task executions consuming more than this predefined level of resources are usually terminated, causing resubmissions. It is commonly witnessed that user requested requirements are demanding the providers to allocate resources 10 times [12] more than the actual requirements. Further, this strategy of the schedulers always overcommits resources for task executions, leading to two immediate implications. Firstly, over-committed resource levels are vulnerable to leave most of the allocated resources idle without actually contributing to the task execution causing undesirable energy consumptions. Secondly, over-allocating the resources restrains the capability of the datacentres to accommodate more task executions. This necessitates the need to investigate the dynamism of user requested resource levels in accordance with the operating business hours of datacentre execution. In general user requests are associated with the required amounts of CPU, memory and disk space requirements. Most often, the allocated-to-usage ratio of both CPU and memory resources varies dynamically with the disk space utilisation remaining consistent. This section investigates the nature of the incoming workloads in accordance with the amounts of resources requested for task execution during different business hours.

Dynamism in workload resource requirements are analysed from two different perspectives. Firstly, by delving into time-of-the-day effects, user requests from a randomly chosen Day 3 are inspected to observe the hourly variations of user requested resources in terms of CPU and memory resources within a single day. Secondly, a clustering analysis is performed by preferentially segmenting the sample into the aforementioned six segments. This cluster analysis is performed based on k-means clustering algorithm for clustering the user requests with similar resource levels together to identify the shifts in the intensity of resource requests levels over time. K-means is a form of disjoint cluster analysis, which finds the optimum number of clusters and maximises the differences among the distinct clusters until convergence is achieved for the purpose of exhibiting the nature of the formed clusters. K-means algorithm with k ranging from 1 to 9 is run firstly to identify the optimum number of clusters for the given user requests and later to analyse the diversity in the resource requests trend of the users over time.

Figure 13.6 presents the requested resource levels based on the job requirements during Day 3 over the period of 24 h. The user requested resource levels are depicted in terms of the core counts for CPU and bytes for RAM. It is clearly evident that the requested resource levels are highly fluctuating during different hours of the observed day, as the resource levels are increasingly high during the first 4 h

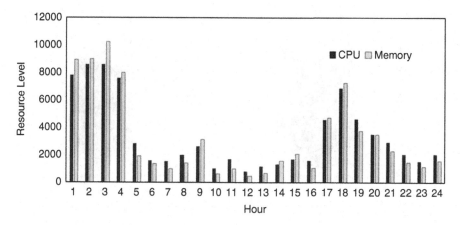

Fig. 13.6 Resource request statistics

when compared to the rest of the day. This higher level of resource requests is postulated to the user activities during such hours submitting increasing number of jobs at the datacentre. In general, increased amounts of job arrival impose higher challenges to the scheduler in scheduling and allocating appropriate resource levels to the incoming jobs, causing increased job terminations and resubmissions. Such resubmissions demand reallocation of resources to execute the terminated jobs successfully. With the increasing/declining trend of resource request levels are the desired inferences from the resource request analysis; the providers might not obtain sufficient inferences from the timely trend of resource request levels. Hence, we postulate that the resource requirements computation at a given time should be given consideration to the user activities during that corresponding time rather than the operating business hours.

Further to the inherent inferences obtained from the hourly-based user requested resource levels, we lead our analyses into the intensity of the requested resource levels during different hours of the day based on the samples of Day 3. Figure 13.7 illustrates the clusters of requested resource levels in terms of CPU and memory during the segmented 6 h within Day 3. It is clearly evident that the resource request levels remain consistent throughout the day. During all the observed six segmented hours within Day 3, both the CPU and memory resource requests are witnessed to be of lower intensities. This corresponds to the fact that Cloud workloads are less computationally intensive. It can thus be concluded that the intensity of resource request levels remain consistent throughout the day. User activities such as the number of concurrent active users and their respective job submissions are the deciding factors of the level of resource provisions at the datacentres. Obviously, increasing numbers of users and job submissions demand more active servers at the datacentres in order to facilitate the providers to provision the appropriate level of resources to the user requests.

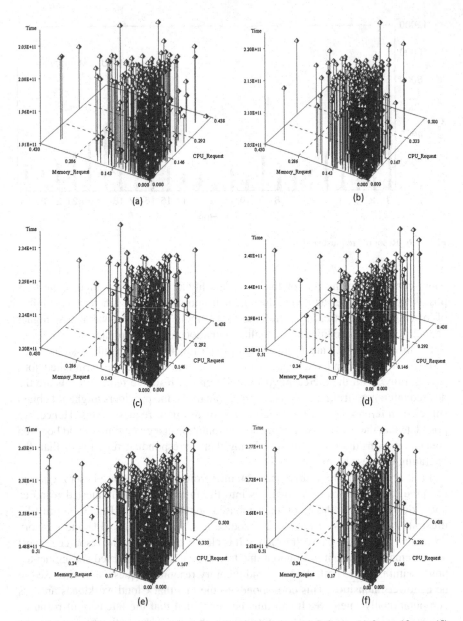

Fig. 13.7 Resource request intensity on Day 3: (**a**) 12–4 am, (**b**) 5–8 am, (**c**) 9 am–12 pm, (**d**) 1–4 pm, (**e**) 5–8 pm, (**f**) 9 pm–12 am

13.8 Conclusion

This chapter analyses the submission events in a large-scale datacentre environment, with the motivation of exhibiting the dynamic nature of Cloud workloads and the machine usage patterns in the server farm. Workload arrival and user behaviours are quantified for different operating business hours and further the machine usage patterns have been analysed in terms of their usage frequency for scheduling the incoming tasks. Extensive analysis conducted on a real-life Cloud trace logs reveals that both Cloud workload and user behaviours are highly dynamic and are bound to periodical effects in accordance to the operating business hours.

Arriving number of job submissions and active number of users follow a diurnal trend and further correspond to the operating business hours with weekday increase and weekend declines. User activities at a given time are the determining factors on the resource request levels during that time rather than the operating business hours. Cloud datacentres usually face a majority of users submitting fewer jobs and fewer jobs characterise a majority of the job submissions. The intensity of requested resource levels are witnessed to be low and remain consistent throughout the day, thus quantifying the number of active concurrent users and their respective job submissions provides contextual clues for the providers to scale and provision the server resources at an optimum level for achieving an efficient trade-off between energy efficiency and QoS. Machines in the server farm exhibit extreme heterogeneity in their usage patterns, with machines characterising one to a few hundred times of utilisations for scheduling tasks. The characterisation of the workload and user behaviours and machine usage patterns presented in this chapter finds applications in prediction analytics, resource provisioning, server management and job allocation, etc., at the datacentres. The inferences presented in this chapter are believed to provide sufficient insights for the Cloud providers to avail proactive services to their clients, by way of balancing the trade-off between energy efficiency and QoS, for prompting eco-friendly sustainable datacentre execution.

References

1. Alam M, Shakil KA, Sethi S (2015) Analysis and clustering of workloads in Google Cluster trace based on resource usage. Cornell University
2. Garraghan P, Moreno IS, Townend P, Xu J (2014) An analysis of failure-related energy waste in a large-scale cloud environment. IEEE Trans Emerg Top Comput 2:166–180
3. Garraghan P, Townend P, Xu J (2013) An analysis of the server characteristics and Resource utilization in Google cloud. In: International Conference on Cloud Engineering. IEEE, Redwood City
4. Google (2011) Google Cluster data V2 [Online]. Google. Available: https://github.com/google/clusterdata/blob/master/ClusterData2011_2.md
5. Jing S-Y, Ali S, She K, Zhong Y (2013) State-of-the-art research study for green cloud computing. J Supercomput 65:445–468

6. Khan A, Yan X, Tao S, Anerousis N (2012) Workload characterization and prediction in the cloud: a multiple time series approach. In: IEEE network operations and management symposium. IEEE, Maui
7. Liu Z, Cho S (2012) Characterizing machines and workloads on a Google cluster. In: 41st international conference on parallel processing workshops. IEEE, Pittsburgh
8. Mahambre S, Kulkarni P, Bellur U, Chafle G, Deshpande D (2012) Workload characterization for capacity planning and performance management in IaaS cloud. In: International conference on cloud computing in emerging markets (CCEM). IEEE, Bangalore
9. Moreno IS, Garraghan P, Townend P, Xu J (2013) An approach for characterizing workloads in Google cloud to derive realistic resource utilization models. In: 7th international symposium on service oriented system engineering (SOSE). IEEE, Redwood City
10. Moreno IS, Garraghan P, Townend P, Xu J (2014) Analysis Modelling and simulation of workload patterns in a large scale utility cloud. IEEE Trans Cloud Comput 2:208–221
11. Panneerselvam J, Liu L, Antonopoulos N, Trovati M (2016) Latency-aware empirical analysis of the workloads for reducing excess energy consumptions at cloud datacentres. In: IEEE symposium on service-oriented system engineering (SOSE). IEEE, Oxford
12. Patel J, Jindal V, Yen I-L, Bastani F, Xu J, Garraghan P (2015) Workload estimation for improving resource management decisions in the cloud. In: Twelfth international symposium on autonomous decentralized systems. IEEE, Taichung
13. Reiss C, Tumanov A, Ganger GR, Katz RH, Kozuchi MA (2012) Towards understanding heterogeneous clouds at scale: Google trace analysis. Intel Science and Technology Center for Cloud Computing, Pittsburgh
14. Wang T, Wei J, Zhang W, Zhong H, Huang T (2014) Workload-aware anomaly detection for web applications. J Syst Softw 89:19–32

Chapter 14
Cloud-Supported Certification for Energy-Efficient Web Browsing and Services

Gonçalo Avelar, José Simão, and Luís Veiga

14.1 Introduction

The software-as-a-service business model relies largely on the capacity for the client to execute rich applications inside a web browser. Parallel to this trend, the Web 2.0 phenomenon also led to the creation of more capable technologies, such as HTML5, enhancements in the JavaScript language and Cascading Style Sheets (CSS), to support blogging platforms, social networks and multimedia streaming sites. As a result, the power consumption in a single end-user device, derived from web browsing, is two to three orders of magnitude larger than in all the intermediate routing equipment, found in the traversed network path [15]. This relation between the different machinery that operates on the Internet suggests much more could be done regarding the way web pages are processed and demanded by browsers. To that effect, two scenarios can be considered:

- Either people start browsing the web more responsibly, requesting each page at a time, lowering the resource consumption on their devices and therefore lowering power consumption rates, (which could be perceived as a loss of convenience and business value); or
- Developers become more responsible for the software they develop, making energy efficiency a primary requirement, taking it into account when they start developing their systems.

G. Avelar • L. Veiga (✉)
INESC-ID Lisboa, Universidade de Lisboa – Instituto Superior Técnico, Lisbon, Portugal
e-mail: luis.veiga@inesc-id.pt

J. Simão
INESC-ID Lisboa, Instituto Superior de Engenharia de Lisboa (ISEL/IPL), Lisbon, Portugal
e-mail: jsimao@gsd.inesc-id.pt

© Springer International Publishing AG 2017

345

N. Antonopoulos, L. Gillam (eds.), *Cloud Computing*, Computer Communications and Networks, DOI 10.1007/978-3-319-54645-2_14

The first scenario is an improbable one. It is hard to instigate environmental responsibility and energy awareness into users' minds, mainly because the financial and energetic incentives, to make people adopt energy management strategies, are minor compared to the constant "desire for always available computing" [10]. In the same study, it is also suggested that "people do not necessarily choose their automated power management settings". Even though this was a study on energy inefficiencies derived from domestic computer usage, it is reasonable to assume that the same ideas hold in more specific cases like the one of web browsers. Another hint of the users' indifference towards green software can be found in several studies [3, 26], suggesting that energy awareness must be delegated to the developer, instead of the user.

Therefore, what *power management strategies* should be employed in order to provide power consumption reductions, while browsing the web? How can environmentally concerned users, or simple-minded users alike, be assured that certain web pages are *greener* than others? How can the related web page processing be used to instigate energy awareness?

Current solutions lack the context at which they were supposed to perform power management actions (the web browser runtime state). Moreover, they typically oversee component metrics, like CPU utilization, disregarding other important components like main memory, which are also responsible for a reasonable slice of the overall energetic waste [8]. An example is Chameleon [24] that brings power management to the application level, adjusting the speed at which applications run. This might be a bad design, since users often impose tight availability constraints on the systems they use, although techniques such as computation offloading [21] or edge computing [5] could be used to improve performance and save energy. These techniques are not always possible to use without hindering the user-experience expected from highly responsive applications.

The main challenge is to provide mechanisms that effectively reduce the energy cost when browsing the web, without sacrificing much of the availability and performance that is expected. This chapter describes and evaluates GreenBrowsing, a system that manages browser access to resources, through the enforcement of different mechanisms that limit resource usage. GreenBrowsing extends the underlying runtime systems and application environments: web browsers, to monitor, promote and certify resource efficiency of running applications, and web pages, based on a cloud-supported certification infrastructure.

On the front-end, GreenBrowsing extends Google's web browser [11] to reach operating system resource management mechanisms in order to enforce our page-aware energy policies. Chrome embodies a full application execution environment with JavaScript just-in-time compilation, garbage collection, thread and process management and component-oriented architecture, in essence a virtual machine for the web. Although it has widespread use, studies also show that it is one of the most power-consuming browsers and, in general, one of the most power-consuming applications [7, 31]. Supported by a back-end infrastructure running cluster and classification algorithms, GreenBrowsing provides means to certify web pages regarding their energy consumption (both during rending and user operation), in order to inform users of the energetic inefficiencies related to different web page visualizations. We show that our system significantly saves browsing-related resources (up to 80% for CPU, memory usage, and bandwidth usage) while keeping delays almost unnoticeable for the user.

In summary, in this chapter we present the following contributions:

- Policies to manage browser access to resources, through the enforcement of different mechanisms that limit resource usage, by taking into account idle tabs (tabs that are open but not being used).
- An extension to a widely used browser, Chrome, in order to decrease the energy costs of browsing, as well as taking advantage of the browser API to perform energy-related optimizations.
- A cloud-based energy-related web page certification scheme, based on computational resource consumption, to the end of raising user awareness in regards to what pages are more resource hungry.

The chapter is organized in the following manner. In Sect. 14.2, both seminal and state-of-the-art energy-reduction systems are surveyed along with energy-related certification systems. In Sect. 14.3, the architectural choices and the algorithms relative to this work will be described, for both the power management extension and the certification subsystem. Section 14.4 explains the details accounting for platform-specific problems and how they were overcome. In Sect. 14.5, the evaluation methodology will be presented, as well as the evaluation testing done in regard to the resource reduction achieved and user-perceived latency impact. To conclude, Sect. 14.6 presents final remarks, and directions for future work will be given.

14.2 Related Work

In this section we present several mechanisms, techniques and systems related to the area of energy-aware web browsing. Section 14.2.1 focuses on techniques to dynamically manage power consumption. Section 14.2.2 presents scheduling algorithms to reduce energy losses, in multitask environments. Section 14.2.3 discusses big data and energy analytic systems.

14.2.1 Dynamic Power Management

Dynamic power management (DPM) is the ability to reduce power dissipation, by selectively turning off or reducing the performance of a system's components when they are idle (or partially unexploited) [29]. These reductions of power dissipation are typically subject to performance and inherent quality of service constraints.

Benini et al. [6] establish a fundamental approach to system-level dynamic power management by providing a high-level architecture, composed by three main

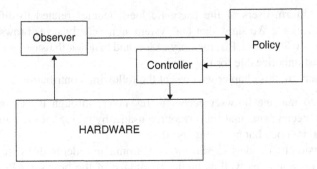

Fig. 14.1 Dynamic power management architecture. As seen in the work of Benini et al. [6]

components: the observer, the controller and the policy (as seen in Fig. 14.1). The latter takes power-management decisions. These decisions are based on the information gathered and transmitted by the observer, as it monitors system activity. The controller is the component through which power management decisions are enforced, on behalf of the policy.

In practice, the observer corresponds to the components that interact with the OS and other device APIs, gathering system properties like CPU and memory usage. The controller is the one who engages devices directly through device drivers. The policy is the component responsible for making sense from the gathered data – by the observer – and issue calls to the right system components – through the controller.

14.2.1.1 Classification of Dynamic Power Management Systems

The decision criteria that allow for a certain system to be adjusted in terms of power consumption, with respect to a systems state change, are embodied in *power models*. Through the enforcement of power models, the policy can adapt to different workload scenarios, adjusting its decision-making mechanisms, in order to perform better power management actions. In essence, power models provide a formal description of the conditions that need to be met, accounting for both system characteristics and other constraints (like performance and availability).

Heuristic Power Models

The more intuitive approach to provide some means of policy adaptation is through the establishment of a static set of rules. These rules are based on common system behaviour and can be implemented as functions, whose parameters correspond to observations and measurements gathered during system's execution. This is the essence of heuristic power models. When modelling simple systems, under near-always-right assumptions, these might suffice in providing good power management capabilities.

Stochastic Power Models

A stochastic model [20] is one that is based on the notion of stochastic process: set of *random variables X(t)*, as a function of time *t*, whose values are called states, and the set of possible values is the state space. In this way, a stochastic model models a process where the current system's state depends on previous states in a nondeterministic way.

Among the many types of stochastic models are the widely used Markov models [18]. In these models, the Markov property [27] holds, hence their name. Intuitively, the Markov property tells us that given a sequence of N events, the value of the probability of the nth event happening after some exact sequence of $N - 1$ previously observed events is approximately equal to the value of the probability of the nth event happening after the $n - 1$th. This approximation is quite useful, since it just requires the computation of the probability of a certain event nth, conditioned to the previous $n - 1$th one, disregarding all the events observed previously.

In a *controlled system*, the Markov model state transitions depend on the current state and on an action that is applied to the system. Therefore, each state is associated to a certain action. In the context of DPM, it means that when the system is in a certain state, the policy will perform the corresponding action over some power-consuming components. Of course, to that effect, there must be some sort of relation among the state set and the components under management, by the policy.

Typically, the stochastic power models used in dynamic power management fall into the Markov decision process category. What Markov decision processes (MDP) try to capture is the relation among sequences of actions in a system and the state transitions that they cause.

Learning Power Models

"An agent is learning if it improves its performance on future tasks after making observations about the world" [34]. This proposition is very relevant to dynamic power management, because there are some power management problems to which solutions are difficult to be programmed or even devised, due to the complexity of the systems at hand. In this way, the policy can be conceived as an agent that learns a new power model from the data it gathers and actions it performs in runtime. This is why machine learning policies tend to be both power model and system model free, since they learn power models dynamically and they might not require any specific system information, in order to execute. They also tend to perform worse than policies that employ heuristic models though.

One particular type of learning process is *reinforced learning* (RL). In this case, the agent learns from a series of reinforcements: rewards or punishments. No direct consequence of the agent actions is observed, even though some feedback is provided in the form of hints, useful for the agent to reason on how it should operate.

It is often desirable to conceive dynamic power management policies that perform actions on a trial-and-error basis, learning from good and bad decisions.

Hence, they can be designed as reinforced learning agents. One common technique of reinforced learning is Q-learning [38] (QL). Q-learning is designed to find stochastic policies that follow the model of Markov decision processes (MDP). This technique is an iterative process with feedback from the previous iterations. At each step of interaction with the environment, the agent observes the environment and issues an action based on the system state. By performing the action, the system moves from one state to another. Based on a value function, the agent decides which action should be taken, given the state the system is in, to achieve the minimum long-term *penalties*. As it is an iterative process, some initial numeral for the value function must be assumed, in order to start the algorithm.

To construct a Markov decision processes through Q-learning, two questions need to be answered: (1) What are the states that compose the state space? (2) How to formulate cost function that depends both on the actions taken and states transited to, from the observed information?

System Models

As shown in the particular cases of heuristic and stochastic models, power models often require information regarding the different power states in which systems can be. More precisely, it is often desirable to know how the power state transitions influence performance and the power consumption of systems. To that end, power models are often based on *system models*.

System models are abstract constructs that describe how a system operates and prescribe functionality and interactions among different system components. They provide a basic framework of system behaviour, facilitating the conception of suitable power models.

An example of a system model is the one of service requester and service provider (SRSP in short). These systems are composed of four components: a *power manager* (PM), a *service provider*, (SP), a *service requester* (SR), and a *service request queue*, (SQ). The idea is such that:

- The service requester sends requests to the service provider;
- The requests are enqueued in the service request queue;
- If the queue of the service provider is empty, then it is in idle mode;
- If the queue of the service provider is not empty, then it is not in idle mode;
- The PM is able to monitor service requests and conclude the mode of the service provider;

Adaptation

Power models can be devised statically, before the execution of the policy, or can be dynamically *adapted*, given the history that is maintained, in order to perfect the model, itself.

This is practical because systems workload changes over time, due to the number and type of applications running, users' use and misuse of applications and other variable concerns that lead to chaotic and, sometimes, unpredictable power dissipation scenarios. In this way, adapted power models can be employed by policies, changing the criteria by which components are put to sleep or have their performance reduced.

Logically, every policy that employs machine learning techniques to devise its power model is an adaptable policy. Heuristic and stochastic models can also be adapted in runtime, by any means other than machine learning. One limitation of a dynamically generated power model is that it incurs additional overheads. This is sometimes problematic, especially if the adaptation is computationally intensive or when there are tight performance constraints.

Synchronization

The way the policy communicates with the observer and the controller is a determining factor on how well the dynamic power manager helps to reduce the power consumption of a system's components. Therefore, it is relevant to classify a policy regarding its communication *synchrony*, towards the other two DPM components, as synchronous or asynchronous. Typically, asynchronous policies perform better than their counterparts, since they do not incur overheads as substantial as synchronous policies, by busily waiting for the observer's responses or the controller's actions to succeed. Therefore, they do not miss as many system events that can be relevant to the act of power management and operate in parallel with the observer and controller, enhancing performance.

Power Reduction Technique

Policies can enforce the reduction of power consumption, according to different *technique* types, either by selectively putting system's components to sleep or by *reducing the performance* of those same components. The notion of sleep state will depend on the system that is being managed. One common way of achieving lower power consumption through performance reductions is through *dynamic voltage and frequency scaling*. DVFS [14, 45] allows the voltage of certain hardware components or the clock frequency of CPUs to be decreased, trading performance for energy. Current architectures provide mechanisms that allow direct access to system components, for DVFS purposes.

Policy Optimality

Policy classification can be done with respect to *optimality*. Benini et al. [6] also point out that observation is indeed essential for devising good policies, i.e. it is strictly necessary to gather system data and adjust policy decisions at runtime. It is not sufficient to greedily put components to sleep as soon as they are idle. There are trade-offs involved that need to be considered: (1) In case of multiple sleep states, the dynamic power management system should choose one sleep state over the others; (2) Since transitions to sleep mode and back to active mode also have a performance cost and inherent overhead, the DPM system should guarantee that the state transitions actually reduce power, compromising performance just up to an acceptable level. This leads to the problem of *policy optimization*, which is the one of choosing a policy that minimizes power consumption, while under performance constraints (or vice versa), based on certain usage patterns. Such a policy is called an *optimal policy*.

14.2.1.2   Relevant Dynamic Power Management Solutions

In the work by Qiu et al. [32], the authors describe the problem of DPM as a continuous-time Markov decision process, applied to a SRSP system model. Qiu et al. propose a continuous time process and included the notion of idle and busy states of the service provider (SP). This is accomplished by adding a transfer state to the service request queue (SQ), to represent the periods when the SP is busy, (since the SP accesses directly the SQ).

On each iteration, a new policy is generated consisting on the cost of performing a sequence of actions, whose probability is weighted and summed to the delay cost of transiting from one system state to another (the actions could be, for instance, to put providers to sleep or wake them up). If the policy is optimal under the performance constraints imposed (an upper bound to the cost function described), it is put in practice. Otherwise, a new iteration of the algorithm is performed, in order to adjust the sequence of actions that are to be made and the respective delay costs state transitions.

In the work by Gerards et al. [14], the authors prove in a theoretical fashion that in order to find an optimal schedule for a set of tasks, it is necessary to consider both DPM and DVFS, instead of just maximizing idle periods' length or minimizing clock frequencies independently. They consider a system model of a number of periodic tasks, in which each of them is invoked the same number of times. The authors conclude that it is best to either start each invocation as soon as possible or as late as possible, with this rationale used to find a globally optimal schedule that minimizes the energy consumption using DPM, for frame-based systems.

In the work by He et al. [16], a simulated annealing (SA)-based heuristic algorithm to minimize the energy consumption of hard real-time systems (real-time system where deadlines must be met) on cluster-based multicore platforms is presented. A technique that allows the power management algorithm to be executed in an online fashion is also proposed, exploring the static and dynamic slack (times of idleness, or amount of time left until a new task is scheduled, during job execution).

The system model follows a classic real-time task model, since this solution is intended for multicore systems. In this way, the system comprehends a task set, where each task corresponds to a pair of its worst-case execution time and the deadline (equal to the period of the job the task is executing). The main idea behind SA is to iteratively improve the solution by investigating the neighbour solutions, generated based on penalty and reward values obtained from the solution of the current iteration. If the number of iterations is sufficiently large, an optimal schedule of tasks can be found.

Shen et al. propose an approach [38] to dynamic power management using reinforced learning, specifically the *Q-learning* algorithm. Even though QL can be applied as a model-free technique, the system under management is known beforehand, which allows for the enhancement of the QL algorithm. In this work, they propose a solution to the management of peripheral devices. The policy chosen will consider states that minimize the delay cost at each state and expected average power wasted, given the observations it has made, over the time the algorithm has been executing, while learning from its decisions and maximizing their quality. After a certain set-up time, the optimal policy can be found.

In the work of Wang et al. [44], the authors propose the use of temporal difference (TD) learning for semi-Markov decision process (SMDP), as a power model-free technique, to solve the system-level DPM problem. Temporal difference learning is a type of reinforcement learning. The system is modelled as a SRSP model. Temporal Difference Learning assumes that the agent-environment interaction system evolves as a stationary SMDP, which is continuous in time but has a countable number of events. The periods at which those events occur are known as epochs.

The key idea is to separate time in decision epochs. At each decision epoch (corresponding to the SP being in a sleep state), actions are taken, depending on the state of the SR. At the next decision epoch, the action is evaluated in order to associate a value to the action taken previously. This will allow to choose from a set of power preserving actions, for each state of the SR, the one with the most beneficial value. Considering the number of requests from the SR and the total execution time to be fixed, the value function is equivalent to a combination of the average power consumption and per-request latency. The relative weight between average power and per-request latency can be changed, over epochs, to obtain an optimal trade-off curve between the average power and latency per request.

In Table 14.1, the different algorithms previously presented are summarized according to the classification criteria established in Sect. 14.2.1.1. The [–] symbol represents that a certain property is not applicable to a particular solution or that the authors did not specified anything regarding that property.

Table 14.1 Dynamic power management scheme classification

| | | | Policy | | | |
Work	PowerModel	SystemModel	Optimality	Adaptation	Synchronization	Technique
Qiu et al.	MDP	SRSP	Optimal	Adaptable	Asynchronous	sleep
Gerards et al.	–	Sporadic tasks	Optimal	–	–	DVFS
He et al.	Heuristic	Real-time tasks	Optimal	Adaptable	–	DVFS
Shen et al.	Q-learning	Peripheral devices	Optimal	Adaptable	Asynchronous	sleep
Wang et al.	TD learning	SRSP	Optimal	Adaptable	–	sleep

14.2.2 Energy-Aware Scheduling Systems

In the classical definition of scheduling, the goal of the scheduler is to determine which task, thread or process should be executed, according to some notion of priority. The idea is to optimize and make the most of CPU utilization.

Energy-aware scheduling is the problem of assigning tasks to one or more cores, so that performance and energy objectives are simultaneously met [37]. In this way, the goal of energy-aware scheduling differs from the one of "vanilla" scheduling, since it is intended to solve a multi-objective optimization problem that comprehends both performance and energy.

Classic techniques include the *first-come first-served* (FCFS) scheduling algorithm [46], where jobs are executed according to the order of their arrival time, to a waiting queue. The major disadvantage of this algorithm is the fact that large jobs greatly delay the execution of the next jobs to execute. This situation is called convoy effect. The *Round Robin* scheduling [42] asserts to each job a time slice where it can run. Finding the proper value for the time slices might be challenging to meet performance constraints, even more if it is intended to achieve both performance and power optimization. *Earliest deadline first* [17] is a dynamic scheduling algorithm where tasks are placed in a priority queue, such that whenever a scheduling event occurs, the queue will be searched for the process closest to its deadline, to be scheduled to execution. Because the set of processes that will miss deadlines is largely unpredictable, it is often not a suitable solution to real-time systems.

Energy-aware scheduling impacts on several levels of the system stack. In the work of Kamga et al. [19], they propose a solution where they extend Xen's default virtual machine scheduler – *Credit*. The goals are to: (i) Induce power reduction in the execution of several consolidated VMs while; (ii) Respecting the agreed service level agreement (SLA) – maintaining acceptable levels of performance. The extension of the credit scheduler is comprised of two modules: *monitoring module* and *cap control module*. At each tick, the monitoring module gathers the current

CPU load for each VM and then computes the optimal frequency to which the CPU should be set to, according to the total VM load and the ratio between current and maximum frequency. After that, the cap control module recalculates new cap values for each VM, adjusting each VM CPU share to the fair percentage, taking into account the CPU load of each VM. In this way, it is possible to redistribute unused CPU cycles from one idle or less active VM to another, while minimizing CPU frequency to save energy, respecting the SLAs imposed.

Yan et al. propose an approach [46] where they introduce a job scheduling mechanism that takes the *variation of electricity price* into consideration as a way to make better decisions of the timing of scheduling jobs with diverse power profiles, since electricity price is dynamically changing within a day and high-performance computing (HPC) jobs have distinct power consumption profiles.

In this approach, the scheduling system is composed by three components: a waiting queue, a scheduling window and a scheduling policy. The waiting queue is where jobs are stored in order to be processed by the HPC system. Rather than allocating jobs one by one from the front of the wait queue, the algorithm allocates a window of jobs. The selection of jobs into the window is based on certain user centric metrics, such as job fairness, while the allocation of these jobs onto system resources is determined by certain system-centric metrics such as system utilization and energy consumption. By doing so, it is possible to balance different metrics, representing both user satisfaction and system performance.

In the work of Datta et al. [12], the authors present two scheduling algorithms that address the utilization of homogeneous CPUs, operating at different frequencies, in order to lower the global power budget in a multiprocessor system. By using *cache miss* and *context switch-CPU migration* indexes, the algorithms are able to exploit the increased performance associated with switching more computationally intensive tasks to higher frequency cores, without suffering from the performance losses associated with cache coherence and context switching overhead. The algorithm assigns static and dynamic priorities to each task. During the schedule stage, the algorithm moves computationally intensive tasks that perform slower, to a higher frequency core or vice versa, based on the number of context switches (or cache misses depending on which of the two algorithms is chosen) and their priority.

14.2.3 Energy-Related Certification and Analytics on the Cloud

In this section we start by analysing the current solutions that assign some sort of energetic rating to computational systems (Sect. 14.2.3.1). We then move to the cloud and big data systems domain (Sects. 14.2.3.2 and 14.2.3.3) in order to study the relevant work that will give us insight on how to incorporate an energy-related certification subsystem into GreenBrowsing, following a cloud-based approach.

14.2.3.1 Energy-Related Certification Computational Systems

To our knowledge, there is no considerable work focusing on the energy-related certification of web pages. There is, however, some work that tries to rationalize and quantify the energy consumption of devices and software, for user visualization purposes.

Siebra et al. propose a scheme [39] to certify mobile devices, regarding their energetic performance. The evaluation is done based on mobile operations (voice call, Internet browsing, message services) and temporal delays between them. Each test case has an energy threshold that cannot be surpassed. If it is, then the mobile device under evaluation is not considered to be green. Amsel et al. developed a tool – GreenTracker [2] – that aims at encouraging users to use software systems that are the most environmentally sustainable. They do this by collecting information about the computer's CPU and by comparing software systems in different classes of software (e.g. browsers are compared with other browsers), based on energy consumption. When all the systems in one class have been tested, Green Tracker creates a chart comparing the CPUs across all the software systems.

Camps et al. propose a solution [9] where a classification of web sites depending of their downloadable content is provided to users, making them aware of the web session costs. The classification is done statistically by computing: (i) The average size of objects embedded on pages; (ii) The rate flow; (iii) The distance from the web browser to the servers. The energy cost should be displayed to final user: this, from the authors' perspective, will allow people to make smarter decisions on how to better manage their energy consumption in their web session.

From these three solutions, the most related to GreenBrowsing is, in fact, the solution presented by Camps et al. However, some disadvantageous characteristics make it less attractive than GreenBrowsing, in particular the fact that it only takes into account the downloadable content of web pages, disregarding important and predominant metrics such as *how heavy the page is* in terms of CPU, memory and I/O performance while rendering and executing JavaScript code. Moreover, all of the required statistical processing is done on the client side of the application, which might turn out to be a dominant overhead, leading to high resource usage and consequent energy consumption.

14.2.3.2 Classes of Big Data Analytic System

There is big variability in terms of big data systems that deal with energy data. In this section attention will be given to systems that gather home energy counters for auditing, analysis and automation purposes.

Features

Singh et al. [41] identify a number of features that can be used to classify a system, regarding its ability to aggregate data from multiple sources and to ubiquitously control data accesses and sharing (from any device and from anywhere).

- Consolidation: To allow a single view into multiple data streams and cross-correlation between different time series, the system should automatically consolidate energy usage data from multiple sources.
- Durability: To allow analysis of usage history, a consumer's energy data should be always available, irrespective of its time of origin.
- Portability: To prevent lock-in to a single provider, data and computation should be portable to different cloud providers.
- Privacy: To preserve privacy, the system should allow a consumer to determine which other entities can access the data, and at what level of granularity, or employ mechanisms that preserve consumers' privacy.
- Flexibility: The system should allow consumers a free choice of analytic algorithms.
- Integrity: The system should ensure that a consumer's energy data have not been tampered with by a third party.
- Scalability: The system should scale to large numbers of consumers and large quantities of time series data.
- Extensibility: It should be possible to add more data sources and analytic algorithms to the system.
- Performance: Data analysis times and access latencies should be minimized.
- Universal Access: Consumers should be able to get real-time access to their data on their Internet-enabled mobile devices.

Design Rationale

At the highest abstraction level, a system's architecture can be divided into the data store (D) components and the application runtime (AR) components that access the data store and perform the execution of analytic algorithms [41]. If we also consider that the system is comprised by two "endpoints" – one residing locally at the client side of the system and other residing remotely – three scenarios for the design of a system are possible:

- *Local-DataStore-Local-Runtime* (LDLR) – Both the data store and application runtime are placed at the client end of the system. There is no remote end.
- *Local-DataStore-Remote-Runtime* (LDRR) – The data store is placed at the client side while the application runtime is executed remotely.
- *Remote-DataStore-Remote-Runtime* (RDRR) – Both the data store and application runtime are placed in the component of the system that operates remotely.

The main disadvantage of the LDLR design is that the application runtime executes on the client side of the system, which can compromise system performance, due to the computational intensiveness of the AR execution.

The LDRR design tries to solve the LDLR disadvantage by moving the application runtime to the component of the system that operates remotely. However, as it also happens in the case of the LDLR design, the *consolidation* feature is harder to attain, since in order to integrate data from various sources into the AR functions, this would incur in greater complexity of the overall system management.

A RDRR design might release the client side of the application from the store and application runtime totally, providing a more lightweight approach to the client end of the system than the LDLR and LDRR designs. However, by moving the data store to the remote end of the system, less control over personal data follows, because the granularity at which users can establish access permissions to their energetic data is greatly decreased. This introduces privacy concerns, since certain energy usage patterns might lead to the disclosure of personal habits the users do not intend to make public.

Business Rationale

This aspect reveals the purpose of the system, which can be classified as a consumer-centric system or a utility-centric one. The latter emphasizes on the usage of energy data by the system, in order to provide utility planning and operation services such as customer billing and home energy waste visualization [41]. On the other hand, consumer-centric approaches emphasize consumer preferences regarding the way their data are handled [25], by integrating their preferences in the decision-making of the services provided.

14.2.3.3   Relevant Energy-Related Big Data Analytic Systems

In the work of Lachut et al. [22], they present the design of a system for comprehensive home energy measurement with the intent of automating the process of adapting energy demand to meet supply. They do this by measuring how the energy consumption is broken down by each appliance, by house, instead of measuring the overall energetic waste of all appliances or just at individual devices. Instead of having one device measuring the energy consumed by each appliance, which might be considered intrusive, the authors state that only minimal collections of energy-related data need to be gathered, in order to measure the actual energy wasted at each appliance. These devices will provide the necessary metrics in order to statistically determine the energy consumption of each appliance, using a technique based on a Markov model.

In the work of Lee et al. [23], the authors propose an analytical tool that can assist in assessing, benchmarking, diagnosing, tracking, forecasting, simulating and optimizing the energy consumption in buildings. This tool is deployed in the cloud, in a software-as-a-service fashion, performing computationally intensive statistical operations on the data it gathers and allowing for the visualization of energy-related data of users' houses. The visualization is done at customers' devices through a dashboard application that summarizes the data outputted by the tool running in the cloud, alleviating any burden to the customer with regard to software maintenance, ongoing operation and support.

In the work of Singh et al. [41], a system that allows consumers to control the access to their energy usage data, from different devices on his/her house, and have it analysed on the cloud, using algorithms of their choice is presented. The analysis of their energy-related data can be done by any third party application in a privacy preserving fashion. In order to allow other applications to access the data stored in the cloud, such as third party applications that can provide different analysis algorithms, privacy protection mechanisms (PPMs) are enforced. PPMs preprocess data by employing mechanisms like noise addition to the data transferred out of the cloud to these applications.

In the work of Balaji et al. [4], the authors present a system called ZonePAC, for the energy measurement of houses with different types of climatization technologies (e.g. variable air volume type heating, ventilation, air conditioning) and energy consumption feedback provision to the house occupants through a web application. The system makes use of existing sensors present on the deployed physical infrastructure of each building to communicate energy consumption counters from the sensors to a building management web service, called BuildingDepot [1]. It relies on a communication protocol for building automation and control networks, BACnet. The network is formed of sensors and the BACnet connector that communicate over a BACnet protocol.

In the work of Oliner et al. [28], the authors propose Carat, a system for diagnosing energetic anomalies on mobile devices. This system consists in a client application, running on a client device, to send intermittent, coarse-grained measurements to a server, which correlates energy use with client properties like the running applications, device model and operating system. The analysis quantifies the error and confidence associated with a diagnosis, suggests actions the user could take to improve battery life and projects the amount of improvement. The server is deployed in a cloud setting, where the samples from client devices are analysed, aggregating the consumption of various mobile devices.

Table 14.2 presents the features that each system has. [*] means that a partial solution is given. [−] means that the authors give no information regarding that particular feature. Table 14.3 exhibits the classification for each system. To represent the fact that the authors gave no information regarding a specific classification property, the [−] symbol will be used.

Table 14.2 Big data system features

Feature	Balaji et al. [4]	Lachut et al. [22]	Lee et al. [23]	Oliner et al. [28]	Singh et al. [41]
Consolidation	Yes	No	Yes	Yes	Yes
Durability	–	–	–	Yes	Yes
Portability	–	–	–	Yes	Yes
Privacy	–	Yes	Yes	–	Yes
Flexibility	No	No	No	No	Yes
Integrity	–	–	Yes	–	*
Scalability	–	–	Yes	Yes	Yes
Extensibility	–	–	Yes	–	Yes
Performance	–	Yes	Yes	Yes	Yes
Universal access	Yes	Yes	Yes	Yes	Yes

Table 14.3 Big data system classification

System	Energy data to visualize	Design rationale	Business rationale
Balaji et al. [4]	Home energy consumption	LDLR	Utility-centric
Lachut et al. [22]	Home energy consumption	RDRR	Utility-centric
Lee et al. [23]	Home energy consumption	RDRR	Utility-centric
Oliner et al. [28]	Mobile device energy anomalies	RDRR	Utility-centric
Singh et al. [41]	Home energy consumption	RDRR	Consumer-centric

14.2.4 Analysis and Discussion

In this section, different energy- and software-related topics were covered, in order to understand how could a browser power management solution be devised. We presented the trade-offs of dynamic power management, in order to understand the advantages of the different policies presented, as well as help perceive the most advantageous situations where one could use those different policies. In particular, the concept of dynamic power management energy-aware scheduling techniques were also discussed because they take into account not only performance constraints but also energetic ones. The rationale of energy-aware scheduling is of great interest to the design of a multitask architecture. Finally, emphasis was given to the fact that it is desirable to move expensive and resource-intensive computations to a cloud-based system when it comes to energy evaluation. These remote systems should be able to process event streams of energy-related counters and give a response in a timely fashion. The data needed to do these computations can sometimes disclose private details of users, and so it should be protected.

14.3 An Architecture for Energy-Efficient Browsing

There are two major subsystems that comprise the GreenBrowsing architecture: a browser extension that will act at a power manager, limiting browser access to resources, and a web page certification back end, to be deployed as a prototypical big data analytic system.

14.3.1 Browser Extension and Power Management

The main roles of the browser extension are to reduce the resource consumption of idle tabs and send to the analytics back-end resource-related data, used to derive energy consumption data, in order to certify web pages in terms of their energy consumption while being accessed.

A layered view of the extensions proposed is presented in Fig. 14.2. *Observer-Controller-Adapter (OCA)* provides interfaces for gathering performance counters of each running tab and the process(es). It is also able to issue commands to reduce tab resource usage through the application of different mechanisms. The *Certification FrontEnd* sends performance data to the back end regarding the open web pages, whose result is rendered by the *Certification Renderer*. The *Policy Enforcer* applies the power reduction algorithms and is configured by the *Policy Manager*. It uses the OCA interface, to gather performance counters and to issue content adaptation and power reduction-related commands. The *Web Page Certifier* module will have code to fetch performance counters, through the OCA. It will also interface with the Certification FrontEnd to send the counters gathered to the

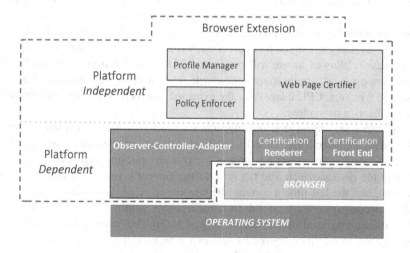

Fig. 14.2 Layered view of the browser extension

back end (for energy-related certification of web pages). Communications with the Certification Renderer are done to inform the user of each web page certification.

In terms of components, the execution of Policy Enforcer's code will be done in parallel with the control and content adaptation of tabs/pages, by two different tasks (comprising one or more threads, each). If they were to be executed sequentially, significant delays could occur in the policy's components execution.

14.3.1.1 Browser-Level Management Policies

We approached the power management problem through simpler heuristics that offer a smaller implementation overhead compared to stochastic or machine learning techniques. This is particularly important to cause the least possible user-perceived delays, while browsing the web. Two *assumptions* are made, regarding general browsing behaviour, serving as basis to the resource-limiting mechanisms to be considered:

- **Last Time Usage.** Tabs that were accessed more recently are more likely to be accessed again and therefore will be less likely to be acted upon. In this way, the tab management policy will make use of a least recently used list for tab energy management.
- **Active Tab Distance.** We also assume that tabs that are closer to the actual tab opened by the user are more likely to be accessed; therefore, they will have lesser probability of being discarded or subject to resource constraints.

The pseudo-code at Algorithm 1 summarizes the extension's behaviour for managing idle tab resource consumption. There is an initial test where, if a certain browser window is not focused (i.e. the topmost user-viewed window), all of the processes that handle its tabs will be halted. In other words, they will stop executing. On the other hand, if a certain window is focused, each of its tabs will be acted upon, individually. Firstly, if a certain tab is active (i.e. selected by the user), it can consume as many resources it needs. If a tab is not active, the maximum resources its process is allowed to use will be limited. If that tab's process ever reaches the limits imposed, a certain *effect/action* will be cast upon that process. Both the resource type (e.g. CPU usage) and the expected effects on resource limit violation are mechanism dependent.

An important aspect that our algorithm considers is the maximum resources allowed for a given tab. Equation 14.1 expresses the resource usage factor (uf) which is used to set the maximum resource usage (for any resource type), by taking into account the distance each idle tab is from the currently visualized tab, at a given moment, and the last time a certain idle tab was selected. Considering i as the tab index distance from a certain tab to the active tab, within a certain window, p as the least recently used index relative to tabs within that same window and a as a controllable/user-defined *aggressiveness* exponent to further intensify reductions, if need be, and where $p >= 1, i >= 1, a >= 0$:

Algorithm 1: Tab management algorithm overview

Data: Windows
Data: Tabs
foreach *window in Browser.Windows* **do**
    if *window is focused* **then**
        foreach *tab in window.Tabs* **do**
            if *tab not active* **then**
                compute tab resource usage allowance ;
                apply resource consumption reduction mechanism ;
            else
                give unconditional resource consumption allowance to tab ;
            end
        end
    else
        foreach *tab in window.Tabs* **do**
            halt tab's process ;
        end
    end
end

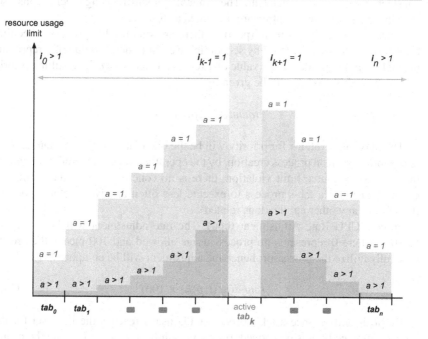

Fig. 14.3 Effects of tab management algorithm on tab resource consumption

$$uf(i, p, a) = \frac{1}{p \times i^a} \qquad (14.1)$$

The value computed by Eq. 14.1 will determine the resources that a given *idle tab* can consume, under the influence of any given resource consumption mechanism (e.g. process priority, CPU and memory cap). The intended effect on focused windows' tabs resource consumption is depicted in Fig. 14.3.

This model allows the possibility that two tabs exist at the same distance i from the active tab and still experience different resource usage limits, for the same value of aggressiveness a, since one of them could have been activated more recently (holding a smaller value for p). One final remark is that some idle tabs may share the same process with the active tab. If this happens, those idle tabs will not be acted upon, since the resource consumption of their process would also constrain the active tab's resource usage (and possibly degrade user experience).

14.3.1.2 Tab Management Mechanisms

Many browsers employ a multiprocess model so GreenBrowsing has to act directly upon the process responsible for handling each tab. This allows to take advantage of some operating system's capabilities, but also implies that some of the mechanisms considered will be OS dependent. The available GreenBrowsing mechanisms used to reduce resource consumption are presented as follows:

Process Priority Adjustment (prio): If there are x adjustable process scheduling priorities, ascendantly ordered by scheduling weight (where a value of x represents the highest priority value and a value of 1 represents the least), the resulting priority of a certain tab's process will be given by

$$round(uf(i, p, a) \times x) \tag{14.2}$$

The maximum value x for priority will be the one that represents a standard/normal priority given on process creation, by the operating system scheduler. Regarding the effect on resource limit violation, there is no concrete action taken. The only expectation is for a tab's process to execute less often relative to other processes (browser or any other applications related).

Process CPU Rate Adjustment (cpu): The rate adjustment will be a value in $[0, 100]$, where 0 represents no process usage allowed and 100 means the process may fully utilize the processor; hence the adjustment will be computed as

$$round(uf(i, p, a) \times 100) \tag{14.3}$$

If **cpu** is active, once a tab's process CPU usage reaches the limit set for that process, its execution is postponed, running again later, when it is given the chance to do so, by the operating system's scheduler.

Process Memory Limitation (mem): With this mechanism, the maximum memory allowed for a process will be the maximum committed private memory up to the time that this mechanism was enforced. The adjusted memory value will be given by

$$round(uf(i, p, a) \times max\_memory\_committed) \tag{14.4}$$

For **mem** there are two versions of this mechanism, with two different possible effect outcomes, once a memory limit is reached by a process: (i) A soft version: The process is halted, and put to a sleep state, returning to execute once its tab becomes active; (ii) A hard version: The process is terminated, releasing all the resources allocated by it, until then.

Process Execution Time Limitation (time): In order to limit the duration a certain tab's process is allowed to run for the average time between consecutive tab activations will be considered. The resource directly managed with this mechanism is execution time. The adjustment formula for allowed process execution time is computed as

$$round(uf(i, p, a) \times average\_tab\_activation\_time) \qquad (14.5)$$

For **time**, the effects employed on limit-breaching processes are the same as with *mem*, once the time for a tab's process to execute expires. It will also wield a soft and a hard version.

14.3.1.3 Enforcing Limits

Once a certain limit is hit, i.e. the maximum value for a tab to consume was reached or surpassed, the effects on the tab depend on the type of mechanism employed. The effects expected once limits are violated are described as follows:

 (i) If **prio** is active, there is no concrete action taken, because changing process execution priorities is not, in itself, a resource-limiting mechanism. The expected outcome would be, however, for a tab's process to execute less often relative to other processes (browser or any other applications related). But, indeed, the arbitration of when a tab's process should be executed is delegated to the operating system's scheduler, entirely.
 (ii) If **cpu** is active, once a tab's processor usage reaches the limit set for that process, its execution is postponed, running again later, when it is given the chance to do so, by the operating system's scheduler.
(iii) For **mem** there are two versions of this mechanism, with two different possible effect outcomes, once a memory limit is reached by a process:

- Soft version: The process is either halted, and put to a sleep state, returning to execute once its tab becomes active, or
- Hard version: The process is terminated, releasing all the resources allocated until then.

(iv) For **time**, the effects employed on limit-breaching processes are the same as with *mem*, once the time for a tab's process to execute expires. It will also wield a soft and a hard version.

By combining the four resource adjustment metrics with the effects on resource usage limit violation, described previously, a total of *six* mechanisms are singled out. Table 14.4 summarizes these mechanisms in terms of the metric that is directly adjusted by the mechanism, the maximum value for resource limits, and action taken on limit violation.

Table 14.4 Mechanisms summarized classification

Model	Metric	Maximum resource value	Action on limit
prio	cpu usage	Normal process priority	–
cpu	cpu usage	100% usage	Postpone execution
mem soft	Memory usage	Max memory committed	Halt execution
mem hard	Memory usage	Min memory committed	Terminate process
time soft	Execution time	avg tab activation time	Halt execution
time hard	Execution time	avg tab activation time	Terminate process

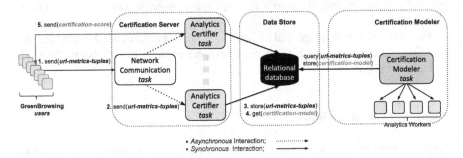

Fig. 14.4 Certification requests sent from GreenBrowsing users to the certification server

14.3.2 Certification Back End

The certification back-end subsystem has the objective of *providing a clear and meaningful notion of how much energy web pages consume*. It is composed of three main components, as depicted on Fig. 14.4:

- A **Certification server** comprised of *network communication tasks* that receive energy-related web page certification requests and forward these requests to tasks specialized in the certification of pages themselves (to avoid service bottlenecks and enhancing the scalability of the system regarding the treatment of requests); those are *analytics certifier tasks* that do the work of certifying a given page, according to a specific certification model.
- A **certification modeller** comprised of *certification modeller tasks* that adjust the certification model, taking into account all the resource data sent from the extension subsystem. For performance purposes, this design emphasizes the usage of specified *worker tasks* to whom parts of the analytical calculations are mapped. The results of processing data at workers are assembled back at the modeller task, as soon as they are ready.
- A **data store** that stores the models used in the certification of pages and tuples with information relative to the performance counters of each page;

14.3.2.1 Performance Counters for Energy-Related Certification

The power consumption induced by web pages will be indirectly determined by some of the performance counters gathered on the browser extension. For each page, the metrics considered will be:

1. CPU usage (in terms of completed clock cycles);
2. Private (main-)memory usage of processes (in Mega-Bytes);
3. Network interface usage (in terms of the bits-per-second), to process and maintain each page open;

These metrics were chosen because they were proved to be highly related to power consumption, in different settings ([8, 30, 33]).

The certification is done at the level of the *web page* and *domain*, but could easily be extended to individual subdomains, subtrees of each domain hierarchy, for instance. Therefore, the information sent from the extension to the certification back end will be a 5 tuple *<id, type, CPU-usage, memory-usage, network-bandwidth-usage>*, where the *type* entry indicates if the performance counters refer to a URL or domain and the *id* refers to its textual representation.

14.3.2.2 Devising Categories and Certifying Pages

Certifying web pages considers the existence of a set of well-defined ranks or certification categories, which in their totality are all inclusive to any web page, i.e. given a certain web page, it is always possible to associate an energy-related classification to it. This might not be trivial, since many different resource usage patterns are expected to be observed while processing web pages, due to the variability of web technologies and richness of web content. Furthermore, it is not known what all resource consumption behaviour inherent to web page processing will entail.

While devising a certification scheme, one should also consider that the entities need to certify change over time. Web pages are no different. What might be considered resource intensive in the present might be considered acceptable in the future (or, most likely, the other way around). So, in essence, the requirements expected for an appropriate certification scheme, in the context presented, are:

1. Group resource consumption from various sources to ensure all-inclusiveness of certification categories;
2. Predict unobserved resource consumption ranges to further ensure completeness/inclusiveness of certification categories;
3. Dynamically adjust the certification scheme to the changes in web-page properties that induce varied resource consumption patterns over time;

To devise certification all-inclusive of categories from multiple sources, the certification modeller uses a method know as *expectation-maximization* [13]. The basic idea is to cluster the observations recorded into, no less than, 8 categories. This is done in a three-dimensional (multivariate) random variable space that comprehends one dimension for the CPU usage, one for the memory usage and another for network usage. Two different data sets will be used to compute parameters for two different models – one comprising resource usage associated with URL and another for web-page domains, being the URL dataset contained in the domain dataset.

The observations belonging to the multivariate resource consumption random variables are assumed to be normally distributed, so multivariate Gaussian mixture models (*MGMM*) are used to fit the data and to iteratively train the parameters for eight random variable's subpopulations, each one corresponding to a cluster. The parameters in question are:

- A *three*-dimensional vector comprising the means of each random variable
- A 3×3 covariance matrix;

After having trained a group of MGMM clusters, a random selection of trained cluster observations is selected from each cluster. The centre of mass (*CM*), or centroid, of each sample is computed, afterwards. The resulting centre of mass vector obtained this way is representative of the category, identifying it unequivocally, and will be used to certify web-page URL or domains while running the certification algorithm. In order to qualify a certain cluster, the vectorial norm of the hypothetical vector space origin to the centre of mass of that cluster will be considered. The greater the norm, the more resource-intensive pages with that norm's certification category will be considered to be. This is done once, per trained model.

In order to certify a page's URL and domain, tasks running at the certification server fetch the clusters' centres of mass, of the last trained certification model, from the data store. The algorithm to certify a URL/domain's web page with respect to its consumption consists in comparing the Euclidean distance (*d*) that goes from each observed resource measurement to the centre of mass of each cluster. If two or more clusters' centres of mass are at the same distance from an observation, the one with the greater norm is associated with the observation. In the end, the cluster/category that is associated with more observations is the final certification category assigned to the URL/domain.

The certification methodology is described more succinctly in Algorithm 2. The input consists of a set of *n* resource consumption values gathered from a single user device and a set of *k* certification categories previously computed.

Algorithm 2: Certification algorithm used to score web-page URL and domains

---

Input: A set $O = \{O_1, O_2, \ldots, O_n\}$ of resource consumption values
Input: A set $C = \{C_1, C_2, \ldots, C_k\}$ of clusters' centers of mass
Output: A pair $\langle s, k \rangle$, where $s \in \{1, k\}$
$S \leftarrow \{S_1, S_2\}$
for $i \leftarrow 1$ *to* n **do**
    $min \leftarrow -\infty$
    $\alpha \leftarrow k$
    for $j \leftarrow 1$ *to* k **do**
        $distance \leftarrow d(O_i, C_j)$
        if $distance < min$ **then**
            $min \leftarrow distance$
            $\alpha \leftarrow j$
        end
    end
    $S_\alpha \leftarrow S_\alpha + 1$
end
$s \leftarrow i$, where $S_i > S_j$, $\forall \langle S_i, S_j \rangle \in S$
return $\langle s, k \rangle$

14.4 Browser-Level Extensions and Certification Back End

14.4.1 Browser Extension

The browser extension was implemented using a Chrome deployment on the Windows operating system. Since Chrome has very limited support for process management, namely, of its tabs, the extension needed to be divided in two main entities: (i) **the browser extension** itself, comprised of JavaScript callbacks and code rather event oriented, whose execution and handling is delegated to the browser, by running from within the browser itself as a Google Chrome extension. (ii) A **background process (BP)** running natively as a service. Through it, browser processes can be directly managed by communicating, beforehand, with the extension.

The extension communicates with the background process issuing mechanism-related commands and in order to allow the latter to keep track of certain browser states, relevant to the tab management algorithm described in Sect. 14.3.1.2. The browser state-related information passed this way is composed of general tab information such as tab identifiers, tab indexes within their windows and corresponding process ids. All communications are handled asynchronously by the background process each time an event is raised by the browser, following a certain tab state update, for instance, when a tab is created, or when a tab is activated.

When on Windows, Chrome uses Windows job objects to employ part of its sandboxing constraints. Job objects are Windows abstractions that allow the grouping of processes and the enforcement of certain limits and restrictions over them. This is exactly what is needed in order to implement the resource limiting mechanisms described in Sect. 14.3.

The sandboxing used by Chrome prescribes the association of a single tab process to a single job. Knowing that these job objects are kept at Chrome's kernel process – i.e., the process that orchestrates all browser activity, from tab creation and management to resource access – the BP retrieves these jobs by enumerating all the Windows kernel objects present at Chrome's kernel process, keeping those that correspond to job objects. Once all job objects are found, the association of jobs to tab processes is done by calling a Win32 API function. Tab processes are retrieved by querying the browser, through its JavaScript API. This is done at the browser extension which, in turn, will pass the tab-to-process associations to the BP, where they are associated with jobs.

The tab management algorithm described in Sect. 14.3 will therefore limit resource usage by acting directly on jobs. Each mechanism is implemented by exploiting the capabilities of job objects. For instance, it is possible to change process priorities or adjust maximum CPU rates for any given tab process belonging to a single job object. This is accomplished in the cases of *prio* and *cpu* mechanisms.

14.4.2   Certification Back End

Concerning the back-end subsystem, all code was developed on Java. Communication between components is done via the certification server web API, transporting messages in JSON format.

The certification server uses the Netty-socketio framework, to serve incoming certification requests. This framework is an implementation of the WebSocket protocol and allows to serve requests efficiently and asynchronously.[1]

The certification modeller runs as a process with two Java threads. Each thread computes the model used to certify either URLs or domains. This is done using a combination of Apache Spark built-in expectation-maximization function, for multivariate Gaussian mixtures and Apache Commons Math library, for the sampling of clusters.[2] For storing resource consumption records, coming from the certification server, and the model's centres of mass, coming from the certification modeller, a PostgresSQL database is deployed at the data store.[3]

14.5   Evaluation

In order to evaluate GreenBrowsing in a systematic way, tests were scripted combining sequences of *mechanisms* with *aggressiveness* values. The aggressiveness values considered will hold values of 1 and 1024, to assess how the intensification of the limits imposed affects resource usage. A set of typical web pages was used,

---

[1]https://github.com/mrniko/netty-socketio, visited 22 November 2016.

[2]https://spark.apache.org/, visited 22 November 2016.

[3]http://www.postgresql.org/, visited 22 November 2016.

comprising pages of news sites, social networks, sports sites, mail clients and multimedia-streaming sites, providing a varied web-page suite.

Scripts were developed to open a set of pages and then navigate through those pages, gathering resource consumption data. Every time a tab is terminated, due to employing *mem hard* or *time hard*, it has its page reloaded once it becomes active again.

Regarding the testing environment, Chrome version was 44.0.2391.0, dev-channel release. The operating system on which Chrome was installed was Windows 8.1 Pro – baseline install, no updates. Hardware wise, the tests were conducted with machines with Intel®Core(TM)2 Duo CPU P8700 running at 2.53 GHz, with 4 GB of RAM memory.

For understanding how the employment of certain mechanism combinations might affect latency, browsing habits are simulated through different *tab selection policies*. These policies state what is the next tab to activate (i.e. what page to visualize next): (i) *Round-robin selection* to navigate sequentially from tab to tab; (ii) *Central tab incidence*, where the tabs at the centre of the tab bar will be selected more often, by following a periodic navigation scheme, from the first tab to the last and from the last to the first one, in a back and forth-fashion; (iii) *Random tab selection* where a certain tab is selected randomly, possibly more than once.

14.5.1   Resource Usage Evaluation

The resource variations induced by *prio* might not be noticeable to the naked eye because of the highly variable values of CPU usage rates, over time. Reductions of 9.92% and 17.56% were recorded, however, being the latter recorded with an higher value of aggressiveness, as shown in Fig. 14.5, in green.

When applying *cpu* (Fig. 14.5), the reductions in CPU usage are intensified even more when compared with *prio*, this time holding reductions that range from 20% to about 47% of CPU time. This advantage over *prio* was expected, since *cpu* directly adjusts the CPU usage allowed for each tab's process, contrary to *prio*, that associates priorities to a process without adjusting the maximum value for CPU usage, itself.

Figure 14.6 depicts how applying *mem soft* and *time soft* influenced CPU usage. The first seems to be the most prominent in reducing CPU usage, with 80% reductions, while the latter is still successful in doing so, even though to a lesser extent, achieving close to 70% reductions.

Concerning memory usage, depicted in Fig. 14.7, *hard* mechanisms induce a substantially lower memory usage, than their *soft* counterparts, achieving reductions of 80% to 85%, when compared to mechanisms being *all off*.

Overall, *mem soft* and *time soft* seemed to be the most capable mechanisms, in terms of managing idle tab resource consumption regarding CPU usage. Even though experiments in Fig. 14.7 seem to disprove its effectiveness in reducing memory usage, (since *soft* mechanisms achieved slight increases when compared

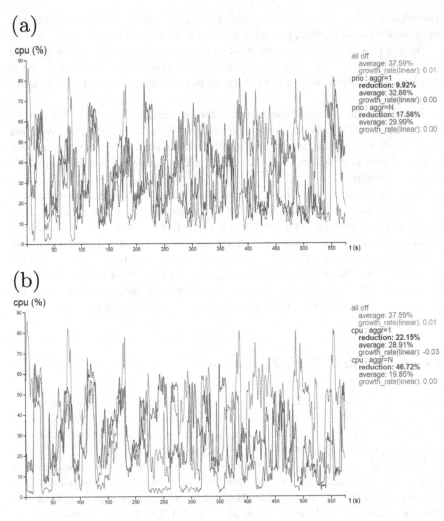

Fig. 14.5 Priority and CPU share mechanisms. (**a**) CPU usage for *prio*. (**b**) CPU usage for *prio* & *cpu*

to *all off*), it is important to notice how stable memory consumption was when compared to the memory variations induced by other mechanisms and *all off*, over time. If it is assumed that memory variations represent system-wide activity, due to having many system entities accessing it, and therefore inducing energy consumption rates proportional to the variations recorded, then *soft* mechanisms effectively help reduce energy consumption, by varying the least.

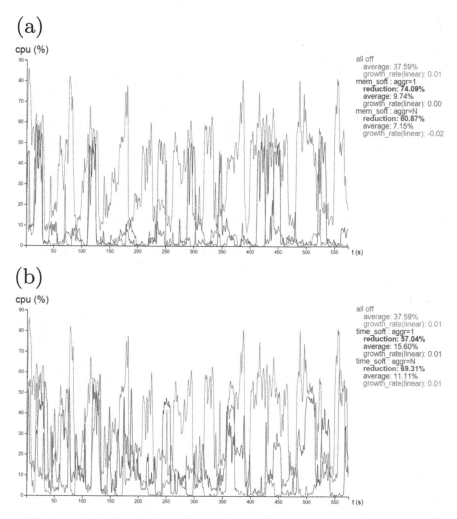

Fig. 14.6 CPU usage when applying memory related mechanisms. (**a**) CPU usage for *mem soft*. (**b**) CPU usage for *time soft*

14.5.2   Perceived Delay Evaluation

In order to assess the implications in terms of user experience-significant requirements, latency was recorded, while running resource consumption tests. Latency, in this context, corresponds to the time period that goes from the moment the active tab starts loading web-page content to the moment that content is totally loaded. This notion of latency is useful to give an idea of how much time is wasted, by enforcing certain mechanisms, in comparison to others.

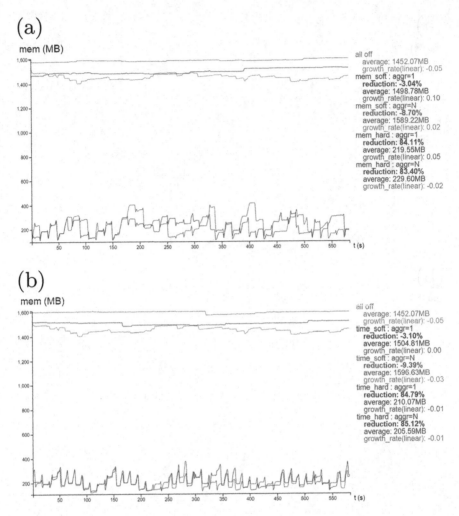

Fig. 14.7 Memory restriction mechanisms. (**a**) Memory usage for *mem soft* & *mem hard*. (**b**) Memory usage for *time soft* & *time hard*

Figure 14.8 presents the latencies experienced on average, as rectangles, for each tab selection policy. Standard deviations correspond to the vertical lines above rectangles. It is possible to see that latencies for *hard* mechanisms were always bigger, on average, when compared to other mechanisms. The experiments comprising *all off*, *prio* and *cpu* held the smaller latency values, as expected, since they tamper very little with process functioning, when compared to other mechanisms (viz. the *soft* and *hard* ones). It is possible to observe that *soft* mechanisms seem to achieve acceptable latencies, when compared to *all off*. The exception is when tabs were chosen randomly, where the latency values are comparable to those recorded for *hard* processes. The standard deviations observed are rather high in value. It has

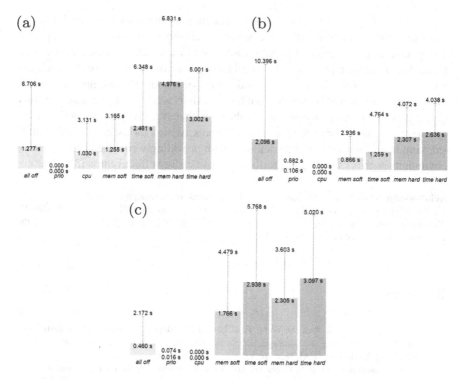

Fig. 14.8 Latency measurements for the 3 tab selection policies considered. (**a**) Latency measurement/round-robin tab selection. (**b**) Latency measurement/central-tab-incidence selection. (**c**) Latency measurement/random tab selection

to do with the wide latency value ranges recorded since; occasionally, some long periods of consecutive busy-tab activations were recorded (where the activated tabs were still processing their pages).

It seems, therefore, negotiable to apply all mechanisms for resource reduction purposes, with the exception of *hard* mechanisms, given the latencies recorded for them, in most experiments.

14.6 Conclusions

This chapter presented GreenBrowsing, a tab-management solution (implemented as a Google Chrome extension) and a cloud-based energy-related certification scheme implemented on a separate subsystem. Evaluation shows *substantial resource usage reductions* on energy consumption-related resource metrics (up to 80% for CPU, 85% for memory usage and 85% for bandwidth usage) while preserving acceptable user-perceived delays (unnoticeable in most cases), all of this when comparing GreenBrowsing-aided web navigations with standard navigations.

Regarding future work, more resource reduction mechanisms could be devised in order to account for bandwidth usage, since studies show it plays a significant part in energy consumption, especially in the case of Wi-Fi-enabled devices. The back end would benefit from improvements at the data store, in order to improve its scalability when it comes to processing reads and writes of resource consumption records. Furthermore, we would like to explore how previous work on differentiated quality of service in the cloud [40] could be combined with declarative policies [43] in order to improve the approach effectiveness and expressiveness for users. Also relevant is studying how this work can be combined with providing web-based services from community networks in order to further improve energy effectiveness [35, 36].

Acknowledgements This work was supported by national funds through Fundação para a Ciência e a Tecnologia with reference PTDC/EEI-SCR/6945/2014 and by the ERDF through COMPETE 2020 Programme, within project POCI-01-0145-FEDER-016883, the Engineering School of the Polytechnic Institute of Lisbon (ISEL/IPL).

References

1. Agarwal Y, Gupta R, Komaki D, Weng T (2012) Buildingdepot: an extensible and distributed architecture for building data storage, access and sharing. In: Proceedings of the 4th ACM workshop on BuildSys. ACM, New York
2. Amsel N, Tomlinson B (2010) Green tracker: a tool for estimating the energy consumption of software. In: CHI'10 extended abstracts on human factors in computing systems, CHI EA'10. ACM, New York
3. Amsel N, Ibrahim Z, Malik A, Tomlinson B (2011) Toward sustainable software engineering (nier track). In: Proceedings of the 33rd international conference on software engineering, ICSE'11. ACM, New York, pp 976–979
4. Balaji B, Teraoka H, Gupta R, Agarwal Y (2013) Zonepac: zonal power estimation and control via hvac metering and occupant feedback. In: Proceedings of the 5th ACM workshop on embedded systems for energy-efficient buildings, BuildSys'13. ACM, New York
5. Beck MT, Werner M, Feld S, Schimper T (2014) Mobile edge computing: a taxonomy. In: The sixth international conference on advances in future internet, Lisbon
6. Benini L, Bogliolo A, Cavallucci S, Riccó, B (1998) Monitoring system activity for os-directed dynamic power management. In: Proceedings of the 1998 international symposium on low power electronics and design, ISLPED'98. ACM, New York
7. Bianzino AP, Raju AK, Rossi D (2011) Greening the internet: measuring web power consumption. IT Prof 13:48–53
8. Bircher WL, John LK (2012) Complete system power estimation using processor performance events. IEEE Trans Comput 61(4):563–577
9. Camps F (2010) Web browser energy consumption
10. Chetty M, Brush AB, Meyers BR, Johns P (2009) It's not easy being green: understanding home computer power management. In: Proceedings of the SIGCHI conference on human factors in computing systems, CHI'09. ACM, Boston
11. Chrome browser. https://www.google.com/intl/en/chrome/browser/
12. Datta AK, Patel R (2013) Cpu scheduling for power/energy management on multicore processors using cache miss and context switch data. IEEE Trans Parallel Distrib Syst 1190–1199

13. Dempster AP, Laird NM, Rubin DB (1977) Maximum likelihood from incomplete data via the em algorithm. J R Stat Soc Ser B 39(1):1–38
14. Gerards M, Kuper J (2013) Optimal dpm and dvfs for frame-based real-time systems. TACO 9(4):1–23
15. Gyarmati L, Trinh TA (2011) Power footprint of internet services. In: Proceedings of the 2nd international conference on energy-efficient computing and networking, e-Energy'11. ACM, New York
16. He D, Mueller W (2012) A heuristic energy-aware approach for hard real-time systems on multi-core platforms. In: Proceedings of the 2012 15th Euromicro conference on digital system design, DSD'12. IEEE Computer Society, Washington, DC, pp 288–295
17. Jansen PG, Mullender SJ, Havinga PJ, Scholten H (2003) Lightweight edf scheduling with deadline inheritance. Technical report, University of Twente, Enschede
18. Kaelbling LP, Littman ML, Cassandra AR (1998) Planning and acting in partially observable stochastic domains. J Artif Intell 101(1–2):99–134
19. Kamga CM, Tran GS, Broto L (2012) Extended scheduler for efficient frequency scaling in virtualized systems. SIGOPS Oper Syst Rev 46(2):28
20. Klebaner FC (2012) Introduction to stochastic calculus with application, 3rd edn. World Scientific, Singapore/London
21. Kumar K, Liu J, Lu YH, Bhargava B (2013) A survey of computation offloading for mobile systems. Mobile Netw Appl 18(1):129–140. doi:10.1007/s11036-012-0368-0. http://dx.doi.org/10.1007/s11036-012-0368-0
22. Lachut D, Piel S, Choudhury L, Xiong Y, Rollins S, Moran K, Banerjee N (2012) Minimizing intrusiveness in home energy measurement. In: Proceedings of the fourth ACM workshop on embedded sensing systems for energy-efficiency in buildings, BuildSys'12. ACM, New York
23. Lee YM, An L, Liu F, Horesh R, Chae YT, Zhang R, Meliksetian E, Chowdhary P, Nevill P, Snowdon JL (2013) Building energy performance analytics on cloud as a service. Serv Sci 5:124–136
24. Liu X, Shenoy P, Corner M (2005) Chameleon: application level power management with performance isolation. In: Proceedings of the 13th annual ACM international conference on multimedia, MULTIMEDIA'05. ACM, New York
25. Liu W, Liu K, Pearson, D. (2011) Consumer-centric smart grid. Innovative Smart Grid Technologies pp 1–6
26. Miettinen AP, Nurminen JK (2010) Analysis of the energy consumption of javascript based mobile web applications. In: MOBILIGHT, Barcelona
27. Norris JR (1998) Markov chains. Cambridge series in statistical and probabilistic mathematics. Cambridge University Press, Cambridge
28. Oliner AJ, Iyer AP, Stoica I, Lagerspetz E, Tarkoma S (2013) Carat: collaborative energy diagnosis for mobile devices. SenSys'13. ACM, New York
29. Paleologo BB, Benini L, Bogliolo A, Paleologo GA, Micheli GD (1998) Policy optimization for dynamic power management. IEEE Trans Comput Aided Des Integr Circuits Syst 18:813–833
30. Park J, Yoo S, Lee S, Park C (2009) Power modeling of solid state disk for dynamic power management policy design in embedded systems. In: Proceedings of the 7th IFIP WG 10.2 international workshop on software technologies for embedded and ubiquitous systems, SEUS'09. Springer, Berlin/Heidelberg, pp 24–35
31. Patel S, Perkinson J (2013) Fraunhofer report – the impact of internet browsers on computer energy consumption
32. Qiu Q, Pedram M (1999) Dynamic power management based on continuous-time markov decision processes. In: Proceedings of the 36th annual ACM/IEEE design automation conference, DAC'99. ACM, New York
33. Rodrigues R, Annamalai A, Koren I, Kundu S (2013) A study on the use of performance counters to estimate power in microprocessors. IEEE Trans Circuits Syst Express Briefs 60:882–886

34. Russel S, Norvig P (2009) Artificial intelligence: a modern approach, 3rd edn. AIPI, Moorpark
35. Sharifi L, Rameshan N, Freitag F, Veiga L (2014) Energy efficiency dilemma: P2p-cloud vs. datacenter. In: IEEE 6th international conference on cloud computing technology and science, CloudCom 2014, Singapore, 15–18 Dec 2014. IEEE Computer Society, pp 611–619. doi:10.1109/CloudCom.2014.137. http://dx.doi.org/10.1109/CloudCom.2014.137
36. Sharifi L, Cerdà-Alabern L, Freitag F, Veiga L (2016) Energy efficient cloud service provisioning: keeping data center granularity in perspective. J Grid Comput 14(2):299–325. doi:10.1007/s10723-015-9358-3. http://dx.doi.org/10.1007/s10723-015-9358-3
37. Sheikh HF, Tan H, Ahmad I, Ranka S, Bv P (2012) Energy- and performance-aware scheduling of tasks on parallel and distributed systems. J Emerg Technol Comput Syst 8(4):1–37
38. Shen H, Tan Y, Lu J, Wu Q, Qiu Q (2013) Achieving autonomous power management using reinforcement learning. ACM Trans Des Autom Electron Syst 18(2):1–32
39. de Siebra C, Costa P, Marques R, Santos ALM, da Silva FQB (2011) Towards a green mobile development and certification. In: 2011 IEEE 7th international conference on wireless and mobile computing, networking and communications (WiMob). IEEE. https://doi.org/10.1109/WiMOB.2011.6085386
40. Simão J, Veiga L (2013) Flexible slas in the cloud with a partial utility-driven scheduling architecture. In: IEEE 5th international conference on cloud computing technology and science, CloudCom 2013, Bristol, 2–5 Dec 2013, vol 1. IEEE Computer Society, pp 274–281. doi:10.1109/CloudCom.2013.43. http://dx.doi.org/10.1109/CloudCom.2013.43
41. Singh RP, Keshav S, Brecht T (2013) A cloud-based consumer-centric architecture for energy data analytics. In: Proceedings of the fourth international conference on future energy systems, e-Energy'13. ACM, New York
42. Tanenbaum AS (2007) Modern operating systems, 3rd edn. Prentice Hall Press, Upper Saddle River
43. Veiga L, Ferreira P (2004) Poliper: policies for mobile and pervasive environments. In: Kon F, Costa FM, Wang N, Cerqueira R (eds) Proceedings of the 3rd workshop on adaptive and reflective middleware, ARM 2003, Toronto, 19 Oct 2004, pp 238–243. ACM. doi:10.1145/1028613.1028623. http://doi.acm.org/10.1145/1028613.1028623
44. Wang Y, Xie Q, Ammari A, Pedram M (2011) Deriving a near-optimal power management policy using model-free reinforcement learning and bayesian classification. Proceedings of the 48th design automation conference on – DAC'11, New York, p 41
45. Weiser M, Welch B, Demers A, Shenker S (1994) Scheduling for reduced CPU energy
46. Yang X, Zhou Z, Wallace S, Lan Z, Tang W, Coghlan S, Papka ME (2013) Integrating dynamic pricing of electricity into energy aware scheduling for hpc systems. In: Proceedings of SC13: international conference for high performance computing, networking, storage and analysis, SC'13. ACM, New York

Author Index

© Springer International Publishing AG 2017
N. Antonopoulos, L. Gillam (eds.), *Cloud Computing*, Computer Communications
and Networks, DOI 10.1007/978-3-319-54645-2

Subject Index

Printed in the United States
By Bookmasters